New Psychiatric Syndromes

DSM-III and Beyond

Edited by Salman Akhtar, M.D.

JASON ARONSON, INC.
New York and London

To Raj, Kabir, and Nishat

Chapters 2 and 4 previously appeared in the *American Journal of
Psychiatry,* 1982, 139:12-20, and 1979, 136:7, 895–900, respectively.

Library of Congress Cataloging in Publication Data
Main entry under title:

New psychiatric syndromes.

  Includes bibliographies and index.
  1. Psychiatry. I. Akhtar, Salman, 1946 July 31–
[DNLM: 1. Mental disorders WM 100 N532]
RC454.N484 1983   616.89   83-3785
ISBN 0-87668-614-5

Manufactured in the United States of America.

Contents

Preface

The recent publication of DSM-III has once again demonstrated that each historical era has its own influence on the form and content of human psychopathology. Many factors account for this effect. The prevalence of a physical disease, for instance, may determine the frequency with which a certain organic brain syndrome is encountered. The disappearance of general paresis from psychiatric practice after syphilis was controlled is an example. Variations in psychopathology may also be related to changes in modes of child rearing. The extended families of the early 20th century and their loving but repressive child-rearing methods produced patients with libidinal conflicts, incestuous anxieties, and symptom neuroses. The contemporary nuclear, and often broken, families and their accelerated, tense child-rearing practices have resulted in more patients with conflicts of aggression, narcissistic concerns, and character disorders. The neurotics of earlier days could love but had sexual inhibitions; today's patients can perform sexually but struggle with an inability to love.

Organic and psychogenic factors interrelate in altering the frequency of certain clinical phenomena. Since the original descriptions of schizophrenia, the progressive increase in the paranoid subtype and a parallel decrease in the catatonic subtype have had both organic-physical and familial-cultural explanations. In addition, political-economic, religious, and aesthetic influences have had a pathoplastic effect. Thus the metaphor of psychotic symptomatology has also changed with increasing industrialization, automatization, and the decline of organized religion. In the persecutory hells of paranoid patients, incubus and succubus have given way to control by computers and hypnosis, and witches and demons have been replaced by remote-control devices and the FBI. More generally, crude hysterical paralysis, neuraesthenic brooding, and bromide intoxication have changed into psychophysiological dysfunction, existential anxiety, and dependence on minor tranquilizers.

Finally, changes in the manifestations of mental illness have resulted also from the discovery of new treatment modalities. And so, with the advent of antidepressants and electroconvulsive therapy, profound depressive stupors have become past history. Unfortunately, the treatments themselves may produce problems. Tardive dyskinesia and benzodiazepine withdrawal syndrome are two such instances.

Isolated case reports herald these changes, followed by the delineation of new syndromes and a revision in nosology. The third edition of *The Diagnostic and Statistical Manual of Mental Disorders* (DSM-III) is the most recent document of this nature, introducing many new diagnostic categories.

Three kinds of "new" psychiatric syndromes can be found in the DSM-III. First are the syndromes that merely have new labels for well-known conditions (e.g., "alcohol amnestic disorder" for "Korsakoff's psychosis"). Second are the reconceptualizations of previously known disorders (e.g., "schizotypical personality disorder" replacing "simple schizophrenia"). Third are the genuinely new syndromes with no phenomenological precursors in earlier psychiatric classifications (e.g., narcissistic personality disorder).

Our book covers this last group of new syndromes, including borderline personality disorder, narcissistic personality disorder, phencyclidine (PCP) psychosis, and cocaine abuse. One chapter discusses multiple personality, which the DSM-III now names as a separate diagnostic entity. Another chapter is devoted to the diagnosis of "attention deficit disorder" in adults. As the DSM-III uses this diagnosis just for children, this chapter is a further refinement and application of the concept of minimal brain dysfunction. Finally, this book considers new psychiatric syndromes *not* included in the DSM-III (e.g., pseudodementia, pathological grief reaction, benzodiazepine withdrawal) and areas of medicine that may yield further new psychiatric entities (e.g., transplantation medicine, chronic dialysis).

But this book does more than provide diagnostic criteria. It discusses the historical evolution of concepts and their status in psychiatric classification, as well as etiology, differential diagnosis, and certain treatment issues. In addition, we present and evaluate contrasting theoretical views, including corresponding DSM-III concepts, of certain syndromes. The detailed bibliographies for each chapter encourage interested readers to expand their knowledge of these relatively unfamiliar areas of psychiatry.

Students of psychiatry, as well as all practicing clinicians, will find in this book detailed discussions of new diagnostic entities, an overview of the DSM-III, and discussions of new areas and potential syndromes in future psychiatry. It is my hope that this book will sharpen readers' diagnostic sensitivity and enhance their therapeutic skills, encourage the already revived interest in descriptive psychiatry, and add theoretical depth to the nosological enterprise in psychiatry.

Acknowledgments

This book is a tribute to two teachers. Dr. N. N. Wig, former chairman of the Department of Psychiatry at the Postgraduate Institute of Medical Education and Research, Chandigarh, India, taught me the love of descriptive psychiatry and the art of teaching. Dr. Vamık Volkan, professor of psychiatry at the University of Virginia School of Medicine, introduced me to psychoanalysis and helped me take my first steps on the road to being a psychotherapist. Both were excellent mentors, and I thank them for their guidance.

The intellectual companionship of Dr. J. Anderson Thomson, Jr., has always enriched my academic pursuits, and I wish to acknowledge this debt. I also wish to thank Drs. Ira Brenner and Harvey Schwartz for their useful comments on this project. I am grateful, too, to the distinguished colleagues who, despite their busy schedules, readily agreed to join this venture. I am confident that their contributions to this volume will lead to a deeper understanding of the newer forms of psychopathology confronting today's psychiatrists. I am also indebted to Mrs. Joan Langs, editorial director at Jason Aronson, Inc., for her helpful advice and constructive criticism throughout this undertaking.

Finally, I wish to thank Mrs. Maxine Rosen and Ms. Lynn Waters for their patient and skillful secretarial assistance.

Contributors

D. WILFRED ABSE, MD
Clinical Professor of Psychiatry
University of Virginia Medical School
Faculty, Washington Psychoanalytic Institute
Director of Education, St. Albans Hospital
Radford, Virginia

SALMAN AKHTAR, MD
Associate Professor of Psychiatry
Jefferson Medical College of the Thomas Jefferson University
Philadelphia, Pennsylvania

PAUL J. FINK, MD
Professor and Chairman
Department of Psychiatry and Human Behavior
Jefferson Medical College of the Thomas Jefferson University
Philadelphia, Pennsylvania

RALPH E. FISHKIN, DO
Clinical Associate Professor of Psychiatry
Jefferson Medical College of the Thomas Jefferson University
Philadelphia, Pennsylvania

EDWARD GOTTHEIL, MD, PhD
Professor of Psychiatry and Human Behavior
Jefferson Medical College of the Thomas Jefferson University
Philadelphia, Pennsylvania

DAVID R. HAWKINS, MD
Director, Consultation-Liaison Service
Michael Reese Hospital and Medical Center
Professor of Psychiatry
Pritzker School of Medicine, University of Chicago
Chicago, Illinois

DILIP V. JESTE, MD

Chief, Unit on Movement Disorders
Adult Psychiatry Branch
National Institute of Mental Health, St. Elizabeth Hospital
Washington, DC

JOHN M. KULDAU, MD

Associate Professor of Psychiatry
University of Florida College of Medicine
Gainsville, Florida

MALCOLM LADER, MD

Professor of Clinical Psychopharmacology
Institute of Psychiatry, University of London
London, UK

LYNNA M. LESKO, MD, PhD

Assistant Attending Psychiatrist
Psychiatry Service
Memorial Sloan-Kettering Cancer Center
Assistant Professor of Psychiatry
Cornell College of Medicine
New York, New York

GERMAN NINO-MURCIA, MD

Clinical Assistant Professor
Director, Center for the Study of Sleep
Jefferson Medical College of the Thomas Jefferson University
Philadelphia, Pennsylvania

HANNES PETURSSON, MD

Senior Lecturer, Department of Pharmacology
Institute of Psychiatry, University of London
London, UK

WARREN PROCCI, MD

Associate Professor of Psychiatry
University of California at Los Angeles
Los Angeles, California

DILIP RAMCHANDANI, MD

Assistant Professor of Psychiatry
Medical College of Pennsylvania
Philadelphia, Pennsylvania

COLLEEN S. W. RAND, PhD

Associate Professor of Psychiatry (Psychology)
University of Florida College of Medicine
Gainesville, Florida

FRED W. REIMHERR, MD

Assistant Professor of Psychiatry
University of Utah School of Medicine
Salt Lake City, Utah

MICHAEL H. STONE, MD

Professor of Psychiatry
University of Connecticut Health Center
Farmington, Connecticut

J. ANDERSON THOMSON JR., MD

Private Practice of Psychiatry
Charlottesville, Virginia

VAMIK D. VOLKAN, MD

Professor of Psychiatry
Medical Director, Blue Ridge Hospital
Director, Division of Psychoanalytic Studies
University of Virginia Medical School
Supervising and Training Analyst
Washington Psychoanalytic Institute
Charlottesville, Virginia

STEPHEN P. WEINSTEIN, PhD

Clinical Associate Professor of Psychiatry and Human Behavior
Jefferson Medical College of the Thomas Jefferson University
Philadelphia, Pennsylvania

KENNETH J. WEISS, MD

Associate Professor of Psychiatry
Jefferson Medical College of the Thomas Jefferson University
Philadelphia, Pennsylvania

CHARLES E. WELLS, MD

Professor and Vice-Chairman, Department of Psychiatry
Vanderbilt University, School of Medicine
Nashville, Tennessee

DAVID R. WOOD, MD

Assistant Professor of Psychiatry
University of Utah School of Medicine
Salt Lake City, Utah

RICHARD JED WYATT, MD

Chief, Adult Psychiatry Branch
National Institute of Mental Health, St. Elizabeth Hospital
Washington, DC

Prologue

Ages are no more infallible than individuals, every age having
held many opinions which subsequent ages have deemed not
only false but absurd, and it is certain that many opinions now
general will be rejected by the present.

On Liberty, John Stuart Mill, 1859

New Diagnostic Entities in the DSM-III

PAUL J. FINK, M.D.

Over the last two decades several important areas of concern have necessitated a greater precision in psychiatric diagnosis. The growing realization that the first step in international research collaboration was a common, operationally clear nosology became the impetus for rethinking in this area. The obfuscation of descriptive psychiatry by widely and loosely used psychoanalytic concepts also demanded a return to phenomenology. As well, the development of specific pharmacologic treatments for specific diseases warranted a clearer delineation of syndromes. Finally, the societal mistrust of the subjective nature of psychiatric diagnoses gave the profession yet another reason for adapting specific and more readily demonstrable criteria for diagnosing various mental disorders.

Although many significant predecessors exist (e.g., DSM-II 1968, Feighner et al. 1972, Spitzer and Endicott 1978), the third *Diagnostic and Statistical Manual of Mental Disorders* (DSM-III) (1980) can be regarded as the latest attempt by American psychiatry to adapt descriptive, concise, and acausal diagnostic criteria that can be replicated and validated. As a result of the major revisions in the classifications of the DSM-II, there now are many new diagnostic categories. Some of these are only newer, more descriptive labels, without any basic change in the underlying concept (e.g., "alcohol amnestic disorder," which is only a new name for the long-recognized condition, Korsakoff's psychosis). But others are new entities that resulted from conceptual shifts, though their precursors existed in the DSM-II (e.g., "simple schizophrenia" is now "schizotypal personality disorder"). Still others are finer tunings of an existing instrument (e.g., the addition of cocaine and PCP to the list of drugs of dependence and abuse). Finally, there are new and original entries that have no counterpart in the DSM-II (e.g., borderline and narcissistic personalities).

This chapter will undertake an overview of these new entities and will also include, when appropriate, comparisons with the DSM-II, pros and cons of certain major changes, references to historical context, and opinions based on clinical experience.

DELETION OF FAMILIAR DIAGNOSTIC TERMS

One striking feature of the DSM-III is its omission of certain diagnostic terms that are part of therapists' everyday vocabulary. Indeed, terms such as manic depressive illness, hebephrenic schizophrenia, hysterical personality, sexual deviation, delirium tremens, and Korsakoff's psychosis do not appear in the DSM-III but are replaced, respectively, by bipolar affective disorder, disorganized schizophrenia, histrionic personality, paraphilias, alcohol withdrawal delirium, and alcohol amnestic syndrome. What necessitated this change? Why were these new diagnostic entities created? At first glance, little seems to have been gained by such changes. Indeed, many therapists will wince at this seemingly callous disregard of history and view these new syndromes as nothing more than a nosological sleight of hand. A careful consideration will reveal that all these alterations emphasize the descriptive and matter-of-fact orientation of contemporary American psychiatry in general and the DSM-III in particular. For instance, Spitzer and colleagues show that "Hysterical Personality was changed to Histrionic Personality Disorder, to avoid confusion caused by the historical relationship of the term "hysteria" to female anatomy . . . and to focus appropriately on the histrionic pattern of behavior" (1980, p. 161).

The terminological change that has caused the most controversy is that pertaining to neurosis. In the DSM-II, all disorders in which anxiety was consciously experienced or "controlled unconsciously" (p. 39) by conversion, dissociation, and various other mental mechanisms were classified together as neuroses. But in the DSM-III, those disorders in which anxiety is directly felt are grouped together in the class of anxiety disorders. Other so-called neurotic disorders are distributed among categories, based on shared, observable symptoms. The attempt is to be purely phenomenological. After all, one cannot argue with the presence of manifest anxiety, phobias, obsessions, or compulsions, but the idea that all of these conditions are in some way connected through unconscious infantile conflicts was anathema to behaviorists and unnecessary in the minds of researchers who found the term neurosis to be confusing and superfluous to their needs.

On the other hand, the majority of therapists in the United States are taught the generic concept of neurosis, which includes a gestalt with implications of etiology and psychoanalytic theory. It also emphasizes that regardless of overt manifestations, the various neurotic disorders have a common core of mental activity. A compromise between the two opposing views and the attempt to satisfy all factions within the profession prevented the term from being deleted altogether from the DSM-III. It was, however, demoted and was retained only in parentheses so that readers could connect the new classification with the old one.

The case of the term *manic depressive illness* is different. The scientific breakthroughs in this area have been remarkable, and it is therefore proper that the labeling process reflect the information in the areas of genetics, biochemistry, and therapeutics that has evolved over the last two decades. Thus, though the DSM-II classification accepted the unity of manic-depressive illness, the DSM-III embraces the more recent evidence (Perris 1966, Winokur et al. 1969) that distinguishes between unipolar and bipolar types of affective disorders. This change is a progressive one with significant research and treatment implications.

OMISSION OF CERTAIN DIAGNOSTIC CATEGORIES

Many diagnostic entities present in the DSM-II have been omitted from the DSM-III. Major categories that met this fate include (1) alcoholic paranoid state, (2) involutional melancholies, (3) involutional paranoid state, (4) neuraesthenic neurosis, (5) asthenic personality, and (6) inadequate personality. These syndromes were found to lack compelling evidence of their occurrence as consistent symptomatic clusters or were considered to be nonspecific functional impairments. Many of these conditions of neuraesthenic neurosis have always been elusive and ill-defined concepts, and so deleting such diagnoses may compel diagnosticians to be more specific in their descriptions.

The status of involutional melancholia seems different, however. Many people would prefer that involutional melancholia had been retained. Since it specifies an age and an etiological connection between that age and disease, the concept ran counter to the DSM-III's generally descriptive and acausal thinking. But involutional melancholia did have features, such as agitation and paranoid tendencies, that distinguished it from other severe depressions. Also distinct was its singular response to electroconvulsive therapy (ECT). Although it is unlikely that a young therapist making a diagnosis of bipolar affective disorder would fail to think of lithium therapy, it is quite possible that the same therapist would now fail to connect a first major depression in late middle life with ECT as the treatment of choice. The omission of involutional melancholia is thus unfortunate.

REFINEMENTS IN SUBCLASSIFICATION OF ESTABLISHED SYNDROMES

ORGANIC MENTAL DISORDERS

One of the most important improvements in the DSM-III, as compared with the DSM-II, is in the broad category of organic disorders. The DSM-II presented a hodgepodge of neurological as well as psychological conditions and failed to give a coherent, well-organized classification that would allow therapists to differentiate among an illness's cause, process, and distinguishing nature. It perpetuated such confusing dichotomies as acute and chronic and psychotic and nonpsychotic in trying to separate one organic condition from another. Acute and chronic, in this one instance in all of medicine, were synonymous with reversible and irreversible and were also loosely equated with delirium and dementia. Thus, acute meant delirious and reversible, and chronic meant demented and irreversible. This method of classification led to inaccuracies and confusion. Some conditions that are chronic are also reversible if proper treatment is applied, and some conditions that start out as deliria deteriorate into chronic and often irreversible conditions. Likewise, attempting to determine if an organically impaired person was also psychotic was difficult and often futile. In contrast, the DSM-III divides all organic conditions into nine categories: intoxication, withdrawal, delirium, dementia, amnesiastic reaction, delusional syndrome, hallucinations, affective syndrome, and personality syndrome. This makes it possible to use a major category to indicate the specific condition and the use of one of the above nine modifiers to describe assorted features which other examiners can identify, recognize, and treat appropriately. In addition, other corrections have been made which include newer information, such as the change from psychoses with cerebral arteriosclerosis to multiinfarct dementia based on the knowledge that dementia is no longer considered to be related to the degree of cerebral arteriosclerosis but, rather, to the presence of multiple infarcts of the brain.

The use of a multiaxial system also allowed for an important change between the two issues of the diagnostic manual. Axis III enables a separate listing of medical diseases, and therefore, delirium caused by a rare endocrinopathy does not call for a specific category to cover such instances.

SUBSTANCE ABUSE DISORDERS

The explosion in information as well as the increase in the use and abuse of multiple substances has led to a much more elaborate classification of these conditions. Perhaps it is a bit overdone. For instance, how many therapists actually intend to use the diagnosis of tobacco dependence? Of course, we should be able to distinguish among opium, cannabis, and alcohol abuse. But the DSM-III takes this several steps further and provides categories in which specific drugs are named as the causative or inducing factor in organic brain disorders, and it also introduces entirely new major categories called *substance abuse disorders*. At first, the lists appear to be similar and may be confusing, but we are now able to specify the exact substance and whether it is an abuse or dependence and also whether it is continuous, episodic, in remission, or unspecified. Within the substance-induced organic brain disorder group there is further refinement that allows the classifier to indicate whether the problem is the result of intoxication or withdrawal and also whether it has additional problems of hallucinations, affective disorders, and the like.

The improved classification of organic conditions and of substance abuse, including alcoholism and alcohol abuse, are remarkable because they have led to simplification, clarification, and a reduction in the confusion and misinformation conveyed by the specific name applied. At the same time, the number of specific categories has been expanded, and the capacity to subdivide and subclassify has been changed. Perhaps this is easier to do with organic conditions when the etiology of the condition is sought and then discovered. The deletion of medical etiologies is also an important improvement, separating mental and behavioral disorders from other specific medical disorders.

SCHIZOPHRENIC DISORDERS

Although the changes in the classification of organic mental disorders have seemed to create order out of chaos, the changes created in the diagnostic divisions and subdivisions of schizophrenia have been viewed with both concern and skepticism. The most dramatic change, which was arbitrary but considered essential in order to determine who should be called schizophrenic, was the use of time in separating those viewed as psychotically impaired with "little chance of recovery" from those who demonstrated short-lived mental disorganization. If patients have a transient psychotic episode of a few days' duration and then return to full functioning, they should be diagnosed as having a serious personality disorder, such as schizotypical, borderline, schizoid, or paranoid. If they have a psychotic episode of less than two weeks' duration, they have either a brief reactive psychosis or an atypical psychosis. The former is used for those whose psychosis is always secondary to a psychosocial stressor, and the latter is used when no such stressor is recognized. If patients have all the signs of schizophrenia, but the duration is between two weeks and six months, the label applied should be schizophreniform disorder. Thus, the term schizophrenia can be used only for those patients whose symptoms, acute or residual, have lasted more than six months.

The second clinical problem that the DSM-III offers to the therapist is the seemingly strong dependence, if not exclusive expectation, that delusions and hallucinations will be present for the diagnoses of schizophrenia. Many fine therapists have taught their residents and students that "one should never make a diagnosis of schizophrenia on the basis of delusions and hallucinations alone." Indeed, this very kind of thinking had originally resulted in Bleuler's concept of schizophrenia (1911), as distinct from Kraepelin's "dementia praecox" (1909). Nevertheless, the diagnostic criteria for the disease center on those perceptual and specific thought disorders. Aside from the requirement that the individual will have deteriorated from his or her previous level of functioning, the symptoms predominate among the observable symptoms needed to make the diagnosis. Even though this narrows the spectrum of those who fall into this category, there will be a great deal of confusion among those who have been trained to look for other signs of impaired thinking, affect, and behavior. The text of the DSM-III reveals that these aspects of schizophrenia are recognized but are considered less important in the final analysis. The DSM-III also considers formal thought disorder and the Schneiderian signs, looseness of associations, affective changes, narcissistic elements in the condition, and disturbances of volitional activity and object relations, all of which should be included in the criteria for the diagnosis. Many of us would have considered those symptoms listed under prodromal or residual symptoms as signs of the active, acute disease and would have made a diagnosis on the basis of those symptoms alone. Though this new system does lead to narrower bands of inclusion, these distinctions are arbitrary, and one wonders how useful they are in actual clinical practice. On the therapeutic side, it is unlikely that one would treat differently a person with a schizophreniform disorder than one with a schizophrenic disorder. The magic six-month period allows one to become the other.

Among the subtypes of schizophrenia, very few of those listed in the DSM-II can be found in the DSM-III. The DSM-II had 15 different types (1968, pp. 7–8), of which only the catatonic, the paranoid, and the residual types remain in the DSM-III. Schizoaffective and childhood schizophrenia are classified elsewhere. The simple, acute, and latent types were abolished, for what appear to be good reasons. Since the term schizophrenia can now be applied only to those who have had the disease for more than six months, acute becomes schizophreniform. Simple and latent cannot exist because the term may be applied only to those who manifest overt psychotic features at that time or have in the past. Most of these patients are now diagnosed as having a schizotypal personality disorder.

The criteria that we used to use to diagnose the hebephrenic type now apply to the disorganized type. Only a single category of catatonic is included and may be applied to the withdrawn, excited, rigid, or negativistic manifestations of the disease. Though the classifying is simpler, the actual diagnosis of schizophrenia is more difficult because of the strictures applied to making the diagnosis.

A word should be included about the concept of schizoaffective disorder. This term was inspired by the growing prevalence of people with thought disorders who also had symptoms resembling mania or depression in lieu of the blunted, flat affect that one was supposed to see in a schizophrenic (for a major review of the schizoaffective disorder, see Procci 1976). It is discussed and included in the DSM-III, but it is clearly not recommended. No criteria for its use are given, but a few examples of how it might be used are included. Instead, the DSM-III indicates that those who were formerly given this label would be better diagnosed from among the following categories: schizophreniform disorder, major depression or bipolar disorder with mood-congruent or mood-incongruent psychotic features, or schizophrenia with a superimposed atypical affective disorder.

PARANOID DISORDERS

Paranoid disorders have been reclassified for a clearer and more precise diagnosis. Once again, the duration of symptoms has been used as a differentiating criterion. In the DSM-II, three subtypes were listed: paranoia, involutional paranoid type, and other paranoid states. In the DSM-III there are four: paranoia, shared paranoid disorder, acute paranoid disorder, and atypical paranoid disorder. The deletion of involutional paranoid disorder is a pity, since it seems to be a characteristic diagnosable condition. The inclusion of folie à deux, or shared paranoid disorder, is a good idea, since the condition has distinct treatment implications. Finally, the paranoia must have lasted for more than six months, and the acute paranoid disorder for less than six months.

AFFECTIVE DISORDERS

Affective disorders, in the DSM-III include the following categories: "bipolar affective disorder" (mixed, manic, depressed) or "major depression," which may be listed either as a single episode or recurrent. Rounding out the list of depressive syndromes are "cyclothymic disorder," included in this section rather than in the one on personality disorders, and finally, "atypical affective disorders," which include atypical bipolar disorder and atypical depression.

The omission of involutional melancholia and the nosological shift from the manic-depressive illness of the DSM-II to bipolar affective disorder have already been commented on. Two other features deserve attention at this point. First is the issue of severity of mood disturbance, and second is the issue of what appear to be quite clearly psychogenic forms of depression.

The DSM-III rejects "neurotic versus psychotic" in the classification of affective disorders. This was never an acceptable division, and comments about the degree of severity were highly speculative and clearly unscientific. Some would say vegetative signs made a psychotic episode, whereas others considered all manic episodes as psychotic. The use of descriptive devices in lieu of these vain attempts at absolute distinctions is preferable. In the DSM-III there is, among the diagnostic criteria for bipolar disease, the opportunity to list with mood-congruent and mood-incongruent psychotic features. Thus, it is possible to fulfill sufficient criteria for the diagnosis of bipolar disease and then to note additional features that recodify it but do not change it. If the patient has gross impairment of reality with delusions and hallucinations or depressive stupor in which he or she is mute and unresponsive, the modifier "with psychotic features" is added.

The psychological forms of affective disorder are, however, not well treated in the DSM-III. The use of dysthymic disorder as both a "neurotic" condition and a personality disorder is a case in point. Also, for instance, the subtleties or differences between a reactive depression and a pathologic grief (Horowitz et al. 1981, Volkan 1981) are not utilized in the phenomenological outlines of depressive syndromes.

NEUROTIC DISORDERS

The discussion regarding the term *neurosis* itself notwithstanding, these so-called neurotic disorders are included in these categories:

1. Anxiety disorders (these include the anxiety, phobic, obsessional, and traumatic neuroses of the DSM-II).

2. Somatoform disorders (these include the hypochondriacal and hysterical conversion neuroses of the DSM-III).

3. Dissociative disorders (these include the hysterical dissociative neurosis of the DSM-II).

Each of these three major categories has been further broken down so that nothing is left to the imagination. Phobias, for example, include agoraphobia with panic attacks, agoraphobia without panic attacks, social phobias, and simple phobias. Anxiety states include panic disorder, generalized anxiety disorder, and obsessive-compulsive disorder. The posttraumatic stress disorder is divided into acute, chronic, or delayed, and finally, there is a category called atypical anxiety disorders. Thus, all the disorders that either do or can elicit overt anxiety are lumped together. The issue of defense mechanisms, etiological conflicts, or somatic symbolic representations of anxiety have no bearing on this classification.

The section entitled "Somatoform Disorders" includes those disorders in which "physical symptoms suggesting physical disorders for which there are no demonstrable organic findings or known physiological mechanisms and for which there is positive evidence or a strong presumption that the symptoms are linked to psychological factors or conflicts" (DSM-III 1980, p. 241). Using this definition, one might think that these are diagnoses made by exclusion; that is, if you cannot find an organic cause, then it must be functional or, in this case, somatoform. This is a style of thinking from which therapists have been trying to escape but is used by those responsible for the DSM-III, since they are seeking a diagnostic system that is criterion based. The section on somatoform disorders is the DSM-III's most confusing and includes somatoform disorder, conversion disorder, psychogenic pain disorder, hypochondriasis, and atypical somatoform disorders.

The text describing conversion disorders gives credence to the term *hysteria* by placing the term *hysterical neuroses, conversion type* in parentheses and describing both primary and secondary gain, both of which are out of voluntary control. Removed from the diagnosis are those conditions that might better be classified as somatoform disorders or psychogenic pain disorders. I have trouble understanding the difference between conversion disorder and somatoform disorder. Somatoform disorder is characterized as a chronic, polysymptomatic disorder that begins early in life. This is apparently the more common condition, whereas conversion reaction is considered rare, usually has neurological symptoms, involves only one or a few symptoms, is temporarily connected with an environmental stimulus, and usually allows the person to avoid pain or get extra attention. This division is arbitrary and represents an effort to deal with a set of diagnoses that require some acceptance of psychodynamic theory. Since there is no wish to give credence to these concepts, the entire chapter seems contrived. Perhaps we can best understand this distinction by viewing somatoform or a new way of classifying those who chronically somatize or use their bodies to express feelings and conflicts: a combination of the old chronic complainer, masochistic character, and psychophysiologic disorders of the DSM-II. By contrast, conversion disorder is one that is brought on by outside influences or traumas or has a specific "psychological" purpose. All of this can be accepted without the idea of unconscious conflict or motivation. The separate listing of psychogenic pain disorder is in keeping with current interest in this condition. The criteria for this diagnosis are almost identical with conversion disorder, except for the specific symptom of pain that cannot be verified as having organic causes. Hypochondriasis is similarly difficult to distinguish from somatoform itself. Even though the criteria suggest pathological preoccupation, they do not stress the defensive or highly irrational quality that most therapists ascribe to this condition.

The chapter on dissociative disorders takes a single neurosis from the DSM-II and creates five new entities. These include psychogenic amnesia, psychogenic fugue, multiple personality, depersonalization disorder, and atypical dissociative disorder. In general, the essential feature of the entire category is a sudden temporary alteration of the normal integrative functions of consciousness, identity, or motor behavior. It is a testimony to creativity that these conditions are described, categorized, and given definite diagnostic criteria without indicating any deep-seated disturbances. There is a heavy reliance on external stimuli in the initiation of these symptom complexes, referred to as psychosocial stress. Although it may be a good idea to subdivide these conditions and describe them as distinct phenomenological entities, it destroys the order that the term hysteria brought to the system of diagnosis that prevailed prior to the DSM-III. Included among the hysterical neuroses were conversion and dissociative reactions, considered conditions that were different expressions of an unconscious conflict with fixation at the oedipal level.

Everyone understood that there could be multiple symptoms and that these were mild, although sometimes debilitating, conditions that represented a characteristic pathological symptomatic method of resolving problems. Unlike the implications in the DSM-III chapter on dissociative disorders, which implies an external stimulus or etiology, all of the neuroses are considered internal, intrapsychic conditions.

PSYCHOSEXUAL DISORDERS

The DSM-III's section on psychosexual disorders provides a good review and an excellent breakdown of sexual problems. There are four subgroups: gender identity disorders, including transsexualism and gender identity disorders of childhood; the paraphilias, which include all of the conditions listed under sexual deviations in the DSM-II with the exception of homosexuality; and the psychosexual dysfunctions, including inhibited sexual desire, inhibited sexual excitement, inhibited female orgasm, inhibited male orgasm, premature ejaculation, functional dyspareunia, functional vaginismus, and, of course, atypical sexual dysfunctions. This last category of psychosexual definitions did not appear in the DSM-II, as this area of study was rudimentary, and its investigation and the development of diagnostic and therapeutic techniques have flourished only in the last decade. The authors of the DSM-III have captured the latest ideas about these conditions and have presented them with a concise set of criteria for making these diagnoses. The use of the term *inhibited* in several of the categories allows us to continue the search for the cause or causes of these inhibitions without either curtailing future research or prematurely assigning categories. In the same chapter is a section called "Other Psychosexual Disorders," and the key diagnostic entity included here is "ego-dystonic homosexuality." In the 1970s, therapists felt that no homosexuals should be labeled as sick, as they seemed to be in the DSM-II. Only those homosexuals who were in conflict over their feelings or felt that their arousal by persons of the same sex was alien would be classified as having an illness. My only criticism of this chapter may be that people who present with these conditions often have other, more significant problems that can lead to either multiple diagnoses or, unfortunately, to failure of the examiner to note a schizophrenic disorder, affective disorder, or neurotic conditions.

ADJUSTMENT DISORDERS

In the DSM-II, adjustment disorders were called transient situational reactions and were organized according to age, e.g., adjustment reactions of childhood, adolescence, and so on. Though usually the result of an identifiable psychosocial stress, in some cases such conditions were neither transient nor situational. Therefore, in the DSM-III the entire category is called adjustment disorders and may be modified according to the accompanying affectives or behavioral symptoms. Thus we have the following modifiers: with depressed mood, with anxious mood, with mixed emotional features, with mixed emotional pictures, with disturbance of conduct, with disturbances of emotions and conduct, with work (or academic) inhibition, with withdrawal, or with atypical features. Such disturbances are expected to remit after the stressor has been removed, but the problem may become chronic. The variation in reaction is manifold, as are the vicissitudes of the stressor. This chapter helps clarify an important set of diagnoses.

PERSONALITY DISORDERS

In the DSM-III, personality disorders are to be diagnosed on a separate "axis." This is clearly a major change from the DSM-II, in which the personality disorders were considered equal to all other psychiatric diagnoses. In the DSM-III, multiple diagnoses can be made, and the personality disorders are placed on a separate axis to indicate their continuity in the face of acute and/or chronic mental illness. The lists of personality disorders in the DSM-II and DSM-III reflect the thinking of the times in which they were created. In the DSM-III, new entities such as narcissistic, borderline, avoidant, and dependent personality disorders are included. Schizotypal is also new and has been discussed with schizophrenia. However, special note should be made of the distinction between schizoid and schizotypal. Schizoid personality disorder is a diagnosis reserved for those in whom there is "a defect in the capacity to form social relationships evidenced by the absence of warm, tender feelings for others and indifference to praise, criticism and the feelings of others" (DSM-III 1980, p. 310). It is no longer viewed as a precursor to schizophrenia. That personality disorder is entitled schizotypal and is characterized by eccentricities of communication or behavior. People with a schizotypal disorder have oddities of thought, perception, speech, and behavior that are not severe enough to meet the criteria of schizophrenia. Cyclothymic, which appeared in the DSM-II under personality disorders, is listed in the DSM-III with the affective disorders. Some of the types that were deleted from the DSM-II, such as inadequate, aesthenic, and explosive, were rarely used and are better excluded. In a way, such simplistic descriptive terminology detracted from the "scientific" intent of the diagnostic manual. The change from hysterical in the DSM-II to histrionic in the DSM-III is consistent with the wish to abolish terms that have a

Freudian flavor. In sum, the DSM-III's chapter on personality disorders is a decided improvement on that in the DSM-II. The criteria for using each term describe more precisely those patients so labeled. The personality disorders listed in the DSM-III are placed in three clusters. The first, which includes paranoid, schizoid, and schizotypal, represents those people who appear odd and eccentric. Those people in the second cluster, which includes histrionic, narcissistic, antisocial, and borderline, often appear dramatic, emotional, or erratic. Those who fall into the final group, including avoidant, dependent, compulsive, and passive-agressive, often appear anxious or fearful.

CONCLUSION

The DSM-III is a vast improvement over the DSM-II. It combines a careful and thoughtful attempt to sort out the essential criteria for making psychiatric diagnoses with a well-reasoned effort to lump together those entities that seem to fall naturally into a system based almost entirely on description and phenomenology. Such a project must, of necessity, be somewhat imperfect. Singerman and associates observed that "indeed, perfection of the diagnostic system is only the first step in creating a scientific, well respected field of endeavor" (1981, p. 426).

I have commented on the areas of the DSM-III that I feel are weaknesses, but overall it is a credit to the field of psychiatry that such a manual has been prepared. The art and science of diagnosis are lively and ever-changing activities. Already we can contemplate the areas of concern for the DSM-IV. No sooner have we completed one task than we discover new entities, new cures, and new problems which not only indicate that we are a growing and exciting field but also represent a new generation of ideas that will benefit our patients and our field.

REFERENCES

Bleuler, E. (1911). *Dementia Precox or the Group of Schizophrenias*. Trans. J. Zinkin, 1951. London: Allen and Unwin.

Diagnostic and Statistical Manual of Mental Disorders (1968). 2nd ed. Washington, D.C.: American Psychiatric Association.

Diagnostic and Statistical Manual of Mental Disorders (1980). 3rd ed. Washington, D.C.: American Psychiatric Association.

Feighner, J. P., Robins, E., Guze, S. B., Woodruff, R. A., Winokur, G., and Munoz, R. (1972). Diagnostic criteria for use in psychiatric research. *Archives of General Psychiatry* 26:57–63.

Horowitz, M. J., Wilner, N., Mormar, C., and Krupnick, J. (1981). Pathological grief and activation of latent self images. *American Journal of Psychiatry* 12:1157–1162.

Kraepelin, E. (1909). *Psychiatrie Ein Lehrbuch für Studierende und Aerzte.* Leipzig: Barth.

Perris, C. (1966). A study of bipolar (manic depressive) and unipolar recurrent depressive psychosis. *Acta Psychiatrie Scandinavica* 194:9–188.

Procci, W. R. (1976). Schizoaffective psychosis: fact or fiction? *Archives of General Psychiatry* 33:1167–1178.

Singerman, B., Stoltzman, R. K., Robins, L. N., Helzer, J. E., and Croughan, J. L. (1981). Diagnostic concordance between DSM-III, Feighner's RDC. *Journal of Clinical Psychiatry* 42:11–16.

Spitzer, R. L., and Endicott, J. (1978). Medicine and mental disorder: proposed definition and criteria in *Critical Issues in Psychiatric Diagnosis.* ed. R. L. Spitzer and D. F. Klein. New York: Raven Press.

Spitzer, R. L., Williams, J. B. W., and Skodol, A. E. (1980). DSM-III: the major achievements and overview. *American Journal of Psychiatry* 12:151–164.

Volkan, V. D. (1981). *Linking Objects and Linking Phenomena.* New York: International Universities Press.

Winokur, G., Clayton, P., and Reich, T. (1969). *Manic Depressive Illness.* St. Louis: C. V. Mosby.

PART I

Psychoanalytic Contributions to Psychiatric Nosology

There is a great deal of unmapped country within us which would have to be taken into account in an explanation of our gusts and storms.

Daniel Deronda, George Eliot

CHAPTER 1

Borderline Personality Disorder
MICHAEL H. STONE, M.D.

HISTORICAL PERSPECTIVE

The notion of "borderland" or borderline states in psychiatry made its first appearance during the closing years of the 19th century. The bipartite division into either the milder "neurotic" or the grossly delusional "psychotic" cases, which had for so long a time held sway in psychiatric taxonomy, was becoming recognized as simplistic. Criminals, for example, often showed aberrations of mental life that as Lombroso (1878) observed, were often not of psychotic proportions, yet still quite far removed from normal or normal/neurotic life. Hence, borderline. Similarly, Rosse (1890) described a number of noncriminal neuropaths whose rather flamboyant symptoms fell just short of what was regarded in his day as clearly (and chronically) psychotic; these cases were also spoken of as borderline.

One could argue that the two great nosologists of the turn of the century, Kraepelin and Bleuler, endorsed the concept of borderline, though neither used the term. In his 1921 monograph on manic depression, Kraepelin spoke of the depressive, irritable, manic, and cyclothymic temperaments as often dilute (i.e., borderline) variants of full-blown manic-depressive psychoses. By the same token, Bleuler (1911) was aware that not all cases of dementia praecox, hereafter called schizophrenic, showed the deterioration that Kraepelin felt characterized this clinical domain. There were, in other words, borderline instances of schizophrenia — into whose ranks Bleuler would, for example, have placed, because of his relatively favorable course, the composer Robert Schumann (Bleuler 1911, p. 210). After the turn of the century, as the psychoanalytic movement began to flourish, a number of its pioneering members began to speak of borderline in relation to the more established categories within their clinical domain (Clark 1919, Moore 1921, Oberndorf 1930). Borderline was now used to designate conditions that seemed outwardly to be amenable to classical psychoanalytic therapy but that turned out not to improve using the classical method.

In a paper that contributed to the popularization of the borderline label, Stern (1938) outlined a number of clinical features he felt typified these intermediate conditions. Among them, he mentioned (severe) narcissism, inordinate hypersensitivity, "negative therapeutic reaction" to certain analytic interpretations (that were meant to be helpful but were experienced by the patient as disapproving or discouraging), a drastically reduced capacity to tolerate stress, projective mechanisms (at times approaching delusory ideation), and difficulties in reality testing (manifest especially in relation to others, such as faulty empathy).

Borderline thus lay between the classical analyzability of the neurotic and the clear-cut nonanalyzability of the chronically psychotic patient. Many of the early analysts thought that the psychosis that these borderline cases resembled was schizophrenia, and so they devised a number of labels not using the term borderline, labels that indicated their prejudice in favor of schizophrenia. We thus heard of pseudoneurotic schizophrenia (Hoch and Polatin 1949), ambulatory schizophrenia (Zilboorg 1941), latent schizophrenia (Bychowski 1953, Federn 1947), as-if personality (as a form of incipient schizophrenia: Deutsch 1942), psychotic character (as resembling schizophrenia; or on occasion, manic-depressive psychosis (MDP): Frosch 1960), and the like. In the early 1950s, Knight moved the concept of borderline in the direction of a distinct syndrome, with characteristic symptoms, psychodynamics, and defenses, even though Knight himself thought many of his borderline patients suffered from an incipient, or in other instances, attenuated form of schizophrenia. By the time Grinker and colleagues wrote their monograph (1968) on borderline inpatients, borderline was well on its way, at least in psychoanalytic circles, to being used as a separate entity. This tendency was perpetuated by Kernberg (1967) and Gunderson and Singer (1975). Kernberg stressed good reality-testing capacity (as distinguished from psychotic structure) and poor integration of the self (as contrasted with the neurotic's good ego integration) as the characteristic features of borderline as a type of psychic structure. Gunderson and Singer emphasized good socialization (to differentiate from manifest schizophrenia) and poor work history (to differentiate from the psychoneuroses), along with predominantly rageful affect, impulsivity, manipulative suicide gestures, and brief psychotic episodes. Both included the attributes of primitive defenses (denial, splitting, and the like) and serious disturbances in close relationships as important to their conception of the borderline state.

In the meantime, some nonanalytically oriented psychiatrists were beginning to speak of a borderline schizophrenia, related to core schizophrenia by virtue of the similarity of symptoms and traits in close relatives (Kety et al. 1968). A few analysts began to recognize that there could be mild depressive or hypomanic conditions in certain borderline patients that ought to be considered within the manic-depressive spectrum rather than the schizophrenic spectrum (Frosch 1964, Jacobson 1953).

Current European definitions of borderline incline toward either the schizophrenia spectrum of disorder (Benedetti 1965) or the inclusion of organic cases with perinatal damage (Aarkrog 1973, 1981). But most of the American definitions by psychoanalytic or clinical therapists (Grinker et al. 1968, Gunderson and Singer 1975, Kernberg 1967, Klein 1977) have been drawn up in such a way that, however unintentionally, the samples of patients who will satisfy their criteria will be composed largely of affectively ill patients.

There are a number of reasons that this peculiar shift has taken place, explaining why the psychosis to which borderline is related is now more often MDP and only occasionally schizophrenia. Partly this is because we are now more careful and more restrictive about whom we call schizophrenic, especially after the advent of lithium (1960s). Once lithium was easily available, one could no longer afford (as was so commonly the custom in the United States) to label all persons with psychotic symptoms (transient or chronic) as schizophrenic. Some patients should have been diagnosed as bipolar manic depressive as they would improve upon being given lithium. Then, too, the newer definitions of borderline tended to exclude cases that were in the schizophrenia spectrum (as outlined in the studies of psychogeneticists like Kety, Rosenthal, and others). Kernberg's insistence on good reality testing in the interpersonal realm excludes both the classical schizophrenics and the majority of the geneticists' borderline schizophrenics. The Kety B-3 borderline schizophrenics, for example, are usually so full of contradictory images of self and others and so inflexible in the way they cling to these distorted views that they emerge as psychotic, according to Kernberg's psychostructural criteria.

In my own studies (1977, 1981) of patients considered borderline by Kernberg's criteria, I was struck by the frequency with which their first-degree relatives exhibited either frank manic depression (unipolar more often then bipolar) or some milder condition that could, because of the prominent affective symptoms, be considered as lying within the manic-depressive spectrum. Many of the close relatives were also alcoholic.

This same correlation between borderline, affective symptomatology and positive family history for affective illness was noted in a study of 100 borderlines by Akiskal (1981), in which the borderline diagnosis rested on Gunderson's rather than Kernberg's criteria.

But even to note this shift from borderline as atypical or dilute schizoprenia to borderline as atypical or dilute MDP does not do full justice to the complexity of the clinical situation. There appear to be not only numerous affective symptoms in the patients we currently call borderline but also numerous meaningful diagnostic subtypes and varieties of affective illness within the borderline domain (as defined by broad criteria such as those of Kernberg or Spitzer and colleagues). Recognition of these subtypes is important, because the treatment is not the same for all, nor is the prognosis.

In this chapter, I shall describe about a dozen such affective subtypes, offering a brief clinical example of each and a brief comment about the therapeutic measures I consider most appropriate for the typical examples of each subtype, which are outlined in Table 1-1 (p. 31).

AFFECTIVE SUBTYPES WITHIN THE BORDERLINE DOMAIN

ENDOGENOMORPHIC DEPRESSION, RELATED TO MDP

A 34-year-old woman was referred for psychotherapy because of a depression that occurred during the breakup of a romantic relationship. She had been the financial editor of a newsmagazine but was currently out of work. A chronic arthritic condition made it difficult for her to find a new job. Though she had experienced insomnia, diurnal mood variation (worse in the morning), tearfulness, and suicidal ruminations, she showed no changes in appetite or weight. Agitation (hand wringing, pacing) was more prominent than the depressed mood was. Borderline features included sharply contradictory notions of self and family members, inability to be alone, chronic ragefulness, ability of mood mistrustfulness, and extreme hypersensitivity to criticism. She was not impulsive. Both of her parents, who divorced when she was 12, were physicians. Both also were severely depressed at one time or another: the father, recurrently so (unipolar MDP).

Although she was referred for analytically oriented psychotherapy, she was unusually resistant to this mode of treatment. She could not free-associate or recall dreams but, instead, would ask over and over, in a rather hostile and petulant manner, "When am I going to get better?" or "What can you do for me?"

I felt that her condition was so close to a classical agitated depression that antidepressants might prove more useful than a verbal approach would. She did not respond to tricyclics but did respond favorably to a monoamine oxidase (MAO) inhibitor. At one point she even became hyperactive and tense until the dosage was reduced. At this point, without any interpretive work having been done, she improved enough that she was able to seek reemployment and find comfort in the company of her friends, whom she had been avoiding for the past six or seven months.

ENDOGENOMORPHIC DEPRESSION, UNRELATED TO MDP

A 29-year-old woman was hospitalized in a state of acute depression, following the death of her 7-year-old son from a congenital heart ailment The year before, her husband had left her, and she was now divorced. During the same year, both her parents had died, and since she was an only child, she now had no family at all. Unable to continue working after her son's death, she became nearly paralyzed with depression and was mute and almost immobile on admission. She had lost 15 pounds. Her previous level of function had been good; she had a responsible position as an editorial assistant. None of her immediate family had suffered any illness within the spectrum of the primary affective disorders.

Several weeks after admission, she became more communicative and gave evidence of sharply polarized thoughts about herself and others: she felt great remorse regarding her son, even though she was in no way to blame for his illness. Likewise, she blamed herself for her other losses and tended to idealize those who had died or left her, despite the callousness of her husband and the unsavory reputation of her father.

She was placed on tricyclic antidepressants. Within two and a half months she made an excellent recovery and was able to see herself and those who had been close to her in a more realistic light. She returned to her job, reestablished ties with her friends, and subsequently remarried. Ten years later, as I learned through a colleague, she is still quite well.

HYSTEROID DYSPHORIA

A 24-year-old law student was referred for psychotherapy because of suicidal ruminations in connection with the breakup of a long relationship with a homosexual partner. This had been the patient's most meaningful and lasting friendship. Previously, his homosexual contacts had been sporadic encounters, such as engaging in fellatio through holes in the partitions of bathroom stalls in subways. He had been apprehended once by the police for such activity.

He had been raised in a family in which his father had been away for many years in the war (he did not see his father until he was 5); his mother had been ambivalent about the pregnancy and had often told him she had wished he had never been born. But once he was, she behaved in an overly protective manner and often was seductive. She bathed him until he was 15 and would fondle his penis while doing so. The patient had become, and remained, exclusively homosexual since age 14.

In the beginning of therapy, he was dramatic and overreacted to rejection by his sexual partners by becoming despondent, tearful, and suicidal. He was negativistic about treatment, deriding it as offering only "words." After the resolution of his negativism, aided by resolution of my countertransference anxieties concerning acceptance of his homosexuality, therapy moved to a different level. He was able to explore deeper early conflicts about paternal rejection and maternal ambivalence. Although he was on tricyclic antidepressants initially, he was comfortable enough after 4 months to be tapered off from the medication. Eventually, he made an excellent academic adjustment and found a partner with whom he could have a more lasting and less sadomasochistic relationship.

PHOBIC-ANXIOUS REACTION

A 34-year-old man entered the hospital in a state of panic following the purchase of a house for himself and his wife. He could not understand why he had become anxious, since he felt that his marriage (of ten years) was "perfect" and that his wife had every right to expect to move to a larger place and to raise a family. The night before his panic attack, he had a disturbing dream in which he saw his penis lying on the ground in front of him and blood coming out of his groin. When admitted to the hospital, he paced the floor and constantly wrung his hands, asking everyone who came near, "When am I going to get better?!" Although he was a psychologist, he had no awareness at first of his negative feelings toward assuming the greater responsibilities of a high mortgage and the even greater responsibilities of parenthood. He was likewise unaware of his strong resentment of his wife for "pressuring" him to do the ordinary things that married couples do. At first he was so anxious that he was unable to engage in any meaningful discussion about his problems and, in fact, denied he had any problems. During this phase of his condition, since verbal psychotherapy seemed not to touch him, it was deemed more appropriate to rely on medication. A tricyclic antidepressant was chosen, because he appeared to suffer from the phobic-anxious syndrome within the spectrum of depressive disorders (manifest dysphoria was not present). After several weeks, his anxiety had largely disappeared, and he was now capable of acknowledging the previously disavowed feelings about his marital situation. He was discharged from the hospital after a month and continued to adjust well, now within the context of an analytically oriented psychotherapy.

CYCLOTHYMIA

A 35-year-old surgeon was evaluated for several weeks at a psychiatric hospital for tests to determine the nature of a depressive condition with phobic features that had resisted six years of psychoanalysis and four more of various forms of supportive therapy.

At the beginning of his illness, he had become so anxious when about to perform surgery that he could not continue the procedure. He quit work and was supported by his wife. At times he became irritable with her or the children to the point of physical abusiveness, without any provocation on their part. At other times he would become weepy and depressed, taking to his bed for a week at a time.

Diagnostic evaluation according to conventional standards suggested a depressive neurosis with obsessional and phobic features. His self-image contained such severe distortions (he was considered by his colleagues a superior surgeon) that by Kernberg's standards, he could be said to be functioning at the borderline level. Analysis of his personality in relation to temperament, however, revealed that he had many traits in three compartments: depressive, manic, and irritable. This, combined with a family history strongly positive for manic depression, made it likely that he was suffering from a mild variant of manic depression; namely, cyclothymia. A trial of lithium was instituted, along with a tricyclic antidepressant. Over a period of six months, he had fewer outbursts of irritability, and there was an improvement in his work-avoidance pattern. He was able to return, at least part time, to his profession.

MASKED DEPRESSION

A 21-year-old graduate student was referred for psychotherapy because of difficulties in his relationships with superiors and with all women. He had developed a peptic ulcer at age 18 while on a trip away from home and had to return to his family, several members of whom had experienced serious depressions.

During the course of analytically oriented therapy, it was revealed that he had been fired from several jobs because of insubordinacy, had been impotent with a number of women, and was given to brief episodes of hypomanic behavior (usually before exams). He was inordinately attached to his mother, calling her for an hour on the phone every night he was away from his home. He became tense and irritable before separations of all kinds, including my vacations. These would be preceded by dreams depicting despair and bleakness; occasionally, he dreamed of being dead. Contradictory views of self and others were of borderline quality. His depressive dynamics and inner life (as characterized by his dreams) were not accompanied by dysphoria. He could therefore be considered to suffer a "masked" depression.

Over a period of two and a half years he responded to therapy, without the addition of medication (though at times, lithium was considered during his rare hypomanic episodes). He made an excellent adjustment, became less contemptuous of superiors at work, made a psychological separation from his mother, and married a suitable girl.

ANACLITIC DEPRESSION

A 26-year-old teacher sought therapy because of depression in connection with the breakup of a romantic relationship. She became tearful, unable to work, and sleepless and immediately after the breakup she began to vomit repeatedly and developed a quasi-delusional idea that she was vomiting out part of her liver and thus dying. Two members of her immediate family had bipolar MDP: one classical (and responsive to lithium) and one atypical.

Her strong tendency to lean excessively on others had been noticeable throughout adolescence and also in recent years. This had been ascribed to the long separations from her parents during her early childhood because of her mother's illness. For several months at a time, she had been cared for by other relatives.

She was seen in thrice-weekly, later twice-weekly, analytically oriented therapy. Throughout the first year she cried during almost every session, often over trivial things. Her tendency to become dependent on others showed itself in relation to her brother, her mother, and a new boyfriend. For some seven or eight months she was prescribed modest doses of Elavil® (25 mg, t.i.d.), which was accompanied by a lessening of dysphoric symptoms. Therapy lasted for two and a half years. By that time she had become engaged to an appropriate man. In the five years that have elapsed since our last session, she has gone to graduate school, entered a new profession, and had two children. She has remained asymptomatic.

ANOREXIA NERVOSA

A 23-year-old graduate student had to stop her studies because of progressive weight loss. She went from 120 to 75 pounds but became hyperactive. She was amenorrheic. At home, where she had remained most of the time sequestered in her room, she made no pretense of doing any useful activity. She spent hours masturbating, at times even in front of her parents. At other times she would become despondent, elaborating schemes for suicide (never carried out). Her parents noted a pronounced preciosity in her speech, as well as some pressured speech. Narcissistic qualities were now very apparent in her personality, in particular, vanity and demandingness. She was hospitalized against her will.

Her mother suffered a severe depression when she was in her thirties but was treated successfully with electroconvulsive therapy.

Not initially receptive to psychotherapy of any sort, the patient was treated with tricyclic antidepressants and a behavior-modification approach, consisting of rewards for gaining weight. On this regimen, her mixed affective and schizotypal borderline condition slowly responded: her weight increased to 105 pounds, her inappropriate behavior stopped, and her dysphoric symptoms abated.

PREMENSTRUAL TENSION

A 23-year-old woman had been found by a roommate as she lay near death from an overdose of sleeping pills. Having been saved by the roommate's unexpected return, she was then hospitalized. Shortly before the attempt, she had had a falling-out with an older man to whom she had become engaged.

Marked mood swings were noted by the hospital staff. At times she would be cheery, friendly with the staff and helpful with the other patients, as though she were quite well and in no need of psychiatric care. At other times, precipitously and without apparent cause, she would descend into the deepest despair and make rash suicide gestures the moment she felt she was not being watched by the nurses. Careful recording of these changes revealed that the depressive episodes always occurred 24 hours before her menses started and ceased several hours after her flow began.

Both of the patient's parents had been treated for serious depressive illnesses; both had received antidepressants; and one had been briefly hospitalized.

The patient showed severe distortions in her self-image, imagining herself to be a loathsome person. Her borderline features (according to Kernberg's and Gunderson's criteria) were much more in evidence premenstrually than at other times. The periodicity of her condition prompted a trial with lithium, to which she did not respond. But she did respond to Nardil® and eventually to intensive psychotherapy without medication.

DEPRESSIVE TEMPERAMENT

A 26-year-old man was referred for psychotherapy because of inability to work, depression, and recurrent bouts of suicidal ruminations.

His mother and a maternal aunt had been treated years earlier for major depressive disorders. His father died of a pulmonary ailment when the patient was six.

The patient had had two bouts of severe depression during college, necessitating leaves of absence. Since his graduation he had not worked, partly out of a kind of phobic avoidance of any kind of employment. The seriousness of this symptom was masked partly by his having come from a wealthy family, and so he did not have to earn his livelihood.

Noticeable during the consultative period of our work was a depressive "temperament," in addition to the history of repeated bouts of crippling dysphoria. He was markedly overscrupulous, pessimistic, worrisome, judgmental of other people's petty foibles, and fearful of exams and job interviews. Markedly obsessional in character, he was largely out of touch with his feelings, but to a degree bordering on caricature. He rarely recalled dreams. For many months, our sessions were filled with dry intellectualizations and endless questions about the "nature of depression." A trial of antidepressants was unsuccessful, largely because of his lack of motivation to take his medication regularly. After a year or so of "cognitive" therapy, a more analytic therapy was possible and was accompanied by the relief of symptoms, the working through of his father's death, and an ability to work (albeit at a part-time level) for the first time in his life.

DEPRESSION WITH SCHIZOAFFECTIVE FEATURES

A 35-year-old housewife and mother of two children had to be admitted briefly to the hospital for what appeared at first to be a paranoid schizophrenic reaction. Persecutory delusions, negativistic behavior, and agitation were present, but these symptoms abated after three or four days of neuroleptic treatment. It was discovered that for many months she had been abusing barbiturates; but after several months she was able to break this habit. Depressive/dysphoric symptoms now surfaced in the context of a joyless and deteriorating marriage. Paranoid/persecutory feelings still emerged periodically, sometimes premenstrually and sometimes after arguments with her husband. She expected the worst from men and was often hostile; these attitudes were manifest in the transference reactions of the analytic therapy she now was undergoing. Tricyclic antidepressants were also used, for approximately one and a half years.

Some of her hostility toward men seemed to come from the hostile/dependent relationship she had with her father, with whom she had briefly had incestuous relations during her adolescence. She was unable to speak of this until after two years of (two to three times weekly) sessions. Her mistrust of men and her sense of entrapment in a hopeless situation then lessened, partly in relation to gains made in therapy and partly in relation to her husband's eventual willingness to enter treatment. At this point, their marriage improved, and her symptoms largely subsided.

"CORE" BORDERLINE WITH DEPRESSIVE, UNSTABLE, AND RAGEFUL FEATURES

A 19-year-old girl was admitted to the hospital after a suicide attempt made while in her first year at college.

During her initial evaluation, severe characterological problems were noted. She was markedly irritable (worse so premenstrually), abusive, rageful, and at times given to screaming fits, slamming doors or physically attacking her therapist or the nurses. Each "crisis" would be followed by depression, uncontrollable crying, and pangs of remorse.

Weekend (let alone longer) separations from her therapist were intolerable to her. She had carried on a homosexual/incestuous relationship with her sister and hoped to recreate this situation with her (female) therapist. The latter she alternately idealized as the "good mother" she felt she never had or depreciated as a rejecting, hateful "witch," the same as she usually experienced her mother. Coercive suicide gestures occurred at frequent intervals for about two years. Hospitalization was needed for almost two years, and even afterwards, her life was often stormy and chaotic. She remained in thrice-weekly, analytically oriented therapy and also took Tofranil® 75 to 100 mgm/day. Slight disappointments, such as being kept waiting for two or three minutes beyond the time a session was to have begun, led to outbursts of anger and vilification. After several years of treatment, she was able to return to school and to work part time. She felt less need to "actualize" the transference than had been noted earlier. Her appealing, dependent personality traits were not more apparent than her irascible and demanding ones. Her family history was remarkable for the large number of both primary depressive and schizoaffective disorders among her first-degree relatives.

DEPRESSIVE CHARACTER SPECTRUM DISORDER

A 29-year-old married woman was referred for psychotherapy by the therapist who was treating her husband. Depressive symptoms — crying spells, despondency, and dysphoric mood — had developed within weeks after their marriage, which was in only its 11th month when she came for therapy herself. She was markedly infantile and dependent. Her husband, a much older man, was largely indifferent to her, rarely wished to have sex, and never offered to go out for entertainment. Despite the absence of gratification in her marriage, she was afraid not only to give it up but even to acknowledge the true state of affairs. As a result, she avoided confrontations by her therapist regarding her unhappiness. After two months she quit treatment, leaving her joyless marriage intact, which offered her nothing except relief from loneliness. At times she was pouty, irascible, and verbally abusive with her husband, though usually meek and self-effacing.

Her character disorder was mainly within the depressive realm but was not considered within the manic-depressive spectrum, because of the absence of any (even mild) vegetative signs and the negative family history with respect to primary affective disorders.

Comment. Though patients with infantile personality who function at the borderline level are often amenable to analytically oriented psychotherapy (and are often the "best-outcome" cases among borderline patients so treated), there are occasional exceptions. The above patient seemed to represent such an exception, largely because of poor motivation. Her poor motivation itself appeared to reflect her dread of being alone, as though the recognition of the barrenness of her marriage would force her to abandon it and then for a time to have to endure being by herself. This was unendurable; hence, any examination of her marital discord was also unendurable. In the absence of any target symptoms, it is not likely that medication would have been beneficial, either.

OTHER VARIETIES OF BORDERLINE CONDITIONS

The Kernberg definition of borderline emphasizes a stable psychic organization or structure which is fairly resistant to change (in the untreated state) or even to temporary fluctuations in state. An exception to the latter is observable in certain cyclothymic persons who usually function at the borderline level but who periodically and spontaneously improve, for several weeks or months at a time, to the level of neurotic personality organization. In cases of this sort, the term borderline as a level of function is of limited value. Such considerations apart, it has been estimated that perhaps 10 percent of the population exhibits the poor identity inte-

Table 1-1. Varieties of depressive and other affective disorders in patients with borderline function

Borderline Structure	Are cases within the MDP spectrum?	Will analytic psychotherapy be useful?	Will antidepressants be useful?	Will lithium be useful?	Will behavior modification be useful?
Endogenomorphic depression, MDP related	Yes	Not as a rule	Yes	No	Occasionally
Endogenomorphic depression, second-degree overwhelming loss	No (or only by coincidence)	Maybe, after acute symptoms subside	In some cases initially	No	No
Hysteroid dysphoria	Usually	Often	Yes, at outset	Rarely	No
Phobic anxious	Often	Not as a rule	Yes	No	Occasionally
Cyclothymia	Yes	Not as a rule	Sometimes	Yes	No
Masked depression	Occasionally	Often	Not often	No	Occasionally
Anaclitic depression, Grinker Type IV	Occasionally	Often	Occasionally	No	No
Anorexia nervosa	Often	In selected cases	Seldom	No	Yes
Severe premenstrual tension	Often in more severe cases	In selected cases	Fairly often	No	Occasionally
Depressive temperament	Yes	Often	Sometimes	No	No
Schizoaffective (affective>Sz.)	Often	Often	Fairly often	Rarely	No
"Core" borderline with depressive, unstable, rageful features	Fairly often	Fairly often, if motivation good	Fairly often, at outset	No	Occasionally
Character spectrum disorder (unrelated to MDP)	No	Fairly often	No	No	No

gration and good reality-testing capacity that together establish border-line function.

A similarly large fraction of the population could be considered borderline if one used as a diagnostic criterion the presence of six or more items from the checklist mentioned by Spitzer and associates (1979) in their survey of American psychiatrists. This checklist combines two lists, each with eight items. One list now appears in the DSM-III (1980) as the "schizotypal personality." The word borderline no longer appears in this label, though it was derived from descriptions of cases felt to be borderline in relation to schizophrenia (Kety et al. 1968). Certain close relatives of unequivocal schizophrenics showed oddities of communica-tion, magical thinking, inordinate suspiciousness, social isolation, and the like but were free of the delusions, hallucinations, and formal thought disorder necessary for the more serious diagnosis. The other list, which made up the "unstable personality" of the Spitzer article, has now been labeled in the DSM-III as the "borderline personality." The merits and drawbacks of this revision will be discussed below. We shall mention here only that the unstable items include many affective traits (inappropriate and intense anger, mood lability) as well as the identity disturbance that Kernberg used as his line of demarcation between the borderline and neurotic levels.

Few patients exhibit exclusively the features of one set of items, and thus there are few pure schizotypal or pure unstable borderlines. The use of half a dozen items, which may be drawn from both lists, especially if one insists on the presence of identity disturbance, defines a territory as broad as (though not completely coextensive with) the Kernberg do-main.

Either of these broad definitions creates a patient sample that is etio-logically heterogeneous. Besides the affective variants we have just outlin-ed, one would have to include other subtypes: the schizotypal, the organic, and the psychogenic. Even these labels are useful primarily for didactic purposes; actual patients are seldom pure with respect to these categories. In the hierarchy of causative influences (to the extent we really know anything definitive about such matters), there are usually primary, sec-ondary, and still other less important influences. A patient may thus be borderline primarily because of organic factors, but with early environ-mental traumata also figuring in the equation. Almost every combina-tion of these factors that is mathematically possible can also be encoun-tered clinically in some particular borderline patient.

The following three vignettes have, for illustrative purposes, been chosen as highlighting the schizotypal, organic, and psychogenic sub-types.

SCHIZOTYPAL BORDERLINE

A 40-year-old musician sought treatment because of anxiety about a failing marriage.

She had come from a family of well-to-do but highly eccentric persons, in several of whom (father, sister, niece, grandmother) overt schizophrenia had been diagnosed (usually with pronounced paranoid features).

During her twenties she had been hospitalized for several weeks following a brief psychotic episode that occurred after a family quarrel. The episode was characterized by intense anxiety and persecutory ideas involving her (actually quite hostile) parents. In the intervening years she had been in psychotherapy for several long periods, primarily because of an inability to separate herself emotionally from her original family.

Characterologically, she was inordinately shy, self-conscious, and ill at ease in social gatherings. She felt both envy and contempt toward ordinary "earthlings" (she could scarcely imagine belonging to the same species), who, though less creative and artistic than she was, were so facile at making friends and achieving material success. She was extremely vulnerable to criticism from her parents, even when she was aware that their remarks were exaggerated or untrue. She had only a small circle of friends, and in their presence she could be quite relaxed and witty. These friends she had maintained for many years, some since childhood. Her manner of speech betrayed a number of peculiarities. She was so terrified of the "power" of her relatives to hurt her that she referred to them almost always by special phrases or secret words, after the manner of the ancient Greeks who called the dreaded Furies the Eumenides (the well-disposed ones). Magical thinking and odd communication were thus combined in this tendency. She would often allude to some past episode via a key word tacked onto the word "thing," thereby creating a kind of private language between patient and therapist (the Carabosse-thing, the Mars-thing, and so forth).

Identity disturbance was manifest in her confusion (which was quite real and not merely "poetic") about what species she belonged to, since ordinary people (whom she saw as smug, indifferent, and insensitive) seemed so unlike her. Likewise, she doubted whether she were a real musician, since (through lack of confidence rather than lack of talent) she did not earn her living through her music. These disturbances in her self-image did not have the force of delusion, however, but merely of "overvalued ideas" (cf. Hoch and Polatin 1949, Kernberg 1967), inasmuch as, upon confrontation, her thinking on these matters became more realistic.

From the preceding, it can be seen that she (1) functioned at the borderline level and (2) showed the schizotypal traits that would also establish her as borderline with respect to schizophrenia. Mood ability, instability of relationships and the other unstable features were not present.

Apart from brief panic-episodes, she rarely showed any of the target symptoms considered amenable to ataractic medications. Occasional use of the minor tranquilizers was sufficient. Psychotherapy, initially twice-weekly, spanned some nine years. The focus shifted between exploration of dynamic issues, during periods of relative calm, to supportive measures, during the many brief crises, designed to help her deal more effectively with her parents and other intimidating authority figures. Sometimes environmental manipulation was employed to reduce anxiety, as when she was advised to get a second, unlisted telephone, permitting her to distinguish between callers likely to unsettle her and those with whom she was comfortable.

BORDERLINE SYNDROME OF ORGANIC ORIGIN

A 17-year-old high school student was admitted to a psychiatric hospital because of rage outbursts that made him unmanageable at home. These attacks had begun the year before and consisted of episodes of uncontrollable anger and abusiveness, sometimes following minor provocations and sometimes for no apparent reason. Not getting his way with his parents, petty frustrations at school, disagreements with his friends all could lead to verbal abuse or, at times, striking out at other people. Both parents had been punched and kicked, as had been several classmates. He had been expelled from two schools because of this behavior, and a counselor at the last school had strongly recommended psychiatric evaluation.

Even before these more serious attacks began, he was noted to have been much more irritable than his two siblings were, ever since childhood. No one in the immediate or extended family exhibited any degree of psychiatric disturbance. The deterioration in the patient's behavior bore no clear relationship to puberty (which began at 14); he did not abuse drugs, like marijuana, that might have affected his habits.

Developmentally, a number of abnormalities had been observed over the years. As an infant, he had been "late for dates" by several months in regard to walking and speech. Clumsiness had been a chronic problem and one that interfered with his ability to play sports. A moderate degree of dyslexia was present, requiring remedial exercises, and he had been enuretic until age six.

He had been born abroad, and no medical records were available about delivery and birth. His mother did report, however, that her labor had been unusually difficult: there had been a placenta previa and apparently some prolonged fetal anoxia.

During the first few weeks of his hospitalization, the nursing staff became aware of his irascibility and demandingness. His speech was coherent and rational, but occasionally he would seem to "scan" for the right word. He complained incessantly of boredom. Unlike many of the other patients, he could not settle into any regular pattern of activities. His attention span was short. After an unsatisfactory visit with his parents and again when someone turned off the television program he was watching, he became violent and had to be subdued, in the process of which he hit members of the nursing staff. He socialized poorly when under tension but could be quite engaging at other times. He made a number of friends among the other patients but was intolerant of criticism, insisting on being the "boss." He had a very imperfect sense of himself, having no idea what he wanted to do after completing school. In matters pertaining to gender he was very touchy: he prided himself on his "macho" image but in other ways made it clear that he felt extremely insecure about his maleness. Others found him empty and lacking in the personal resources of his age-mates.

His history suggested perinatal minimal brain damage, and suspicions of this grew even stronger when he was noted on a number of occasions to become distracted and uncommunicative for brief moments, losing the thread of conversation as well as any sense of connectedness to those around him.

Psychological tests showed a verbal IQ of 97 and a performance IQ of 88, substantially less than might have been expected, considering the high levels at which the others in his family performed. Conventional electroencephalography (EEG) was inconclusive, showing some evidence of mild and not focused abnormality. But EEG with nasopharyngeal leads suggested an irritable focus in the right temporal region.

At this point the patient was given anticonvulsant medication. The results were equivocal. There seemed to be some diminution in the frequency of rage outbursts, though these did not abate entirely. Furthermore, there was a residuum of low frustration tolerance, poor motivation for psychotherapy, and an abrasive personality, all of which combined to hamper his chances for making an adequate social and occupational adjustment.

ADVERSE PSYCHOGENIC FACTORS CONTRIBUTING TO A BORDERLINE CONDITION

A 19-year-old woman was admitted to a psychiatric hospital because of suicidal ruminations and depression. The severity of her symptoms caused her to drop out of junior college. She had begun to withdraw from her friends, for reasons not immediately discernible, ending up as something of a recluse in her own home. By the time she came to the hospital, she could barely speak above a whisper, and that only when urged to talk. There was no spontaneous speech. Her facial expression suggested a severely depressed state, but she offered no verbal confirmation of this clinical impression. Within the first six weeks of her stay she was seen by three consultants, who proposed three different diagnoses: "schizophrenia, catatonic type, with schizoid personality"; "psychotic depression"; and "elective mutism in a borderline personality."

It was three months before she spoke without prodding; her voice was now audible, though feeble. Whereas there had initially been some measure of psychomotor retardation, her gait and movements were now normal, just as her speech remained quite impaired. What she said was coherent and rational, free of any signs of a thought disorder. But even to her therapist, whom she saw three times a week, she told few details of her life before coming to the hospital. By the fourth month she had settled into the role of a model patient: quiet, cooperative, helpful, and undemanding. She seemed prudish and immature and had no hobbies or interests.

On two occassions, each occurring several days before her therapist's vacation, she suddenly became wild: her attack consisted of hostile flailing gestures with her arms, screaming, and delusions of being menaced by the ward staff. These paranoid episodes, seemingly out of character for this patient, subsided after a few hours following a phenothiazine injection. As a result of these rage attacks, it became clear that there was another side to her nature than she had thus far revealed: because she looked as fearful as she was intimidating, one had the impression that she was abreacting some experience of great terror. But of this she gave no hint.

It was not until she had been on the unit for a year that she felt comfortable enough with her therapist to speak candidly about what had happened before her hospitalization. She had come from a large family. Her father died when she was eight, and so she and several of her younger siblings were sent to live with an uncle. Soon thereafter she became the victim of sadistic beatings and bizarre forms of sexual molestation at the hands of this relative. The scenes took place in a remote part of the house out of the earshot of her aunt, to whom she was, under threat of her life, to reveal nothing. After the patient's menarche, the nature of the incestuous approaches changed: intercourse (without beatings) took the place of the torture sessions. At one point she became pregnant by her uncle, who then drove her to an abortion clinic far away from home, leaving her to get back by her own devices. This was the stress that overwhelmed her and precipitated her hospitalization.

Despite the severe character pathology manifest in the uncle's behavior, he did not suffer from any clear-cut psychiatric disorder within either the schizophrenic or manic-depressive spectra. The same was true for her other first- and second-degree relatives. If the patient had any predisposition to such illnesses, it was not a quality that could be inferred from an abnormal pedigree. In her case, however, borderline function (especially her sharply contradictory, idealized/denigrated images of herself and of men) seemed readily ascribable to the brutalization that had been part of her daily experience over a span of 11 years.

DIFFERENTIAL DIAGNOSIS

One cannot with the same ease write about the differential diagnosis of borderline conditions as one can of schizophrenia. There now exist widely accepted inclusion and exclusion criteria for schizophrenia (viz., those of Carpenter et al. 1973, Feighner et al. 1972). Though not unitary etiologically, schizophrenia is predominantly a heredofamilial condition, the very heritability of which contributes to its validation as a nosologic entity.

Borderline, in contrast, is not the name of a unitary condition that enjoys anything like the agreement on criteria or the validation by external (viz., genetic, biologic) frames of references and that may be said to be true of schizophrenia or mania.

If borderline is used to denote a level of function (the Kernberg usage), then differential diagnosis should concern itself, properly speaking, only with other meaningful levels of function. Kernberg set forth in his 1967 paper the psychostructural criteria demarcating borderline from neurotic and psychotic structures, as mentioned above in "Historical Perspective." Therapists are sometimes at pains, however, to differentiate a borderline condition, having defined it according to Kernberg's criteria, from clinical entities like schizophrenia or anorexia nervosa. Now one is comparing (unwittingly, in the usual case) a level of function with a syndrome. Because these reflect two different universes of discourse, some confusion is inevitable. True, the vast majority of core schizophrenics exhibit a psychotic rather than a borderline psychic structure. But this does not mean that we have successfully differentiated schizophrenia from borderline (i.e., in level of function). Switching momentarily, if we may, to a quite different realm of comparison, we could note that oranges are usually heavier than tangerines and that both items are in the same class of objects and thus can be legitimately compared. But there are some small oranges that one cannot differentiate from tangerines by means of weight (corresponding to our level of function) alone. Similarly, schizophrenics are usually psychotic in structure. A few can, nevertheless, be found (not core cases, but spectrum cases, i.e., some schizotypal persons) who function typically at the borderline level (Stone 1979a).

If one speaks of borderline as a syndrome or otherwise distinct clinical entity, then differential diagnosis, in the traditional sense, becomes a meaningful exercise. Even here, however, there are several competing usages (Gunderson, Grinker, Bergeret, Benedetti, Aarkrog, the DSM-III), each with areas of overlap and disjunction with respect to the others. The Gunderson criteria were sketched above; a semistructured interview, the DIB (Diagnostic Interview for Borderlines), was developed by Gunderson and his colleagues to improve the reliability of diagnosing the borderline personality disorder (BPD) as they elaborated it. BPD is more narrowly defined than Kernberg's borderline personality organization. Most patients exhibiting the Gunderson BPD function at the (Kernberg) borderline level demonstrate borderline structure and are thus borderline twice over. But the Gunderson domain (answering to a clinical syndrome couched more in phenomenological and less in psychoanalytical terms) excludes sociopaths, severe alcoholics, and other (severe) substance-abusing patients, the bulk of whom happen to function at the borderline level. The Kernberg domain is thus much larger than the Gunderson domain.

A number of other clinical syndromes have been defined in such a way as to be discriminable for BPD, even though the typical instance of the condition in question shows borderline function. Most hospitalized cases of anorexia nervosa and severe premenstrual tension are borderline in Kernberg's terms, but nosologically distinct from BPD. Some patients, however, satisfy the Gunderson criteria simultaneously with their exhibiting anorexia or one of the other syndromes.

The syndrome of hysteroid dysphoria (HD), defined by D. F. Klein (1977), derived from his observations of certain female patients who showed marked dysphoric responses to interpersonal rejection, along with a number of other symptoms, mostly involving mood. HD is probably best viewed as an atypical affective disorder. Some cases, on follow-up, turn into quite typical bipolar or unipolar manic depression. Many satisfy the Gunderson criteria (but only a few BPD cases also have the Klein syndrome), and almost all function at the borderline level.

This leads us to a discussion of borderline conditions from still another vantage point: proximity to one of the classical psychoses. We have already alluded to the notion of a borderline schizophrenia, such as that adumbrated in the study of Kety and colleagues (1968) and objectified in the schizotypal checklist developed by Spitzer and his colleagues (1979). The latter has surfaced as the DSM-III's schizotypal personality, the adjective *borderline* no longer affixed to this label. A generation ago, psychoanalysts coined a variety of terms meant to indicate atypical, incipient, or mild (i.e., nonpsychotic) forms of schizophrenia: ambulatory schizophrenia (Zilboorg 1941), latent psychosis (Bychowski 1953), borderline schizophrenia (Ekstein 1955), as-if personality (Deutsch 1942), and pseudoneurotic schizophrenia (Hoch and Polatin 1949), to cite but a few examples. According to contemporary diagnostic criteria, many of the patients subsumed under these labels have only a tenuous relationship to heredofamilial schizophrenia (Stone 1980); some are now viewed as within the spectrum of affective disorders (Klein 1975). Many of these atypical patients are borderline in Kernberg's terminology. The few that are schizotypal could be said to be borderline in two frames of reference: the one relating to function or structure and the one relating to hereditary predisposition. This was true of the schizotypal borderline patient in the above vignette.

A much larger percentage of Kernberg's borderline patients exhibit affective (especially depressive) symptoms (Stone 1980, 1981), to such a degree that the notion of being borderline with respect to (i.e., in the spectrum of) manic depression is also applicable. Akiskal (1981) found something similar in a sample of Gunderson's borderlines. Since the age of risk for primary affective disorders is usually later than the age at which many patients are first appraised as showing borderline structure, it is not surprising that some Kernberg borderlines, at follow-up, have developed clear-cut affective illnesses that now meet (but did not at initial evaluation) hard criteria for one or another form of manic depression (Fard et al. 1978). Despite Kraepelin's generally valid claim about manic depressives' showing a *restitutio ad integrum* between attacks, these interpsychotic phases are not always characterized by normality. Indeed, some manics show a borderline structure during these intervals. Bipolar patients, as a rule, however, fluctuate between their (usual) neurotic level and their (transient psychotic level. In the realm of depressive conditions, the presence of many vegetative signs and psychomotor retardation indicates a diagnosis of a primary depressive disorder (within the manic-depressive family of illnesses). Such patients will not ordinarily exhibit all of the Gunderson criteria for BPD, though some will show borderline function. There is an uncomfortable degree of overlap among most of the currently popular definitions of borderline and the major depressive disorders, complicated further by the already mentioned tendency of the former to shade into the latter as they evolve over the years. The DSM-III definition exemplifies this tendency: derived from the checklist of unstable items in the Spitzer questionnaire (1979), the DSM's borderline personality contains mostly affective traits (mood lability, self-damaging acts and suicidal ruminations, unstable relationships, angry affect). For those relying on this method of diagnosing a borderline case, the cards will be stacked heavily in favor of affective disturbances, some of which will nearly, or eventually, meet conventional criteria for a primary affective illness, as well. A certain percentage of patients with cyclothymic personality or with irritable temperament (Stone 1980) are Gunderson negative but Kernberg positive; they will also manifest many of the (unstable) DSM borderline items. It is worth noting that the current DSM definition of borderline is narrow. Most Kernberg borderlines as Spitzer and colleagues (1979) demonstrated, emerge as mixed types, exhibiting a few schizotypal plus a few unstable items rather than only schizotypal or only unstable items. This leads to the curious situation in which most patients that Kernberg would call borderline fall between two chairs with respect to the DSM: unless they show many of the old unstable features, they must forfeit, once they are viewed by DSM criteria, their borderline label.

The intermingling of borderline character traits (ragefulness, demandingness, impulsivity) and serious depressive symptoms may be balanced in such a way that the depressive condition is (for longer or shorter periods) overshadowed and overlooked. Life stresses (e.g., acute loss) or biological factors (e.g., menses) may push this condition to the forefront. In many patients of this sort, abnormal results may be recorded upon measurement of several biological markers. A positive (abnormal) dexamethasone suppression test was noted in over half of Carroll's and colleagues' borderline sample (1981), suggesting an affiliation, in this large subgroup, with classical manic depression. Shortened REM latency was reported (Akiskal 1981) in a similar group of borderlines, half of whom appeared at the same time to be in the manic-depressive spectrum.

Andrulonis and associates (1981) collected a large sample of adolescent patients who, though functioning at the borderline level, suffered from a form of minimal brain damage. Subtle manifestations of temporal lobe epilepsy were present in some cases (tending to mimic affective disorders if localized in the nondominant hemisphere, schizophrenia if in the dominant hemisphere: cf. Rockford et al. 1981), of a sort producing "episodic dyscontrol" (unprovoked rage outbursts, and so on). These patients, though often Kernberg positive, do not often show the

Gunderson syndrome. They do respond favorably in many instances to antiepileptic medications, such as Tegretol® or Dilantin®.

Therapists are sometimes at pains to differentiate borderline from narcissistic disorders. The utility — or to my way of thinking, the futility — of this exercise reflects the same sort of semantic confusion over the various universes of discourse that we have just been examining in regard to the classical psychoses.

If one is wedded to a nosology consisting solely of discrete and mutually distinguishable syndromes, then one must employ only those usages of the term borderline that rely on lists of objectifiable items (Gunderson and Singer 1975, DSM-III 1980). Definitions of narcissistic and other serious character disorders are available, permitting fairly good discrimination from these syndromal definitions of borderline. If one finds greater usefulness in the concept of borderline as a level of function (Kernberg 1967), then within this broader patient population it will be noticed that many borderline patients exhibit, from the standpoint of personality diagnosis, strong narcissistic traits. These may, indeed, predominate in some cases over infantile, obsessive, paranoid, or other pathological personality attributes. In such a situation, one speaks of a borderline personality organization with narcissistic features. The borderline level can be found in conjunction with just about any of the common personality types (phobic, passive-aggressive, infantile, schizoid, antisocial, hypomanic, and so forth: cf. Stone 1980) in which the latter becomes a second and co-existing diagnosis. The personality profiles of a borderline patient sample will differ from those of a neurotic sample, in that the more pathological personality traits (paranoid, schizoid, severe narcissistic, antisocial) will be overrepresented among the borderlines, whereas the healthier types (histrionic, depressive, obsessive) will be overrepresented among the neurotics.

ETIOLOGY OF BORDERLINE CONDITIONS

Even the narrower, syndromal definitions of borderline relate to a domain of patients that, however similar clinically, are heterogeneous when appraised from the standpoint of etiology. The broader definitions of borderline answer to an even greater degree of etiological diversity.

A few conditions of interest to therapists stem from fairly well delimited and well understood genic errors (Huntington's chorea, phenylpyruvic oligophrenia); others may derive from abnormalities at a single major locus or within a polygenic system (classical idiopathic schizophrenia and mania). But no such neat correlations are discernible within the realm of borderline conditions (no matter how defined). More often one is dealing with an interaction, a confluence of biological and psychological factors, whose various weights will differ from case to case. Not all the possible factors will be relevant to each particular case.

Among the biological factors, one thinks of hereditary factors specific to some form of psychopathology and others that are nonspecific, though capable of influencing the severity or type of eventual psychiatric condition. Factors affecting intelligence, physical stature, and attractiveness, for example, may modify other genic influences, causing within our frame of reference a borderline condition either more or less likely to develop. Organic factors, such as perinatal damage to certain centers in the central nervous system that subserve affect or cognition, may also play a role, especially in the kinds of borderline cases that Andrulonis and associates (1981) described. Alcohol or drug abuse in adolescence may aggravate underlying tendencies toward emotional illness and may contribute to the formation, discovery, or aggravation of a borderline condition. This applies to the broader, functional definitions of borderline; the Gunderson syndrome specifically excludes the severer forms of substance abuse. Whatever factors lead to premenstrual tension (Stone 1982), and these are themselves heterogeneous etiologically, may similarly influence the development or intensification of a borderline condition in certain women.

We mentioned a number of psychological influences that, especially under extreme circumstances, appear to foster the development of borderline function in adult life. One can distinguish between acts of commission (child beating of a severe and chronic nature, incest) and acts of omission (severe parental neglect), but fate may play a hand as well, as in the instance of overwhelming loss. The death of a parent between the ages of two and ten, when need is maximal and the capacity to grasp the meaning of death minimal, may seriously hamper development. Presumably, breakup of the family, especially when there have been ugly scenes and a chaotic home life, may similarly affect younger children and early adolescents.

Many researchers, especially those whose background is psychoanalytic and who have devoted themselves to long-term psychotherapy with borderline patients, believe that borderline-to-be persons have suffered from poor nurturance — usually because of deficits in maternal care — during the separation-individuation phase of early childhood (Mahler 1971, Masterson 1972, Rinsley 1978). Masterson, in fact, characterized the mothers as themselves customarily borderline, with a tendency to be cold,

absent, or actively hostile (cf. Gunderson and Englund 1981). The im-
plication is that these mothers may have adequately handled the earliest
infancy of their children but during their toddler years (two to three and
a half) interacted with them in such a way as to undermine their burgeoning independence and autonomy. The mother of the borderline person
is seen as excessively dependent on the child for certain emotional supplies and, consequently, is unable to let the child go. The family atmosphere is said to be charged with intense affect, which supposedly differentiates it from the atmosphere that is said to be typical of homes from
which schizophrenics emerge. Skewed patterns of communication and
schism have often been noted in the latter (Lidz 1963).

The evidence to support these theories of specific family constellations
for borderline conditions is weak. Speculation has filled the void where
hard data should be but are missing. In a way, one could hardly expect
there to be any convincing data on the subject, because there are as yet
only the most rudimentary biometric scales for assessing what mothering
or parenting existed in any given family. Prospective studies are just getting under way, which means that claims have thus far rested on retrospective studies. These are subject to errors of memory and inadvertent
falsification and are also at the mercy of what are often serious gaps in
information (teachers' observations no longer available, psychological test
results from childhood now inaccessible, and the like). We should not
rely too heavily on what our (adult) borderline patients tell us about their
past. Those of us who have often seen their families, either in periodic
consultations or in the context of family therapy, know how difficult it is
to obtain, even in this wider network, an accurate picture of past family
life. A few adult borderline patients appear to have had parents who provided a family environment, through their emotional stability and good
empathic capacities, that one could scarcely distinguish from that of
a normal family. Often, all the siblings have done well, and the patient
stands out as an inexplicable phenomenon, given the harmony and in-
tegratedness of the rest of the family. This state of affairs was present,
as best I could determine, in the homes of 3 out of 48 adolescent and
adult borderline-level patients I have seen in office practice, on whom
I maintain careful records of family psychopathology. But I cannot present this as hard evidence that at least some borderlines come from
families that would fail to fit the hypotheses of Masterson and Mahler.
Also, my data are retrospective and prone to the same kinds of error as
are other retrospective data. But my observations have inclined me
toward a less rigid view of borderline etiology. There may indeed have
been traumata during the separation-individuation phase of many future

borderline patients. How these traumata, or unfavorable patterns (mother's constant verbal abuse, father's alcoholic scenes, older brother's sadistic assaults, and the like), were negotiated largely depends, nevertheless, on a number of constitutional givens — temperament (Stone 1979b), a degree of liability for classical psychosis, and so forth — that make a significant difference in whether the child takes the negative influences in stride or whether he or she succumbs. Only in some cases, I believe, can etiological primacy be accorded to environmental factors. Many other children who later develop a borderline condition came into the separation-individuation phase already handicapped, already predisposed, that is, to handle separations from the parents less adaptively than could some of their constitutionally better endowed siblings. Since a number of prospective studies are already in progress, focusing mainly on children at high risk for schizophrenia (Erlenmeyer-Kimling 1975) or manic depression (Carlson and Strober 1978, Cytryn and McKnew 1974), we may be only a decade away from having some answers regarding the role of psychogenic factors in borderline patients that stem more from rigorous and objective methodology than from clinical intuition.

SUMMARY

As a diagnostic term, borderline first appeared in the psychiatric annals a century ago, as a label for conditions intermediate between the then current notions of neurosis and psychosis. The borderline concept did not achieve popularity until some 40 years ago, when psychoanalysts designated certain cases as borderline that were not only between neurosis and psychosis but also between classic analyzability and clear-cut nonanalyzability. These usages relate to a general level of adaptation or function. Kernberg's psychostructural criteria grew out of an effort to define this borderline level in more precise terms. The Gunderson criteria represent an advance in the objectification of a borderline condition defined primarily as a syndrome rather than as a level of adaptation. A number of psychogeneticists have used borderline in still a different way, to designate certain atypical nonpsychotic cases that appear to be within the spectrum of schizophrenia or manic depression. Despite the different ways in which these definitions arose, there is a considerable degree of overlap, so that at the clinical level, a patient diagnosed borderline according to one formulation will be so considered according to another. It is important to know the areas of disjunction, as well, lest a therapist familiar with one system fail to communicate effectively with a therapist who employs the term differently.

Even the narrower, syndromal definitions of borderline do not mark out a diagnostic domain that is etiologically homogeneous. A variety of constitutional and psychogenic factors are of potential significance and their relative importance will vary from case to case. These factors include, on the biologic side, predisposition to schizophrenia, a primary affective disorder (manic depression), perinatal or other early central nervous system damage, or severe premenstrual tension; on the psychogenic side, parental brutality (verbal or physical), incest, severe parental deprivation, or overwhelming loss during childhood. Faulty development during the separation-individuation phase is often present and may be spurred on by poor maternal nurturance. How often this is of etiological importance, and how often it is an epiphenomenon related to preexisting handicaps are open questions.

Whereas borderline cases were once thought to be dilute or incipient manifestations of schizophrenia, the changes over the past 15 years, both in the popular definitions of borderline and in the accepted definitions of schizophrenia, mania, and the like, have led to a shift: borderline cases, if they show any affiliation at all to a classical psychosis, will more often be found to resemble an affective, rather than a schizophrenic disorder. A number of affective subtypes within the borderline domain were discussed in order to illustrate this shift in usage.

REFERENCES

Aarkrog, T. (1973). Conditions in adolescents who were borderline psychotics as children. *Acta Psychiatrica Scandinavica* 49:377–385.

———. (1981). The borderline concept in childhood, adolescence and adulthood. *Acta Psychiatrica Scandinavica Supplement* 64:293.

Akiskal, H. (1981). Subaffective disorders: dysthymic, cyclothymic and bipolar II disorders in the "borderline" realm. In *Borderline Disorders,* ed. M. H. Stone, pp. 25–46. Philadelphia: Saunders.

Andrulonis, P. A., Glueck, B. C., Stroebel, C. F., Vogel, N., Shapiro, A. L., and Aldridge, D. (1981). Organic brain dysfunction and the borderline syndrome. In *Borderline Disorders*, ed. M. H. Stone, pp. 47–66. Philadelphia: Saunders.

Benedetti, G. (1965). Psychopathologie und Psychotherapie der Grenzpsychose. Report of the Dikemark Seminar, Dikemark Sykhuset, pp. 1–29, Norway. April 29–May 1.

Bergeret, J. (1974). *La Depression et les États-Limites*. Paris: Payot.

Bleuler, E. (1911). *Dementia Praecox oder Gruppe der Schizophrenien*. Leipzig: F. Deuticke.

Bychowski, G. (1953). The problem of latent psychosis. *Journal of the American Psychoanalytic Association* 4:484–503.

Carlson, G. A., and Strober, M. (1978). Manic-depressive illness in early adolescence. *Journal of the American Academy of Child Psychiatry* 17: 138–153.

Carpenter, W. T., Jr., Strauss, J. S., and Bartko, J. J. (1973). Flexible system for the diagnosis of schizophrenia: report from the W.H.O. International Pilot Study of Schizophrenia. *Science* 182:1275–1277.

Carroll, B. J., Greden, J. F., Feinberg, M., Lohr, N., James, N., Steiner, M., Haskett, R. F., Albala, A. A., deVigne, J., and Tarika, J. (1981). Neuroendocrine evaluation of depression in borderline patients. In *Borderline Disorders*, ed. M. H. Stone, pp. 89–99. Philadelphia: Saunders.

Clark, L. P. (1919). Some practical remarks upon the use of modified psychoanalysis in the treatment of borderland neuroses and psychoses. *Psychoanalytic Review* 6:306–308.

Cytryn, L., and McKnew, D. H., Jr. (1974). Factors influencing the changing clinical expression of the depressive process in children. *American Journal of Psychiatry* 131:879–881.

Deutsch, H. (1942). Some forms of emotional disturbance and their relationships to schizophrenia. *Psychoanalytic Quarterly* 11:301–321.

Diagnostic and Statistical Manual of Mental Disorders (DSM-III) (1980). 3rd ed. Washington, D.C.: American Psychiatric Association.

Ekstein, R. (1955). Vicissitudes of the "internal image" in the recovery of a borderline schizophrenic adolescent. *Bulletin of the Menninger Clinic* 19:86–92.

Erlenmeyer-Kimling, L. (1975). A prospective study of children at risk for schizophrenia. In *Life History Research in Psychopathology*, vol. 4, ed. R. D. Wirt, G. Winokur, and M. Roff, pp. 22–46. Minneapolis: University of Minnesota Press.

Fard, K., Hudgens, R. W., and Welner, A. (1978). Undiagnosed psychiatric illness in adolescents. *Archives of General Psychiatry* 35: 279–282.

Federn, P. (1947). Principles of psychotherapy in latent schizophrenia. *American Journal of Psychotherapy* 1:129–139.

Feighner, J. P., Robins, E., Guze, S. B., Woodruff, R. A., Jr., Winokur, G., and Munoz, R. (1972). Diagnostic criteria for use in psychiatric research. *Archives of General Psychiatry* 26:57–63.

Frosch, J. (1960). Psychotic character. *Journal of the American Psychoanalytic Association* 8:544–551.

———. (1964). The psychotic character. *Psychiatric Quarterly* 38:81–96.

Grinker, R. R., Sr., Werble, B., and Drye, R. C. (1968). *The Borderline Syndrome*. New York: Basic Books.

Gunderson, J. G., and Englund, D. W. (1981). Characterizing the families of borderlines: a review of the literature. In *Borderline Disorders,* ed. M. H. Stone, pp. 159–168. Philadelphia: Saunders.

Gunderson, J. G., and Singer, M. T. (1975). Defining borderline patients: an overview. *American Journal of Psychiatry* 132:1–10.

Hoch, P. H., and Polatin, P. (1949). Pseudoneurotic forms of schizophrenia. *Psychiatric Quarterly* 23:248–276.

Jacobson, E. (1953). Contribution to the metapsychology of cyclothymic depression. In *Affective Disorders*, ed. P. Greenacre, pp. 49–83. New York: International Universities Press.

Kernberg, O. F. (1967). Borderline personality organization. *Journal of the American Psychoanalytic Association* 15:641–685.

Kety, S. S., Rosenthal, D., Wender, P. H., and Schulsinger, F. (1968). Mental illness in the biological and adoptive families of adopted schizophrenics. In *Transmission of Schizophrenia*. ed. D. Rosenthal and S. Kety, pp. 345–362. Oxford (England): Pergamon Press.

Klein, D. F. (1975). Psychopharmacology and the borderline patient. In *Borderline States in Psychiatry*, ed. J. E. Mack, pp. 75–92. New York: Grune & Stratton.

———. (1977). Psychopharmacological treatment and delineation of borderline disorders. In *Borderline Personality Disorders: the Concept, the Syndrome, the Patient*, ed. P. Hartocollis, pp. 365–383. New York: International Universities Press.

Knight, R. P. (1953). Borderline states. *Bulletin of the Menninger Clinic* 17:1–12.

Kraepelin, E. (1921). *Manic-Depressive Insanity and Paranoia*. Edinburgh: E. and S. Livingstone.

Lidz, T. (1963). *The Origin and Treatment of Schizophrenic Disorders*. New York: Basic Books.

Lombroso, C. (1878). *L'uomo Delinquente*. Rome: Bocca Bros.

Mahler, M. S. (1971). A study of the separation-individuation process, and its possible application to borderline phenomena in the psychoanalytic situation. *Psychoanalytic Study of the Child* 26:403–424.

Masterson, J. F. (1972) *Treatment of the Borderline Adolescent*. New York: Wiley Interscience.

Moore, T. V. (1921). The parataxes: a study and analysis of certain borderline mental states. *Psychoanalytic Review* 8:252–283.

Oberndorf, C. F. (1930). The psychoanalysis of borderline cases. *New York State Journal of Medicine* 30:648–651.

Rinsley, D. B. (1978). Juvenile delinquency, a review of the past and a look at the future. *Bulletin of the Menninger Clinic* 42:252–260.

Rockford, J. M., Weinapple, M., and Goldstein, L. (1981). The quantitative hemispheric EEG in adolescent psychiatric patients with depressive or paranoid symptomatology. *Biological Psychiatry* 16:47–54.

Rosse, I. (1890). Clinical evidences of borderland insanity. *Journal of Nervous and Mental Disease* 17:669–683.

Spitzer, R. L., Endicott, J. and Gibbon, M. (1979). Crossing the border into borderline personality and borderline schizophrenia. *Archives of General Psychiatry* 36:17–24.

Stern, A. (1938). Psychoanalytic investigation and therapy in the borderline group of neuroses. *Psychoanalytic Quarterly* 7:467–489.

Stone, M. H. (1977). The borderline syndrome: evolution of the term, genetic aspects and prognosis. *American Journal of Psychotherapy* 31:345–365.

————. (1979a). Assessing vulnerability to schizophrenia or manic-depression in borderline states. *Schizophrenia Bulletin* 5:105–110.

————. (1979b). A psychoanalytic approach to abnormalities of temperament. *American Journal of Psychotherapy* 33:263–280.

————. (1980). *The Borderline Syndromes: Constitution, Adaptation and Personality*. New York: McGraw-Hill.

————. (1981). Borderline syndromes: a consideration of subtypes and an overview, directions for research. In *Borderline Disorders*, ed. M. H. Stone, pp. 3–24. Philadelphia: Saunders.

————. (1982). Borderline conditions and the menstrual cycle. In *Behavior and the Menstrual Cycle,* ed. R. Friedman, pp. 317–344. New York: Marcel Dekker.

Stone, M. H., Kahn, E., and Flye, B. (1981). Psychiatrically ill relatives of borderline patients: a family study. *Psychiatric Quarterly* 53 (2):71–84.

Zilboorg, G. (1941) Ambulatory schizophrenia. *Psychiatry* 4:149–155.

CHAPTER 2

Narcissistic Personality Disorder

SALMAN AKHTAR, M.D.
J. ANDERSON THOMSON, JR., M.D.

The diagnosis of narcissistic personality disorder has been used with increasing frequency in recent years; the third *Diagnostic and Statistical Manual of Mental Disorders* (DSM-III) lists it as a distinct character disorder. Yet the concept remains poorly defined and controversial. It depends largely on data derived from clinical psychoanalysis and lacks phenomenological documentation from extensive patient samples. In this chapter we survey the literature relevant to narcissistic personality disorder with the goal of developing a composite picture of the syndrome. Similar efforts to clarify another controversial diagnosis, the borderline personality (Gunderson and Kolb 1978, Gunderson and Singer 1975, Perry and Klerman 1978), have been useful in identifying diagnostic criteria and defining areas for continued research.

HISTORY

According to Greek mythology, Narcissus fell in love with his own reflection in a pool; unable to tear himself away from it, he died of languor. Havelock Ellis (1898) first used this myth to illustrate a psychological state in reporting a case of male autoeroticism. In commenting on Ellis's work, Nacke (1899) first used the term *narcissmus*. The term *narcissistic* was first used by Freud in a 1910 footnote to "Three Essays on the Theory of Sexuality" (1905). Otto Rank wrote the first psychoanalytic paper on narcissism in 1911, and Freud's paper "On Narcissism" was published in 1914.

In a 1925 paper that foreshadowed more recent work, Waelder reported in detail on an individual with a "narcissistic personality." Waelder characterized such individuals as displaying condescending superiority, intense preoccupation with their self-respect, and marked lack of empathy and concern for others while maintaining an adequate external adaptation to reality. Their lack of empathy is often most apparent in their sexuality. Intercourse is a purely physical pleasure, the partner being less a person than a means to an end. Waelder also pointed out the narcissistic motives that underlie even the morality of these individuals. Unlike the usual superego dictate, "I must not do or think this, for it is immoral; my parents have forbidden it," narcissistic morality prompts something like, "This may not be, for it would humiliate me; it does not accord with my lofty and noble personality." Waelder indicated that these individuals often displayed a "narcissistic mode of thought," which included "libidinization of thinking" (thinking for thinking's sake), preference of concepts to facts, and an overvaluation of their mental processes.

Following these early papers, the term narcissism was used with various meanings. Pulver (1970) and van der Waals (1965) who catalogued the various meanings of narcissism from 1911 to the 1960s, pointed out that it was first used to denote a sexual perversion. Later, the word's connotations were expanded and changed to include an early stage of infant development, placement of psychic energy (the libidinal cathexis of the self), a type of interpersonal relationship, and, most recently, a synonym for self-esteem. In this overview we use Moore's and Fine's definition of narcissism as "a concentration of psychological interest upon the self" (1967).

Tracing the evolution of the concept of narcissistic personality disorder (see Rothstein 1979) is further complicated by the early interchangeable use of the terms *narcissistic neuroses, psychoses, dementia praecox,* and *schizophrenia.* Waelder (1925) considered narcissistic personality a muted variant of schizophrenia. In "On Narcissism," Freud (1914) avoided character typology but pointed out that some people "compel our interest by the narcissistic consistency with which they manage to keep away from their ego anything that would diminish it" (p. 218). In 1931 Freud defined the narcissistic character type:

The subject's main interest is directed to self preservation; he is independent and not open to intimidation. His ego has a large amount of aggressiveness at its disposal, which also manifests itself in readiness for activity. In his erotic life loving is preferred above being loved. People belonging to this type impress others

as being "personalities"; they are especially suited to act as a
support for others, to take on the role of leaders and to give
a fresh stimulus to cultural development or to damage the established state of affairs. (p. 218)

Annie Reich (1960) emphasized that "narcissistic pathology cannot
be viewed as restricted to psychosis" and pointed out the "compensatory
narcissistic self-inflation" in certain nonpsychotic individuals. These
individuals, according to Reich, have "exaggerated, unrealistic —
i.e., infantile — inner yardsticks" and constantly seek to be the object of
admiring attention "as a means to undo feelings of inferiority" (pp.
289–291).

In 1961 Nemiah described individuals with a narcissistic character
disorder as displaying great ambition, highly unrealistic goals, tolerance
of failures, and imperfections in themselves, and an almost insatiable
craving for admiration. Such individuals, according to Nemiah, do very
little in life because they want to; their actions are constantly influenced
by what they think will make others like them.

Nemiah postulated that if the parents set unrealistically high standards for their children and if the children cannot live up to those standards, the parents will treat them with harsh criticism. The children in-
ternalize these parental attitudes, and as adults they demand too much
of themselves and become very ambitious. They also criticize themselves
and react to even an ordinary setback with a dismal sense of inadequacy.
Such an individual becomes "a prisoner of his aspirations, his needs, and
his harsh self-criticism" (p. 163).

In 1967 Kernberg presented a coherent clinical description of the narcissistic personality structure. In a later paper Kernberg (1970) cited
several early authors who had contributed to the concept. Ernest Jones
(1913) had described patients with a God complex, and Abraham (1919)
and Riviere (1936) had described patients who deprecated and defeated
the analyst, behaviors observed by Kernberg in his narcissistic patients.
Kernberg also acknowledged Rosenfeld's contributions (1964), particularly
the latter's emphasis on the rigid, pathologic ideal self-image and unconscious envy in these patients. Tartakoff (1966) wrote of the Nobel
Prize complex among people who are intellectually gifted and uniformly
preoccupied with the pursuit of applause, wealth, power, or social pres-
tige.

The term narcissistic personality disorder was introduced in the literature by Kohut in 1968. Since then, Kernberg and Kohut have been
the major theoreticians examining the concept of narcissistic personality
disorder.

KERNBERG'S CONTRIBUTIONS

Kernberg's description of narcissistic personality (1967) is derived from clinical psychoanalysis. Although most of his writings on pathological narcissism (1975, 1976) are theoretical, he does offer explicit descriptions of clinical characteristics and bases the diagnosis on readily observable behavior. Kernberg portrays patients with this condition as having excessive self-absorption; intense ambition; grandiose fantasies; an overdependence on acclaim; and an unremitting need to search for brillance, power, and beauty. He stresses the pathological nature of their inner world, regardless of their superficially adaptive behavior. This pathology is manifest in an inability to love; a lack of empathy; chronic feelings of boredom, emptiness, and uncertainty about identity; and exploitation of others. Kernberg also emphasizes the "presence of chronic intense envy, and defenses against such envy, particularly devaluation, omnipotent control, and narcissistic withdrawal" (1975, p. 264). These defenses appear in their contempt for, anxious attachment to, or avoidance of secretly admired or envied others. There is also a tendency toward sexual promiscuity, homosexuality, perversions, substance abuse, a peculiarly corruptible conscience, and a readiness to shift values quickly to gain favor.

According to Kernberg, individuals with narcissistic personalities possess a capacity for consistent work and may even become socially quite successful, yet their work and productivity are in the service of exhibitionism, and these individuals lack genuine, in-depth professional interests. Kernberg calls this tendency "pseudosublimatory" (1975, p. 229) in order to distinguish it from mature forms of productivity.

Kernberg holds that as children, these narcissistic individuals were left emotionally hungry by chronically cold, unempathic mothers. Feeling unloved and "bad," these children projected their rage onto their parents, who were then perceived as even more sadistic and depriving. The children's sole defense then was to take refuge in some aspect of themselves that their parents, particularly their mother, valued. Thus the grandiose self developed.

Kernberg proposes that the grandiose self (a term he borrowed from Kohut but uses with different etiological formulation) is formed by fusion of the children's admired aspects, the fantasied version of themselves that compensated for frustration and defended against rage and envy, and the fantasied image of a loving mother. These three psychic structures coalesce in the grandiose self. The unacceptable image of oneself as a hungry infant is dissociated or split off from the main functioning self, although an experienced eye can discern its presence behind the boredom, emptiness, and chronic hunger for excitement and acclaim.

Kernberg selectively integrated certain concepts from analysts of the British object-relations school, including Klein (1948) Fairbairn (1952), Guntrip (1968), Rosenfeld (1964) and Khan (1974), and American psychoanalysts such as Mahler (1968), Jacobson (1976) and van der Waals (1965). Kernberg maintains agreement with classical psychoanalytic theory, recognizing the contribution of instinctual drives to psychopathology and not proposing a "narcissistic libido" independent of early object relations, as Kohut suggests.

KOHUT'S CONTRIBUTIONS

Kohut's extensive writings on narcissism (1966, 1968, 1971, 1972, 1977, 1979) are based on the psychoanalytic treatment of patients with narcissistic personality disorder. Although his writings are clear articulations of psychoanalytic technique, they do not contain empirical diagnostic criteria. Kohut (1971) specifically disavows "the traditional medical aim of achieving a diagnosis in which a disease entity is identified by clusters of recurring manifestations" (pp. 15–16), holding that "the crucial diagnostic criterion is based not on the evaluation of the presenting symptomatology or even of the life history, but on the nature of the spontaneously developing transference" (p. 23), mobilized during the analysis of these patients.

One can extract behavioral descriptions of narcissistic patients from Kohut's writings, however. He notes that these patients may complain of disturbances in several areas: sexually, they may report perverse fantasies or lack of interest in sex; socially, they may experience work inhibitions, difficulty in forming and maintaining relationships, or delinquent activities; and personally, they may demonstrate a lack of humor, little empathy for others' needs and feelings, pathologic lying, or hypochondriacal preoccupations. These patients also display overt grandiosity in unrealistic schemes, exaggerated self-regard, demands for attention, and inappropriate idealization of certain others. Reactive increase in grandiosity because of perceived injury to self-esteem may appear in increased coldness, self-consciousness, stilted speech, and even hypomanic-like episodes.

Profoundly angry reactions are characteristic of these individuals, as Nemiah (1961) noted. Kohut eloquently describes this narcissistic rage as the reaction to an injury to self-esteem (1972). Its central features are the need for revenge — the undoing of hurt by whatever means — and compulsion in this pursuit, with utter disregard for reasonable limitations. The irrationality of this vengeful attitude is frightening because reasoning is not only intact but sharpened. Narcissistically angry individuals see the "enemy" as a flaw in reality and a recalcitrant part of the self, the mere existence of which is an offense. They disregard the limits and definite goals characteristic of mature aggression in the service of a sound cause.

Kohut, who suggests that primary infantile narcissism is injured by inevitable maternal shortcomings, believes that the narcissistic personality stems from a developmental arrest. He sees children defensively denying the narcissistic disequilibrium and then developing an even more megalomanic self-image, the grandiose self, to regain their narcissism. The children also defensively idealize their parent and then regain self-esteem from association with this idealized parent imago.

Kohut considers these maneuvers typical of normal development, in which they are followed by affective neutralization of these psychic structures. The grandiose self is gradually made more realistic and age-specific by the mother's mirroring responses to her child's archaic grandiosity. For example, a 2-year-old's accomplishment of a task such as riding a tricycle receives enthusiastic approval from the mother. Similar accomplishment would elicit little applause a few years later, the mirroring enthusiasm now being reserved for more mature tasks. The idealized parent imago is internalized through phase-specific, nontraumatic disappointments in the parents as the children are exposed to realistic limitations. They gradually incorporate their earlier idealization into their own ideals and values to contribute to the superego system.

According to Kohut, the narcissistic personality disorder results from disruption of this normal developmental sequence. Archaic grandiosity may remain untamed if the mother's confirming responses are deficient. The idealized parent imago may not be internalized if the children are suddenly exposed to huge disappointment in their parents or, conversely, if they are never permitted to appreciate their real limitations. Then grandiosity and the seemingly contradictory tendency to idealize others and draw strength from them will persist.

Efforts are being made to document Kohut's descriptions on the basis of more clinical material (Goldberg 1978), but the focus is on metapsychological and therapeutic issues rather than on the phenomenology of the disorder. Kohut has been criticized (Kernberg 1975, Volkan 1976) for his radical disregard of the traditional analytic theory of the part played by instinctual drives — especially aggressive ones — in the formation of character pathology and for his proposal of a narcissistic libido independent of early investment in objects. This theoretical stance accounts for the lack of congruence between Kohut's and Kernberg's views.

THE KOHUT-KERNBERG CONTROVERSY

Kohut and Kernberg agree on the grandiose characteristics of the narcissistic personality. Their theoretical differences, however, substantially influence their suggested therapeutic techniques. Kohut sees the disorder as a developmental arrest. He posits a separate narcissistic libido, which follows a developmental sequence independent of object relations determined by libido and aggression. Kohut's suggested treatment initially allows the patients to display their grandiosity and to idealize the therapist. The therapist then empathetically points out the realistic limitations of the patients and themselves. The childhood determinants of such fixations are then highlighted. The purpose is to complete the arrested developmental tasks of taming archaic grandiosity and internalizing early idealizations. When narcissistic rage appears as anger in treatment, Kohut sees it as a reactive, secondary phenomenon: "I am angry because my supremacy is questioned."

Kernberg emphasizes the coexistence of feelings of inferiority with notions of grandiosity. He sees the grandiosity as purely pathological and defensive rather than as a halt in normal development. His treatment method centers on interpreting the defensive nature of grandiosity and mending the fragmented or split self-representations. This is accomplished through exploration of the dissociated hungry-infant self-images and their attached angry emotions. Kernberg applies the dual instinct theory of psychoanalysis to his object-relations theory. Kernberg sees aggression, specifically early childhood or oral rage, as the inciting agent in the formation of a narcissistic personality disorder: "I am grandiose because I feel unlovable and hateful, and I fear I cannot be loved unless I am perfect and omnipotent."

Kohut's position is shared by Goldberg (1972, 1973, 1975), the Ornsteins (1975), and Schwartz (1973), who see narcissism as separate from drive-determined conflicts. Prominent among Kernberg's supporters are Volkan (1976) and Hamilton (1978), who assert that aggression reflecting early deprivation is at the core of such a character disorder, and not an epiphenomenon, and that narcissistic investment and object investment occur simultaneously, influencing each other, so that one cannot study the vicissitudes of narcissism without studying those of object relations as well.

Spruiell (1975) suggested that narcissistic patients may in fact be of two distinctly different types, one suffering from developmental arrest (with a fixation arising from parental failure to tame the child's archaic grandiosity) and the other with defenses against paranoia (consequent on projection of rage over early childhood frustrations). Our own experience in psychoanalytic psychotherapy makes us favor Kernberg's theoretical stance. However, many factors may be at work, with the possibility of etiological heterogeneity and as yet undetermined mechanisms.

OTHER PSYCHOANALYTIC CONTRIBUTIONS

Here we limit ourselves to those investigators who provided substantial additional insights into narcissistic personality disorder; Bach, Volkan, Modell, Horowitz, and Bursten seem representative of the major contributors in this area.

Bach's main contributions (1975, 1977a, 1977b) are in phenomenology. More than any other investigator, Bach has delved into the intricacies of what he calls the "narcissistic state of consciousness" (1977b). He indicates that the narcissistic person has defects in five crucial areas: (1) perception of self, including body-self; (2) language and thought organization; (3) intentionality and volition; (4) regulation of mood; and (5) perception of time, space, and causality. The disturbance in self includes a splitting of self, and the split-off self-representation may even have a distinct psychophysical embodiment such as a double. Even when such a personification does not occur, the split-off self shows a "mirror complementarity" with conscious complaints. An individual who has feelings of weakness and vulnerability may secretly harbor a grandiose and dangerously powerful split-off self, and one who exhibits paranoid arrogance may secretly fear the timid, dependent child-self. Among these individuals there is also relative predominance of self-oriented reality perception, and they display a tendency toward excessive self-stimulation.

The narcissistic individual uses language in a predominantly autocentric manner for well-being and self-esteem rather than for communicating or understanding. There is a peculiar gap between words and percepts, and such persons give the impression that they are talking to themselves or that their words endlessly circle. A loss of flexibility in perspective results in overabstractness, concretization, or fluctuations between these extremes. The narcissist often uses impersonal subjects: for example, "the thought occurred . . .," "one feels that. . . . " Bach points to subtle learning problems and memory defects; the learning process, in its assumption of ignorance, inflicts an intolerable narcissistic injury. Along with these defects are restrictions in volition, spontaneity, and intentionality, often disguised by fruitless pseudoactivity. Mood regulation seems excessively dependent on external circumstances, with many ups and downs. Bach differentiates these mood swings from the classical cyclothymia insofar as these are

> . . . characterized by limited duration and rapid vacillations, with relative maintenance of insight and the general integrity of the personality. Typically, the depressions follow a narcissistic loss or defeat, have a primary quality of apathy and show a predominance of shame over guilt. . . . [However, the patient fears] he may overshoot the mark and become "too excited," lose contact, be unable to stop, be consumed and die. This *hyper*-arousal is associated with physical transcendence, grandiosity, and megalomania. (1977b, pp. 224–225)

Bach also points out that for narcissistic individuals, time loses its impersonal and abstract quality and is reckoned by its internal personal impact. Similarly, a causal relationship may be seen to exist between events solely because they occur simultaneously.

Volkan's main contributions (1973, 1976, 1979) are his descriptions of the maneuvers used to protect the grandiose self from the assaults of reality. He points to three such mechanisms: externalization of the conflict and restructuring of reality, the glass-bubble fantasy, and the use of transitional fantasies. He notes that narcissistic individuals, particularly those in positions of power, may restructure their reality by devaluing or even eliminating those on whom their vulnerable self-representations have been projected. Also, they may surround themselves with admirers — extensions of the grandiose self for whom they have little empathy or concern. Volkan (1979) finds that narcissistic individuals use the glass-bubble fantasy, which resembles what Modell (1976) described as the initial cocoon phase of psychoanalytic treatment. Narcissists feel that they live by themselves in a glorious but lonely way, enclosed by impervious but transparent protection. Volkan notes that sometimes this fantasy is not readily disclosed but appears only in psychoanalytic treatment. He notes also the use of transitional fantasies (1973), imaginary and rather stereotyped dramas of personal glory that narcissistic persons may habitually indulge in when faced with psychic trauma or even when falling asleep. Their manner of using these fantasies is reminiscent of a child's use of transitional objects (Winnicott 1953).

Volkan suggests that such a person's mother has treated her child as "special" while staying unempathic and unnourishing and that, indeed, some narcissistic individuals were born as replacement children (Cain and Cain 1964, Poznanski 1972) and became living linking objects (Volkan 1981b) for mothers bereaved by the death of a significant person who had been regarded with ambivalence. Such a mother allegedly treats her child as special insofar as he or she becomes the replacement of the one lost, but she falls short of providing adequate mothering because of her ambivalence and her unresolved and chronic mourning.

Modell (1976) bases his formulation largely on Winnicott's work (1965) and holds that narcissistic individuals were traumatized as children when their sense of self was developing. Deficient maternal empathy at that stage necessitates the establishment of a precocious and vulnerable sense of autonomy, which is supported by fantasies of omnipotence and around which the grandiose self develops.

Horowitz (1975) offers three sets of criteria for the diagnosis of narcissistic personality. The first two refer to traits and interpersonal relations and include the clinical characteristics described by Kohut and Kernberg. The third refers to the information-processing style, which Horowitz sees as consisting of paying undue attention to sources of praise and criticism, maintaining incompatible psychological attitudes in separate clusters, and using characteristic coping devices when faced with threats to self-esteem. The narcissist denies, disavows, or negates disappointing experiences or "slides around the meaning of events in order to place the self in a better light" (p. 171). Such fluid shifts in meanings, while permitting an apparent logical consistency, lead to a shaky subjective experience of ideas.

Bursten (1973) has attempted definition and even subclassification of narcissistic personality disorder. His definition is similar to those outlined above. However, his subclassification of the disorder into four subtypes (craving, paranoid, manipulative, and phallic) seems too inclusive in that it subsumes such diverse character pathologies as passive-aggressive, antisocial, and paranoid under one nosological rubric.

SOCIAL AND EXISTENTIAL PERSPECTIVES

Some sociological studies (Johnson 1977, Lasch 1978, Lifton 1971, Macoby 1977) provide graphic descriptions of what could be seen as narcissistic personality disorder. For instance, in a study of contemporary corporate leaders, Macoby noted that the modal character in this group "wants to be known as a winner . . . is seductive . . . has little capacity for personal intimacy and social commitment . . . feels little loyalty . . . lacks conviction." He likes a "sexy atmosphere," and, "once his youth, vigor, and even the thrill in winning are lost, he becomes depressed and goalless," finding himself "starkly alone" (1977).

Lifton's "protean man" lives with "an interminable series of experiments and explorations . . . a certain kind of polymorphous versatility . . . a profound inner sense of absurdity . . . a severe conflict of dependency . . . a vague but persistent kind of self condemnation . . . a nagging sense of worthlessness . . . resentment and anger [and] . . . hunger for chemical aids to expand consciousness" (1971, pp. 301–303).

Contemporary fiction sometimes portrays such protagonists — the work of Joseph Heller (1979) and Saul Bellow (1975) for example. Klass and Offenkrantz (1976), in a review of Jean-Paul Sartre's contributions to the understanding of narcissism, find the protagonist of *Nausea* stabilizing his fragmenting self with mechanisms they have seen in narcissistic patients: reflection (a process by which consciousness tries to adopt an external viewpoint about itself), temporality (the establishment of one's continuity through time), and being for others (how one experiences another's view of himself or herself). They consider the narcissist's hyperreflectiveness, acute sense of the passage of time, and inordinate sensitivity to others' assessment of him or her as defensive measures buttressing a fragile self-system.

Johnson's descriptive profile of the alienated person (1977) also resembles that of the narcissist. Johnson reviewed the contributions of major existential thinkers in picturing the alienated person as "sitting in his own private theater at once the projectionist and the sole audience," feeling like "an actor, a player, or impersonator but never a person" with an ever-present "feeling of inauthenticity and meaninglessness." Concepts of sincerity or authenticity seem absurd to such an individual. Relating to others is accompanied by "such intense self consciousness that any kind of action seems overwhelmingly synthetic." Johnson portrays the alienated person as living in "caves, cocoons, containers, and bell jars . . . with the inevitability of this counterbalanced by the splendid private awareness of his own internal equipment" (pp. 140–141).

All these descriptions bear a striking resemblance to the clinical picture of narcissistic personality disorder. Whether this likeness validates the existence of the disorder is not the issue; what is important is a synthesis of description from various sources — psychoanalytic, psychiatric, literary, sociologic, and existential — in order to grasp the essential phenomenology of this disorder.

DSM-III

The DSM-III lists narcissistic personality disorder as a separate entity, giving the following diagnostic criteria and specifying that these are characteristic of the subject's long-term functioning and may not be limited to episodic behavior: (1) grandiose sense of self-importance or uniqueness; (2) preoccupation with fantasies of unlimited success, power, brilliance, beauty, or ideal love; (3) exhibitionism (the person requires constant attention and admiration); (4) cool indifference or marked feelings of rage, inferiority, shame, humiliation, or emptiness in response to criticism, indifference of others, or defeat; and (5) at least two of the following characteristics of disturbances in interpersonal relationships: (a) entitlement (expectation of special favors without assuming reciprocal responsibilities), (b) interpersonal exploitiveness (taking advantage of others to indulge one's own desires or for self-aggrandizement and disregard for the personal integrity and rights of others), (c) relationships that characteristically oscillate between the extremes of overidealization and devaluation, and (d) lack of empathy (inability to recognize how others feel).

Clearly, this is the first major attempt to develop diagnostic criteria for the narcissistic personality disorder. As a landmark in the evolution of a definition of this syndrome, the attempt deserves recognition and praise. Even the inclusion of the disorder as a separate entity in the DSM-III, although it is yet to be mentioned in major textbooks of psychiatry, is a progressive step.

The diagnostic criteria themselves are quite detailed. However, including certain other clinical features mentioned in the literature may have rendered them deeper and more comprehensive. These features are chronic, intense envy and defenses against it; pseudosublimation or exhibitionistic motivation to work; the corruptibility of value systems; and cognitive pecularities. Also, the DSM-III's description does not emphasize the coexistence of mutually contradictory stances, seen in almost all areas of functioning, that is to us a central feature of the condition. We hope to cover these areas clearly in the following composite picture of the narcissistic personality.

AN ATTEMPT AT SYNTHESIS

For our diagnostic criteria of the narcissistic personality disorder (see Table 2-1), we drew on three sources: the literature, our own clinical experience, and the experience of our colleagues. We assigned the clinical

Table 2.1. Clinical features of the narcissistic personality disorder

Clinical Features	Overt Characteristics	Covert Characteristics
Self-concept	Inflated self-regard; haughty grandiosity; fantasies of wealth, power, beauty, brilliance; sense of enlightenment; illusory invulnerability	Inordinate hypersensitivity; feelings of inferiority, worthlessness, fragility; continuous search for strength and glory
Interpersonal relations	Shallow; much contempt for and devaluation of others, occasional withdrawal into "splendid isolation"	Chronic idealization and intense envy of others; enormous hunger for acclaim
Social adaptation	Social success; sublimation in the service of exhibitionism (pseudosublimation), intense ambition	Chronic boredom; uncertainty; dissatisfaction with professional and social identity
Ethics, standards, and ideals	Apparent zeal and enthusiasm for moral, sociopolitical, and aesthetic matters	Lack of any genuine commitment; corruptible conscience
Love and sexuality	Seductiveness; promiscuity; lack of sexual inhibitions; frequent infatuations	Inability to remain in love; treating the love object as extension of self rather than as separate, unique individual; perverse fantasies; occasionally, sexual deviations
Cognitive style	Egocentric perception of reality; articulate and rhetorical; circumstantial and occasionally vague, as if talking to self; evasive but logically consistent in arguments; easily becoming devil's advocate	Inattention to objective aspects of events, resulting at times in subtle gaps in memory; "soft" learning difficulties; autocentric use of language; fluctuations between being overabstract and overconcrete; tendency to change meanings of reality when self-esteem is threatened

findings to six areas of psychological functioning: (1) self-concept; (2) interpersonal relationships; (3) social adaptation; (4) ethics, standards, and ideals; (5) love and sexuality; and (6) cognitive style. We tried to distinguish between the overt, or readily observable, and the covert characteristics of the disorder. (In this context, overt and covert do not refer to conscious and unconscious; both types of clinical features are consciously held, but some can be more easily noticed than others can.) These diagnostic criteria are more comprehensive than those in the DSM-III. We regard our conceptualization of the clinical features as overt and covert as a forward step serving to underline the centrality of splitting in narcissistic personalities and to emphasize their divided self. This not only gives sounder theoretical underpinnings to the disorder's phenomenology but also prepares the therapist for the mirror complementarity of the self that Bach (1977b) noted. Patients with narcissistic personality disorder may sometimes initially display some of the usually covert features, whereas most of the usually overt ones remain hidden in the first few interviews, but the therapist's awareness of the dichotomous self will encourage further inquiry and prevent misdiagnosis.

DIFFERENTIAL DIAGNOSIS

There are superficial resemblances between the narcissistic and other personality disorders. The DSM-III recognizes this but condones multiple diagnostic labels in such cases. We take exception to this; multiple labels allow for the coexistence of metapsychologically incompatible, psychogenetically heterogeneous, and experientially distinct psychiatric conditions in one person. We also disagree with the DSM-III's omission of obsessional personality from the differential diagnosis. We think that narcissistic personality disorder should be distinguished, on the one hand, from borderline and antisocial personality disorders and, on the other, from developmentally "higher" forms of personality disorders such as the obsessional and the hysterical. One important differential diagnosis, we feel, is the rather uncommon one involving atypical affective disorders.

BORDERLINE PERSONALITY

Splitting, or active dissociation of mutually contradictory self and object representations, is the central defensive mechanism in both borderline and narcissistic personality disorders (Kernberg 1975). Patients with both disorders may exhibit shaky interpersonal relationships, inability to love, deficiencies in empathy, egocentric perception of reality, and solipsistic claims for attention. But there are important differences. In the narcissistic disorder the self is more cohesive, albeit pathological, and less in danger of regressive fragmentation (Bursten 1973, Kernberg 1975, Kohut 1971); in borderline personality the self is poorly integrated and at greater risk of dissolution into psychoticlike states, especially under stress (Gunderson and Kolb 1978, Gunderson and Singer 1975). Because of the greater cohesion of the self, a person with narcissistic personality is able to achieve better social adjustment and greater capacity for work and social success than the person with borderline personality. In addition, the narcissistic person shows better impulse control and greater anxiety tolerance than the borderine person does. Self-mutilation and persistent overt rage, often seen in the borderline personality (Gunderson and Singer 1975), are not features of the narcissistic disorder.

Adler (1981) pointed out that narcissistic patients differ from borderline patients in that they have greater cohesion of the self, more stable narcissistic transferences, and greater ability for mature aloneness.

OBSESSIONAL PERSONALITY

The narcissistic personality may resemble the obsessional personality: both display high ego-ideals; great need for control; perfectionism; and a compulsive, driven quality; but important differences exist in the subjective experience and inner lives of the two (Kernberg 1975, Volkan 1976). The obsessional seeks perfection; the narcissist claims it. The obsessional does not devalue others whereas the narcissist shows contempt for others. The obsessional is modest, the narcissist haughty. Moreover, the value system of the latter is generally corruptible in contrast with the rigid morality of the obsessional. Finally, although somewhat bland on the surface, the obsessional individual has genuine and deep moral and sociopolitical beliefs; the narcissist shows apparent zeal and enthusiasm for such issues without having any inner commitment to them.

HYSTERICAL PERSONALITY

Many authors (Bursten 1973, Volkan 1976) have stated that narcissistic individuals seem like hysterical individuals: both tend to be demonstrative, exhibitionistic, dramatic, and, at times, seductive. However, the narcissistic patient's exhibitionism and seductiveness have a haughty, exploitive, and cold quality; the hysterical persona is more human, playful, and warm. Indeed, both obsessional and hysterical individuals, unlike narcissistic individuals, retain the capacity for empathy, concern, and love for others.

ANTISOCIAL PERSONALITY

The DSM-III includes antisocial personality in the differential diagnosis of narcissistic personality disorder. The narcissistic person may indulge in substance abuse, promiscuity, manipulativeness, and antisocial behavior. However, these behaviors are sporadic. The narcissistic patient is also devoid of the consistent, pervasive, calculated, and ruthless disregard for social standards evident in the sociopathic individual (Kernberg 1975, Kohut 1971). Unlike the sociopathic individual, the narcissistic patient retains the ability for consistent work and job-related success.

ATYPICAL AFFECTIVE DISORDERS

Narcissistic personality disorder, due to its tendency toward mood fluctuation, is sometimes confused with a mild and atypical affective disorder. These two conditions are, however, quite different and must be differentiated for the sake of appropriate treatment.

Individuals with an affective disorder have a positive family history of the disorder and display mood changes of endogenous origin and relatively long duration. They suffer from depressions with a quality of genuine, guilt-ridden sadness and from manias that are ego-syntonic, pleasurable states of elation. Between episodes, these individuals have fairly stable lives.

Narcissistic patients rarely have a family history of bipolar affective disorder and display mood changes of reactive origin and short duration. Their depressions have a quality of impotent rage, and their manias are ego-dystonic, anxious excitements. Between episodes, narcissistic patients display seriously pathologic character traits.

These distinctions, based on limited data, await research for validation.

COMMENT

There is a consensus regarding the existence of the nosological entity of narcissistic personality disorder and agreement on phenomenological characteristics, with only minor differences in emphasis. This certainly warrants the inclusion of the disorder in the DSM-III. A relatively small number of patients have been studied, however, and all the clinical samples seem weighted with the affluent and articulate. Sociodemographic correlates remain unknown, and the differential diagnosis is incomplete. The characteristics of narcissistic individuals on various psychological tests also remain to be studied. These lacunae will perhaps be filled once a larger data base becomes available with increasing use of the DSM-III.

One of our observations not in the literature is that most of the patients who have been reported on are men. Is this simply a reflection of the predominance of men currently undergoing psychoanalysis (Pulver 1978)? Is there a diagnostic bias involved? Are male children at greater risk of being treated as ambivalently "special" in our culture? Finally, is the predominance of men evidence that the development of the narcissistic personality is somehow intertwined with male psychosexual development?

Insights from the study of pathologic narcissism are being applied to such diverse topics as administrative and political leadership (Kernberg 1979, Volkan 1981a); literature (Geidman 1975); creativity (Kohut 1976); and religion, cults, and mystical states (Horton 1973, Johnson 1977). Kohut's concepts of narcissistic rage are being used to study terrorism and political turmoil in the Middle East (GAP 1978). These admittedly important matters are, however, beyond the scope of this overview.

ACKNOWLEDGMENTS

The authors thank Drs. Andre Derdeyn, Paul J. Fink, Joseph Mooney, and Jeffrey Dekret for critical comments on earlier drafts of this paper. They also thank their fellow members of the Charlottesville Study Group for Psychoanalytic Psychotherapy (Drs. Amelia Burnham, Ron Heller, William Rheuban, Vamık Volkan, and Paul Wilkins) for their helpful suggestions and Mrs. Virginia Keenan and Ms. Lisa Marzo for editing the manuscript.

REFERENCES

Abraham, K. (1919). A particular form of neurotic resistance against the psychoanalytic method. In K. Abraham, *Selected Papers on Psychoanalysis,* pp. 303–311. London: Hogarth Press, 1949.

Adler, G. (1981). The borderline-narcissistic personality disorder continuum. *American Journal of Psychiatry* 138:46–50.

Bach, S. (1975). Narcissism, continuity and the uncanny. *International Journal of Psychoanalysis* 56:77–86.

⸺. (1977a). On narcissistic fantasies. *International Review of Psychoanalysis* 4:281–293.

⸺. (1977b). On the narcissistic state of consciousness. *International Journal of Psychoanalysis* 58:209–233.

Bellow, S. (1975). *Humboldt's Gift.* New York: Viking.

Bursten, B. (1973). Some narcissistic personality types. *International Journal of Psychoanalysis* 54:287–300.

Cain, A., and Cain, B. S. (1964). On replacing a child. *Journal of the American Academy of Child Psychiatry* 3:443–456.

Ellis, H. (1898). Auto-eroticism: a psychological study. *Alienist and Neurologist* 19:260–299.

Fairbairn, W. R. D. (1952). *An Object Relations Theory of the Personality.* New York: Basic Books.

Freud, S. (1905). Three essays on the theory of sexuality. *Standard Edition* 7:123–243.

––––––. (1914). On narcissism: an introduction. *Standard Edition* 14:73–107.

––––––. (1931). Libidinal types. *Standard Edition* 21:215–220. London: Hogarth Press, 1974.

Geidman, H. K. (1975). Reflection on romanticism, narcissism, and creativity. *Journal of the American Psychoanalytic Association* 23:407–423.

Goldberg, A. (1972). On the incapacity to love. *Archives of General Psychiatry* 26:3–7.

––––––. (1973). Psychotherapy of narcissistic injury. *Archives of General Psychiatry* 28:722–726.

––––––. (1975). Narcissism and the readiness for psychotherapy termination. *Archives of General Psychiatry* 32:695–699.

––––––. (1978). *The Psychology of the Self: A Case Book.* New York: International Universities Press.

Group for the Advancement of Psychiatry (1978). *Self-Involvement in the Middle-East Conflict*, G.A.P. Report 103. New York: G.A.P.

Gunderson, J. G., and Kolb, J. E. (1978). Discriminating features of borderline patients. *American Journal of Psychiatry* 135:792–796.

Gunderson, J. G., and Singer, M. T. (1975). Defining borderline patients: an overview. *American Journal of Psychiatry* 132:1–10.

Guntrip, H. (1968). *Schizoid Phenomena, Object Relations and the Self.* New York: International Universities Press.

Hamilton, J. W. (1978). Some remarks on certain vicissitudes of narcissism. *International Review of Psychoanalysis* 5:275–284.

Heller, J. (1979). *Good as Gold.* New York: Simon & Schuster.

Horowitz, M. J. (1975). Sliding meanings: a defense against threat in narcissistic personalities. *International Journal of Psychoanalytic Psychotherapy* 4:167–180.

Horton, P. C. (1973). The mystical experience as a suicide preventive. *American Journal of Psychiatry* 130:294–296.

Jacobson, E. (1976). *The Self and the Object World.* New York: International Universities Press.

Johnson, A. B. (1977). A temple of last resorts: youth and shared narcissisms. In *The Narcissistic Condition,* ed. M. C. Nelson, pp. 27-65. New York: Human Sciences.

Johnson, F. A. (1977). The existential psychotherapy of alienated individuals. In *The Narcissistic Condition,* ed. M. C. Nelson, pp. 127-153. New York: Human Sciences.

Jones, E. (1913). The God complex. In E. Jones, *Essays in Applied Psychoanalysis,* vol. 2, pp. 244-265. New York: International Universities Press, 1964.

Kernberg, O. F. (1967). Borderline personality organization. *Journal of the American Psychoanalytic Association* 15:641-685.

———. (1970). Factors in the treatment of narcissistic personality disorder. *Journal of the American Psychoanalytic Association* 18:51-85.

———. (1975.) *Borderline Conditions and Pathological Narcissism.* New York: Jason Aronson.

———. (1976). *Object Relations Theory and Clinical Psychoanalysis.* New York: Jason Aronson.

———. (1979). Regression in organization leadership. *Psychiatry* 42: 24-39.

Khan, M. M. R. (1974). *The Privacy of Self.* New York: International Universities Press.

Klass, D. B., and Offenkrantz, W. (1976). Sartre's contribution to the understanding of narcissism. *International Journal of Psychoanalytic Psychotherapy* 5:547-565.

Klein, M. (1948). *Contributions to Psychoanalysis (1921-1945).* London: Hogarth Press.

Kohut, H. (1966). Forms and transformations of narcissism. *Journal of the American Psychoanalytic Association* 14:243-272.

———. (1968). The psychoanalytic treatment of narcissistic personality disorders. *Psychoanalytic Study of the Child* 23:86-113.

———. (1971). *The Analysis of the Self.* New York: International Universities Press.

———. (1972). Thoughts on narcissism and narcissistic rage. *Psychoanalytic Study of the Child* 27:360-400.

———. (1976). Creativeness, charisma, group psychology: reflections on the self-analysis of Freud. In *Freud: The Fusion of Sciences and Humanism. The Intellectual History of Psychoanalysis,* ed. J. E. Gedo and G. H. Pollack. Psychological Issues Monograph, vol. 9. New York: International Universities Press.

————. (1977). *The Restoration of the Self.* New York: International Universities Press.

————. (1979). Two analyses of Mr. Z. *International Journal of Psychoanalysis* 60:3–27.

Lasch, C. (1978). *The Culture of Narcissism: American Life in an Age of Diminishing Expectations.* New York: Norton.

Lifton, R. J. (1971). Protean man. *Archives of General Psychiatry* 24: 298–304.

Macoby, M. (1977). *The Gamesman: The New Corporate Leaders.* New York: Simon & Schuster.

Mahler, M. S. (1968). *On Human Symbiosis and the Vicissitudes of Individuation.* New York: International Universities Press.

Modell, A. (1976). The holding environment and the therapeutic action of psychoanalysis. *Journal of the American Psychoanalytic Association* 24:255–307.

Moore, B. E., and Fine, D., eds. (1967). *A Glossary of Psychoanalytic Terms and Concepts.* New York: American Psychoanalytic Association.

Nacke, P. (1899). Die sexuellen perversitaten in der irrenstalt. *Psychiatrische en Neurologische Bladen* 3.

Nemiah, J. C. (1961). *Foundations of Psychopathology.* New York: Oxford University Press.

Ornstein, A., and Ornstein, P. H. (1975). On the interpretive process in psychoanalysis. *International Journal of Psychoanalytic Psychotherapy* 4:219–271.

Perry, J. C., and Klerman, G. L. (1978). The borderline patient. *Archives of General Psychiatry* 35:141–150.

Poznanski, E. O. (1972). The replacement child: a saga of unresolved parental grief. *Behavioral Pediatrics* 81:1190–1193.

Pulver, S. E. (1978). Survey of psychoanalytic practice 1976: some trends and implications. *Journal of the American Psychoanalytic Association* 26:615–631.

Rank, O. (1911). Ein beitrag zum narcissmus. *Jarbuch fur Psychoanalytische und Psychopathologische Forschungen* 3:401–426.

Reich, A. (1960). Pathologic forms of self-esteem regulation. *Psychoanalytic Study of the Child* 15:215–232.

Riviere, J. A. (1936). A contribution to the analysis of the negative therapeutic reaction. *International Journal of Psychoanalysis* 17:304–320.

Rosenfeld, H. (1964). On the psychopathology of narcissism: a clinical approach. *International Journal of Psychoanalysis* 45:332–337.

Rothstein, A. (1979). An exploration of the diagnostic term "narcissistic personality disorders." *Journal of the American Psychoanalytic Association* 27:893-912.

Schwartz, L. (1973). Panel report on the technique and prognosis in the treatment of narcissistic personality disorder. *Journal of the American Psychoanalytic Association* 21:617-632.

Spruiell, V. (1975). Three strands of narcissism. *Psychoanalysis Quarterly* 64:577-595.

Tartakoff, H. H. (1966). The normal personality in our culture and the Nobel Prize complex. In *Psychoanalysis: A General Psychology. Essays in Honor of Heinz Hartmann*, ed. R. M. Lowenstein, L. M. Newman, M. Schur, and A. J. Solnit, pp. 222-252. New York: International Universities Press.

van der Waals, H. G. (1965). Problems of narcissism. *Bulletin of the Menninger Clinic* 29:293-311.

Volkan, V. D. (1973). Traditional fantasies in the analysis of a narcissistic personality. *Journal of the American Psychoanalytic Association* 21:351-376.

———. (1976). *Primitive Internalized Object Relations*. New York: International Universities Press.

———. (1979). The "glass bubble" of the narcissistic patient. In *Advances in Psychotherapy of the Borderline Patient*, ed. J. Leboit and A. Capponi, pp. 405-431. New York: Jason Aronson.

———. (1981a). Immortal Ataturk: narcissism and creativity in a revolutionary leader. In *Psychoanalytic Study of Society*, vol. 9, ed. W. Muensterberger, L. B. Boyer, and S. Grolnick, pp. 221-255. New York: Psychohistory Press.

———. (1981b). *Linking Objects and Linking Phenomena: A Study of the Forms, Symptoms, Metapsychology and Therapy of Complicated Mourning*. New York: International Universities Press.

Waelder, R. (1925). The psychoses, their mechanisms and accessibility to influence. *International Journal of Psychoanalysis* 6:259-281.

Winnicott, D. W. (1953). Transitional objects and transitional phenomena: a study of the first not-me possession. *International Journal of Psychoanalysis* 34:89-97.

———. (1965). *The Maturational Process and the Facilitating Environment*. New York: International Universities Press.

CHAPTER 3

Complicated Mourning and the Syndrome of Established Pathological Mourning

VAMIK D. VOLKAN, M.D.

This chapter examines recent findings concerning the complications that can occur in mourning the death of someone of psychological importance to the bereaved. This examination will identify a syndrome known as *established pathological mourning*.

I believe that the psychodynamic state of most mourners whose responses to bereavement are complicated eventually leads to either depression or established pathological mourning. Both of these states reflect mental conflict, but depression indicates that the course of mourning is set in a pathological direction, whereas established pathological mourning is evidence of a fixation impeding the course of mourning. Various neurotic, psychotic, or psychosomatic symptoms may at first conceal either of these two states, but careful scrutiny usually shows that both rest on a foundation of chronic complications in the response to a death.

Freud (Breuer and Freud 1893–1895) suggested in the early days of the psychoanalytic movement a relationship between bereavement and symptom formation, and he later (Freud 1917) made a critical distinction between "normal" mourning and the reactive depression (melancholia) that sometimes follows the death of a person important to the bereaved. With Abraham (1911, 1916, 1924), Freud emphasized the role of introjection and identification as they are reactivated in the mourning process. In the normal process of mourning the person reacts to a real object loss by effecting a temporary introjection of the loved person. Its main purpose is to preserve the person's relation to the lost object. "My loved object is not gone, for now I carry it within myself and can never lose it" (Abraham 1924, p. 437).

With the establishment of structural theory (Freud 1923), other analysts—notably Rado (1928), Lewin (1950), and Jacobson (1954)—elaborated and extended Abraham's and Freud's concepts. In uncomplicated grief, the mourners loosen their ties to the internalized representation of the dead person by means of mourning. We know that in completing this process, mourners identify with selected "good" aspects of the representation of the dead person and adopt these perceived good traits as their own. This enriches the mourners' self-concept and ego functions. Thus an adaptive restitution (Pollock 1961, Rochlin 1965) takes place, and the good identifications help build a "solid bridge between the generations" (Volkan 1981).

The mourning process of some individuals does not, however, follow an uncomplicated course. Fenichel (1945) summarized the basic reasons for its taking a complicated course: (1) the lost object has not been loved on a mature level but has been chiefly perceived as a provider of narcissistic supplies; (2) the mourner's relationship to the dead person was highly ambivalent before his or her death; or (3) the mourner is orally fixated and "has unconscious longings for sexualized 'eating'." In the third situation, introjection (eating) is intense, and the mourner tries to keep within himself or herself the ambivalently regarded representation of the deceased. When identification occurs, it is not selective, as in uncomplicated mourning; the mourner identifies in an indiscriminate and "*in toto*" (Ritvo and Solnit 1958) way with both good and bad aspects of the dead individual's representation. Since both the libido and aggression invested in the deceased are now turned against the representation of the dead that is now part of the self by means of identification, there follows an internal battle of the kind classically considered a psychodynamic cause for depression. In 1917 Freud noted, "If the love for the object—a love which cannot be given up . . . takes refuge in narcissistic identification, then the hate that is felt for the dead person comes into operation on his substitutive object, abusing it, debasing it, making it suffer and deriving sadistic satisfaction for its suffering" (p. 251).

The classic psychoanalytic understanding of the depression that follows a death refers to an intersystemic conflict within the mental apparatus. The mourner ambivalently identifies with the representation of the dead person, and sadism, enlisting on the side of the superego, attacks the mourner's ego, which is also changed by identification with the libidinally invested aspect of the dead person's representation. In other words, it is usual in depression for a battle to occur between the individual's superego and ego. But Bibring (1953) objected to this view, stating that oral and aggressive strivings in depression are not universal. He studied the condition as an ego-psychological phenomenon, so his emphasis is on the intrasystemic conflicts within the ego. I agree with Jacobson (1971) that certain depressions, especially psychotic depressions in which the "conflict is between the wishful self image and the image of the failing self" are the kind that mainly reflect tension within the ego. Jacobson (1971), Mahler (1968), and I (1981) believe that Bibring leaves out the role of object relations, aggression, and hostility in neurotic depression, a classification into which most depressions after a death fall — unless, of course, the mourner's mental structure is primitive and one in which death triggers a psychotic response.

Although the literature offers examples of complicated mourning that has given rise to somatized responses (i.e., Cobb et al. 1939, Lidz 1949, McDermott and Cobb 1939, Schmale 1958), the purely psychodynamic aspects of such patients still refer to the internalization of the representation of the dead person (accompanied by the contamination of this representation with drives) as well as to the somatization of drive derivatives. The literature also notes specific types of complicated mourning. For example, Deutsch (1937) wrote of those patients who initially do not display a grief reaction, and Wahl (1970) wrote about those who exhibit chronically manifestations of "normal" grief reactions. In general, though, since Freud's 1917 description of melancholia, psychological complications in mourning the death of an important other are referred to in terms of depression or pathological grief, which are often (still) used interchangeably. What I describe here as a "new" syndrome — *established pathological mourning* — has its own clinical characteristics and, what is more important, its own psychodynamic state which differentiates it from depression. In this state, the internalization of the deceased's representation indicates a different situation than it does in normal mourning or in depression after a death. In fact, established pathological mourning more directly reflects a fixation in the mourning process and represents the bereaved's persistence in limbo: the mourner wants to complete the mourning and tries to do so, but at the same time he or she wants to undo the reality of the death and makes every attempt to do that also.

RECOGNIZABLE STAGES OF MOURNING

Different investigators studying the sequential behavior patterns of persons suffering the loss of an important other have synthesized these patterns into schemata, all of which I find generally similar from a phenomenological viewpoint, despite some theoretical differences among them.

For example, Pollock (1961) classified the mourner's reactions into two stages, the acute and the chronic. The first stage has three sequential steps: (1) shock, accompanied by denial of the death; (2) acute grief (affective reaction); and (3) separation reaction, the beginning of withdrawal of psychic interest in the internal representation of the dead. This is followed by a chronic stage with "various manifestations of adaptive mechanisms attempting to integrate the experiences of the loss with reality so that life activities can go on" (Pollock 1961, p. 352). Pollock seems to equate his chronic stage with Freud's (1917) work of mourning. Most observers suggest that the work of mourning may take about a year, although Freud spoke of a year or two.

Some systems of classifying the sequential phases of mourning fail to distinguish between an acute and a chronic stage. Among such schemata, the one of Bowlby and Parkes (1970) is well known. This has four stages. The first involves numbness, usually lasting from a few hours to a week, which is interrupted by outbursts of intense distress and/or anger. Bowlby and Parkes see the second stage as one of yearning and searching for the lost figure; this stage may last for months or years, during which the mourner will not only yearn for the one he or she has lost but be aware of an urge to search for that person. Then comes a phase of disorganization (the third stage), which is followed by the fourth and last stage, consisting of at least some degree of reorganization.

These schemata refer only to adult mourning, since there is considerable controversy in psychoanalytic writings as to whether — or when — a child is capable of mourning. Obviously, the psychological response to losing someone depends not only on the ability to experience someone as an entity separate from oneself but also on the attainment of a level of psychic development at which the mental representation of the other can be maintained despite his or her physical absence. Thus the achievement of so-called object constancy is a prerequisite for the mourner's psychological ability to represent internally that person whose physical presence has been destroyed by death. The better able a child is to maintain object constancy, the more closely he or she can approximate adult grief, which includes an intrapsychic process dealing with the representation of the lost one. Nonetheless, there is some reason to agree with Wolfenstein (1966) that the capacity to mourn in the adult sense requires completion of the developmental experience of adolescence, which brings to the individual both obligatory regression and a review of his or her relationship with the representation of parents (or important others) as known in childhood (Blos 1979, A. Freud 1965). Since this produces a gradual withdrawal from one's investment in such representations, a modification of them, and a fresh investment in new representations that enrich the internal world, adolescence is a natural developmental model of mourning as it will be encountered in adult life. Passage through adolescence without complications is thus a prerequisite for the ability to mourn in an adult sense the death of an important other.

Because mourning, once initiated, moves through recognizably different stages, one may assume that if the passage through any one of these is complicated, the individual may be fixated at that particular stage. In that event, the clinical characteristics of that stage will be exaggerated, and the clinical picture will be further complicated. My own clinical research (1970, 1981) suggests that whenever a complication contaminates the chronic stage, the mourner may begin what I call established pathological mourning. Before describing this, I shall outline how one may detect complications in the earlier, or acute, stage. It is important to note that the severity of complication manifested in the initial stage of mourning does not necessarily mean that the mourner cannot work through it, since some people settle down into a normal mourning process after an exaggerated initial reaction. But if complications evident in the initial stage persist, they will become part of the psychodynamic pattern of established pathological mourning or depression.

EARLY DETECTION OF COMPLICATIONS

The reasons for particular responses to death were summarized by Fenichel (1945) and include the mourner's ego maturity and the nature of the rapport he or she had with the deceased. It has long been recognized that when the relationship between the mourner and the deceased was ambivalent and stormy, the mourner's reactions are apt to be complicated by various component feelings. The more loving the relationship was, the more likely it is that the mourner will feel sadness but no guilt and that this sadness will be personal and intimate, like love, and more difficult to convey than depression (Smith 1971).

The true circumstances of the death are also important. Reaction to death is influenced by its being sudden and unexpected and/or violent; by the mourner's view of the deceased as someone heroic who has been transported to some kind of Valhalla; by the kind of arrangements made for the funeral and burial; and by the mourner's participation in these rites.

The death of an aged person or a chronic invalid is less shocking than a sudden and entirely unexpected death is. For example, I believe that a young mother never gets over the sudden death of a healthy child, however many creative/adaptive ways she may find to help assuage her loss. Lindemann (1944), who offered an excellent description of acute grief, pointed to what he called *anticipatory grief*, the gradual accommodation that one makes to the loss of a significant other whose life is clearly coming to a close; and to the passage through some or all of the stages of grief that may in such circumstances take place before death actually occurs. Such anticipatory grief may even be worked out in a fantasied situation. I had as a patient a young woman whose husband had been sent to Vietnam soon after their marriage. She was certain that he would not return alive. I learned later that as a young girl she had suddenly lost someone close and hence had a genetic reason for her fear. When her husband did return from Vietnam without a scratch, she perceived him as a stranger, a virtual "ghost" to whom she did not want to be married. They were soon divorced. Although she had kept in her mind an idealized image of her husband, it did not correspond to the real man just back from the war zone.

I have found that a violent death is often unconsciously connected with the mourner's aggressive drive derivatives. It fosters a guilt that precludes any expression of the angry and aggressive reactions that are "natural" after the death of an important other. Or the dead person may be too greatly idealized to be "killed," and the expected stages of mourning cannot be initiated. This is often the case when an idealized leader dies suddenly, perhaps at the hands of his or her enemies; or when the mental representation of slain soldiers viewed as saviors are memorialized in the minds of those who mourn them. I earlier (1978) described this situation as I saw it on the island of Cyprus after the 1974 war there.

I (1970) also noted that the type of funeral, the nature of the mourner's participation in it, and even the type of coffin chosen can influence the mourner's initial responses. As psychoanalytic studies show, funeral rites and religious services are attempts to deal with the common psychological components of acute grief, among these the emergence of aggressive feelings. Thus the mourner should be allowed to indulge fully in mourning rituals of whatever kind his or her culture and religion support. It often happens, however, that those most likely to have difficulty in dealing with their grief, such as the young, are not allowed to participate in the funeral rites.

Often a teenaged boy who has just lost his father will be made the male family head and, paradoxically, be kept busy and "protected" from playing any active part in the funeral service itself. (One also should not overlook the effect of any drastic change the death may have brought to the survivors, such as the loss of a home or financial support.)

My patient Solomon was a young teenager when his father died. The rather extended Jewish religious rites for the dead man were well under way when his mother decided that young Solomon should be sent to the country "to get fresh air." While in the country he caught a snake and put it in a glass bottle with some kind of acid; having been interrupted in the religious ceremonies for his father, he created his own ceremony for "killing" (mourning) his parent. The dead snake represented the dead man, and the son made a daily ritual out of observing its progressive deterioration in the bottle. His unfinished (psychological) business with his father was so complicated, however, that he could not go through the mourning process successfully. As the snake rotted away, Solomon himself fell victim to severe dermatitis. His skin became infected and gave him considerable pain and inconvenience. Although one cannot know all of the particulars and etiological factors involved in his skin trouble, it is safe to assume that it reflected some identification with the decaying father.

The influences on the initial response to death mentioned thus far are rather readily observable. It is obvious that only a psychological examination, such as takes place during psychoanalytic treatment, will reveal any idiosyncratic perception of the loss by death, as well as its condensation in the representation of important psychic events, such as those related to separation and/or castration anxiety. If one is to understand the patient's responses on this level one must grasp the symbolism the patient is using.

For example, a young man who knew that his cancer-ridden father would die shortly took his wife into a room just beneath his father's death chamber and had intercourse with her while his father died. He knew that his wife could be made pregnant at this time, and in fact she did conceive their first child on this occasion. During his analysis some years later, he spoke of this with embarrassment, saying that it puzzled him. After much time in analysis it was possible to understand the many meanings of his behavior. He had been a sickly child who had received radiation therapy. His mother had insisted that he wear a hat while outdoors so that the sun's radiation would not add to what he had received therapeutically. The hat was a constant reminder of her anxiety about his health, of which he was so aware that he could not psychologically tolerate being apart from her lest something horrible overtake him. By the time he reached the oedipal stage, he had sexualized this mother-son relationship, and even after his marriage he fantasied, while masturbating, sexual union with his mother. He wanted his father to disappear or die so that he could possess his mother without competition. Early physical trauma and ritualistic beating by his father had greatly exacerbated his castration fear. During puberty he assimilated these early traumas into his character, and he behaved in a self-castrating way when he became an adult: he "accidentally" amputated his toe as if to ensure his not having to face castration and/or separation caused by others. When his father's cancer was diagnosed, his childhood fantasies were reactivated, along with the accompanying guilt. By having intercourse with his wife as his father lay dying, he was trying to say, "Look, Dad, I have my own woman now, and I leave Mother to you. Please forgive me!" Such thoughts and behavior were a defense against his castration anxiety, and on a lower level his sexual union was a defense against his separation anxiety. As might be suspected, this young man had been preoccupied with death throughout his life, and when his father's impending death turned this guilt against himself, it heightened his fear of death/separation. He fantasied that by impregnating his wife he would ensure the continuation of his life as her child.

Complication of initial reactions to death may be evidenced in the clinical picture as a denial of the death, the absence of the expected affective responses, or numbness. It may also take the opposite form, being displayed in exaggeration of affective responses, especially in angry outbursts. Such manifestations may persist on and off over the years or may appear at anniversaries of the death, and if normal mourning is not established, these symptoms will be absorbed into the total syndrome of established pathological mourning.

ESTABLISHED PATHOLOGICAL MOURNING

I noted that internalization taking place at the culmination of uncomplicated mourning is healthy and selective and that in depression it is disruptive and total rather than selective. In either situation, internalization of the deceased's representation has advanced to the point of identification, but it is pathological only in the second situation. Such identification does not occur in established pathological mourning; the mourner makes of the representation an unassimilated *introject* that he or she speaks of as an inner presence and perceives as located within his or her bosom, either representing the totality of the deceased or a part such as the head. Thus the dead person, although existing within the mourner's body, is perceived as a separate entity — an encapsulated foreign body.

The metapsychological explanation of this is that the whole or partial representation of the deceased is taken in through the mechanism of introjection but then results in an introject rather than in identification. The introject is a specific kind of object representation that the mourner strives to assimilate in his or her self-representation but cannot. It is functional in that it exerts great influence on the self-representation. Unlike identification, it does not cause structural change but continues to use ego energy to maintain an inner relatedness.

My argument here is that the kind of clinical picture that will follow the death of an important other depends on what mourners eventually do with the representation of the dead. In established pathological mourning they will maintain an introject of the deceased in a state between healthy identification and depression due to death. The ambivalent relationship of the past continues in the mourners involvement with their introject; they are torn between a strong yearning for the restoration of the departed and an equally strong dread that the dead might actually return. Thus the mourners' aggressive drives are not gratified; the introject's presence provides the illusion that they can choose between the two possibilities and reduces their anxiety thereby. The syndrome of established pathological mourning reflects this state of affairs and may be described as a condition of chronic hope of a return along with a chronic dread of such a return. Mourners in these circumstances may speak for years of the continued presence within them of the departed and say such things as "I have inner conversations with my father whenever I need advice" the father in question having been dead for six years. One patient said of such a presence, "I actually feel his head beneath my ribs. I actually talk to him. I know he is dead — and I know I am not crazy. I need him, but at the same time I wish he (his head) would disappear, die. I don't seem to be able to change the situation of his being half-dead and half-alive."

Such patients are typically interested in topics such as reincarnation and compulsively read obituary notices, betraying by this compulsiveness not only fear of their own demise (due to guilt over wishing the deceased to be "killed," among other reasons) but also a continued attempt to deny the death of the one they mourn by finding no current mention of it. The memory of the death notice that did appear at the appropriate time makes the death seem final and "kills" the lost one.

A glimpse of a stranger resembling the dead person often leads one in established pathological mourning to anxious pursuit of that stranger with the idea of establishing or ruling out the possibility that the one mourned continues somehow to be among the living. The mourner uses the present tense in speaking of the departed, such as "My mother likes to buy flowers." The mourner's mind seems to be populated by the dead person's image and those of others, dead or alive, who represent the deceased. The mourner seems now to relate more closely to the dead than to the living, and he or she often refers to tombs, graveyards, and the like.

Dreams with typical *manifest* content give diagnostic clues and may be classified as follows:

1. *Frozen dreams.* The term *frozen* is often used spontaneously by patients themselves to describe dreams composed of one tableau after another, with no action. One patient likened his dreams to a slide series, and another compared hers to slices of bread slipping out of their wrapping. "Frozen" also indicates "lifeless." Associations to such dreams reflect fixation in the work of mourning, a defensive situation in which patients try to deny their aggression toward the dead person while at the same time finding a way to bring him or her back to life; the conflict between the wish to do so and the dread of success are handled by "freezing" the conflict and averting resolution.

2. *Dreams of a life-and-death struggle.* In this kind of dream, the dreamer sees the dead person as living but engaged in a life-and-death struggle, perhaps on the point of drowning, for example. The dreamer tries to save him or her but usually awakens with anxiety before succeeding. Such a dream leaves the mourner again in the indeterminate position of being faced with "killing" or "saving" the one he or she mourns.

3. *Dreams of death as an illusion.* The dreamer dreams of meeting the one whom he or she mourns as dead but who exhibits such paradoxical signs of life as sweating or twitching and so the mourner's doubt about his or her being truly dead persists.

These three kinds of dreams often recur for years after the death that is mourned.

LINKING OBJECTS AND PHENOMENA

The maintenance of an introject is not the only means whereby persons in established pathological mourning remain in contact with the one they mourn. They invest some object (which may be as tangible as a ring or as intangible as a song) with the magical ability to establish external contact with the representation of the dead. These I (1972, 1981) refer to as *linking objects* and *linking phenomena*. They are a useful diagnostic indication of established pathological mourning, evidence that there is not only a specific kind of internalization product — the introject — but also another such product — the linking object or phenomenon — that results from externalizing the representation of the dead and connecting it with the corresponding representation of the self, as evident in my patients in this state.

Psychoanalysts have long been able to demonstrate (Mahler 1968) that it takes the first 36 months of life for the infant to individuate, to break out of the mother-child unit, and to feel and behave on his or her own behalf and not simply as an extension of the mothering figure. In their clinical practices, therapists see many adult patients whose problems stem from this separation-individuation process and some who have never achieved a complete differentiation from the mother-child unit in spite of their advance in chronological age.

One of the familiar devices employed by young children to handle the problem of separation from the mother is the "security blanket," which readers of Peanuts comics will connect with Linus. Typically, children adopt and cling to an object like a blanket — something soft and recognizable by its odor — for solace, especially at bedtime. These are called *transitional objects* (Winnicott 1953) in recognition that each represents a bridge across the chasm that is opening between the child and mother and the child, as well as a place for pondering the first blurred awareness of the outside world (Greenacre 1970). The transitional object is a manifestation of a normal developmental phase, and it is laid aside spontaneously when it has served its purpose.

The anxiety of some children over psychic separation from the mother is so intense, however, that their comforting objects are used in bizarre ways and with undue concentration. In this case we call them childhood fetishes. Adult patients in established pathological mourning reactivate, as it were, a new version of the transitional object when they make an object magically able to link them externally to the representation of the one they mourn. I have considered elsewhere (1981) the similarities and differences of transitional and linking objects, as well as the fetish and the linking object. The latter are chosen from among:

1. Belongings of the dead, sometimes something he or she wore, like a watch.

2. Something the dead person once used as an extension of his or her senses, like a camera (an extension of seeing).

3. A symbolic or realistic representation of the dead person, the simplest example of which would be a photograph.

4. A gift given by or received from the one now dead.

5. Something at hand when the news of death was received or when the mourner viewed the body. These I call *last-minute objects*, since they recall the last moment during which the full impact of the living personality of the other was available. For example, one patient got word of his brother's accidental death just as he was sitting down to play a stack of phonograph records, and so these became his linking objects (Volkan 1981).

Linking objects should not be confused with the kind of keepsake that is simply treasured and perhaps put to appropriate use. Anyone might value and use his or her father's watch, perhaps attaching considerable sentiment to it. But the patient who clings to a linking object would put the watch away, be fastidious about knowing exactly where it was at all times, and at the same time be certain of being able to avoid it when this suited him or her. It is as important to be able to avoid the linking object as it is to touch it. One of our patients had her linking object in a car that was wrecked. She took extravagant pains to rescue it, and it was the only thing she did salvage from the wreckage.

Since a linking object represents a place external to the self in which the mourner can magically reunite with the dead, he or she can, by avoiding it, reduce the anxiety generated by the thought of such reunion. The deceased is not resting in peace; the mourner is engaged in the dilemma of killing or saving that person.

One version of a linking object can be seen in any unusual way of memorializing the dead, such as keeping his or her room exactly as it was when the person died, as though he or she might return — but putting this possibility to the test. The more "normal" memorial — a sublimated version — is a statue, plaque, or tablet that effectively acknowledges the reality of the death.

SUICIDE

In depression that follows a death, mourners keep the representation of the deceased in an *in toto* identification by investing it with their libido. At the same time their aggression is turned toward the representation that identification has made a part of the mourners' own self. Accordingly, they feel a clash between the need to cling to and, simultaneously, to destroy this internal representation. If destructive forces gain the upper hand, suicide will result. The risk of suicide is not as great in established pathological mourning as it is in reactive depression, since individuals in the former condition are *protected* from the self-destructive impulse by a stable linking object or introject. They have not identified in the manner of the depressed person but maintain the illusion of contact with a representation of the dead that remains outside their own self-representation. Although they may be aggressive toward their introject or linking object, their aggression is not directed toward themselves. Moreover—and more importantly—the illusion they maintain manages their feelings of guilt by enabling them to "bring back the dead" if they choose.

In the rather rare circumstance of those in established pathological mourning who attempt suicide, their effort is not of the melancholic type, but one that reflects their wish for magical reunion with the representation of the dead. The anniversary reaction of persons in established pathological mourning may initiate such a strong desire to merge with the representation of the dead (which exists independently of the self-representation) that suicide becomes compelling.

TREATMENT

I generally do not use drugs to suppress the symptoms and signs of the initial stage of grief. In fact, one should support rather than suppress these initial responses; it is an economical move, since it prevents the need of further or recommenced grieving at some later time. The development of various religious rituals to deal with death and the emotions it generates is no accident. They provide external help for the internal process of mourning, and we advise mourners to indulge fully in them, since they will find them beneficial. When initial reaction is strikingly absent, however, help should be sought, if only on the grounds of preventive medicine. At this phase help may appropriately come from a religious adviser, but if the symptom persists, someone able to assess the reason for negative responses and able to give psychotherapy should be sought out. Should short-term therapy prove unsuccessful, it will at least give the patient the option to obtain more intensive therapy and encourage him or her to think of obtaining professional help should he or she need it in the future.

Grief-stricken persons are initially distant from others and are, at times, hostile. Their hostility may be "projected" onto the professional care-giver, who, being familiar with this symptom, is able to "absorb" the patient's hostility without returning it. Whenever the anger is highly exaggerated, however, it should be taken seriously, although I still prefer to refrain from using drugs, if possible, in such a case. But the therapist should set limits, perhaps insisting that the patient enter a hospital. Once the patient is in the protective hospital environment, the therapist can respond to his or her anger by assuming a role in which he or she can bear the patient's narcissistic hurt. The therapist must reject using drastic measures in response to the patient's behavior patterns and allow him or her to experience pain, anger, and other emotions, empathically helping the patient to heal the "wound," always remembering that he or she is responding to a natural process. Some mourners may even be relieved by little more than an educational and therapeutic effort to assure them that anger is an expected initial reaction to the death of someone close.

I repeat that the appearance of severe signs and symptoms in the initial stage does *not* necessarily mean that the patient will have complications in the second stage, that of the work of mourning. Statistically speaking, 98 percent of those experiencing bereavement seek no psychiatric assistance, and of that 98 percent, 81 percent begin to improve from six to ten weeks after the death. Four percent do not improve (Clayton et al. 1968).

A depressive constellation or established pathological mourning develops once the complication becomes chronic and reflects difficulties in the work of mourning. The psychotherapy recommended for the depressed patient is long term, intensive, and insight related, dealing with the individual's underlying matrix. Those with established pathological mourning may also benefit from insight psychotherapy on a long-term basis. The short-term therapy called *re-grief therapy* (Volkan 1971, 1981; Volkan and Josephthal 1979; Volkan and Showalter 1968; Volkan et al. 1975) was originally developed to care for patients hospitalized for established pathological mourning (sometimes coexisting with a depressive constellation).

Patients in re-grief therapy have a strong and persistent hope of seeing again the one they mourn, but they also want to "kill" him or her in order to complete their mourning. Thus they urgently want to be in psychological contact with the representation of the dead that they may perceive as an introject. Those able to externalize the representation onto their linking objects may not report having an introject, but in any event they are clearly trying to relate ambivalently to an unassimilated representation of the one they lost.

Therapists are well advised at the start of re-grief therapy not to question the patients vigorously when taking their history. They should instead develop a nondirective exchange in which they can help their patients begin differentiating their own thoughts, attitudes, and feelings from those influenced by their introject. Anyone in established pathological mourning can be counted on to broach the subject of death and the lost one himself or herself. Focusing on the history and associations pertaining to the relationship between the patient and the one he or she mourns enables the therapist to help the patient see what he or she has taken in and thus feels about the introject or representation of the other and which of its aspects are so bothersome that he or she wants to reject them.

Although the patients themselves may use the kind of physical terminology we have used in referring to an introject, what is actually involved is an affective-dynamic *process*. Therapists treating patients of the kind discussed here should be sufficiently experienced to refrain from intellectual gymnastics. The manifest content of the patients' dreams helps show how their mourning became arrested and why they feel that they embody a special representation of the one they mourn. It can, in short, help them understand their fixation. But the therapist who shares too quickly his or her formulation of the reasons for the patient's fixation may find that he or she has slowed the affective-cognitive process involved in the activation of a forward-moving mourning process. During this exchange, which may take several weeks, the therapist does not encourage an outpouring of great emotion but helps the patient prepare for it.

Meanwhile the therapist has expanded the formulation that will later guide his or her clarifications and interpretations and has learned more now about the psychological reasons for the patient's arrest and inability to grieve. The therapist encourages the patient to reminisce about the deceased, the circumstances of the final illness or fatal accident, the conditions in which he or she heard of the death, reactions to the sight of the body, the particulars of the funeral, and so on. Again, direct questioning is far less productive than encouraging the patient to offer such particulars himself or herself and permitting the display of appropriate feelings as he or she does so.

The ambivalence felt toward the dead person is clarified. Instead of commenting that such ambivalence is normal, the wise therapist conveys the appropriate message through therapeutic neutrality and empathy. He or she promotes the patient's curiosity about this ambivalence and the insight that is largely responsible for being torn between wanting to "save" the deceased or to "kill" him or her once and for all. As soon as the patient can rather readily alternate between positive and negative aspects of the ambivalence, he or she is apt to become angry. This anger may be diffuse and directed toward others, but it authenticates the reality of the death, much as though the patient had returned to the initial stage of his or her dilemma. By understanding the patient's need to have the dead "alive," the therapist then slowly clarifies the relationship between the two and interprets it, along with the reasons for anger being so expectable. Abreaction — "emotional reliving" (Bibring 1954) — arising from the recall of certain past experiences involving the deceased or his or her death may occur at this point if everything goes well. Such abreactions reflect the (re-)visiting of the initial response to death and the (re-)commencement of the work of mourning. The patient has begun to "re-grieve." It can be assumed that certain impulses, such as death wishes, are now surfacing, and the patient's readiness to have them interpreted, and to reduce his or her guilt feelings, can be assessed.

Our patients often report problems regarding the funeral and say that they did not actually see the coffin lowered into the grave. When the therapist asks at an appropriate time, "How do you know that he (or she) was buried?" the patients are likely to surprise themselves by realizing that one part of their awareness never did hold that the burial had been accomplished. They are then likely to be angry at those who stood in the way of their participation in the funeral rites. It has been made clear that although they felt — and even knew — that death had occurred, they had paradoxically continued to behave as though nothing had happened.

The most important part of this phase of confrontation — clarification and interpretation of death-related impulses, fantasies, and wishes, as well as of the defenses the patients have been using against them — is the focus on the linking object. Because it has physical existence, with properties that reach the senses, the linking object has greater "magic" than the introject does. Once the patients grasp that they have been using their linking object to maintain absolutely controlled contact with the image of the dead person, as well as to postpone mourning and keep it frozen, they will use it to activate their mourning. The therapist suggests that they bring the linking object to a therapy session. At first the patients will usually avoid it after bringing it in. The therapist then asks permission to keep it and points out that its magic exists in the patient's perception of it. When it is finally introduced into a therapy session, it is placed between patient and therapist long enough for the former to feel its "spell." The patients may then be asked to touch it and to report what comes into their mind. I am even now astonished at what intense emotion is contained in the linking object and warn others about this. This emotion serves to unlock the psychological processes that until then were contained in the linking object itself. Emotional storms so triggered may continue for weeks. At first diffuse, they then become differentiated, and the therapist and patient can then together identify such emotions as anger, guilt, and sadness. The linking object then at last loses its power, whether or not the patient chooses to dispose of it.

Clarifications and interpretations concerned with death and the deceased, and the sharper focus on these subjects made possible by the use of the linking object, lead to the final phase of the treatment — disorganization. This is then followed by organization and the appearance of sadness. A sort of graft of secondary-process thinking then is required to help heal the wound that this experience has torn open; patients who had never visited the grave of the one they mourn do so now, as if to say goodbye, and those who had been unable to arrange for the tombstone make arrangements to have one put in place. The mourner can feel sad, but he or she no longer needs to feel guilty. Many patients at this point spontaneously plan some memorial rite, and many consult priests, ministers, or rabbis for religious consolation toward the end of their treatment as they begin accepting the death.

I have been able to use the manifest content of the serial dreams of suitable patients coming to the end of their therapy to indicate where they were in their re-griefing. These patients seem to feel that their introject has departed, leaving them in peace, and they feel free, even excited, at the lifting of their burden, beginning to look for new objects for their love. My experience has been that the re-griefing that so liberates the patient can be completed within two to four months with frequent sessions, that is, three or four times a week.

I believe that elucidating some of the important meanings of the patient's loss will be of little benefit if emotions and ideation are not blended. Throughout the treatment, patients experience a variety of emotions as they gain insight into their inability to let the dead person die. This insight is arrived at by the clarifications and interpretations given, the therapy being designed to loosen up and reactivate the arrest of the mourning process. It should be noted that the patient's resistance to acknowledging his or her fixation in the work of mourning is interpreted on such levels that the interpretations do not necessarily resolve the infantile conflicts underlying the fixation. One must assume that these patients may indeed further repress such conflicts, even as they loosen whatever condensations into such conflicts they have made on a higher level. The use of linking object brings about special emotional storms that are not curative without interpretation engaging the close scrutiny of the patient's observing ego. Thus the link to the representation of the dead, externalized onto the linking object, is brought into the realm of the patient's inner experience.

Despite the use of a special device—the linking object—in re-grief therapy, the transference relationship becomes the vehicle whereby insight into ambivalence and the conflict between longing and dread may be gained and resolution accomplished. Thereby the therapist offers himself or herself as a new object—a healer—for the patient's consideration, aiming, as in psychoanalytic therapy, to develop a therapeutic alliance without encouraging an infantile transference neurosis.

Rado (1956) used the term *interceptive interpretations*, which I modified in describing my interception of the development of infantile transference neurosis by premature interpretation of the transference phenomena whenever I thought it could lead to a ripened infantile transference neurosis. For example, one interferes with full displacement of the dead person's representation onto the therapist, so that the patient is kept aware of being faced with complications in his or her mourning of the lost one. But the patient's reactions to parallel situations of loss involving the therapist—separation at weekends, for example—are interpreted in due time, and such interpretation makes it possible to work through past conflicts while focusing on the dead person. Also, the fresh grief caused by the imminent separation from the therapist when therapy is about to terminate can be used appropriately. Transference reactions are inevitable, but infantile transference neurosis is not; and selected reference to and interpretations of the transference reactions may be therapeutic by providing close and intimate contact within the therapeutic setting as the patient's coflicts are understood. Thus, although re-grief therapy is brief and lasts for months rather than years, it is intense, intimate, and certainly not superficial.

SUMMARY

Accomodation to a loss by death unfolds in expectable stages when complications do not interfere. If the process of mourning becomes complicated and remains so, one of two basic psychodynamic constellations will occur. One is a depression in which the mourner has identified *in toto* and disruptively with the representation of the dead. This chapter considered the second constellation, one that appears on the clinical level as a syndrome of established pathological mourning. In the latter situation, the patients remain in limbo, chronically preoccupied with "killing" the representation of the dead while at the same time hoping to bring

him or her back to life. They maintain contact with the internal representation of the dead through an introject, a special object representation
of the deceased, and externally through the linking object (or phenomenon) which provides a symbolic locus in which the mourner and the
mourned can meet.

I then described the syndrome of established pathological mourning
and a treatment method specifically designed to deal with it.

REFERENCES

Abraham, K. (1911). Notes on the psycho-analytical investigation
and treatment of manic-depressive insanity and allied conditions. In
Selected Papers, ed. D. Bryan and A. Strachey, pp. 137–156. New
York: Basic Books, 1960.

————. (1916). The first pregenital stage of libido. In *Selected Papers,*
ed. D. Bryan and A. Strachey, pp. 248–279. New York: Basic Books,
1960.

————. (1924). A short study of the development of the libido, viewed
in the light of mental disorders. In *Selected Papers,* pp. 418–501. London: Hogarth Press, 1927.

Bibring, E. (1953). The mechanism of depression in affective disorder. In *Affective Disorder,* ed. P. Greenacre, pp. 13–48. New York: International Universities Press.

————. (1954). Psychoanalysis and the dynamic psychotherapies.
Journal of the American Psychoanalytic Association 2:745–770.

Blos, P. (1979). *The Adolescent Passage.* New York: International Universities Press.

Bowlby, J., and Parkes, C. M. (1970). Separation and loss within the
family. In *The Child in His Family,* vol. 1, ed. E. J. Anthony and C.
Koupirnik, pp. 197–216. New York: Wiley Interscience.

Breuer, J., and Freud, S. (1893–1895). Studies on hysteria. *Standard
Edition* 2.

Clayton, P., Desmarais, L., and Winokur, G. (1968). A study of
normal bereavement. *American Journal of Psychiatry* 125:168–178.

Cobb, S., Bauer, W., and Whiting, K. (1939). Environmental factors in rheumatoid arthritis. *Journal of the American Medical Association*
113:668–670.

Deutsch, H. (1937). Absence of grief. *Psychoanalytic Quarterly* 6:12–23.

Fenichel, O. (1945). *The Psychoanalytic Theory of Neurosis.* New York:
Norton.

Freud, A. (1965) Normality and pathology in childhood. In *The Writings of Anna Freud*, vol. 6. New York: International Universities Press.

Freud, S. (1917). Mourning and melancholia. *Standard Edition* 14: 237–258.

————. (1923). The ego and the id. *Standard Edition* 19:3–59.

Greenacre, P. (1970). The transitional object and the fetish, with special reference to the role of illusion. *International Journal of Psychoanalysis* 51:447–456.

Jacobson, E. (1954). Contributions to the metapsychology of psychotic identifications. *Journal of the American Psychoanalytic Association* 2:239–262.

————. (1971). *Depression*. New York: International Universities Press.

Lewin, B. D. (1950). *The Psychoanalysis of Elation*. New York: Norton.

Lidz, T. (1949). Emotional factors in the etiology of hyperthyroidism. *Psychosomatic Medicine* 11:2–9.

Lindemann, E. (1944). Symptomatology and management of acute grief. *American Journal of Psychiatry* 101:141–148.

McDermott, N. T., and Cobb, S. (1939). A psychiatric study of fifty cases of bronchial asthma. *Psychosomatic Medicine* 1:203–245.

Mahler, M. S. (1968). *On Human Symbiosis and the Vicissitudes of Individuation: Infantile Psychosis*. New York: International Universities Press.

Pollock, G. H. (1961). Mourning and adaptation. *International Journal of Psychoanalysis* 42:341–361.

Rado, S. (1928). The problem of melancholia. *International Journal of Psychoanalysis* 9:420–438.

————. (1956). Adaptational development of psychoanalytic therapy. In *Changing Concepts of Psychoanalytic Medicine*, pp. 89–100, ed. S. Rado and G. E. Daniels. New York: Grune & Stratton.

Ritvo, S., and Solnit, A. (1958). Influences of early mother-child interaction on identification process. *Psychoanalytic Study of the Child* 13:64–85. New York: International Universities Press.

Rochlin, G. (1965). *Grief and Discontents: The Forces of Change*. Boston: Little, Brown.

Schmale, A. H. (1958). Relationship of separation and depression on disease. I. A report on a hospitalized medical population. *Psychosomatic Medicine* 20:259–277.

Smith, J. H. (1971). Identificatory style in depression and grief. *International Journal of Psychoanalysis* 52:259–266.

Volkan, V. D. (1970). Typical findings in pathological grief. *Psychiatric Quarterly* 44:231–250.

——. (1971). A study of a patient's re-grief work through dreams, psychological tests, and psychoanalysis. *Psychiatric Quarterly* 45:255–273.

——. (1972). The linking objects of pathological mourners. *Archives of General Psychiatry* 27:215–221.

——. (1978). *Cyprus — War and Adaptation*. Charlottesville: University Press of Virginia.

——. (1981). *Linking Objects and Linking Phenomena: A Study of the Forms, Symptoms, Metapsychology and Therapy of Complicated Mourning*. New York: International Universities Press.

Volkan, V. D., Cillufo, A. F., and Sarvay, T. L. (1975). Re-grief therapy and the function of the linking objects as a key to stimulate emotionality. In *Emotional Flooding*, pp. 179–224. ed. P. T. Olsen. New York: Human Sciences Press.

Volkan, V. D., and Josephthal, D. (1979). The treatment of established pathological mourners. In *Specialized Techniques and Psychotherapy*, pp. 112–142. ed. T. B. Karasu and L. Bellak. New York: Jason Aronson.

Volkan, V. D., and Showalter, C. R. (1968). Known object loss, disturbance in reality testing, and "re-grief work" as a method of brief psychotherapy. *Psychiatric Quarterly* 42:358–374.

Wahl, C. W. (1970). The differential diagnosis of normal and neurotic grief following bereavement. *Psychosomatics* 11:104–106.

Winnicott, D. W. (1953). Transitional objects and transitional phenomena: a study of the first not-me possession. *International Journal of Psychoanalysis* 34:89–97.

Wolfenstein, M. (1966). How is mourning possible? *Psychoanalytic Study of the Child* 21:93–123. New York: International Universities Press.

PART II

Diagnostic Refinements in Neuropsychiatry

It ought to be generally known that the source of our pleasure, merriment, laughter, and amusement as of our grief, pain and anxiety, and tears, is none other than the brain.

Hippocrates

CHAPTER 4

Pseudodementia
CHARLES E. WELLS, M.D.

Pseudodementia is the syndrome in which dementia is mimicked or caricatured by functional psychiatric illness. Patients with pseudodementia present symptoms and give responses to mental status examination questions that are much like those seen in verified cases of dementia, but their clinical distress is the result of functional psychiatric disorders and not primarily of underlying organic brain disease. Although the topic has been little noted in either the psychiatric or the neurological literature, the syndrome is not rare, especially to those whose practices include significant numbers of elderly patients or patients with neuropsychiatric problems. From published reports it can be inferred that pseudodementia is usually recognized only after the patient has unexpectedly recovered. Thus as Kiloh (1961) observed, pseudodemented patients are in danger of both therapeutic neglect and diagnostic procedures that are not only superfluous but possibly dangerous.

Growing evidence suggests that the mimicry of dementia by functional psychiatric disorders occurs with some frequency and that as a result, dementia is overdiagnosed. In a study comparing the psychiatric diagnoses assigned elderly patients in New York, Toronto, and London, Duckworth and Ross (1975) found that organic brain disorders were diagnosed 50 percent more frequently in New York than in either Toronto or London. Although differences in the patient populations might account for some discrepancy, it is more likely that the elderly New York patients with functional disorders were incorrectly labeled as demented, whereas in Great Britain, where Roth and his group (1955) emphasized the importance of functional geriatric disorders, elderly patients with functional disorders were more often recognized as such.

Other studies have confirmed that the diagnosis of dementia is often incorrect. Marsden and Harrison (1972) studied 106 consecutively admitted patients who were hospitalized, after preliminary screening by a consultant neurologist, psychiatrist, or both, for thorough neurological investigation of dementia. The diagnosis of dementia could not be substantiated in 19 cases (18 percent), and specific functional disorders were identified in 10 of these. Nott and Fleminger (1975) followed up 35 patients who were diagnosed as having presenile dementia after thorough inpatient evaluation on the psychiatry ward of a London teaching hospital; in only 15 cases (43 percent) did progressive mental deterioration confirm the initial diagnosis. Haward (1977) reported that of 49 patients with a provisional diagnosis of presenile dementia who were referred to a county mental hospital, "17 produced a psychometric picture incommensurate with an organic state and suggestive of an endogenous depression, and under appropriate treatment showed a reversal of the apparent cognitive impairment."

One must conclude, therefore, that errors in the recognition of dementia are not unusual even when patients are carefully evaluated by competent neurologists and psychiatrists. Much of what at first glance appears to be dementia turns out not to be and can best be described as pseudodementia. The clinical recognition of pseudodementia and its differentiation from true dementia are the focus of this paper.

PREVIOUS STUDIES

In 1961 Kiloh wrote what is still the most comprehensive paper on pseudodementia. He noted that the term pseudodementia "is purely descriptive and carries no diagnostic weight" and went on to distinguish the Ganser syndrome from pseudodementia, pointing out that the psychiatrist "seldom has much difficulty in differentiating between the Ganser symptomatology and true dementia." Kiloh then described ten patients with functional disorders who manifested to varying degrees the classic changes of dementia — impairment of orientation, memory, judgment, and intellectual functions such as comprehension, calculation, and knowledge. Although he noted the presence of hysterical features and schizophrenic elements in some patients, he emphasized depressive illness in the etiology of pseudodementia.

Kiloh made several clinical observations of diagnostic relevance. He noted that in pseudodementia the dysfunction was often of somewhat abrupt onset and short duration before medical evaluation. "Any suggestion that the illness is of short duration virtually eliminates the possibility of dementia; exceptions of this rule are rare" (1961). Kiloh went on to emphasize the dangers of relying on either air encephalograms or psychological testing to establish the diagnosis of dementia. The findings from either of these diagnostic procedures might be typical of dementia, although the dementia be spurious, as proved by its subsequent disappearance.

Roth (1975) and Roth and Myers (1975) at Newcastle-upon-Tyne emphasized the frequency with which depressions, especially in the elderly, present features that strongly suggest dementia. In differentiating depressive pseudodementia from dementia they suggested, in addition to the points made by Kiloh, that depressed patients with pseudodementia often communicate a sense of distress, whereas with dementia their emotions are often shallow; they do poorly on some tests of memory and intelligence but unexpectedly well on others; and they have a personal or family history of depression. Post (1975) pointed out that in cases of depressive pseudodementia, the patient's history usually indicates that the symptoms of depression preceded those of cognitive loss. In contrast, symptoms of depression due to dementia usually follow the development of cognitive failure. However, Liston's study of the presenile dementias (1977) indicated that this course of progression does not always occur. Post (1975) also observed that "near-miss" answers to questions testing cognitive function suggest organic defects, whereas "don't know" answers are typical of pseudodementia. Folstein and associates (1975) described a group of depressed patients with significant impairment of cognitive function (as measured by their Mini-Mental State Test) whose cognitive function improved with resolution of the depression. They did not state whether these patients presented a clinical picture easily confused with dementia or whether their symptoms led easily to the diagnosis of depression.

Rhoads (1977) described a group of patients whose psychiatric symptoms were precipitated largely by overwork. Some of these patients had a pseudodementia "severe enough" that "organic dementia" was initially considered a serious possibility.*

CLINICAL FEATURES

None of the above studies focused on the clinical features that might be used to differentiate pseudodementia from true dementia. Rather, in these studies the diagnosis of pseudodementia was made because the cognitive dysfunction eventually disappeared after resolution of the underlying depression or other functional disorder (with or without treatment).

---

*Rhoads J. M., personal communication, July 6, 1977.

During the past two years I have seen ten patients with a fully developed pseudodementia syndrome, in each of whom a diagnosis of dementia was seriously considered; in addition, I have seen many others with functional disorders in whom the possibility of dementia was at least entertained. These patients have been studied for clinical features that might differentiate them from patients with true dementia, i.e., for features that would permit recognition of pseudodementia on clinical grounds without the necessity of waiting for the diagnosis of dementia to be disproved by the passage of time. The clinical observations on these ten patients provide the basis for this report.

The patients' symptoms had been present from several months to two years before the patients came to psychiatric attention. Only one patient had an abrupt onset of symptoms. In the others the onset was insidious, and the symptoms progressed slowly. Thus the duration and the course of illness in these patients were consistent with those usually seen in dementia and were not therefore helpful in the differential diagnosis. On the other hand, the single instance of abrupt onset suggested pseudodementia. True dementia is usually insidious in onset, but this is not always the case. It is not unusual in the elderly for dementia to become evident abruptly during an episode of pneumonia, congestive heart failure, or other acute medical illness.

Eight of these subjects were hospitalized on the inpatient psychiatric service and one on the neurology service at Vanderbilt University Hospital; one was seen for outpatient neuropsychiatric consultation. Their ages ranged from 33 to 69, with seven in their fifties or sixties. Poor memory, along with other symptoms of cognitive dysfunction, was a prominent symptom in all of the subjects, but in only one could it be considered the chief complaint. Most had many complaints, dysmnesia being one among them. However, in each patient difficulty with memory was prominent and could be described in considerable detail by the patient. Other symptoms of cognitive dysfunction included disorientation to time and place, confusion about the purpose of hospitalization, inability to learn the layout of the ward and the names of staff and other patients, inability to perform previously well learned tasks, difficulty understanding questions and instructions, limited funds of information, failure to recall overlearned data (such as home telephone numbers and names of family members), and poor concentration and easy distractibility. Prominent among the patients' many other complaints were depression, anxiety, agitation, confusion, paranoid delusions, social withdrawal, inability to perform usual daily tasks, ruminations of guilt, headaches, "falling out" spells, anorexia, weight loss, insomnia, and episodes of crying. It was doubtless this panoply of symptoms that led to the admission of most of these persons to the psychiatry service rather than the neurology service.

All of the patients complained of their memory loss with vigor and feelings. Whereas the patient with true dementia often appears oblivious to memory defects that are quite apparent to the examiner, the opposite is more often true in pseudodementia; i.e., the patient complains of memory loss that is not at all apparent to the examiner. Most of the patients complained of memory loss for remote events that was equal to that for recent events. Several patients mentioned memory loss for specific periods of time and specific events; this is an unusual observation in genuine dementia. One patient's complaints included an inability to recognize certain persons and to cook certain dishes. Another complained bitterly of her forgetfulness but maintained that she always knew when she had forgotten something. Thus patients complained of memory loss that was both more diffuse and more circumscribed than that usually encountered in cases of organic disease.

Five of the patients cooperated fully in providing a history, and the family members and past medical records of the other patients provided complete anamneses. Although the patients complained of cognitive losses, in response to open-ended questions they gave clear, detailed, logical, and temporally coherent accounts of their present illnesses and past lives. Their imagined attentiveness and alertness to detail frequently belied their conspicuous complaints of poor concentration. In striking contrast was their response to direct, specific questions. To these, "I don't know" and "I can't remember" responses were the rule, and near-miss responses or avoidance of the questions was rare. Usually these negative responses emerged readily, with little indication that the patient had diligently sought the correct answer and with no indication that he or she had tried to conceal the diability. Indeed, these patients often pointed to their "don't know" answers as irrefutable evidence of their dysfunction, and on the unit they repeatedly called attention to their failures, errors, and limitations.

These patients' acknowledged awareness and open demonstration of their disabilities stand in striking contrast to what is usually seen in cases of organic brain disease. Demented patients commonly appear unaware of the extent and severity of their cognitive dysfunction, and they usually employ a variety of stratagems to conceal the dysfunction from others (and perhaps from themselves as well). "I don't know" answers are often virtually unobtainable from the organically ill patient in response to questions that the patient would normally have been able to answer. However, organically amnestic patients may give "I don't know" responses to questions that they would not normally have been expected to answer (Mercer et al. 1977).

Loss of social skills was prominent in eight patients. In contrast, the common Alzheimer form of dementia is often marked by retention of social skills, even with advanced disease. A depressive affect was pervasive in seven of the ten patients; anxiety predominated in three. There were no signs of the lability and especially the shallowness of affect so characteristic of dementia.

Seven of the patients were disoriented for place; they all stated that they did not know where they were or why they were there. In cases of organic dementia, on the other hand, the disoriented patient usually offers some answer, even if it is erroneous, to questions of orientation, and the organic patient usually misperceives the unusual for the usual, i.e., the hospital for home or another familiar spot. These pseudodemented patients also failed to experience the nocturnal worsening of cognitive functions so often observed in organically ill patients.

Close attention to the performance of the patients in this group always revealed profound inconsistencies. For example, in conversation one patient recounted recent and remote events in meticulous detail and in correct temporal sequence, but when items on a psychological test questionnaire were read to her, she insisted that she could not "hold on to the questions long enough to get answers." Another man in conversation provided complex and specific details about his financial problems but failed on inquiry to solve mathematical problems of minimal difficulty.

In the patients who did not cooperate verbally, incongruency between cognitive dysfunction and behavior usually became evident by observation of behavior alone. For example, one patient insisted that he was incapable of performing or learning the simplest of tasks, but he repeatedly found his way to the kitchen, easily assembled desired snacks, and skillfully found hiding places just at the moment he was scheduled to perform assigned chores. This lack of fit between symptoms and performance was repeatedly the key to the clinical recognition of pseudodementia.

Table 4.1, modified from Wells (1977), lists the major clinical features that have been identified to help differentiate pseudodementia from dementia. The presence of one of these differentiating point is not diagnostically conclusive; rather, it is the totality of the clinical picture that is important.

ANCILLARY DIAGNOSTIC PROCEDURES

Psychological testing (including neuropsychological evaluation and projective tests) was performed with nine patients: in none did the psychologists suggest that the clinical picture resulted from diffuse cerebral dysfunction such as is characteristic of dementia (Wells and Buchanan 1977). All of these patients performed poorly on one or more of the tests usually used to measure organic dysfunction, but it was their inconsistent performance from test to test that argued most strongly against attributing their clinical dysfunction primarily to organic disease (as it was in part their inconsistency in clinical performance that led the clinicians to question the diagnosis of dementia). Two patients had IQs within the range for mild mental retardation. The psychological test findings for one patient suggested mild diffuse cerebral disease; the findings for another patient pointed to some degree of left hemisphere dysfunction. However, in neither case were the abnormalities adequate to explain the clinical dysfunction. The findings from psychological testing thus agreed in large measure with those from clinical evaluation.

The results of psychological testing in this group thus differ from those reported by Kiloh (1961) and Post (1975), although the findings are not necessarily incompatible. My observations suggest that these patients differed clinically from patients with true dementia, and psychological testing (which is, after all, standardized testing of behavior) bore out this difference. The patients described by Kiloh and Post may have resembled more closely those with true dementia or may have been patients with mild dementia greatly accentuated by depression, in which case psychological testing might understandably have been less accurate in picking up the difference. An equally plausible explanation is that the psychological tests were more skillfully interpreted in this group of nine patients because the psychologists were more sensitive to the nature of the clinical problem.

Computerized cranial tomographic (CT) scans were carried out in eight patients and were normal in seven. In one patient, whose case has been previously reported (Wells and Duncan 1977), the CT scan was interpreted as showing mild cortical atrophy. This patient, who complained of severe cognitive impairment, was clearly not demented on clinical examination or on psychological testing. The key to the recognition of this patient's pseudodementia lay in the lack of fit between his symptoms and his performance on psychiatric examination and psychological testing. Tomlinson and associates (1968) demonstrated some years ago that mild cortical atrophy and ventricular dilatation could be found in nondemented aged subjects. They also showed that visually detectable cerebral atrophic changes could be minimal in the presence of significant dementia (1970). Dementia and pseudodementia must be recognized, therefore, on clinical grounds. Mild widening of the cortical sulci or minimal enlargement of the cerebral ventricles is not conclusive diagnostic evidence of dementia.

Table 4-1. The major clinical features differentiating pseudodementia from dementia

Clinical Features	Pseudodementia	Dementia
Course and history	Family always aware of dysfunction and its severity	Family often unaware of dysfunction and its severity
	Onset can be dated with some precision	Onset can be dated only within broad limits
	Symptoms of short duration before medical help is sought	Symptoms usually of long duration before medical help is sought
	Rapid progression of symptoms after onset	Slow progression of symptoms throughout course
	History of previous psychiatric dysfunction common	History of previous psychiatric dysfunction unusual
Complaints and clinical behavior	Patients usually complain much of cognitive loss	Patients usually complain little of cognitive loss
	Patients' complaints of cognitive dysfunction usually detailed	Patients' complaints of cognitive dysfunction usually vague
	Patients emphasize disability	Patients conceal disability
	Patients highlight failures	Patients delight in accomplishments, however trivial
	Patients make little effort to perform even simple tasks	Patients struggle to perform tasks
	Patients do not try to keep up	Patients rely on notes, calendars, and the like to keep up

Table 4-1 (Continued).

Clinical Features	Pseudodementia	Dementia
Memory, cognitive, and intellectual dysfunctions	Patients usually communicate strong sense of distress	Patients often appear unconcerned
	Affective change often pervasive	Affect labile and shallow
	Loss of social skills often early and prominent	Social skills often retained
	Behavior often incongruent with severity of cognitive dysfunction	Behavior usually compatible with severity of cognitive dysfunction
	Nocturnal accentuation of dysfunction uncommon	Nocturnal accentuation of dysfunction common
	Attention and concentration often well preserved	Attention and concentration usually faulty
	"Don't know" answers typical	Near-miss answers frequent
	On tests of orientation, patients often give "don't know" answers	On tests of orientation, patients often mistake unusual for usual
	Memory loss for recent and remote events usually equally severe	Memory loss for recent events usually more severe than for remote events
	Memory gaps for specific periods common	Memory gaps for specific periods unusual*
	Marked variability in performance on tasks of similar difficulty	Consistently poor performance on tasks of similar difficulty

*Except when due to delirium, trauma, seizures, and so forth.

Electroencephalograms were recorded in seven of the patients in the present study and were normal in all cases.

One patient was interviewed with the aid of sodium amytal. This patient, who was disoriented, withdrawn, and uncooperative to questioning, showed striking temporary clinical improvement under the influence of the barbiturate rather than the worsening that might have been expected with organic brain disease. Ward and associates (1978) recently added to the evidence that the amytal interview can be useful in the differential diagnosis of confusion. It probably should be used more often when differentiation between dementia and pseudodementia is difficult on clinical grounds alone.

PSYCHIATRIC DIAGNOSES

I was the primary attending physician for only one of these ten patients and served as neuropsychiatry consultant for the others. Final diagnoses were made after extensive patient evaluation by the attending physicians. In general, the diagnostic criteria of DSM-II (1968) were used, although as will be seen below, most of the patients did not fit neatly into the diagnostic categories enumerated there.

Previous studies (Kiloh 1961, Post 1975, Roth and Myers 1975) have emphasized the frequency with which depressive disorders present a dementialike picture, especially in the elderly. The association with primary affective illness was not so close in this group, although a depressive affect was pervasive in seven patients. For only three of these patients was the pseudodementia part of a typical episode of depressive illness. One of these patients, a 47-year-old man whose symptoms of cognitive dysfunction were the most glaring of the lot, had had an almost identical episode about ten years previously (as revealed through hospital records). In three of the others in whom depressive affect predominated, the pattern of illness was much more typical of long-standing passive dependency with depression than of a discrete episode of depressive illness.

In two patients the symptoms of cognitive dysfunction appeared to be conversion reactions. In one of these there was a history of multiple conversion reactions; in the other the pseudodementia evolved slowly as the patient emerged from a dissociative reaction.

One patient was diagnosed as having a posttraumatic neurosis. The last had a very complex psychiatric illness with features of both depression and schizophrenia; although no definite psychiatric diagnosis could be established, the pseudodementia disappeared with improvement in the patient's overall psychiatric symptomatology.

Six of the ten patients had histories of psychiatric dysfunction that long antedated the onset of pseudodementia.

DYNAMIC AND ETIOLOGICAL FEATURES

Aside from the pseudodementia, the most striking feature common to all of these patients was their marked dependency for both physical care and emotional support. This dependency dated back many years in seven patients; in only one was it based on serious somatic illness. In these seven patients the appearance of the pseudodementia accentuated their demands on others for care. In the other three the dependency evolved along with the pseudodementia. For patients whose dependency needs were marked, it might be speculated that the choice, however unconsciously determined, of the symptoms of dementia would be especially apt. Few patients require such total care as the severely demented, and pseudodemented patients were striking in the demands they made on the nursing staff for care and concern. Pseudodementia might thus be viewed as an active means of communicating a sense of helplessness. However, there is no evidence at present to support this speculation, and there is little known about the exact determinants of pseudodementia.

Another factor that must be considered is the possible relationship between the clinical syndrome of pseudodementia and underlying brain disorders, even if those disorders are not of the sort or severity that are expected to produce dementia. Two of the ten patients had mild mental retardation; another had evidence pointing to mild left hemisphere dysfunction; and psychological test findings from another patient suggested mild diffuse cerebral dysfunction. Finally, one patient had a history of subarachnoid hemorrhage without residual cognitive impairment. In none of these five were the abnormalities uncovered by psychological testing sufficient to explain the clinical presentation, but did these underlying disorders form the framework on which the spurious symptoms of dementia were elaborated? This question raises intriguing possibilities about relationships between the brain and behavior in this condition of which we have little understanding at present.

COURSE

Nine of the ten patients were followed up for periods varying from several weeks to many months. In four (three with depressive episodes and one with hysterical neurosis, conversion type), the symptoms and manifestations of pseudodementia disappeared quickly with treatment. These included the two patients with mild mental retardation, the patient whose psychological testing suggested disease of the left hemisphere, and the patient with a previous subarachnoid hemorrhage; i.e., four of the five in whom there was some evidence of an underlying brain disorder. In four other patients the symptoms did not disappear completely but tended to move from the center of attention into the background, to become simply one more feature in the pattern of chronicity and dependency. In none of these four patients was there evidence from psychological testing that seriously suggested significant organic disease. In the one patient whose pseudodementia did not improve, the pseudodementia was believed to be an aspect of severe, long-standing passive dependency that did not respond to treatment. In differentiating this patient's disorder from dementia, it is noteworthy that although she did not improve, neither did she worsen during the two years after her initial evaluation.

DISCUSSION

In the past the diagnosis of pseudodementia has been made largely after the unanticipated recovery of a patient who had previously been diagnosed as demented. My thesis is that with attention to the features listed in Table 4-1, pseudodementia can usually be differentiated from dementia on clinical grounds alone. Pseudodementia can be described most succinctly as a caricature or burlesque, not an imitation, of dementia. The recognition of this caricature permits a prediction of improvement or recovery in pseudodemented patients, in contrast to the predictably downhill course of most demented patients.

The syndrome described here is not so closely related to depressive disorders as suggested earlier (Haward 1977, Kiloh 1961, Post 1975). It did appear as part of a depressive episode in three of the ten patients, but in the others it was a manifestation of chronic characterological disorders, conversion reactions, posttraumatic neurosis, and a complex undiagnosable psychotic process. I have also observed the syndrome in cases of manic illness, although such a patient was not included in this series. The caricaturing of dementia may thus occur in a wide variety of psychiatric specificity.

I do not believe that pseudodementia is a myth, as recently suggested by Shraberg (1978). He hypothesized that pseudodementia is the process of "dementia and depression occuring as parallel and interrelated processes in the senium" (p. 120), with the underlying dementia being

accentuated by a superimposed depression. This situation certainly occurs. I have observed it, and Shraberg's analysis of his patient's dysfunction appears to be accurate. It does, indeed, appear unjustified to describe these patients as having pseudodementia. However, the syndrome
of pseudodementia as described in this paper differs clinically, occurs
in a variety of psychiatric disorders other than depression, is not confined to the aged, and is not necessarily associated with underlying brain
damage. Its recognition should result in the use of fewer neurological
diagnostic procedures and in more vigorous and accurate treatment of
the underlying psychiatric disorders.

REFERENCES

Diagnostic and Statistical Manual of Mental Disorders (1968). 2nd ed.
Washington, D.C.: American Psychiatric Association.

Duckworth, G. S., and Ross, H. (1975). Diagnostic differences in
psychogeriatric patients in Toronto, New York and London. *Canadian
Medical Association Journal* 112:847–851.

Folstein, M. F., Folstein, S. E., and McHugh, P. R. (1975). "Mini-
mental state." A practical method for grading the cognitive state
of patients for the clinician. *Journal of Psychiatric Research* 12:189–
198.

Haward, L. R. C. (1977). Cognition in dementia presinilis. In *Aging
and Dementia,* ed. W. L. Smith and M. Kinsbourne. New York: Spectrum.

Kiloh, L. G. (1961). Pseudo-dementia. *Acta Psychiatrica Scandinavica*
37:336–351.

Liston, E. H., Jr. (1977). Occult presenile dementia. *Journal of Nervous and Mental Disease* 164:263–267.

Marsden, C. D., and Harrison, M. I. G. (1972). Outcome of investigation of patients with presenile dementia. *British Medical Journal* 2:
249–252.

Mercer, B., Wapner, W., Gardner, H., et al. (1977). A study of
confabulation. *Archives of Neurology* 34:429–433.

Nott, P. N., and Fleminger, J. J. (1975). Presenile dementia: the difficulties of early diagnosis. *Acta Psychiatrica Scandinavica* 51:210–217.

Post, F. (1975). Dementia, depression, and pseudodementia. In *Psychiatric Aspects of Neurologic Disease,* ed. D. F. Benson, and D. Blumer.
New York: Grune & Stratton.

Rhoads, J. M. (1977). Overwork. *Journal of the American Medical Association* 237:2615-2618.

Roth, M. (1955). The natural history of mental disorder in old age. *Journal of Mental Science* 101:281-301.

―――. (1975). Mental disorders of the aged: diagnosis and treatment. *Medical World News,* October 27, pp. 35-43.

Roth, M., and Myers, D. H. (1975). The diagnosis of dementia. *British Journal of Psychiatry,* Special Publication 9:87-99.

Shraberg, D. (1978). The myth of pseudodementia: depression and the aging brain. *American Journal of Psychiatry* 135:601-603.

Tomlinson, B. E., Blessed, G., and Roth, M. (1968). Observations on the brains of non-demented old people. *Journal of Neurological Sciences* 7:331-356.

―――. (1970). Observations on the brains of demented old people. *Journal of Neurological Sciences* 11:205-242.

Ward, N. G., Rowlett, D. B., and Burke, P. (1978). Sodium amylobarbitone in the differential diagnosis of confusion. *American Journal of Psychiatry* 135:75-78.

Wells, C. E. (1977). Dementia, pseudodementia, and dementia praecox. In *Phenomenology and Treatment of Schizophrenia,* ed. W. E. Fann, I. Karacan, A. D. Pokorny, et al. New York: Spectrum.

Wells, C. E., and Buchanan, B. C. (1977). The clinical use of psychological testing in evaluation in dementia. In *Dementia,* ed. C. E. Wells, 2nd ed. Philadelphia: Davis.

Wells, C. E., and Duncan, G. W. (1977). Danger of overreliance on computerized cranial tomography. *American Journal of Psychiatry* 134:811-813.

CHAPTER 5

Minimal Brain Dysfunction (Attention Deficit Disorder) in Adults

DAVID R. WOOD, M.D.
FRED W. REIMHERR, M.D.

Minimal brain dysfunction (MBD) is one of many terms used to describe a common behavioral syndrome of childhood. Other terms that have been used include the hyperactive child syndrome, hyperactivity, hyperkinesis, and minimal brain damage. In the recent Diagnostic Statistical Manual-III (DSM-III) it was renamed attention deficit disorder (ADD), and the adult form of this disorder was formally recognized as attention deficit disorder, residual type (ADD, RT). In keeping with the new nomenclature, we shall use the term attention deficit disorder (ADD) throughout this discussion.

ADD in children is a syndrome that has provoked considerable controversy. Some feel the condition does not exist, and others regard it as an extremely common behavioral problem of children. Numerous theories, including lead poisoning, red food dyes, excessive dietary sugar, intrauterine trauma, and a genetic illness with biochemical abnormalities have been suggested. Not only has its etiology been controversial, but there also has been wide disparity in its diagnostic features and treatment. This would appear to be related to a clinical variability, the setting in which it presents or is first noticed, and the different professional viewpoints of the disorder (Wender and Eisenberg 1974). For example, the conceptualization of the disease by a neurologist may be markedly different from that of an elementary school counselor. It may present clinically under various guises: as a learning disorder, a case of vandalism, a class disrupter, a neurological abnormality, or an ungovernable and incorrigible child in the home. It is not hard to imagine that if such variability exists in children, the clinical picture in adults could be even more variable and evoke more controversy. Despite theoretical and clinical disputes, we believe that (1) ADD in adults represents a distinct clinical entity with diagnosable signs and symptoms; (2) it is relatively common among certain populations; (3) and specific treatment can provide remarkable and long-lasting improvements in selected patients. This discussion will give an overview of the syndrome and the necessary diagnostic and therapeutic information to recognize and treat the disease.

HISTORY

Traditionally, ADD has been considered a disorder that disappeared with the onset of adolescence. Despite this common view, there is considerable evidence to suggest that ADD may continue into adult life and be associated with adult psychopathology (Arnold et al. 1972, Laufer and Denhoff 1957, Morrison and Minkoff 1975, Pincus and Glaser 1966, Shelley and Riester 1972). The evidence suggests that although there may be some symptomatic transformations in adults, the basic abnormalities manifested in children are the same as for adults. The following is a review of the evidence that led to this conclusion. First, it has been noted at many clinics where large numbers of ADD children are treated that in certain patients it is important to continue treatment through adolescence into early adulthood. Second, an increasing number of prospective and longitudinal studies have revealed the persistence of many ADD symptoms into late adolescence and early adulthood (Ackerman et al. 1977, Hammar 1967, Hechtman et al. 1976, Huessy et al. 1974, Mendelson et al. 1971, Weiss et al. 1979). Mendelson and associates (1971), in a follow-up study of MBD children during their adolescence, noted that 77 percent had difficulties with concentration, 71 percent continued to be overactive, and 74 percent were impulsive.

There are two studies that report a continued therapeutic effect of stimulant medication on ADD throughout adolescence (MacKay et al. 1973, Safer and Allen 1975). This stimulant response with the absence of tolerance and dependence is typical of the response in ADD children. This specific drug response also suggests the persistence of ADD into adulthood. Hill in 1944 reported the successful treatment of certain adult psychopaths with amphetamines. He described this group as aggressive, ill tempered, hostile, alcoholic, and antisocial. They also had the interesting associated disturbances of persistent enuresis and deep sleep, which are not uncommon clinical manifestations of childhood ADD. Hill found that when cooperation was elicited, he was able to maintain them on amphetamines, which relieved their symptoms. Hartocollis (1968) and Quitkin and Klein (1969) independently reported an association among soft neurological signs, a history of ADD in childhood, and adult impulsive character disorders. In further studies an increased frequency of the symptoms of childhood hyperactivity was found in a number of cases of adult psychiatric problems (Borland and Heckman 1976, Mann and Greenspan 1976, Menkes et al. 1967, Morris et al. 1956, Morrison and Minkoff 1975, O'Neal and Robins 1958, Richmond et al. 1978, Rybak 1977, Shelley and Riester 1972, Tarter et al. 1977), including impulsive character disorders; early onset of severe alcoholism; lability and impulsivity in young adults; explosive personality; violent dyscontrol; depression; low self-esteem and anxiety; and aggressive, destructive, and unmanageable behavior.

Finally, family studies employing adoptive and nonadoptive methodologies suggest a linkage between childhood ADD and adult psychopathology. Morrison and Stewart (1971) and Cantwell (1972) found that the parents of hyperactive children have an increased prevalence of alcoholism, sociopathy, and hysteria. Since familial association may be mediated by either genetic or psychosocial transmission, Morrison and Stewart turned to the adoption methodology of Wender and associates (1968) to resolve this difficulty. They found that the adopting parents of hyperactive children had an incidence of alcoholism and sociopathy no higher than that of the controls.

Cantwell replicated this study in greater detail, comparing the parents of three groups of children: biological parents who reared their own ADD children, adoptive parents of ADD children, and the parents of 50 children chosen at random from a pediatric practice. He found that parental psychopathology in the adoptive parents and the parents of pediatric controls were equivalent, but that there was a substantial increase in psychopathology in the biological parents, with a higher prevalence of alcoholism and sociopathy in biological fathers and hysteria in biological mothers. This is of interest because studies conducted at Washington University (Arkonac and Guze 1963, Woerner and Guze 1968) indicate a familial association among male alcoholism, sociopathy, and Briquet's syndrome (hysteria). Taken together, these studies suggest that certain adult alcoholics, sociopaths, and hysterics may be "grown up" ADD children.

The persistence of ADD-related behaviors may be theoretically explained in at least two ways. First, the adult abnormal behaviors may represent learned behaviors, and the putative physiologic abnormality underlying ADD may have been outgrown. A second explanation is that the abnormal physiology may have persisted into adulthood, causing behavior patterns similar to those seen in childhood. If the latter is the correct explanation, one might expect that ADD adults would respond to stimulant medication in the same manner that ADD children do. Our research, which was reported in two studies (Wender et al. 1981, Wood et al. 1976), suggests the latter as the more likely explanation. This does not mean that learned abnormalities might not be a factor, but it is our impression that certain patients develop behavioral patterns as a way of adapting to the continuing underlying biological abnormalities.

Our interest in adult ADD started in 1975 when we independently studied two patients, one in her early twenties and the other in the early forties, both of whom had long past histories of emotional difficulties. We were impressed by the strong similarity between their symptom patterns and those of ADD children. Previous medication (antianxiety agents, neuroleptics, and antidepressants), along with psychotherapy, had failed to alleviate significantly their abnormal behaviors. Each was given a trial of methylphenidate to which both had a striking beneficial response, with practically a complete reversal of abnormal behaviors. Since then, we have been engaged in various studies of ADD in adults, including drug trials, family history studies, identification of the clinical picture, psychological testing, and biochemical investigations. The remainder of this chapter is a summation of our research findings.

CLINICAL CHARACTERISTICS

The following abnormalities represent the main components of this disorder. We shall describe both the childhood and the adulthood forms to demonstrate the continuity of the traits.

Attention Difficulties. We believe that one of two basic abnormalities of ADD adults is their short attention span or poor ability to concentrate. As children, these individuals will give histories of being unable to focus on one activity for a reasonable period of time. Their teachers may have complained that they had a short attention span, were easily distracted, and did not listen in class. The complaint of "you couldn't get his or her attention" is common. As adults, these individuals' poor attention spans are often most noticeable when they have to complete a task that is not pleasurable or interesting. For example, college students may have difficulty concentrating on a lecture; business people may have trouble keeping their minds on their reports; and skilled craftspeople may find it difficult to attend to fine detail, often having to repeat the work. In addition to educational and vocational difficulties, this trait may cause significant marital or family problems, since the patients are unable to focus their attention on conversations with their spouse or are unable to attend to their children.

Commonly, one finds that the attention deficits were much worse when the patient was a child than as an adult. There is one caution: it is not uncommon for adults and children to focus attention fairly well on enjoyable items such as a television show. Consequently, the examiner must ask questions related to onerous tasks. Another trait is the difficulty in shifting attention from one focus to another.

Motor Behavior. Hyperactivity appears to be the second basic abnormality of ADD adults. A typical history of motor abnormalities may begin in infancy with children described as extremely active and poor sleepers. Upon entering the toddler stage, they are described as constantly into things, always touching and needing constant attention. As older children, they are motorically driven, fidgety, unable to keep still, unable to lie down and relax, unable to sit through a motion picture without getting up, or unable to sit and watch television for long. In school they cannot sit still and frequently leave their seat to walk about in the classroom, disrupting the other children. They constantly play with paper, drum their fingers on the desk, or doodle in their notebook.

As they age, the hyperactivity may lessen, but typically these individuals continue to be more restless than other people are. They often need to be doing things and find it difficult to sit down and relax. Their spouses will frequently describe them as "always on the go" and often will comment that they are "tired out" trying to keep up with them. In contrast to childhood, these patients often "overwork," putting in extra hours or assuming additional part-time work. During the diagnostic interview, hyperactive adults may frequently squirm in their chair, tap their leg, drum their fingers, play with their hands, or pick at their face and hair. At times this motor restlessness may be easily confused with agitation.

A second aspect of abnormal motor behavior is impaired coordination. Fine motor coordination, especially hand-eye skills, are the most impaired. As a child, a girl may have had difficulty playing jacks, whereas a boy is often chosen last to play games like baseball or basketball. In addition, simple coordination tasks such as buttoning shirts, tying shoelaces, coloring, and writing all may have been difficult for them. Poor handwriting is often seen in adults. Frequently, when reflecting upon their childhood, adults will describe themselves as "spastics."

Poor Organization.   Adults will have difficulty organizing or structuring their lives. Histories of moving from one task to another before completion are typical. If they do complete the task, they often find that it takes them longer than it does others to do it. A woman may state that it is impossible for her to do all of her housework, go to the market, and fix meals in one day. The common problem of balancing one's checkbook may be turned over to the other spouse because "it's too trying." As children, this poor organization is most frequently manifested by difficulties in school. They were unable to complete their homework or to keep up with the rest of the class in carrying out daily activities. Consequently, they were frequently late and often fell behind.

Short Temper or Irritability.   During childhood, there is a history of quick and explosive temper tantrums and frequent fights in school. As adults, these individuals may describe their temper as quick, short, and/or explosive. Frequent fights and histories of violence and beatings are not uncommon. Child abuse may be one unfortunate consequence of the ADD adult's temper. Many adults will have learned to "leave the scene" to prevent their tempers from erupting. Our patients commonly report this as one of the most serious problems in their personal lives, producing marital conflicts, distancing them from their children, and ending friendships.

Difficulty with Impulse Control.   Another common characteristic of the ADD adult is poor impulse control, manifested by a low frustration tolerance and an inability to delay gratification. There is a tendency to do things on the spur of the moment, only to regret the actions later. These individuals seem unable to postpone decisions and frequently are unable to anticipate consequences. Impulsive buying often leads to financial difficulties, and a tendency to talk first and think later may impair interpersonal relations. These people are often difficult to converse with in a crowd, as they are always butting in and interjecting their comments as if theirs were the most important.

As children, a history of impaired early sphincter control (enuresis and encopresis) is often found. In addition, poor impulse control in children may be manifested by antisocial behaviors, such as destructiveness, stealing, lying, fire setting, and sexual promiscuity.

Abnormalities of Mood.   Hyperactive adults typically have mood lability. As children they report frequent "ups and downs" that usually last from hours to days and persist into adulthood. Generally, the depressions last at most for a few days. However, if ADD individuals experience pain or stress, they may be depressed for longer periods. Typically, depression appears as a reaction to outside stress or disappointment, but it can be quite severe. Unlike those individuals with a major mood disorder, the ability to enjoy pleasurable situations remains intact. Suicidal gestures and attempts are usually a manifestation of overreaction and poor impulse control. The biological abnormalities of a major mood disorder—a diurnal mood change, early morning awakening, and a significant weight change—are not typical. In many ways these individuals resemble "emotional unstable character disorders" (EUCD) as reported by Rifkin and colleagues (1975). However, unlike EUCD, the mood lability of ADD, RT typically appears and is noticed before adolescence. Not uncommonly, many of the ADD adults will have used lithium for mood instability.

Another abnormality of mood is a low-grade, pervasive anhedonia which generally is not as severe as that seen in schizophrenia or major mood disorder. Some will describe themselves as not enjoying life, being chronically pessimistic, and lacking the gratifications and pleasures of life seen in their normal counterparts. Risk taking or stimulus-seeking behavior may be their way of compensating.

Low Stress Tolerance—Overreactivity.   ADD adults seem to be those who have inherited an "emotionally thin skin." Typically, they are easily flustered and often will describe themselves as hassled, tense, or uptight. They overreact to the ups and downs of life and appear to handle pressure poorly. "Making mountains out of molehills" is common, and crises seem to occur frequently. As children they tend to overreact to frustration and excitement with easy laughter, tears, and/or anger.

These seven major abnormalities, we believe, represent the core symptoms upon which a diagnosis of ADD, RT can be made. Additional abnormalities are seen in the areas of cognition and learning but are not necessary for a diagnosis. Often there is an abnormality with orientation in space manifested by right-left difficulties which may be demonstrated by the reversal of letters and numbers. There may be difficulties in auditory discrimination (using similar sounds), difficulties in auditory synthesis, and difficulties in transferring information from one sensory modality

to another. For example, it may be difficult for ADD individuals to recognize the equivalence between printed Morse code and its sounding out,
or they may clearly understand a class lecture but be unable to transcribe
it into written notes. The attentional and perceptual-cognitive difficulties often impede academic progress. Most commonly, they have difficulty in learning to read and also have problems in arithmetic and writing. As a consequence ADD children frequently fall behind and "never
live up to their potential." In adults these difficulties may interfere with
job performance and career advancement.

Other common abnormalities in hyperactive adults are that they tend
to be bossy, strong willed, and stubborn. Because of their multiple handicaps, these individuals often develop a very low self-esteem and are often
dissatisfied with their lives in general. The poor control of temper and
increased impulsiveness commonly lead to unstable relationships. These
people tend to have few close social contacts. Divorces are common. Because of these major behavioral disadvantages, such individuals may be
shunned from normal society and can drift into a life of antisocial behaviors.

One interesting variant of the childhood ADD picture should be
noted. ADD girls usually give the typical history and are often described as tomboys. But we have found many ADD women to have been shy
and reserved. Although they may have had difficulties with attention and
hyperactivity, they were not class disrupters. The more typical patterns
of ADD may not be observed until midadolescence.

Psychological Tests.   Although ADD adults can have learning disabilities, they do not necessarily have low IQs. The mean Wexler IQs in our
studies have been 110 ± 10. The Wide Range Achievement Test scores
are significantly lower than expected on the basis of the subjects' IQ and
education. ADD men, particularly, seem to do poorly in spelling and
arithmetic. The Lincoln Oseretsky Test, the only available coordination
test for which normative data are available, showed hyperactive adults
(both male and female) to be below the fifth percentile for their respective sexes. Although the Minnesota Multiphasic Inventory (MMPI) demonstrates no diagnostic pattern for these individuals, it is clearly abnormal. The most common pattern is that of the psychopathic, but neurotic
and psychotic patterns have also been found.

Neurological and Physical Abnormalities.   There is an increased prevalence of minor or soft neurological signs in children with ADD (Wender
and Eisenberg 1974). This has been estimated to be as high as 50 to 60

percent in some series. These include difficulties in fine motor coordination, visual coordination, balance, choreoform movements, clumsiness, and poor speech. Their electroencephalograms often are abnormal, but there is no specific diagnostic pattern. In addition to the neurologic abnormalities, there is an increased prevalence of minor anatomic abnormalities. These are similar to those seen in schizophrenic children and may overlap those seen in Down's syndrome. There may be abnormalities of the epicanthus and ears; a high-arched palate; a short incurving fifth finger; a single palmar crease, strabismus; and a large, small, or abnormally shaped skull. These physical abnormalities have been reported only in ADD children, but we assume their presence in adults.

DIAGNOSIS

Currently, we use the following requirements to diagnose ADD, RT:

1. A history of childhood ADD with hyperactivity as defined by the DSM-III. In order to meet this criterion, the adult as a child must have had a history of inattention, impulsivity, and hyperactivity; an onset before the age of seven; a duration of at least six months; and the absence of schizophrenia, affective disorder, or profound mental retardation.

2. A current history of ADD, as defined by the presence of the following symptoms.
   A. Hyperactivity
   B. Poor attention span
   C. Any two of the following additional attributes
      1) Poor organization skills and/or inability to complete tasks efficiently
      2) A short, quick, and/or severe temper
      3) Prominent affective lability
      4) Impulsivity
      5) Abnormally poor or low stress tolerance and/or over-reactivity to stress

The diagnosis is not made in a person with major mood disorder, schizophrenia, or schizotypal or borderline personality.

These Utah criteria were developed by Wender and associates (1981), based on our research, and are more stringent than the DSM-III criteria for attention deficit disorder, residual type (adult ADD).

A third criterion, although not necessary for diagnosis, is a score of 12 on the Conners Abbreviated Rating Form as rated by the subjects' mothers. Figure 5-1 is the Parent's Rating Scale, which we send to the mother if she is alive. The Conners Abbreviated Rating Scale is used if we need to have a parental description of the patient's childhood behavior, since many patients are unable to remember their childhood accurately. Normative data are available for this scale when rated by teachers, but recently Wender* obtained normative data using the parents' judgments. He used a sample of 500 normal children who were judged not to have ADD and then asked their grandparents to rate the children's parents. This procedure allowed him to collect retrospective data on parents. Wender found that a score of 12 represented the 95th percentile. Subsequently, we demonstrated that a score of 12 or greater on this scale has a high correlation with the treatment response to stimulate medications (Wender et al. 1981).

In making the diagnosis, each suspected ADD adult is asked to complete a series of screening questions, as seen in Figure 5-2. If there is sufficient evidence from the answers to these questions to suggest ADD, the individual is then interviewed, preferably in the presence of his or her spouse. We have found the spouse history to be of great benefit, since ADD adults are typically poor observers of themselves. Not only is this history useful for diagnosis, but we also have found it useful in gauging treatment results. If there is a positive history obtained in this interview, a Conners Rating Scale is then sent to the mother. If both parents are alive, we frequently ask that both parents, independently, rate the child. If no parental history is available, we try to get a history from siblings or significant others with whom the patient may have lived as a child.

Finally, in order to be a candidate for treatment, we insist that symptoms not only be present but that they also clearly contribute to the patient's impaired psychosocial adjustment. Long-term treatment is generally necessary, and there must be present such factors as an encouraging spouse, a sense of ambition, or unpleasant psychological or psychosomatic symptoms that motivate the patient to stay in treatment.

DIFFERENTIAL DIAGNOSIS

As one may imagine, these behavior patterns present a variety of possible clinical pictures. This clinical diversity was reflected in our first study (Wood et al. 1976), in which the following Research Diagnostic Criteria

---

*Wender, P. H., personal communication, 1982.

Figure 5-1. Parents' Rating Scale

Patient's Name _____ Number _____

Date _____ Physician _____

To be filled out by the mother of the patient (or father only if mother not available).

Instructions. Listed below are items concerning children's behavior and the problems they sometimes have. Read each item carefully and decide how much you think you were bothered by these problems *when your child was between 6 and 10 years old.* Rate the amount of the problem by putting a check in the column that describes your child at that time.

	Not at all	*Just a little*	*Pretty much*	*Very much*
1. Restless (overactive)				
2. Excitable, impulsive				
3. Disturbs other children				
4. Fails to finish things he or she starts (short attention span)				
5. Fidgets				
6. Inattentive, distractible				
7. Demands must be met immediately; gets frustrated easily				
8. Cries				
9. Mood changes quickly				
10. Frequent temper outbursts (explosive and unpredictable behavior)				
	0	1	2	3

Figure 5-2. Questionnaire Used to Screen Suspected ADD Adults

Please circle number when problem applies to you.

Attention span   More than other people, I
1. Have trouble with my mind wandering.
2. Have trouble keeping my attention on one thing at a time.
3. Do not pay careful attention to someone else talking in a conversation.
4. Am distractible.
5. Lose or misplace things.
6. Forget plans.
7. Can't keep my mind on a job or activity.
8. Don't enjoy reading.
9. Find it hard to do only one thing at a time.

Hyperactivity
1. I am much more restless than other people are.
2. I feel a constant need to be doing things.
3. It is difficult for me to sit down and relax.
4. Compared with other people, I am always on the go.
5. I have nervous habits more than other people (my foot is always moving; I am always drumming my fingers).

Organization
1. I often start things and take too long to finish them.
2. I find it hard to stay with things.
3. I have a tendency to be disorganized.
4. Frequently I start something new before I have finished something else.
5. My housekeeping is not as well organized as I would like it to be.
6. At work, I tend to be disorganized.

Short temper
1. Compared with other people, I have a hot temper.
2. I blow up easily.
3. Compared with other people, I have a short fuse.

Affect
1. My mood changes easily and frequently.
2. I have frequent ups and downs.
3. I am easily bored.
4. I am very often discontented.
5. I get depressed easily.
6. I get excited more easily than other people do.

Impulsivity
1. I have a tendency to do things on the spur of the moment and later regret the action.
2. I don't like to postpone decisions.
3. I don't look ahead as much as I should when I am making decisions.
4. I buy on impulse.
5. I have a tendency to talk or act first and think later.

Figure 5-2 (Continued).

Stress
1. I am easily flustered.
2. Often I feel I am hassled more easily than other people are.
3. I react too strongly to the ups and downs of life.
4. When I am under pressure, I become angry or anxious or sick more than other people seem to do.

Self-image
1. I have a low opinion of myself.
2. I am dissatisfied with myself.

Stubbornness
1. I tend to be bossy.
2. Once I have made my mind up, it's very hard for me to change my opinion.

Relationships
1. I have damaged or destroyed good relationships by acting impulsively.
2. I seem to make or break relationships more often than other people do.

Miscellaneous
1. I have never achieved up to my potential.

Circle the numbers that describe you between the ages of approximately 6 and 12 years.

Compared with other children, I was (or I was told that I was)
1. Very active.
2. Very restless.
3. Always on the go.
4. Always talking excessively (a chatterbox).
5. Always wearing out my shoes very fast.
6. Unable to sit through a meal.

Compared with other children, I was
1. Said to be inattentive.
2. Distractible.
3. Unable to finish school work or assignments on time.
4. Never performing up to my ability in school.

Compared with other children, I
1. Fought more than others.
2. Disrupted the class more than others.
3. Was disciplined more frequently by the teacher and the principle.
4. Got into fights.

Compared with other children, I
1. Would do things on the spur of the moment and get into trouble.
2. Would do stupid things for which I knew I would be punished or which I knew were wrong.
3. Would not think before I acted.
4. Would call out of turn in class.

Figure 5-2 (Continued).

Compared with other children, I was
   1. Very thin-skinned.
   2. Was easy "to get a rise out of."
   3. Was easily angered or upset.
   4. Would cry or blow up easily.

---

were satisfied: generalized anxiety disorder, cyclothymic disorder, drug and alcohol abuse, antisocial behavior, and minor depressive disorder. As these diagnoses suggest, certain symptoms and behaviors are frequently seen: anxiety, dysphoria and depression, mood lability, impulsivity, substance abuse, and chronic difficulties in interpersonal relations. Consequently, ADD adults may be identified under a wide range of traditional diagnostic categories, i.e., the hysterical female, the antisocial male, the alcoholic; the drug abuser, the child abuser, and the psychosomatic patient. Other common presenting complaints are an inability to maintain friendships, marital or family problems, suicide attempts, and histories of education or vocation difficulties. These individuals often have past histories of drug abuse and jail terms. ADD adults prefer alcohol, amphetamines, and cocaine as their drugs of abuse, and they generally avoid central nervous system depressants and narcotics. These individuals may also present with complaints that "life is getting too much for me," "I can't handle the stress," or "I can't cope."

Because of this wide range, a high degree of suspicion for ADD must be kept in mind when complaints of depression, quick temper, impulse control, or attention difficulties are encountered. Populations in which we believe this disease may be prevalent are (1) the young alcoholic, (2) the child abuser, (3) the criminal, and (4) the conflicted marital couple. In one study we found (Wender et al. 1983) the prevalence of ADD in a young male alcoholic inpatient population to be 30 percent. On a number of occasions we have seen cases of child abuse in which the abusing parent turned out to be hyperactive. One of our case histories demonstrates this. In one survey (unpublished data) of a criminal population, we found a high number to be young hyperactive adults.

Depressed ADD adults are frequently misdiagnosed as having major or atypical depression. We saw several hyperactive adults wrongly treated with tricyclic antidepressants. The difficulty in distinguishing the ADD adult from the atypical depressive may be considerable. The atypical depressive, though displaying many of the characteristics of ADD,

RT, usually lacks the motor hyperactivity. As previously mentioned, emotionally unstable character disorder may be easily confused with ADD. Many ADD adults who were treated unsuccessfully with lithium had a beneficial response to stimulants. Occasionally, we also made this mistake in reverse, trying stimulants in EUCD in which lithium would have been the drug of choice.

TREATMENT

Our research demonstrated that, like ADD in children, the backbone of therapy for ADD adults is stimulant medication. Currently, we favor methylphenidate as the drug of choice and usually begin therapy with a b.i.d. or t.i.d. dosage of 5 or 10 mgm. The dose is gradually elevated until there is considerable or entire reduction of the ADD signs. Although the range is large, with doses varying between less than 5 mgm up to 60 mgm daily, the common dose appears to be between 20 and 45 mgm total per day.

Initially patients may do well on one dose but after approximately two weeks to a month, they may notice a return of their symptoms. Generally, a small increase in dose will eradicate this, and further elevations are usually unnecessary. As is true in children, one does not see escalating tolerance. We often find individuals who will have a partial response to methylphenidate but one that is less than satisfactory. If this occurs, we switch to dextroamphetamine or sodium pemoline. Although both of these drugs may be effective when methylphenidate is not, each has some disadvantages. Dextroamphetamine has been widely abused, and consequently, we are reluctant to use it because of its potential for drug abuse, either by the subjects or their receptive friends. Sodium pemoline may also be effective, but we have found it difficult to use. Although it is not abused, a slow onset of action and its accumulative effects make determining an accurate dose difficult. In addition, it has the potential for liver toxicity, which we saw in a number of cases.

We found it useful to inquire about individuals' past drug responses to stimulants. If they have a low tolerance for caffeine and find stimulants activitating, then it is doubtful that they will respond to these medications. Likewise, individuals who are able to tolerate large amounts of caffeine are more likely to respond favorably. Typically, these individuals tolerate CNS depressants poorly. This history also may indicate whether stimulants will be effective. Patients who have prominent sleep disturbance may be helped by small amounts of phenothiazine at bedtime. Stimulants seem more effective than tricyclic antidepressants in treating the depression of ADD.

We are cautious in selecting patients for stimulant treatment because of this country's abuse of amphetamines. Particularly at risk are those individuals who have past histories of drug and alcohol abuse or criminal behavior. We have been examining new compounds that may be useful in treating the ADD, RT patient. We tried 1-dopa (Wood et al. 1982) (see "Etiology" for our rationale) with discouraging results. More recently, we found pargyline and phenelzine to be effective in some of these individuals, particularly if they have a history of depression. Pargyline has the unfortunate disadvantage of causing hypotension, and both MAO inhibitors mandate diet restrictions. Needless to say, we are reluctant to employ MAO inhibitors in a group of individuals who may impulsively drink or use stimulant drugs.

One can expect a response rate of 60 to 70 percent with proper use of the stimulants, which raises the question of how to treat the remaining one-third. Unfortunately, there are no clear guidelines, and although other medications may be of benefit, the therapist must guess as to where to start. As mentioned, phenelzine may be effective, but it does not appear to reduce greatly the hyperactivity and attention abnormalities. Imipramine has occasionally proved effective. Some would claim lithium carbonate to be of value, although this has not been our experience. Currently, we cannot recommend a specific therapy for this group.

Although we believe drug therapy to be the mainstay of treatment for this disorder, certain forms of psychotherapy may be very beneficial when combined with medication. In particular, we believe that it is helpful to teach such individuals the manifestations of their disease and how to correct them. As a consequence of the disorder, most of these individuals have extremely low self-esteem. Although the stimulants can correct the physiology, psychotherapy may help the patients understand the reasons for their failures. Education that previously had been formidable or unsuccessful can now in many cases be undertaken, providing the individuals with the qualifications for a future career. For those who have had marital problems, marital therapy may be needed. We find it helpful to meet jointly with the patients and their spouses and to help each describe freely how he or she views the other. We try to help them discuss how changes in medication effect the patient's temperament and their interactions. Traditional insight-oriented psychotherapy may benefit those individuals who have personality problems or conflicts above and beyond those caused by the disease. And finally, since ADD, RT may represent a genetic illness, education for the parent regarding the recognition and treatment of ADD in childhood seems warranted. We believe psychotherapy without stimulant medication to be of little value.

The following case histories amplify our previous descriptions.

CASE HISTORIES

CASE 1

A. B. is a 23-year-old white male referred by the court for psychiatric evaluation because of child abuse. At the time of his initial intake, he stated that when his 3-year-old daughter started crying, he changed, claiming he was like the "Hulk" of the TV show. "I just go crazy; I get angry; a rage comes over me. I don't know why it is, I just can't tolerate her crying." He would subsequently beat her. In addition, he had beaten his wife on numerous occasions during the three years they had been married. The most striking aspect of A. B.'s behavior was his constant fidgeting in his chair, drumming his fingers, moving about, shifting his legs, and the like. Because of this and his explosive temper, he was referred to us to rule out ADD.

A. B. was the product of a broken home and an abused childhood. Both his parents were alcoholics. His father, who had beaten him, had been jailed for three years for almost killing a man because of his severe temper. His parents fought frequently and abandoned their children when the patient was 3 years old. This resulted in his being placed in numerous foster homes. As a child he was uncontrollable, could not stay with any one thing for long, was always on the go, had a very short attention span, and apparently had a poor memory. He described himself as "the clown of the class." At age 9 he was placed on a drug called Ritalin®, although he was unable to remember why. He did remember taking it for about three years. At the age of 12 he was transferred from one foster home in Georgia to another in South Carolina. During this transfer, his methylphenidate therapy was discontinued, for an unknown reason.

Other attributes he remembered were that he was known as "wild' and had a bad temper. He recalls being so angry at times that he would put his fist through walls and break down doors. He did poorly in school and in early adolescence fell into a life of sociopathy. He states that he was constantly running away from his foster homes, that he was incorrigible, and that on numerous occasions he had been placed in jail for brief durations. At age 13 he ran away from the foster home and has been on his own since that time. His criminal behavior increased, and at age 15 he was placed in jail for two years for stealing food and car radios. Unfortunately, his criminal behavior did not end at the completion of his jail term but became more serious. His crimes included stealing cars, abusing drugs, selling drugs, and stealing sundry items. He remembers that he used "speed" frequently because it calmed him down. At age 18 he was sentenced to a 15-year prison term because of auto theft, attempting to evade arrest, and shooting at an officer. He was released after two years of prison, put on probation, and has remained free of crime since that time. He states that he has held over 20 jobs, primarily of a semiskilled nature, the longest of which lasted two months. He would quit because of boredom and "move on" to something more interesting. Although his marriage has had a calming effect on his sociopathic behaviors, it has not helped his employment.

Additional attributes that he described were moodiness and becoming easily upset. He stated that he no longer puts his hands through doors and walls; he just throws ashtrays at them. He described a recent incident in which he was unable to get his TV to work and, in a moment of rage, smashed it. Depsite his antisocial history, during the interview he was warm and likable. We felt that he felt badly about abusing his daughter and very much wanted her returned to his home. We were touched by his statement that he had spent approximately half his life in jail; yet he did seem to care for his fellow beings, which is not typical of sociopathy. Rather, he acted on the spur of the moment and used extremely poor judgment. When the nature of his illness was explained to him, he readily agreed to begin methylphenidate therapy and asked for the directions to be written down because of his "poor memory" (attention span).

He has now been on methylphenidate therapy (25 mgm per day) for about six months. During this time he has been able to maintain the same job, which is the longest he has ever held employment. In addition, his home visits with his daughter have proved entirely satisfactory to the court, and they have allowed her to return to his home. He tolerates her crying without the previous anger. The therapist believes that he has greatly benefited from his medication and appears to be on the road to a productive life. A. B. realizes the importance of his medication and is aware that without it the likelihood of his again abusing his daughter is high.

This case history demonstrates several common properties of attention deficit disorder. First, the recognition and treatment of ADD in childhood are discontinued in early adolescence. Second, the family history, particularly on the father's side, includes uncontrollable temper, child abuse, and alcoholism. Third, a broken home and hyperactivity appear to lead to school failure and, in turn, a life of crime. Finally, hyperactivity in adults appears to be partially responsible for poor employment history, marital difficulties, and child abuse. Time will tell whether A. B.'s drug therapy will remedy the majority of these problems, but certainly the first six months of therapy have resulted in a very positive outcome.

CASE 2

C. D. is a 32-year-old white male who was initially seen in 1976 and given the diagnosis of adult attention disorder. Since 1974 he had been in conjoint marital therapy with another therapist. Despite two years of marital therapy, the difficulties continued. He was described by his wife as withdrawn, moody, and quick to anger. In addition, he was depressed much of the time. His marriage at age 18 had been one of constant conflict. Despite difficulties, the couple managed to stay together, and his wife described him as a caring father. Their marriage was complicated when at age 22 he started drinking approximately two quarts of wine per day, which persisted for the next five years. He found that the wine gave him moderate relief from his dysphoric feelings; however, the only time he "felt good" was when he was playing baseball with his friends. The marriage was also troubled by job changes which he made every two to three years. His daughters, although fond of him, described him as usually moody. C. D. felt that he was a good friend and a good father but that he had always received the "short end" in relationships and that people took more from him than they gave.

The most striking aspects of his childhood were that he was enuretic until age 12, was overemotional, and did "lousy" in school, especially in those courses requiring much concentration, science, and mathematics. He was well liked in school because he was an exceptionally good athlete. He appeared as the champion of the underdog and was constantly in fights to protect them. Despite difficulty in "the hard classes," he constantly read escapist fantasies. In time his athletic powers diminished, and he became more socially isolated. He remembers being the "class clown" throughout school, but as his social relations deteriorated, the "drinkers and smokers" became his pals. He always felt inferior to his peers because of his poor academic performance. There were disciplinary problems in high school until finally he was briefly expelled after knocking a peer down a flight of stairs. He was forced to enter therapy at that time in order to return to school and recalled his therapist challenging him to "do something with my life."

After completing high school, he had no idea where his future would lie, since he had never thought much about the future but, rather, acted on the spur of the moment. He started college but stopped because of his inability to concentrate. After the diagnosis of ADD was made, he was placed on Ritalin® and noticed an immediate benefit. His marriage improved greatly; he was able to return to college and graduate; and subsequently he was elected vice-president of his fishing club, in which for the first time in his life he felt that he had lived up to his potential.

As sometimes happens in the therapy of ADD adults, C. D. discontinued his medications for a period of nine months. His wife subsequently forced him to seek another evaluation and help because of a reappearance of his old behaviors. She described him as not finishing tasks, being withdrawn and irritable, and having attempted suicide. He could not explain why he discontinued his medications other than that he felt well and believed he no longer needed them. The medicine was resumed, and there was an immediate improvement. He and his wife are now getting along well. He appears to be a good father and seems competent and satisfied with his job.

This case demonstrates further typical features of the ADD adult. C. D.'s school difficulties, rather than leading to a life of crime, were resolved by the use of alcohol. As is frequently seen, the marital difficulties and family discord quickly surface without medication. Finally, the moodiness and attempted suicide demonstrate the specific mood abnormalities characteristic of ADD in adults. As in the first case, C. D.'s pathology greatly changed with the addition of methylphenidate to his daily life.

CASE 3

E. F. is a 42-year-old white mother of three adult children, seen because of social withdrawal and episodes of intense anxiety. She was initially seen in a western rural clinic because her complaints had gradually worsened over the last few years. The patient had had a 15-year history of psychiatric impairment. When first interviewed, she was socially isolated and withdrawn and did literally nothing. She was drinking up to several fifths of wine a day. She had gained almost 100 pounds and frequently felt terrified.

The patient was born in the West. Her mother was a successful artist, and her father was a highly successful magazine editor. She was the result of an unexpected pregnancy and felt ignored during her early childhood. During her early years, World War II was under way, and she frequently was scared of the possibility of enemy bomb attacks on the West Coast or imprisonment in a concentration camp because of her Jewish heritage. As a child she was kept out of kindergarten because her overactivity made her uncontrollable. She hated school. She was poor in sports. She was very independent and stubborn, could not sit still, and could not concentrate. She had very few friends but nevertheless did well academically. Her home life was plagued by a great deal of marital discord. Both parents were alcoholics, and her mother later died of cirrhosis. Her father had previously divorced her mother and is now in his ninth marriage. Both grandfathers and several siblings were alcoholics. She cut school frequently during adolescence, continued to isolate herself, and had few friends. During one period she semistarved herself for several months and lost 40 pounds. At 18 she became pregnant, felt rejected by her family and her church, but married the child's father and had two more children soon thereafter. At age 25 more severe psychiatric problems began. In a suicide gesture she shot herself in the abdomen. She described 12 hospitalizations, generally in state psychiatric wards, during the next 13 years, the length varying from several weeks to several months. Between hospitalizations she drank heavily and used large doses of drugs. She was diagnosed as a chronic schizophrenic. During this time she made a number of suicide attempts, slicing her forearms, once requiring 150 stitches to repair. She was given a wide variety of medications, but with little benefit.

Two years ago, we decided to give her a trial of methylphenidate because of her childhood history. This decision was made despite her rather atypical past history. On methylphenidate she was gradually able to discontinue her alcohol use. She was able to lose weight and has lost 90 pounds, seemingly without effort. She has been maintained on 10 mgm of Ritalin®, three times a day. Her energy and concentration have improved remarkably. She describes her head as "being clear," and her memory and mental organization are much better. She learns more easily and uses more appropriate social behavior. She has gradually discontinued psychotherapy and has an improved self-image. She is now actively involved in the community, recently was cochairman of the American Cancer Society Fund Raising Drive, and is editor of her church newspaper. She believes that the methylphenidate has enhanced the benefit from counseling with a local priest. Periodically she has tried to go without the methylphenidate but has always become restless and sleepless. Her emotional reactions become inappropriate and excessive, and she becomes anxious and overactive.

ETIOLOGY

Although the etiology of the ADD syndrome is unknown, it is probable that the syndrome represents a final common expression of distinct and separate causal factors (Wender 1981). Extrinsic brain insults, genetic transmission, intrauterine factors, and/or fetal maldevelopment may represent different etiologies. ADD behavior was first described in the early 1920s following von Economo's encephalitis epidemic (Bond and Smith 1935). Many of the children who developed this disease subsequently displayed symptoms characteristic of ADD. Knobloch and Pasamanick (1966) demonstrated an association among prematurity, perinatal complications, and various psychological, behavioral, and neurological abnormalities in children. The highest association between reproductive pathology and behavioral abnormalities was found in the group of children who were motorically hyperactive, confused, and disorganized—a group with many ADD symptoms. In premature infants and monozygotic twins, increased ADD pathology is repeatedly seen in the lower birthweight infants (Rogers et al. 1955).

Another possible cause for ADD is genetic. In addition to the family studies already cited, Safer (1971) located 14 MBD children whose siblings or half-siblings had been reared in foster homes. This allowed him to disentangle the effects of nature versus nurture. He found that approximately 50 percent of the full siblings, versus 14 percent of the half-siblings, were characterized by short attention span and repeated behavior problems and were given the diagnosis of ADD by an independent rater.

If the most common cause of ADD is genetic, what is the probable underlying mechanism? Currently, there is considerable evidence to suggest that an underactivity of the dopamine system may at least in part be the responsible abnormality. This theory is supported by evidence from varying sources. First, many of the adults who were afflicted with von Economo's encephalitis developed a severe form of Parkinson's disease (Bond and Smith 1935). Since abnormalities in the dopaminergic nervous system have been found in Parkinson's disease, one can hypothesize that the pathogenic viral agent attacked dopamine tracts in the central nervous system. Why in older patients Parkinson's disease was produced and in younger patients a syndrome like ADD was caused is unknown. Second, in recent years several researchers (Shekim et al. 1979a, 1979b; Shetty and Chase 1976) have investigated cerebral spinal fluid (CSF) monoamine metabolism in ADD. Shaywitz and colleagues (1977) examined the concentration of the main metabolites of dopamine and serotonin in the cerebral spinal fluid of a group of children with ADD. After probenecid loading, homovanillic acid, dopamine's main metabolite, was 47 percent lower in ADD children compared with a control group, and there was no difference in the concentration of serotonin's main metabolite 5-hydroxyindolacidic acid. Third, although a variety of medications have been tried in ADD, the one known neurochemical property that has separated effective from ineffective medications has been the ability to potentiate the activity of dopamine. Fourth, a number of animals with hyperactivity have been created by manipulation of the central nervous system (CNS) dopaminergic pathways. Shaywitz and associates (1976) treated rat pups with 6-hydroxydopamine to induce permanent reduction in brain dopamine. In the young rat, this produces a transient increase in activity that can be reduced by the administration of dextroamphetamine or methylphenidate. Bareggi's and colleagues' (1979) experiments with telominian-beagle hybrids also suggest impaired dopamine metabolism. In this canine subspecies, they were able to breed a group of dogs who show hyperactivity, distractibility, and learning impairments. These animals could be further subdivided into amphetamine responders and nonresponders similar to the human syndrome. In comparing the CSF fluid homovanillic acid concentrations in the responders with those of nonresponders, the responders to dextroamphetamine showed a significantly lower level of cerebral spinal fluid homovanillic acid. Currently, we are trying to replicate the Shaywitz data by obtaining CSF samples of homovanillic acid in ADD adults. As yet, our results are inconclusive.

PREVALENCE AND COURSE

Although the exact incidence of ADD in childhood is unknown, it has been estimated to be between 5 and 10 percent of the child population. What percent of the afflicted children go on to develop ADD, RT is also unknown. In addition, the percentage of an adult psychiatric population that becomes ADD adults is unknown. Borland and associates (1976) reported a 25-year follow-up of 20 adult males who had been given the diagnosis of ADD as children. Fifty percent continued to show symptoms of ADD. Our very rough guess of the prevalence in adults is that 20 to 30 percent of the child ADD population will continue to have ADD beyond adolescence. Using the prevalence figures for children of 5 to 10 percent, if one-third of these go on to become hyperactive adults, then somewhere between 1 and 3 percent of the adult population may be afflicted with this disorder—but this is only a guess. Undoubtedly, the prevalence will vary in different subpopulations, as indicated by the study of alcoholics previously quoted and by our initial evaluation of a criminal population.

It has been our impression that the course of ADD in adults is one of gradual lessening. This is based on three observations. First, we have found that hyperactive adults commonly report histories of greater disease intensity in childhood than in adulthood. Second, in those patients whom we have followed for more than two years, some have required smaller doses of medication than originally needed. And, third, we have failed to find many ADD adults beyond the age of 50. In our first study, the mean age was 28 years.

Although ADD in children is reported more frequently in boys than in girls, in our samples women have outnumbered men 3 to 2. Possible reasons for the discrepancy are that that subgroup of women who as children are shy and withdrawn may not be recognized as having ADD, and adult males may not seek treatment as frequently as females do; whereas in children, boys are brought for help by concerned parents.

FAMILIAL HISTORY

Based on our data collected from the ADD adults, there appears to be a high prevalence of psychopathology in the families of the ADD adult. One-third of their parents and one-fifth of their sibs were described as having serious problems with alcohol and drugs (Wender 1981). In one study, only one of the females did not have a dysphoric disorder and of those females with dysphoric disorders, half had alcoholic fathers. These findings are in keeping with the previously cited family history studies.

CONCLUSIONS

There are numerous unanswered questions and many opportunities for the future researcher. Prevalence data, particularly in different subpopulations, are badly needed. The underlying biochemical abnormalities remain a mystery. Fortunately, many of the difficulties encountered in doing biological studies on children can be avoided by using an adult population. Cerebrospinal fluid levels in children are difficult to obtain. Adults, on the other hand, can give informed consent and are more likely to follow specific diets and activity levels and thereby should provide more accurate CSF analyses. The response of some adults to monoamine oxidase inhibitors suggests that perhaps in a subpopulation the monoamine oxidase system may be at fault, but this needs further investigation. Because of the abuse potential of the stimulants, newer and more potent drugs are needed. The problem of how to treat the one-third who do not respond to stimulants remains unresolved.

ADD taps major social problems. Could the prevalence of alcoholism in many young adults be lessened by proper treatment of their underlying ADD? Could child abusers who have ADD be identified and treated? Could certain types of crimes be reduced by treating ADD children throughout their early adult period? Are many stimulant abusers, or so-called abusers, hyperactive adults who are in part self-medicating? Better, nonabusable drugs may allow treatment of these populations. Finally, we believe that the therapist's awareness of this disease may allow him or her to treat many people who were previously treatment resistant.

Those readers who wish a more thorough understanding of ADD in childhood — its prognosis, clinical signs, and symptoms — and a greater discussion of the theoretical aspects are referred to Wender and Eisenberg (1974) and Wender (1971).

ACKNOWLEDGMENT

The authors wish to thank Eugene L. Bliss, M.D., for editorial assistance.

REFERENCES

Ackerman, P. T., Dykman, R. A., and Peters, J. E. (1977). Teenage status of hyperactive and nonhyperactive learning-disabled boys. *American Journal of Orthopsychiatry* 47:577–596.

Arkonac, O., and Guze, S. B. (1963). A family study of hysteria. *New England Journal of Medicine* 268:239–242.

Arnold, E. L., Strobl, D., and Weisenburg, A. (1972). The hyperkinetic adult. *Journal of the American Medical Association* 222:693–694.

Bareggi, S. R., Becker, R. E., Ginsburg, B. E., and Genovese, E. (1979). Neurochemical investigation of an endogenous model of the "hyperkinetic syndrome" in a hybrid dog. *Life Sciences* 24:481.

Bond, E. D., and Smith, L. H. (1935). Post-encephalitic behavior disorders. *American Journal of Psychiatry* 92:17–33.

Borland, B. L., and Heckman, H. K. (1976). Hyperactive boys and their brothers: a 25-year follow-up study. *Archives of General Psychiatry* 33:669–675.

Cantwell, D. P. (1972). Psychiatric illness in the families of hyperactive children. *Archives of General Psychiatry* 27:414–417.

Hammar, S. L. (1967). School underachievement in the adolescent: a review of 75 cases. *Pediatrics* 40:373–381.

Hartocollis, P. (1968). The syndrome of minimal brain dysfunction in young adult patients. *Bulletin of the Menninger Clinic* 32: 102–114.

Hechtman, M. D., Weiss, G., Finklestein, F., and Schneider, D. U. (1976). Hyperactives as young adults: preliminary report. *Canadian Medical Association Journal* 115:625–630.

Hill, D. (1944). Amphetamine in psychopathic states. *British Journal of Addiction* 44:50–54.

Huessy, H. R., Metoyer, M., and Townsend, M. (1974). Eight- to 10-year follow-up of 84 children treated for behavioral disturbance in rural Vermont. *Acta Paedopsychiatrica* 40:230–235.

Knobloch, H., and Pasamanick, B. (1966). Prospective studies on the epidemiology of reproductive casualty. *Merrill-Palmer Quarterly of Behavior and Development* 12:27–43.

Laufer, M. W., and Denhoff, E. (1957). The hyperkinetic behavior syndrome in children. *Journal of Pediatrics* 50:463–473.

MacKay, M. C., Beck, L., and Taylor, R. (1973). Methylphenidate for adolescents with minimal brain dysfunction. *New York State Journal of Medicine* 73:551–554.

Mann, H. B., and Greenspan, S. I. (1976). The identification and treatment of adult brain dysfunction. *American Journal of Psychiatry* 133:1013–1017.

Mendelson, W., Johnson, N., and Stewart, M. D. (1971). Hyperactive children as adolescents: a follow-up study. *Journal of Nervous and Mental Disease* 153:273–279.

Menkes, M. H., Rowe, J. S., and Menkes, J. H. (1967). A 25-year follow-up study on the hyperkinetic child with MBD. *Pediatrics* 39: 393–399.

Morris, H. H., Escoll, P. J., and Wexler, R. (1956). Aggressive behaviors of childhood: a follow-up study. *American Journal of Psychiatry* 112:991–997.

Morrison, J. R., and Minkoff, K. (1975). Explosive personality as a sequel to the hyperactive child syndrome. *Comprehensive Psychiatry* 16: 343–348.

Morrison, J. R., and Stewart, M. A. (1971). A family study of the hyperactive child syndrome. *Biological Psychiatry* 3:189–195.

O'Neal, P., and Robins, L. M. (1958). The relation of childhood behavior problems to adult psychiatric status. A 30-year follow-up study of 150 patients. *American Journal of Psychiatry* 114:961–969.

Pincus, J., and Glaser, G. (1966). The syndrome of "minimal brain damage" in childhood. *New England Journal of Medicine* 275:27–35.

Quitkin, F., and Klein, D. F. (1969). Two behavioral syndromes in young adults related to possible minimal brain dysfunction. *Journal of Psychiatric Research* 7:131–142.

Richmond, J. S., Young, J. R., and Groves, J. E. (1978). Violent dyscontrol responsive to D-amphetamine. *American Journal of Psychiatry* 135:365–366.

Rifkin, A., Quitkin, F., Carrillo, C., et al. (1975). Lithium carbonate in emotionally unstable character disorder. In *Progress in Drug Treatment,* ed. D. K. Klein and R. Gittelman-Klein, pp. 617–628. New York: Brunner/Mazel.

Rogers, M. E., Lilienfeld, A. M., and Pasamanick, B. (1955). Prenatal and paranatal factors in the development of childhood behavior disorders. *Acta Psychiatric et Neurologica Scandinavica,* Supplement 102.

Rybak, W. S. (1977). More adult brain dysfunction. *American Journal of Psychiatry* 134:96–97.

Safer, D. J. (1971). The familial incidence of minimal brain dysfunction. Unpublished manuscript.

Safer, D. J., and Allen, R. P. (1975). Stimulant drug treatment of hyperactive adolescents. *Disease of Nervous System* 36:454–457.

Shaywitz, B. A., Cohen, J., and Bowers, M. B. (1977). CSF metabolites in children with minimal brain dysfunction: evidence for alterations of brain dopamine. *Journal of Pediatrics* 90:67.

Shaywitz, B. A., Yaeger, R. D., and Kloppen, J. M. (1976). Selective brain dopamine depletion in developing rats: an experimental model of minimal brain dysfunction. *Science* 191:305.

Shekim, W. O., et al. (1979a). Norepinephrine metabolism and clinical response to dextroamphetamine in hyperactive boys. *Journal of Pediatrics* 93:389.

Shekim, W. O., DeKirmenjian, H., and Chapel, J. L. (1979b). Urinary MHPG excretion in minimal brain dysfunction and its modification by d-amphetamine. *American Journal of Psychiatry* 136:667.

Shelley, E. M., and Riester, A. (1972). Syndrome of MBD in young adults. *Disease of Nervous System* 33:335–339.

Shetty, T., and Chase, T. N. (1976). Central monoamines and hyperkinesis of childhood. *Neurology* 20:1000.

Tarter, R. E., McBride, H., Buonpane, N. (1977). Differentiation of alcoholics: childhood history of minimal brain dysfunction, family history and drinking pattern. *Archives of General Psychiatry* 34:761-768.

Weiss, G., Hechtman, L., Perlman, T., Hopkins, J., and Wener, A. (1979). Hyperactives as young adults: a controlled prospective ten-year follow-up of 75 children. *Archives of General Psychiatry* 36:675-681.

Wender, P. H. (1971). *Minimal Brain Dysfunction in Children.* New York: Wiley.

————. (1977). Speculations concerning a possible biochemical basis of minimal brain dysfunction. In *Learning Disabilities and Related Disorders,* ed. J. G. Millichap, pp. 13-24. New York: Year Book Medical Publishers.

Wender, P. H., and Eisenberg, L. (1974). Minimal brain dysfunction in children. In *American Handbook of Psychiatry,* ed. S. Arieti. New York: Basic Books.

Wender, P. H., Reimherr, F. W., and Wood, D. R. (1981). Attention deficit disorder ("minimal brain dysfunction") in adults: a replication. *Archives of General Psychiatry* 38:449-456.

Wender, P. H., Rosenthal, D., and Kety, S. S. (1968). Psychiatric assessment of adoptive parents of schizophrenics. In *The Transmission of Schizophrenia,* ed. D. Rosenthal and S. S. Kety, pp. 235-250. Elmsford, N.Y.: Pergamon Press.

Woerner, P., and Guze, S. B. (1968). A family and marital study of hysteria. *British Journal of Psychiatry* 114:161-168.

Wood, D. R., Reimherr, F. W., and Wender, P. H. (1976). Diagnosis and treatment of minimal brain dysfunction in adults. *Archives of General Psychiatry* 33:1453-1460.

————. (1982). Effects of levodopa on attention deficit disorder, residual type (ADD, RT). *Psychiatry Research* 6:13-21.

Wood, D. R., Wender, P. H., and Reimherr, F. W. (1983). The prevalence of attention deficit disorder, residual type (ADD, RT) or "minimal brain dysfunction" in a population of male alcoholics. *American Journal of Psychiatry* 140:1.

CHAPTER 6

Narcolepsy and Associated Neuropsychiatric States

G. NINO-MURCIA, M.D.
RALPH E. FISHKIN, D. O.

Why include a discussion of narcolepsy, a neurological disease, in a volume devoted to new psychiatric syndromes? Our reasons are that, first, the clinical manifestations of narcolepsy, particularly sleep paralysis, hypnogogic hallucinations, automatisms, frequent terrifying dreams, impotence, and reduced sexual interest could suggest major psychiatric entities. Second, narcolepsy, like any chronic and disabling illness, is accompanied by secondary psychiatric symptoms that may require psychiatric attention in addition to skillful medical management. Third, the similarity in symptomatology between narcolepsy and schizophrenia, the polysomnographic similarities between narcolepsy and depression, and the new explanations of the mechanisms involved in narcolepsy could offer new insight into our understanding of mental illness.

For these reasons we believe that a good understanding of narcolepsy is important. In this chapter we shall discuss the history of narcolepsy, its clinical manifestations, its psychiatric aspects, some of the important neurophysiological studies, and differential diagnosis and important treatment issues.

HISTORY

In 1877, narcolepsy was first described by Westphal (Westphal 1877). Three years later, in France, Jean-Baptiste E. Gelineau (Passouant 1981) published in the *Gazette des Hopitaux* his observations on his patient, a 38-year-old male wine-barrel retailer with sudden and repetitive sleep attacks and falls or muscle weakness that he called "astasia." A year later, in 1881, Gelineau published a monograph, *De la Narcolepsie,* in which he analyzed 14 cases from the literature and his own observations.

Adie (1926) began to use the term *cataplexy* to describe the abrupt, reversible, and short-lived paralysis in patients with narcolepsy. The symptoms that constitute the main criteria for the diagnosis of narcolepsy (sleep attacks, cataplexy, hypnagogic hallucinations, and sleep paralysis) were defined by Yoss and Daly (1957).

Electroencephalography (EEG) and more recently, sleep polygraphy have allowed sleep researchers to clarify the nature of the major symptoms of narcolepsy. This began with the discovery by Aserinsky and Kleitman (1953, 1955) of rapid eye movement (REM) sleep and its differentiation from nonREM (NREM) sleep, and continued with the description of the cyclic variations of EEG during sleep and their relation to eye movements (Dement and Kleitman 1957).

Vogel (1960), while studying dreams in narcoleptics, reported the presence of REM sleep at the onset of sleep. Rechtschaffen and associates (1963) were the first to explain the symptomatology of this disorder as a disorder in the regulation of REM sleep (lack of normal inhibition of REM sleep phenomena in narcoleptics). This hypothesis has been confirmed by many studies of narcoleptics with electroencephalography and telemetry. Dement and associates (1966) described the nature of the narcoleptic attack as a result of dissociated REM sleep.

More recently, diagnostic procedures such as the Multiple Sleep Latency Test (Carskadon and Dement 1977; Mitler 1982; Richardson et al., 1978) and electronic pupillography (Schmidt and Fortin 1982) have have become valuable tools in evaluating patients with narcolepsy.

CLINICAL MANIFESTATIONS

The four symptoms mentioned above, sleep attacks, hypnogogic hallucinations, cataplexy, and sleep paralysis, constitute the classic narcoleptic tetrad characteristic of this disorder. Disturbances of nocturnal sleep are so frequent and troublesome that they have come to be considered as the fifth characteristic of narcolepsy (Vogel 1960, Yoss and Daly 1957).

SLEEP ATTACKS

Excessive daytime sleepiness may be the first and only manifestation of narcolepsy, and its severity varies from patient to patient and results in irresistible episodes of sleep. Because excessive daytime sleepiness may be the first and only manifestation of narcolepsy, it can be confused with depression, withdrawal, epilepsy, intracranial disease, viral encephalitis, hypothyroidism, and laziness (Yoss and Daly 1957).

Carskadon (1982) believes that the obscurity of this symptom in youngsters is a major cause of the delay in the diagnosis of narcolepsy during the second decade. The insidious appearance of the symptoms sometimes makes it difficult to establish the early existence of the disease (Carskadon 1982). Yoss and Daly (1960) found that among 16 children with narcolepsy, 3 had an onset at age 3, and all had an onset by age 14. Some of these patients presented diplopia, especially those with a high degree of exophoria. In some cases this could cause confusion with multiple sclerosis (Yoss and Daly 1960).

Carskadon, with the Stanford group (1982), studied and followed seven children with a family history of narcolepsy and diagnosed the illness in some of them. Among the ones with a history of narcolepsy, they found several who were somewhat sleepier than were normal controls.

CATAPLEXY

After the sleep attacks, cataplexy is the second most common symptom in narcolepsy. It consists of a sudden but temporary loss of muscle tone, without impairment of consciousness, precipitated by a sudden, intense movement or strong emotions such as laughter, anger, joy, or surprise. The extent of muscle involvement varies from simple ptosis, diplopia, involuntary slackness of the jaw, or buckling of the knees to complete paralysis leading to falling and possible injury. It is possible, also, to see attacks of cataplexy without a strong emotion preceding it. During the attack, patients report feeling as if they are floating in the air and at times experience hallucinations concomitantly with the cataplectic attack. Cataplexy can begin many years after the onset of the sleep attacks.

Marco (1978) reported a case of a 55-year-old man with tinnitus that started 60 to 90 seconds before a cataplectic attack. We wonder if this auditory phenomenon is related to the middle ear muscle activity (MEMA) described initially by Pessah and Roffwarg (1972) as a physiological event that occurs more frequently during REM and in stage 2 sleep immediately preceding REM (Ogilvie et al. 1982, Roffwarg et al. 1973). Lamstein and associates (1977) found MEMA in narcoleptics at sleep onset before REM-onset sleep, strong evidence that MEMA is a precursor of REM.

SLEEP PARALYSIS

Sleep paralysis, although occasionally experienced by nonnarcoleptic patients, occurs as one of the tetrad in 28 percent of narcoleptics (Soldatos et al. 1979) and in less than 5 percent of them as an isolated symptom (Kales and Kales 1974). This transient inability to move occurs during the transition from wakefulness to sleep or the opposite and can be seen at night or related to daytime naps. It usually disappears after one to ten minutes and can be relieved by strong movements of the eyes or external stimuli such as talking or touching the patient. At times much stronger stimulation is necessary. Sometimes sleep paralysis appears concomitantly with hypnogogic hallucinations. Once the patient learns about the reversibility of the symptom, the anxiety related to its development decreases. The frequency of the appearance of these paralyses varies from only a few episodes in life to every day. Cataplexy and sleep paralysis are similar, since both produce loss of muscle tone. The latter, however, is not associated with strong emotions, but with the sleep-wake transition. Electrophysiological techniques have determined that sleep paralysis occurs at times of bursts of REM periods simultaneously with the presence of low-voltage mixed-frequency EEG. It is, therefore, considered to be a manifestation of dissociated REM sleep.

Some narcoleptics, especially while trying to control the sleepiness, exhibit automatic behavior such as walking, talking, or driving. These are also short episodes of dissociated REM sleep.

HALLUCINATIONS

Hallucinations, the fourth symptom in the narcoleptic tetrad, can be experienced while falling asleep (hypnogogic hallucination), while awakening (hypnopompic hallucinations), or during cataplexy. The hallucinations can be visual, auditory, or tactile.

In a study of 54 narcoleptics, Van den Hoed and colleagues (1979) found that among patients who reported episodes of cataplexy lasting more than one minute, 67 percent reported having experienced hallucinations or dreams during the episode, primarily during the longer attacks.

Yoss and Daly (1960) consider the hypnogogic hallucinations "analogous to the dreams that may occur in normal persons just prior to sleep" (p. 1026). Narcoleptics, however, experience more vivid hallucinations than do normal individuals.

We mentioned earlier, the sleep attacks, cataplexy, sleep paralysis, impotence in men, and loss of libido in both sexes as symptoms of narcolepsy. Broughton and associates (1981), in an international study of 180 narcoleptic patients and 180 matched controls, found many other symptoms that although not present as frequently as is the tetrad mentioned above, are equally debilitating. These symptoms include intermittent diplopia, blurred vision, excessive snoring, and memory impairment mainly for recent events.

NEUROPHYSIOLOGY OF NARCOLEPTIC SYMPTOMS

All the polygraphic studies demonstrated that the night sleep, in most cases, starts with REM sleep or, if not, with an abnormally short REM latency (Dement et al. 1966, Hishikawa and Koneko 1965, Rechtschaffen et al. 1963, Roth 1980, Vogel 1960). The latter can also be seen in patients with affective illness, depressive type. In polysymptomatic narcolepsy, this phenomenon is also observed during daytime napping (Roth 1980), providing one of the characteristics of the polygraphic studies of narcoleptics during the day (specifically the Multiple Sleep Latency Test — MSLT) (Carskadon and Dement 1977; Mitler 1982). Signs of REM sleep are observed during episodes of sleep paralysis and hypnogogic hallucinations (Roth 1980). During the cataplectic attack, a reduction in muscle tone activity, similar to the one seen during REM sleep, is present. The EEG is one of wakefulness, and there is no REM.

The nature of the sleep attacks is less well defined. We mentioned the REM onset episodes. At times, however, the patient falls asleep, but the accompanying sleep is NREM (Roth 1978, 1980). In fact, drowsiness or sleepiness is definitely a symptom of narcolepsy. These patients are excessively sleepy during the entire day, and so the idea of the narcoleptic going from short sleep periods to complete wakefulness needs revision.

It is important at this point to discuss the impact of the disordered sleeping patterns of narcoleptics on the circadian rhythms of some hormones.

Normally, there is a rise in the level of prolaction (PRL) which begins 60 minutes after the onset of sleep and continues to increase until it reaches its highest point during the last third of the night. This increase is related to the stages of sleep, with the nadir during REM sleep and an increase during NREM (Parker et al. 1980).

The growth hormone (GH), on the other hand, reaches its highest secretion level during the first third of the night and is directly related to slow-wave sleep (SWS) (Parker et al. 1980).

Parker and associates (1980) determined that daytime naps in normal subjects are associated with an increase in the level of prolactin. However, Higuchi and associates (1979) studied the 24-hour secretory pattern of PRL in four narcoleptics and did not find a relationship with REM and NREM sleep, mentioned above. Some of their patients presented peaks during REM and a decrease in the secretions of PRL at the beginning of the night, reaching a nadir one to one and a half hours after a REM-onset nocturnal sleep, with normalization of the secretory patterns by the end of the night.

Different from normal subjects, who present the highest peak of GH secretion in the 24-hour period during the first third of the night, Higuchi's and associates' narcoleptics showed a decrease during the first third of the nocturnal sleep. A functional disturbance of the hypothalamus of narcoleptic patients was their explanation for the abnormal secretory patterns.

Clark and associates (1979) also found an absence of the normal peak in the GH secretion during SWS (within two hours of sleep onset), as well as normal diurnal GH secretion in their narcoleptics. The normal increase in GH levels following L-DOPA or arginine was not observed, and the secretory patterns of PRL were significantly lower than in normal controls. L-DOPA failed to suppress PRL secretion in their narcoleptic patients.

Further studies of secretory patterns of hormones in relation to sleep-wake cycle abnormalities in narcoleptics promise a better understanding of the pathophysiology of this disorder. We wonder if, besides the medications used in its treatment, PRL abnormalities and their relation to testosterone could contribute to the erectile dysfunction and the lowered sexual drive observed in some narcoleptics.

DIFFERENTIAL DIAGNOSIS

A careful history is diagnostic in many patients with narcolepsy. The differential diagnosis includes a variety of medical conditions. These include several sleep disorders in which excessive daytime somnolence (EDS) is an important symptom (ASDC 1979). Sleep apnea is one of them. The frequent episodes of obstruction of the upper airways and the arousals by the end of the apneic episode result in considerable disruption of sleep in these patients, with consequent sleep deprivation and excessive daytime sleepiness. This is most probably why patients with sleep apnea can present sleep attacks and/or REM-onset episodes. These sleep attacks in the sleep apnea patient produce long, unrefreshing naps, quite different from those most commonly seen in the narcoleptic, in which short naps produce a sense of being refreshed. Other symptoms of sleep apnea include loud snoring with pauses, often witnessed by the bed partner; hypertension, both systemic and pulmonary; early morning confusion sometimes confused with toxic states; headaches in the morning; enuresis; nocturia; impotence and personality changes characterized by jealousy; irritability; and quite frequently, depression (ASDC 1979).

Periodic movements in sleep (nocturnal myoclonus) can produce frequent arousals and considerable distortion of the sleep architecture. Patients suffering from this disorder can develop excessive daytime somnolence (ASDC 1979) and can therefore be confused with narcoleptics.

Idiopathic central nervous system hypersomnia is characterized also by excessive daytime sleepiness; lengthy naps that are not refreshing, but with no evidence of cataplexy; obstructive or central sleep apnea; and sleep attacks.

The differential diagnosis of narcolepsy also includes other medical conditions in which the symptom of hypersomnia is present, such as brain tumor, encephalitis, multiple sclerosis, Kleine-Levin syndrome, and myasthenia gravis. Niedermeyer and associates (1979) reported a case of hypersomnia with sudden sleep attacks in the clinical context of vertebrobasilar artery insufficiency. Their patient also had, however, episodes of unsteadiness, dizziness, diplopia, and dysarthria.

Yoss and Daly (1960) pointed out that narcolepsy can be confused with hypothyroidism and akinetic seizures, particularly when the symptoms appear in latency or early adolescence.

Cases of functional hypersomnia with short sleep cycles, which were studied by Roth (1981), are characterized by excessive sleepiness, but the attacks are usually longer than in the narcoleptic (lasting from one to several hours) and present in about 60 percent of the cases with sleep drunkenness at awakening. Narcoleptics feel refreshed after a short nap and have a period of a few hours free of sleep attacks.

Patients with Kleine-Levin syndrome evaluated with an MSLT can present REM-onset sleep if the test is done during a symptomatic period (Roth 1980). However, these patients have a history of periods of time free of symptoms and periods in which hypersomnia, bulimia, polydipsia, hypersexuality, and other psychological changes are observed. Fever can precede or accompany the periods of hypersomnia (Roth 1980). Female patients can develop hypersomnia associated with menstrual periods (ASDC 1979).

Finally, some patients with EDS display no abnormality in the physical exam, polysomnography, or psychological examination (ASDC 1979).

PSYCHIATRIC ASPECTS OF NARCOLEPSY

The psychiatric aspects of narcolepsy were listed, in the introduction and in the description of the disease's clinical symptoms. We now shall discuss these symptoms in more detail with a view toward differentiating narcolepsy from some of the psychiatric entities that may be suggested in evaluating a narcoleptic.

The appearance of narcolepsy in a previously vigorous individual is startling and puzzling. The parents of adolescents and young adults with narcolepsy are apt to interpret this sleepiness as a result of the adolescent's rapid physical growth or emotional turmoil. The clinician should be aware that the patients use the terms *sleepiness* and *tiredness* interchangeably.

The sleep attacks of narcolepsy can last a few seconds or as long as 30 minutes. Typically, a narcoleptic takes a nap that lasts for about 15 to 30 minutes and awakes to feel refreshed and alert for about 2 hours. This manifestation helps in the differential diagnosis between narcolepsy and hypersomnia of a different etiology, in which the naps are usually longer and do not produce the same alertness as seen in narcoleptics. The narcoleptic's sleep attacks are usually irresistible and occur more frequently in circumstances conducive to sleep, such as after meals, in monotonous situations, or in the late afternoon (Kales and Kales 1974). Patients complain of drowsiness preceding the sleep attack. The number of attacks varies from a few to many attacks dispersed during the day or in clusters.

In contrast with the sleepiness of the narcoleptic, the neurotic patient complains of physical exhaustion. Neurotics will not generally feel refreshed by short naps. Their hypersomnolence is related to psychological stress that will be obvious to the trained clinician, though generally not to the patient.

As mentioned above, cataplexy is often precipitated by strong emotions. Patients soon learn this and begin to avoid strong feelings. The clinician may be struck by the narcoleptic's blandness and denial of emotion and may develop the false impression that the patient has either the blunted affect of a schizophrenic or la belle indifference, as seen in hysteria. The terrifying hypnogogic hallucinations and loosened associations of the drowsy narcoleptic may be confused with psychotic symptomatology, though the thought processes of the narcoleptic between attacks are normal (Soldatos et al. 1979).

Shapiro and Spitz (1976) reported on a narcoleptic patient initially diagnosed as schizophrenic and suggested that misdiagnosis of narcolepsy can be avoided if clinicians are aware that this disorder can simulate a psychiatric disorder. Another case of a patient with narcolepsy, paranoid psychosis, and tardive dyskinesia (Pfefferbaum and Berger 1977) illustrates the difficult problems in psychopharmacological management faced by clinicians treating narcoleptics. Amphetamines and tricyclic antidepressants used to treat narcolepsy can produce or precipitate symptoms of anxiety, drug dependence, insomnia, and frank psychosis. See, for example, the organic mental disorders associated with the amphetamines and similarly acting sympathomimetics described in the third *Diagnostic and Statistical Manual of Mental Disorders.*

Broughton and associates (1981) emphasized the high frequency of depression in narcoleptic patients and postulated that the pathophysiology of this condition "may be endogenously expressed by depression as well as by the major symptoms" (p. 103). In other words, depression may be a major symptom of the disease, not only the by-product of a chronic illness. It is interesting to note, in this connection, that both depression and narcolepsy improve with amphetamines and tricyclic antidepressants and that on polysomnography, both show short REM latencies or sleep-onset REM periods.

Psychiatric conditions such as unipolar depression and a variety of personality disorders may also be erroneously considered, usually because the clinician is not aware of the entity of narcolepsy and its symptoms and does not take a sleep history. This is particularly true when the therapist is not a medical person and fails to obtain medical or psychiatric consultation.

Besides affective illness, hypersomnia can be seen in patients who, when confronting stress, tend to remain in bed and sleep during the day. Patients with obsessive personality traits can engage in work to the extent of inducing sleep deprivation and disorders of the sleep-wake cycle, with consequent excessive daytime somnolence (EDS). EDS can also be observed in patients who use or abuse psychostimulants. Although rare, patients can present a fictitious disorder with physical symptoms (DSM-III 301.51) after becoming aware of some of the symptoms and signs of narcolepsy. Nowadays this information is readily available to the public. This is particularly true in patients trying to obtain prescriptions for amphetamines. Polygraphic recordings (specifically the Multiple Sleep Latency Test) are most helpful in the diagnosis and management of these cases.

Symptoms such as automatisms can lend themselves to misinterpretation. Zorick and associates (1979) reported a case of shoplifting as "a particularly troublesome sort of automatic behavior" (p. 194) in a narcoleptic. The lack of self-control during these amnesic episodes can be particularly frightening to the narcoleptic after the incident and may also lead the clinician to entertain the diagnosis of dissociative, impulsive, or antisocial character disturbance.

Indeed, patients may believe that they are suffering from a serious psychiatric disturbance, and clinicians may be confronted with a narcoleptic whose anxiety or reactive depression is striking and requires treatment. They should consider the possibility that there may be other factors in the patient's life and mind that can produce psychiatric illness that coexists with narcolepsy (Pfefferbaum and Berger 1977, Salzman 1976). Symptoms such as sexual dysfunction are often tenacious, despite resolution of the crisis in which they began. These deserve careful evaluation, since they may stem from an organic etiology. If psychogenic, they may respond to brief active intervention, such as sex therapy, or they may reflect underlying neurotic or characterologic symptomatology that requires psychotherapy (Kernberg 1975). It is important to remember that in addition to a thorough review of symptoms and sleep history, the patient should undergo a thorough psychiatric evaluation so that the concomitant psychopathology can be assessed and appropriately treated in conjunction with the treatment of narcolepsy, as part of a comprehensive treatment plan.

SPECIAL STUDIES

When the sleep attacks constitute the first and often the only manifestation of this disorder, or in more atypical cases, special studies are necessary. The most frequently used diagnostic tool is the Multiple Sleep Latency Test (MSLT) (Carskadon and Dement 1977, Mitler 1982, Richardson et al. 1978). In this test, the patient is monitored in the sleep laboratory while given five opportunities of 20 minutes each to fall asleep. These naps are scheduled at 2-hour intervals. These recordings allow a clear determination of the time of sleep onset, the sleep latency (amount of time between the beginning of the recording session and sleep onset), the presence or absence of REM sleep and the REM latency (amount of time between sleep onset and the appearance of REM sleep).

It is important that the patient be tested after being drug-free and without evidence of sleep deprivation, which could produce false positive results during the MSLT.

Evidence of abnormally short sleep latencies demonstrate objectively excessive sleepiness. In a study using the MSLT to evaluate narcoleptics as compared with nonnarcoleptics with excessive daytime sleepiness and controls, Mitler (1982) found a mean sleep latency of 2.91 minutes, S.D. 2.7 in 49 narcoleptics with excessive daytime sleepiness and 13.38 minutes, S.D. 4.3 for controls. The presence of more than one REM-onset sleep period during the recording sessions is helpful in confirming the diagnosis of narcolepsy. Mitler (1982) found one REM sleep episode in 8 percent of his nonnarcoleptic patients with excessive sleepiness, but only narcoleptics presented more than one REM-onset episode.

In evaluating the polygraphic recordings, other conditions must be considered, such as sleep deprivation, sleep apnea, and depression or withdrawal from REM-suppressant medications that can result in REM-onset sleep.

Kendel (1978) found onset REM-sleep in 17 percent of cases with caudal brain-stem lesions. Weitzman and associates (1980) detected sleep-onset REM episodes during the first third of the circadian sleep episode in subjects studied while allowed to sleep freely without any clues to time of day.

Electronic pupillography was recommended by Schmidt and Fortin (1982), who confirmed the findings of Yoss and associates (1969) in narcoleptics demonstrating a very unstable pupillary diameter, and they also described a paradoxical response to light stimulation (a very small contraction of the pupil) suggesting a "sleepy cortex and a hyperaroused brainstem" (p. 134).

TREATMENT

The comprehensive treatment of patients with narcolepsy includes pharmacotherapy, treatment of the patients' psychosocial problems, and education of the patients and their families regarding the disease, particularly in order to prevent accidents that might occur because of symptoms such as sleep attacks and cataplexy. Because of their medical background, skill in using psychoactive medications, and training in a variety of psychotherapies, psychiatrists are uniquely qualified to provide primary care in narcolepsy.

PHARMACOLOGY

The pharmacotherapy varies according to the symptoms of narcolepsy present and the coexistence of other medical or psychiatric conditions. The initial approach is the use of amphetamines. These sympathomimetics help prevent sleep attacks and should be used in low but increasing doses until the minimal amount necessary to treat successfully the excessive sleepiness or the sleep attacks is found. Both the racemic form and the dextroisomer of amphetamine are powerful stimulants of the central nervous system. The dextroamphetamines have greater central effects and smaller cardiovascular effects than the levoisomer does. Methylphenidate (Ritalin®), a compound chemically and pharmacologically similar to amphetamines, was recommended by Yoss and Daly (1959) as the drug of choice, for they found that the incidence of undesirable side effects from amphetamines is greater than that from methylphenidate. Methylphenidate is not without unpleasant characteristics, however, particularly its short duration of activity. Amphetamines are well absorbed from the gastrointestinal tract. Yoss and Daly (1959) advised patients to take the drug 30 minutes before meals. Soldatos and associates (1979) believe that this medication should be taken "at least 45 minutes before or not less than one hour after eating" (p. 135) and recommended the use of methylphenidate 5 mg in the morning, at noon, and at 4:00 p.m., increasing one or all doses depending on the clinical response and the needs and activities of the particular patient during the weekday or weekends.

A combination of methylphenidate and "elective" programmed naps seems to work effectively for many patients. The total daily dose can then be increased or decreased to find the minimum necessary to control the sleep attacks and excessive daytime sleepiness so that the incidence of side effects and complications of the amphetamines is minimized.

The use of elective naps makes it possible to reduce the dose of amphetamines. This is particularly important in treating children and adolescents with narcolepsy, since the consequences of long-term therapy with sympathomimetics is not known.

Broughton and Mamelak (1980) treated 14 patients having narcolepsy-cataplexy with gammahydroxy-butyrate (GHB) at night, with considerable reduction or disappearance of sleep attacks. They observed an improvement in these patients' sleep at night, characterized by increases in delta sleep and in the amount of sleep obtained by patients while in bed and a reduction in latency and fragmentation of REM sleep, number of periods of short sleep, and stage 1.

Mamelak and Webster (1981) used GHB to treat a patient with narcolepsy and sleep apnea and obtained improvement in the narcoleptic symptoms and a decrease in the number of apneic episodes.

Considering previous theories of narcolepsy that propose a tendency of the sleep subsystems to dissociate (Broughton and Mamelak 1979, Dement 1976) and explaining the episodes of sleep apneas seen in this illness, Mamelak and Webster (1981) proposed that GHB would act by promoting integration of the sleep subsystems, resulting in a stabilization of respiratory patterns.

Although GHB needs further evaluation as a treatment of patients with narcolepsy or narcolepsy and sleep apnea, this medication could become useful. This is especially true in the treatment of those patients who have developed psychiatric disorders as a result of amphetamines, those who need increasing doses of amphetamines, or those in whom the coexistence of another sleep disorder such as sleep apnea has been demonstrated. The use of GHB for narcoleptic patients who have developed erectile dysfunction associated with the use of amphetamines deserves investigation.

Monoamino oxidase (MAO) inhibitors such as nialamide (Baumgarten and Bushart 1970) and phenelzine (Wyatt et al. 1971) have also been used to treat narcolepsy. Phenelzine produced improvement, not only in the excessive sleepiness and sleep attacks, but also in the cataplectic attacks, the sleep paralysis, and the hallucinations. Unfortunately, this medication also produced hypertension, impaired sexual function, and edema.

Parkes and Schachter (1979) treated 34 patients with mazindol, obtaining considerable amelioration of sleep attacks but no effects on the cataplexy or sleep paralysis.

Kales and associates (1979a, 1979b) reported successful treatment of narcolepsy with propranolol hydrochloride. This medication could be helpful in treating narcoleptics suffering also from hypertension. A serotonin antagonist, methysergide, has also been used to reduce sleep attacks (Wyler et al. 1975). The possibility of retroperitoneal fibrosis and calf claudication makes this medication undesirable.

If, besides excessive sleepiness and sleep attacks, the patient presents cataplexy, the drugs of choice in addition to the amphetamines are tricyclic antidepressants such as clomipramine or imipramine. All the side effects and complications of tricyclics and amphetamines ought to be considered during the management of narcoleptics. These two drugs are known to suppress REM sleep and increase the level of catecholamines at the neuronal synapse (Kales and Kales 1974). In some cases, imipramine is effective a few hours after the first dose (Soldatos et al. 1979) as a treatment for cataplexy but is minimally effective in decreasing sleep attacks. The usual dose of imipramine is 50 mgs in the morning.

PSYCHOTHERAPEUTIC CONSIDERATIONS

It is easy to understand the difficulties that a narcoleptic has in adapting to society. The irresistible sleep attacks produce voluntary restriction in social activities, loss of jobs, low productivity, and difficulties in relationships with family and friends. Narcoleptics are often misunderstood and are regarded as lazy, irresponsible, incompetent, intoxicated, dependent, or psychiatrically ill. A lack of emotional expressiveness, reflecting a tendency to control feelings that may produce sleep attacks or cataplexy may make narcoleptics seem remote or uninterested and may cause them to feel frustrated and emotionally unfulfilled (Kales et al. 1982).

Feelings of embarrassment, low self-esteem, anxiety, and depression occur in patients affected by irresistible sleep attacks and/or cataplectic attacks, especially if they occur at inopportune times such as while visiting friends, making love, or engaging in sports.

Beutler and associates (1981) reported the presence of psychopathology in narcoleptics. In a more recent study, Kales and associates (1982) found that narcoleptics present more psychopathology than controls do, but they explained this as secondary to the illness.

Salzman (1976) wrote a beautiful paper, the case report of a 40-year-old male narcoleptic referred for depression. The paper is a primer for psychiatrists treating narcoleptics because Salzman clearly delineated the interplay of symptoms, psychosocial and marital consequences, and secondary gain. He described his treatment — consisting of a blend of education, pharmacotherapy, individual, and couple therapy — and discussed quite frankly the advantages and the limitations of each modality. Salzman divided the psychologic consequences of the patient's narcolepsy into three phases. The first was the development of depression. Here Salzman's goal was to help the patient recognize the depression and confront a real compromise in performance due to his chronic illness. The second phase of the patient's illness was the deterioration of the patient's marriage because of his wife's frustration and inability to understand the illness. Here he extended the blend of support, education, and specific suggestion to the wife as well, permitting both to express their feelings about the effects of narcolepsy on their lives. In the third phase, Salzman addressed the erosion of marital and sexual intimacy by exploring the couple's interpersonal psychodynamics and helped them understand that their loss of satisfaction "was a mutual problem, and as such necessitated mutual efforts at resolution" (p. 51). The result would satisfy any therapist.

The diagnosis of any chronic illness often has disastrous consequences for the patient's marriage and sexual life. The sleep attacks, the cataplexy, and the medications used can interfere severely with the narcoleptic's sexual function. Broughton and his associates (1981) found that

15.2 percent of male narcoleptics reported impotence and that 16.7 percent of narcoleptics of both sexes reported a decrease in their sexual drive since the onset of the illness.

EDUCATION OF THE PATIENT

Once patients know and accept that they have a neurological condition that explains most of their symptoms, their anxiety and difficulties in interpersonal relationships will diminish somewhat. Patients need to understand that the frightening sleep paralysis is another symptom of their condition and that it is completely reversible, spontaneously or by external stimulation. In the same way, they should be aware that the hallucinations are not a symptom of psychosis.

Patients can learn to distribute brief naps through the day according to their needs and opportunities at work and at home in order to avoid sleep deprivation and to reduce their need for stimulant medication.

Both narcoleptics and their families should understand the need for caution in operating hazardous machinery or other activities that require sustained alertness. Long-distance driving should be avoided completely. If patients feel drowsy while driving, they should pull off the highway and nap before continuing the trip (Soldatos et al. 1979).

CONCLUSIONS

Because of the initial difficulties in diagnosing narcolepsy, the patients may have suffered for a long time from the consequences of their illness and may have sustained serious psychiatric morbidity. The symptoms of narcolepsy may resemble those of psychiatric conditions and may require careful differential diagnosis. The treatment of narcolepsy requires psychoactive medications such as amphetamines, methylphenidate, the tricyclic antidepressants, and others with side effects and complications which can include serious psychiatric problems such as drug dependence, anxiety, and psychosis. They should be prescribed by clinicians familiar with and able to treat these adverse effects.

The increased incidence of psychopathology in narcoleptics, as well as the severe marital, sexual, social, and financial problems produced by the illness, must be recognized and treated by therapists skilled in the appropriate mode of psychotherapy. For these reasons, psychiatrists are ideally equipped to treat narcoleptics and their families. Every team involved in the diagnosis and treatment of narcolepsy should have a psychiatrist, and every narcoleptic deserves a thoughtful and thorough psychiatric evaluation.

REFERENCES

Adie, W. J. (1926). Idiopathic narcolepsy: a disease sui generis: with remarks on the mechanisms of sleep. *Brain* 49:257–306.

Aserinsky, E., and Kleitman, N. (1953). Regularly occurring periods of eye motility and concomitant phenomena during sleep. *Science* 118: 273–274.

_____. (1955). Two types of ocular motility occurring in sleep. *Journal of Applied Physiology* 8:1–10.

Association of Sleep Disorders Centers (ASDC) (1979). Diagnostic classification of sleep and arousal disorders. 1st ed. prepared by the Sleep Disorders Classification Committee, H. P. Roffwarg, chairman. *Sleep* 2:58–86.

Baumgarten, H. G., and Bushart, W. (1970). Treatment of narcolepsy with monoamino oxidase inhibitors and sympathomimetic agents. *European Neurology* (Basel) 3:97–104.

Beutler, L. E., Ware, J. C., and Karacan, I. (1981). Differentiating psychological characteristics of patients with sleep apnea and narcolepsy. *Sleep* 4:39–47.

Broughton, R., Ghanem, Q., Hishikawa, Y., Sugita, Y., Nevsimalova, S. and Roth, B. (1981). The socioeconomic and related life effects in 180 patients with narcolepsy from North America, Asia, Europe compared to matched controls. In *Psychophysiological Aspects of Sleep,* ed. I. Karacan, pp. 96–105. Park Ridge, N.J.: Noyes Medical Publications.

Broughton, R., and Mamelak, M. (1979). The treatment of narcolepsy-cataplexy with nocturnal gammahydroxy butyrate. *Canadian Journal of Neurological Science* 6:1–6.

_____. (1980). Effects of nocturnal gammahydroxy butyrate on sleep-waking patterns in narcolepsy-cataplexy. *Canadian Journal of Neurological Science* 7:23–31.

Carskadon, M. (1982). The second decade. In *Sleeping And Waking Disorders: Indications and Techniques,* ed. C. Guilleminault. Reading, Mass.: Addison-Wesley.

Carskadon, M., and Dement, W. (1977). Sleep tendency: an objective measure of sleep loss. *Sleep Research* 6:200.

Clark, R. W., Schmidt, H. S., and Malarkey, W. B. (1979). Disordered growth hormone and prolactin secretion in primary disorders of sleep. *Neurology* 29:855–861.

Dement, W. (1976). Daytime sleepiness and sleep "attacks." In *Narcolepsy*, ed. C. Guilleminault, W. Dement, and P. Passouant, pp. 17–42. New York: Spectrum.

Dement, W., and Kleitman, N. (1957). Cyclic variations in EEG during sleep and their relation to eye movements, body motility, and dreaming. *Electroencephalography and Clinical Neurophysiology* 9:673–690.

Dement, W., Rechtschaffen, A., and Gulevitch, G. (1966). The nature of the narcoleptic sleep attack. *Neurology* 16:18–33.

Higuchi, T., Takahashi, Y., Takahashi, K., Yoshizumi, N., and Miyashita, A. (1979). Twenty-four-hour secretory patterns of growth hormone, prolactin, and cortisol in narcolepsy. *Journal of Clinical Endocrinologic Metabolism* 49:197–294.

Hishikawa, Y., and Koneko, Z. (1965). Electroencephalographic study on narcolepsy. *Electroencephalography and Clinical Neurophysiology* 18:249–259.

Kales, A., Cadieux, R., Soldatos, C. R., and Tan, T. L. (1979a). Successful treatment of narcolepsy with propranolol: a case report. *Archives of Neurology* 36:650–651.

Kales, A., and Kales, J. (1974). Sleep disorders: recent findings in the diagnosis and treatment of disturbed sleep. *New England Journal of Medicine* 290:487–499.

Kales, A., Soldatos, C. R., Bixler, E. O., Cadwell, A., Cadieux, R. J., Verrechio, J. M., and Kales, J. D. (1982). Narcolepsy. Cataplexy II. Psychosocial consequences and associated psychopathology. *Archives of Neurology* 39:169–171.

Kales, A., Soldatos, C. R., Cadieux, R., Bixler, E. O., Tan, T. L., and Scharf, M. (1979b). Propanolol in the treatment of narcolepsy. *Annals of Internal Medicine* 91:741–743.

Kendel, K. (1978). Analysis of sleep stage sequence. *Waking and Sleeping* 2(3):181–185.

Kernberg, O. (1975). *Borderline Conditions and Pathological Narcissism.* New York: Jason Aronson.

Lamstein, S. M., Spielman, A. H., Weitzman, E., Pollak, C., and Roffwarg, H. P. (1977). The recording of middle ear muscle activity in narcolepsy. *Sleep Research* 6:175.

Mamelak, M., and Webster, P. (1981). Treatment of narcolepsy and sleep apnea with gammahydroxy butyrate: a clinical and polysomnographic study. *Sleep* 4:105–111.

Marco, L. (1978). Narcolepsy with tinnitus aura: interpretation. *International Journal of Psychiatric Medicine* 9:275–280.

Mitler, M. (1982). The multiple sleep latency test as an evaluation for excessive somnolence. In *Sleeping and Waking Disorders,* ed. C. Guilleminault, pp. 145–153. Reading, Mass.: Addison-Wesley.

Niedermeyer, E., Coyle, P. K., and Preziosi, T. S. (1979). Hypersomnia with sudden sleep attacks ("symptomatic narcolepsy") on the basis of vertebrobasilar artery insufficiency: a case report. *Waking and Sleeping* 3:361–364.

Ogilvie, R. D., Hunt, H. T., Sawicki, C., and Samahalskyi, J. (1982). Psychological correlates of spontaneous middle ear muscle activity during sleep. *Sleep* 5:11–27.

Parker, D. C., Rossman, L. G., Kripke, D. F., Hershman, J. M., Gibson, W., Davis, C., Wilson, K., and Pekary, E. (1980). Endocrine rhythms across sleep-wake cycles in normal young men under basal conditions. In *Physiology in Sleep,* ed. J. Orem and C. Barnes, pp. 146–179. New York: Academic Press.

Parker, D. C., Rossman, L. G., and Vanderban, E. F. (1973). Sleep related, nyctohermeral and briefly episodic variation in human plasma prolactin concentrations. *Journal of Clinical Endocrinologic Metabolism* 35: 1119–1124.

Parkes, J. D., and Schachter, M. (1979). Mazindol in the treatment of narcolepsy. *Acta Neurologica Scandinavica* 60:250–254.

Passouant, P. (1981). Historical note. Doctor Gelineau (1828–1906) narcolepsy centennial. *Sleep* 3(3):241–246.

Pessah, M. A., and Roffwarg, H. P. (1972). Spontaneous middle ear muscle activity in man: a rapid eye movement sleep phenomenon. *Science* 178:773–776.

Pfefferbaum, A., and Berger, P. A. (1977). Narcolepsy, paranoid psychosis and tardive dyskinesia: a pharmacological dilemma. *Journal of Nervous and Mental Diseases* 164:293–297.

Rechtschaffen, A., Wolpert, E., Dement, W., Mitchell, S., and Fischer, C. (1963). Nocturnal sleep of narcoleptics electroencephalograph. *Clinical Neurophysiology* 15:599–609.

Richardson, G., Carskadon, M., Flagg, W., Van den Hoed, J., Dements, W., and Mitler, M. (1978). Excessive daytime sleepiness in man: multiple sleep latency measurement in narcoleptic and control subjects. *Electroencephalography of Clinical Neurophysiology* 45:621–627.

Roffwarg, H., Adrien, J., Herman, K., Lamstein, S., Pessah, M., Spiro, R., and Bowe-Anders, C. (1973). The place of middle ear muscle activity in the neurophysiology and psychophysiology of the REM state. *Sleep Research* 2:36.

Roth, B. (1978). *Narcolepsy and Hypersomnia*, ed. R. L. Williams and I. Karacan, pp. 29–59. New York: Wiley.

_____. (1980). *Narcolepsy and Hypersomnia*, rev. and ed. R. Broughton. Basel and New York: Karger.

_____. (1981). Classification of states of excessive sleep: a critical evaluation of the present situation. In *Psychophysiological Aspects of Sleep*, ed. I. Karacan, pp. 88–95. Park Ridge, N.J.: Noyes Medical Publications.

Salzman, C. (1976). Interpersonal problems in narcolepsy. *Psychosomatics* 17:49–51.

Schmidt, H. S., and Fortin, L. D. (1982). Electronic pupillography in disorders of arousal. In *Sleeping and Waking Disorders*, ed. C. Guilleminault, pp. 127–143. Reading, Mass.: Addison-Wesley.

Shapiro, B., and Spitz, H. (1976). Problems in the differential diagnosis of narcolepsy versus schizophrenia. *American Journal of Psychiatry* 133:1321–1323.

Soldatos, C., Kales, A., and Cadieux, R. (1979). Evaluation and treatment. In *Amphetamine Use, Misuse and Abuse*, ed. D. E. Smith, D. R. Wesson, M. E. Buxton, et al., pp. 128–140. Boston: G. K. Hall.

Van den Hoed, J., Lucas, E., and Dement, W. (1979). Hallucinatory experiences during cataplexy in patients with narcolepsy. *American Journal of Psychiatry* 136:1210–1211.

Vogel, G. (1960). Studies in psychophysiology of dreams III. The dream of narcolepsy. *Archives of General Psychiatry* 3:421–428.

Weitzman, E. D., Czeisler, C. A., Zimmerman, J. C., and Ronda, L. M. (1980). Timing of REM and stages 3 and 4 sleep during temporal isolation in man. *Sleep* 2:391–407.

Westphal, C. (1877). Eigetumliche, mit Einschlafen verbundene Anfalle. *Archiv für Psychiatrie und Nervenkrankheiten* 7:631–635.

Wyatt, R. J., Fram, H., Buchbinder, R., and Snyder, F. (1971). Treatment of intractable narcolepsy with a monoamino oxidase inhibitor. *New England Journal of Medicine* 285:987–991.

Wyler, R., Wildus, R.J., and Troupin, A. (1975). Methysergide in the treatment of narcolepsy. *Archives of Neurology* 32:265–268.

Yoss, R. E., and Daly, D. D. (1957). Criteria for the diagnosis of narcoleptic syndrome. *Staff Proceedings Meeting of the Mayo Clinic* 32:320–328.

————. (1959). Treatment of narcolepsy with ritalin. *Neurology* 9:171.

————. (1960). Narcolepsy in children. *Pediatrics* 25:1025–1033.

Yoss, R. E., Moyer, N. J., and Ogle, K. N. (1969). The pupillogram and narcolepsy: a method to measure decreased levels of wakefulness. *Neurology* 19:921–928.

Zorick, F. J., Salis, P. H., Roth, T., and Kramer, M. (1979). Narcolepsy and automatic behavior: a case report. *Journal of Clinical Psychiatry* 40:194–197.

PART III

Drug-related Syndromes

We are ever in pursuit of pleasure: that is what we want, greater and greater pleasure. And when we pursue pleasure, inevitably there must be pain and fear.

You Are the World, J. Krishnamurti, 1972

CHAPTER 7

Phencyclidine Intoxication and Abuse

KENNETH J. WEISS, M.D.

Rarely in the history of drug abuse has a substance caused as much psychiatric morbidity as has phencyclidine (PCP). Having reached a peak in the late 1970s, the relatively new diagnoses of PCP intoxication and abuse remain significant considerations in the practice of psychiatry. Phencyclidine was a prototype of a class of dissociative anesthetics whose fate could not have been predicted. Its unique psychotomimetic properties, coupled with ease of manufacture and the drug-abusing population's suggestibility, set the stage for a true epidemic. This chapter will explore the historical, pharmacologic, and clinical aspects of PCP.

HISTORY

The history of PCP began in the mid-1950s (Domino 1978, Maddox 1980). At that time pharmacologists were working on the preparation of ketones or stable imino compounds with analgesic properties. An anomalous chemical reaction occurred when combining piperidines with the Grignard reagent phenylmagnesium bromide. This ultimately yielded a compound with unique properties, 1-(1-phenylcyclohexyl) piperidine or phencyclidine.

The pharmacologic activity of PCP was recognized immediately and was studied in animals and humans. Cats given PCP in low doses were rendered cataleptic for 24 hours, only breathing and moving their eyes. A rhesus monkey, ordinarily quite unruly, was made serene, hence the trade name Sernyl® or Sernylan®. It was also noted that the therapeutic index was 10, whereas it is 2 for most anesthetics. Naturally, there was a great deal of enthusiasm for using Serynl® as an anesthetic for humans.

PCP was first studied in humans at Wayne State University's Department of Anesthesiology. In a study by Greifenstein and colleagues (1958), intravenous PCP was administered to seven volunteers at a dosage of 0.5 mg per kg. Larger doses caused agitation and seizures. All subjects had analgesia with 8 to 11 mg. At this dose no other anesthesia was needed. They all had amnesia afterward. In 12 patients, mild excitation during anesthesia was a side effect. In 5 patients, excitation reached near mania, though less so in 8 others. Despite this degree of behavioral toxicity, Greifenstein and his associates were optimistic about the use of Sernyl® in surgery.

One of the earliest reports of the adverse behavioral effects of PCP was by Meyer and associates (1959), who cited PCP as causing symptoms of sensory deprivation and other difficulties. Low doses of PCP gave rise to impaired sense of touch, pain, and proprioception. Higher doses produced ataxia, nystagmus, anxiety, depression, difficulty in thinking, delusions, and hallucinations. Meyer and his colleagues performed a study in which they gave intravenous PCP to 80 medically healthy persons and as an oral drug to 22 neurologic patients. Thirteen of the 80 normals experienced a psychotic state of confusion, unreality, anxiety, and so on, lasting one to four days. Patients who had had postencephalitic Parkinsonism did poorly. Many of them became withdrawn, but this effect was variable and some tremors improved. The pain improved in four cases of thalamic pain treated with oral PCP. There was no effect on rubral tremor or Huntington's disease. Meyer and his colleagues felt that the site of action of PCP was in the sensory cortex, brain stem, and thalamus.

Another early study of the psychological effects of PCP was performed by Luby and colleagues (1959), who were interested in drug-induced models of schizophrenia. They studied 18 subjects, 9 normals, and 9 psychiatric patients, including 5 with schizophrenia. They gave PCP intravenously at 0.5 mg/kg and measured psychological and physiological parameters. All of the subjects experienced body image changes, estrangement, thought disorders, and drowsiness. Two-thirds had negativism or hostility, and 78 percent of the normals but 22 percent of the patients felt inebriated. Neurologically, diminished pain, touch, and position sense occurred in all subjects. Some had nystagmus, diplopia, ataxia, and decreased auditory and visual accuity, and a few became nauseated. The schizophrenics' symptoms became worse, even up to one month later. It is now generally accepted that PCP psychosis is the best model for schizophrenia (Snyder 1980).

A number of compounds related to PCP were synthesized. There are five commonly sold analogues of PCP: PCE, N-ethyl-1-phenylcyclohexylamine; TCP, 1-(1-2-thienylcyclohexyl) piperidine; PHP, 1-(1-phenylcyclohexyl) pyrrolidine; PCC (1-piperidinocyclohexane) carbonitrile; and Ketamine, 2-(0-chlorophenyl)-2-methylamine cyclohexanone (Snyder 1980). Ketamine is shorter acting and less likely to produce seizures or delirium. Combined with diazepam for muscle relaxation, it is safe for humans and remains the only PCP derivative in use.

The use of PCP as a street drug began around 1967 (Fauman and Fauman 1980, Smith and Wesson 1980). Not surprisingly it made an appearance at a rock and roll concert in San Francisco as the "peace pill" (Smith and Wesson 1980). Toxic reactions numbered 25 to 30 and were similar to LSD intoxications, but with more physical manifestations and paranoia. The drug became known as "angel dust," and the illicit manufacturing of PCP proliferated over the next decade. Ironically, a drug with as much potential for toxicity as PCP has is quite simple for the amateur chemist to synthesize and usually has a high profit margin, as it is sold as any number of more expensive drugs. The most notable of these misrepresentations has been as THC (tetrahydrocannibinol), the euphoriant in marijuana. It has also been sold as amphetamine, cocaine, LSD, mescaline, peyote, and psilocybin (Lerner and Burns 1978).

Domino (1980) listed many street names for PCP including synthetic THC, angel dust, dust, hog, crystal, animal tranquilizer, horse tranquilizer, peace pill, crystal joint, CJ, KJ, sheet, rocket fuel, peace, peace weed, supergrass, superkools, superweed, elephant tranquilizer, horse tracks, seams, surfer, snorts, scuffle, Cadillac, mist, goon, ameba, cyclones, DOA (dead on arrival), killer weed, synthetic marijuana, lovely, and lovely high. Its appearance as a street drug is also variable, as it can be sold as a liquid, powder, or tablet and is frequently sprinkled on marijuana or parsley to be smoked (Petersen and Stillman 1978).

The use of PCP by teenagers in the 1970s became epidemic (Newmeyer 1980). Between 1976 and 1978, PCP use increased by 50 to 100 percent per year, especially among males aged 15 to 25, with a higher proportion of nonwhites and city dwellers. Some of the factors related to these statistics were summarized by Dogoloff (1980): (1) availability secondary to easy synthesis and low price, (2) potent effect with high abuse potential, (3) expanding use among heroin users as an opiate substitute, and (4) relatively light sentences for conviction for sale. Now the penalties for possession of PCP with intent to sell are severe, and piperidine itself is tightly controlled. As of 1978, PCP has no longer been manufactured or sold legally and is a Class II drug according to the Drug Enforcement Administration.

DIAGNOSIS

PCP found its way into the third *Diagnostic and Statistical Manual of Mental Disorders* (DSM-III) (1980) as a cause of organic mental disorders and substance abuse. The organic diagnoses include phencyclidine or similarly acting arylcyclohexylamine *intoxication* (305.90), *delirium* (292.81), and *mixed organic mental disorder* (292.90). The latter two are as specified for any organic condition, with PCP alone as the causative agent. The diagnostic criteria for PCP Intoxication can be summarized as (1) recent PCP use; (2) within an hour at least two of the following physical symptoms: nystagmus, increased pulse and blood pressure, numbness, ataxia, and dysarthria; (3) within an hour at least two of the following psychological symptoms: euphoria, psychomotor agitation, marked anxiety, emotional lability, grandiosity, sensation of slowed time, and synesthesias; and (4) maladaptive behavioral effects, e.g., belligerence, impulsivity, unpredictability, impaired judgment, and assaultiveness. The diagnosis of PCP abuse (305.9) is similar to that for other substance abuse disorders. The criteria include a pattern of pathological use and impairment of social or occupational functioning over a period of at least one month. There is no listing for PCP dependence, since withdrawal or tolerance has not been demonstrated for the drug. I shall describe its clinical signs and symptoms, course, treatment, and prognosis later in the chapter.

Improvements in laboratory methods for detection of PCP in blood and urine have made the diagnosis more easily verifiable. The kinetics of PCP are such that blood sampling should be done within several hours. Under conditions of urinary acidification, it is feasible to detect the drug in the urine after a longer period. PCP is lipophilic and is redistributed in the tissues, dropping serum levels. The laboratory method for analyzing bodily fluids described by Aniline and associates (1980) can detect concentrations of PCP to 5pg/ml. At this date general hospitals and commerical laboratories are equipped to assay for PCP. The timely collection of blood or urine will assist the therapist in the diagnostic process. For example, Yago and colleagues (1981) studied 145 consecutive psychiatric emergency visits and drew blood for PCP determination. Sixty-three (43.4 percent) were positive. Although the most common clinical signs were auditory hallucinations, sleep disturbances, paranoid delusions, hostility, and disorientation, a wide variety of psychiatric symptoms were found, including mania, depression, and schizophreniform disorders with relatively few other signs of intoxication. A similarly high yield from PCP blood levels was obtained by Aniline and associates (1980) in which 78.5 percent of 135 consecutive psychiatric admissions were positive. Although the effects of PCP are clearly dose related, it is debatable whether quantitative analyses are useful in an emergency setting (Walker et al. 1981). A positive screening test and a keen eye for the telltale signs of level of intoxication remain the surest way to proper treatment planning.

DIFFERENTIAL DIAGNOSIS

There are a number of diagnostic possibilities for the patient presenting with an acute organic brain syndrome suspected to be drug induced. Obviously, a confirmed history of PCP ingestion or a positive blood or urine assay will facilitate treatment planning. Anyone attempting to take a history for PCP should keep in mind the various forms in which PCP is found, its typical routes of administration, and time course. For example, a patient who is a moderate marijuana user with no adverse effects and who smokes some "supergrass," probably unwittingly, may present with a toxic psychosis. This patient should be provisionally diagnosed as a PCP case, and the usual precautions taken (see below). It would be overly optimistic to suggest that the classic signs of PCP intoxication are consistent enough to make the differential diagnosis a simple one. The patient with a psychotic, panicky, or violent presentation, who has nystagmus, elevated pulse and blood pressure, and analgesia, will be as clear-cut a case as will be found. As McCarron and colleagues (1981) pointed out, however, the "hallmark" signs may be absent in over 40 percent making history and laboratory findings indispensable.

The age concentration of PCP users is in the 15- to 25-year range. The list of medical causes of organic brain syndromes is shorter in this group, and drugs are always a top item in the differential. There are several types of drugs that must be considered, as their treatments for abuse vary. Di Sclafani and associates (1981) outlined the decision trees in the differential diagnosis of toxic psychosis. They listed the hallmark signs of PCP intoxication and noted that "minimal intervention," and not "talking down," is the recommended interpersonal treatment. If the patient shows a more sensorally florid picture with disortions, illusions, and visual hallucinations, the hallucinogenic drugs should be considered.

These are divided between those producing sympathetic excess (STP, mescaline, and nutmeg) and those without it (LSD and psilocybin). With these drugs, talking down is indicated. Intoxication with amphetamine or cocaine should be considered in patients who exhibit primarily schizophreniform signs, hypomania or stereotypy, and signs of sympathetic excess. When the patient presents with what Di Sclafani and associates call "undistinguished acute delirium," and signs of muscarinic blockade are present (dilated and sluggish pupils, blurred vision, flushed face, paralytic ileus, constipation, urinary retention, fever, and hyperpyrexia), they recommend a cholinergic challenge test with physostigmine. If the signs are reversed, physostigmine becomes the treatment (see also Castellani et al. 1982).

The signs and symptoms of acute PCP intoxication are so variable that a number of psychiatric diagnoses must be considered apart from drug intoxications. These include brief reactive psychosis, schizophreniform disorder, anxiety disorder with or without panic, conversion symptoms, and mania (Rosen 1979). One should also remember that many PCP users are polydrug abusers and that many have a preexisting psychiatric disorder. One of the more difficult differentials is between chronic PCP use and schizophrenia, since the age of onset, psychiatric symptoms, and course can be identical. This point is controversial, since it may be that the patient with prolonged PCP psychosis is in fact a schizophrenic, making the distinction academic. Treatment with antipsychotic drugs would be indicated in either case.

PHARMACOLOGY

Phencyclidine is a white, stable solid with a melting point of 234° to 236°C and is soluble in water (Domino 1964). Its effects have been extensively studied in a variety of species. It appears that mice and rats are excited by PCP, whereas pigeons, guinea pigs, hamsters, rabbits, cats, dogs, and monkeys are tranquilized. The effects are always dose related and follow a predictable pattern from analgesia to anesthesia, seizures, and death. Domino (1978, p. 20) reviewed the major properties of the arylcyclohexylamines:

1. Central nervous system
   A. Small doses produce a drunken state with numbness of the extremities.
   B. Moderate doses produce analgesia and anesthesia.

C. Psychological state resembles sensory isolation, except that sensory stimuli reach the neocortex and then are distorted.

D. Cataleptoid phenomena.

E. Large doses produce convulsions.

F. Marked species differences — primates are mostly depressed.

2. Autonomic nervous system and cardiovascular system
   A. Sympathomimetic.
   B. Tachycardia.
   C. Hypertension.
   D. Potentiation of catecholamines via cocaine-like action.

A great deal of research has addressed the neurochemical effects of PCP. It has been said to interact with the neurotransmitters epinephrine, norepinephrine, dopamine, serotonin, and acetylcholine in the brain and to be an uncoupler of oxidative phosphorylation in the energy mechanisms of the brain. Ary and Komiskey (1980) demonstrated that PCP reduced the accumulation of dopamine in synaptic vesicles in pig caudate. This effect is similar to that of amphetamine. The effect of PCP on the behavior and motor systems in the rat was studied by Garey and associates (1980). Behavioral and motor dysfunctions were antagonized by apomorphine and to a lesser extent by haloperidol. This suggests a presynaptic action on dopamine autoreceptors supporting apormorphine as a possible antidote for PCP poisoning (Garey et al. 1980). Similarly Meltzer and colleagues (1980) found that haloperidol antagonized PCP-induced behaviors in a dose-dependent manner, whereas atropine potentiated those behaviors. They felt that the action of PCP was similar to that of methylphenidate, i.e., an indirect dopamine agonist. Menon and colleagues (1980) noted that a number of drugs that are gamma-aminobutyric acid (GABA) agonists blocked PCP effects in mice. Although diazepam was not effective, baclofen, a GABA analogue, was. Hence, baclofen may be considered for use in toxic states. It appears that the effects of PCP as a schizophrenomimetic are consistent with the dopamine hypothesis of schizophrenia and similar in many ways to that of amphetamine, which also produces a schizophreniform psychosis. Dopaminergic mechanisms seem to predominate, and Snyder (1980) suggested that anticholinergic effects alone are too weak to be explanatory. A recent report, however, on the use of physostigmine to reverse PCP toxicity asserted that anticholinergic factors cannot be overlooked (Castellani et al. 1982). Indeed, for this reason, most sources recommend against using antipsychotic drugs with high anticholinergic potency. As will be apparent from our discussion of treatment, there is no "naloxone" for PCP, implying that a PCP overdose is still a potentially life-threatening situation.

There has been some controversy over whether PCP receptors exist in the brain. Meibach and associates (1979) measured PCP activity in rat brain via ^{14}C-labeled 2-deoxy-D-glucose. The major site of activity was the limbic system (hippocampus followed by the cingulum, thalamus, and substantia nigra). The binding studies of Zukin and Zukin (1980) corroborated by using receptor-binding assays the activity of PCP at hippocampal and other limbic areas. In a fascinating demonstration Altura and Altura (1980) performed an in vitro study of the effects of several hallucinogens on dog cerebral arteries. LSD, mescaline, and PCP, in descending order of potency, all produced spasms in concentrations consistent with psychotomimetic doses. They further demonstrated the existence of PCP receptors on the arteries, which were distinguishable from those for LSD or mescaline. The concentrations of PCP producing the most spasms were similar to those found at autopsy in PCP-related deaths in humans. Altura and Altura also found that a calcium antagonist, verapamil, reversed and/or prevented PCP-induced spasm, indicating a possible role for this drug in emergency treatment. The significance of PCP receptors in the brain remains mysterious. The question of tolerance and dependence with PCP in humans has not yet been resolved. Although there is a variable tolerance effect (Balster and Woolverton 1980), there is no well-documented withdrawal; hence PCP is not generally thought to produce physiological dependence.

CLINICAL PHARMACOLOGY

At least in the early stages of PCP intoxication, the mental state produced by the drug is schizophreniform, in contrast to that produced by LSD or mescaline. This is most evident in the relative absence of visual hallucinations with PCP and in the predominance of auditory hallucinations and paranoia. Its action also seems to be less dependent on the user's personality than other drugs are (Showalter and Thornton 1977). PCP users are also more likely to have an unpleasant experience, with unclear thinking, anxiety, and agitation. Showalter and Thornton (1977) reviewed the psychological and physiological effects of PCP in humans and found that a predictable sequence of events can be observed, depending on the dose. First are body-image changes. The limbs are felt to be changing in size and may feel as if they are floating away from the body. These are not formal hallucinations. Depersonalization and depression frequently accompany these bodily changes. Anxiety progressing to thought disorganization, as well as ataxia, tremulousness, parasthesias, and analgesia, may be present in some subjects at low dose, and others may experience euphoria similar to mild ethanol intoxication. In larger doses, negativism, hostility, anesthesia, and catalepsy may appear.

The stages of PCP toxicity, in terms of basic clinical signs were outlined by Gallant (1980). In the behavioral stage, produced by 1 to 5 mg of PCP, with serum levels of 10 to 70 ng/ml, the patient experiences one to eight hours of nystagmus, dysarthria, ataxia, anesthesia, drooling, bizarre vocalization, hypersalivation, nausea, and mild pulse and blood pressure elevations. In the stuporous stage, with 5 to 20 mg and blood levels of 70 to 200 ng/ml, the patient is still responsive but may be catatonic, with myoclonus and rigidity; analgesia to pain, touch, and proprioception; neck spasms; excessive secretions; fever; and elevated pulse and blood pressure. In the comatose stage, with more than 20 mg and more than 200 ng/ml in the blood, the patient is unresponsive to stimulation. The pupils are fixed and dilated, and the eyes are closed. There is an adrenergic crisis, and gag and corneal reflexes may be absent. This state may last from one to four days and can be fatal. In Gallant's experience, these syndromes are most frequently diagnosed as something other than PCP intoxication. McCarron and colleagues (1981) reviewed the clinical findings in 1,000 cases of PCP toxicity and found somewhat less than classic pictures of this syndrome. Nystagmus and hypertension, for example, were found in 57 percent, bizarre behavior in 29 percent, and agitation in 34 percent. Thirty-five percent were violent. All the other signs of "typical" PCP poisoning were found in lesser degrees.

Whereas psychological effects of PCP intoxication are the rule, prolonged psychosis following its use is much rarer. Erard and associates (1980) feel that such a state is unusual and is intertwined with schizophrenia in such a way as to make it difficult to determine whether the drug alone caused the psychosis or whether a schizophrenia-prone individual was chemically pushed into psychosis. They note that schizophrenics are more sensitive to PCP than to LSD or mescaline and that PCP is more likely to produce a formal thought disorder, social withdrawal, and autism. Some points of differentiation from schizophrenia are that in PCP intoxication there is a lack of a prodrome, a high incidence of violence, anxiety bordering on panic, and gross visual distortions.

There are many case reports of prolonged PCP psychosis. Most cases involve disorganization, bizarre psychiatric and neurologic signs, and a treatment course suggesting that antipsychotic drugs do little to alter the time course (Allen and Young 1978, Rainey and Crowder 1975). Aside from chronic psychosis, other symptoms associated with chronic PCP use include recent memory and speech impairment, with stuttering and dysarthria, anxiety, depression, and social and vocational withdrawal.

Smith and Wesson (1980) outlined four types of adverse psychiatric reactions to PCP: (1) acute PCP toxicity. The time frame here is minutes to hours. The symptoms are dose related and recalled by the 4 C's of combativeness, catatonia, convulsions, and coma. The first two occur at low doses, the third and fourth at higher doses. (2) PCP toxic psychosis. This condition carries the highest risk for prolonged psychosis in chronic users. Present are impaired judgment, hallucinations, delusions, paranoia, and agitation, and the patient may be destructive to self or others. The blood is negative but the urine positive for PCP (after acidification). (3) PCP-precipitated psychotic episode. A predisposed individual may become psychotic for one to four weeks or more. Urine and blood are usually negative. (4) PCP-induced depression. This state may follow a psychotic episode and can include a suicide attempt. The depression may be secondary to the perceived cerebral dysfunction. Tricyclic antidepressants are not usually helpful.

In addition to the typical cases, there are many gruesome tales of PCP-related mutilations and deaths. Chronic users seem to be at great risk for this. Fauman and Fauman (1979) interviewed 16 chronic polydrug abusers and found that 12 were violent to themselves or others and that 7 were the objects of violence. It is interesting to note that one of the most common causes of PCP-related deaths is provoked homicide. Grove (1979) reported a case of a man with PCP psychosis who had command hallucinations to bite his hands and proceeded to bite his forearms almost to the bone, seemingly without pain. He sought medical attention for pain only after infection had set in. Another common cause of PCP-related death is drowning, since the apparently pleasant sensation during immersion is followed by a loss of control (Noguchi and Nakamura 1978). Hypertension is another potentially lethal effect of PCP (Eastman and Cohen 1975), which has led to the recommendation of continuous blood pressure monitoring of intoxicated patients. Assorted other reports of PCP-related toxicity include rhabdomyolysis and renal failure (Barton et al. 1980) and birth defects in the infant of a PCP user (Golden et al. 1980).

TREATMENT

Recognition that a patient has PCP intoxication, especially in an emergency setting, should set in motion a set of medical and psychiatric measures designed to limit both physiologic morbidity and harm to the patient and others. As mentioned, the effects of PCP are dose related, although fluctuations in level of toxicity can occur with recirculation of the drug and corresponding blood levels. Since analysis of blood takes time, the physician's reaction must be swift and based on clinical signs. A rule suggested by Rappolt and colleagues (1979) is that the patient should be treated for the deepest level of anesthesia as indicated by any one sign. They outlined treatment strategies based on three stages of intoxication, roughly equivalent to Gallant's, described above.

In stage 1 intoxication, the patient has smoked or snorted 2 to 5 mg of PCP to achieve a blood level of 25 to 90 ng/ml. Except for intentional overdoses, most patients will be in stage 1. They rarely reach coma, since they are too incapacitated to take more. Clinical signs are comparable to those of Gallant's behavioral stage. In working up the patient, try to obtain a history for the possibility of an overdose, to determine if the patient may be progressing to deeper stages. The treatment approach is a conservative one. Vital signs should be monitored continuously, but instrumentation such as nasogastic suction or endotracheal intubation should be avoided. External stimulation should be reduced, and gentle interpersonal contact can be made. Medical treatment consists of alkalinization of the urine with ascorbic acid 0.5 to 1.5 mg orally (this can increase excretion 100-fold) and symptomatic treatment of anxiety and sympathetic signs with diazepam (10 to 30 mg) and propranolol (40 to 80 mg), respectively. The use of antipsychotic drugs in these patients is controversial, since they apparently do little to alter the course of intoxication. Phenothiazines, especially with anticholinergic properties, must be avoided, and haloperidol has been recommended when unavoidable for behavioral management (Di Sclafani et al. 1981).

In stage 2, the patient has ingested or inhaled 5 to 25 mg of PCP with a serum level of 90 to 300 ng/ml. These patients will be unable to communicate and may be comatose but can be recognized by their response to pain. The general measures in stage 1 apply, including now an intravenous infusion through which drugs will be administered. The key elements in the treatment are support of vital signs, prevention of hyperthermia, alkalinization of the urine, and diuresis. Drug treatment consists of diazepam 5 to 15 mg in 2.5 mg increments, ascorbic acid 0.5 to

1.5 gm over five to ten minutes, furosemide 40 mg, and propanolol 1 mg every one to five minutes up to 10 mg, all intravenously. Instrumentation such as deep suctioning and urinary catheterization may be necessary. The patient should revert to stage 1 in an hour or two, and if not, hospitalization is indicated.

Stage 3 intoxication, with a dose of 25 mg or more and serum levels upwards of 300 ng/ml, is commonly associated with a suicide attempt. These patients are comatose and not responsive to deep pain. All initial efforts are aimed at maintaining vital signs. One sees tachypnea, tachycardia, hypertension, hyperpyrexia, seizures or myoclonus, and dilated pupils, or some combination of these. Gastric suction is recommended because of the recovery of large amounts of PCP in the stomach due to ion trapping (Done et al. 1980). Activated charcoal is instilled via nasogastric tube to hasten gastrointestinal transit. Aggressive pulmonary drainage may be necessary, as may be diazoxide 300 mg for hypertensive crisis. Urine pH should be maintained at 5.0 to 5.5 by ascorbic acid (other therapists have used ammonium chloride).

Rappolt and colleagues also noted that there are emergence phenomena that need to be identified during treatment. For example, a patient emerging from stage 2 may become violent. They identify two syndromes of emergence, an anxiety-depression-confusional state and a dopaminergic storm. The first is treated with diazepam and/or haloperidol for a week. The second, potentially life threatening, is marked by hypertension, hyperthermia, or psychosis and can be treated with propranolol 40 mg t.i.d. for a week.

Another treatment consideration is what to do with polydrug abusers who seem to crave PCP. Bolter (1980) claims that these patients are unlike the typical addict in that they are younger and less mature and do not tolerate confrontation. Hence Synanon-type programs are not successful. Bolter feels that PCP abusers should be treated like persons with learning disabilities who have poor concentration and lack interpersonal skills and suggests the following for inpatient treatment: (1) set firm rules, (2) require minimum decision making, (3) tolerate inattention and repeat things, (4) give patient a short list of tasks and a regular routine, (5) avoid stressful situations, and (6) set realistic positive and negative consequences and be consistent.

It would not be realistic to discuss the social or psychological rehabilitation of the PCP abuser as if the disorder were found in pure form. Most likely, the chronic PCP abuser is a troubled adolescent with a basic psychiatric disorder such as depression, with polydrug abuse and a variety of encounters with the criminal justice system (De Angelis and Goldstein

1978). Unless the underlying condition warrants it, there is little need for psychotropic drugs. There is a report of several patients whose PCP craving was reduced by desipramine (Tennant et al. 1981). Further subtyping of PCP abusers by response to psychotropics merits further consideration.

CONCLUSIONS

Phencyclidine began as an anesthetic with great promise. Its psychotomimetic properties were recognized early, but the drug emerged on the street at a time of tremendous polydrug experimentation. Far from being "angel dust" or the "peace pill," PCP conveyed many of its users not into the psychedelic fantasy world but into a state resembling schizophrenia and a host of medical complications. Fortunately, such effects have occurred in a minority of users. Many "recreational" users shun PCP because of initial negative reactions, whereas chronic "dusters" probably self-medicate with whatever is available.

This chapter, having focused on a diagnosis and not on a sociologic phenomenon, has by necessity underscored the morbidity associated with PCP. Although there is little to say in defense of PCP use, the sense of panic or hopelessness by professionals, parents, journalists, and bureaucrats seems unjustified. Ungerleider (1980) put this into perspective:

Our nation continues to declare war on drug abuse and authorities repeatedly pronounce that we are turning the corner on the drug abuse problem. Yet turning the corner repeatedly is but going in circles. Indeed, we feature a "drug of the month" philosophy; the concern moved from heroin to LSD, then it was methadone, then methaqualone (Quaalude®), then parquat-laced marijuana and the propxyphene (Darvon®). Now it is PCP, and already there are rumblings of the future wave of hysteria, with coca-paste smoking and diazepam (Valium®) abuse as our drug worries for the coming season. (p. 193)

By this time, the epidemic of PCP-related morbidity has declined. Already the concern over teenage alcohol abuse has all but eclipsed it. Clearly, mental health professionals are always in a catch-up situation, as there is little in the way of effective prevention. Educational scare tactics may keep some youths from going astray, but the psychodynamic and sociologic forces in drug abuse will continue unchecked until a means of identifying dysfunctional persons is discovered. Until that time it behooves therapists to become familiar with the range of behavioral disturbances associated with drugs such as PCP, so that secondary preventive measures can be applied in a timely manner.

REFERENCES

Allen, R. M., and Young, S. J. (1978). Phencyclidine-induced psychosis. *American Journal of Psychiatry* 135:1081-1083.

Altura, B. T., and Altura, B. M. (1980). Phencyclidine, lysergic acid diethylamide, and mescaline: cerebral artery spasms and hallucinogenic activity. *Science* 212:1051-1052.

American Psychiatric Association (1980). *Diagnostic and Statistical Manual of Mental Disorders*. 3rd ed. Washington, D.C.: American Psychiatric Association.

Aniline, O., Allen, R. E., Pitts, F. N., Yago, L. S., and Pitts, A. F. (1980). The urban epidemic of phencyclidine use: laboratory evidence from a public psychiatric hospital inpatient service. *Biological Psychiatry* 15:813-817.

Ary, T. E., and Komiskey, H. L. (1980). Phencyclidine: effect on the accumulation of ^{3}H-dopamine in synaptic vesicles. *Life Sciences* 26:575-578.

Balster, R. L., and Woolverton, W. L. (1980). Tolerance and dependence to phencyclidine. *Psychopharmacology Bulletin* 16:76-77.

Barton, C. H., Sterling, M. L., and Vaziri, N. D. (1980). Rhabdomyolysis and acute renal failure associated with phencyclidine intoxication. *Archives of Internal Medicine* 140:568-569.

Bolter, A. (1980). Issues for inpatient treatment of chronic PCP abuse. *Journal of Psychedelic Drugs* 12:287-288.

Castellani, S., Adams, P. M., and Giannini, A. J. (1982). Physostigmine treatment of acute phencyclidine intoxication. *Journal of Clinical Psychiatry* 43:10-11.

De Angelis, G. G., and Goldstein, E. (1978). Long term treatment of adolescent PCP abusers. In *Phencyclidine (PCP) Abuse: An Appraisal*, ed. R. C. Petersen and R. C. Stillman, pp. 254-271. National Institute on Drug Abuse Research Monograph 21. Rockville, Md.: National Institute on Drug Abuse.

Di Sclafani, A., Hall, R. C. W., and Gardner, E. R. (1981). Drug-induced psychosis: emergency diagnosis and management. *Psychosomatics* 22:845-855.

Dogoloff, L. I. (1980). Federal response to the PCP problem, 1979. *Journal of Psychedelic Drugs* 12:185–190.

Domino, E. F. (1964). Neurobiology of phencyclidine (Sernyl), a drug with an unusual spectrum of pharmacological activity. *International Review of Neurobiology* 6:303–347.

———. (1978). Neurobiology of phencyclidine—an update. In *Phencyclidine (PCP) Abuse: An Appraisal,* ed. R. C. Petersen and R. C. Stillman, pp. 18–43. National Institute on Drug Abuse Research Monograph 21. Rockville, Md.: National Institute on Drug Abuse.

———. (1980). History and pharmacology of PCP and PCP-related analogs. *Journal of Psychedelic Drugs* 12:223–227.

Done, A. K., Aronow, R., and Miceli, J. N. (1980). Pharmacokinetic bases for the diagnosis and treatment of acute PCP intoxication. *Journal of Psychedelic Drugs* 12:253–258.

Eastman, J. W., and Cohen, S. N. (1975). Hypertensive crisis associated with phencyclidine poisoning. *Journal of the American Medical Association* 231:1270–1271.

Erard, R., Luisada, P. V., and Peele, R. (1980). The PCP psychosis: prolonged intoxication or drug-precipitated functional illness? *Journal of Psychedelic Drugs* 12:235–251.

Fauman, M. A., and Fauman, B. J. (1979). Violence associated with phencyclidine abuse. *American Journal of Psychiatry* 136:1584–1586.

———. (1980). Chronic phencyclidine (PCP) abuse: a psychiatric perspective. Part I: general aspects and violence. *Psychopharmacology Bulletin* 16:70–71.

Gallant, D. M. (1980). Clinical and laboratory diagnostic problems with phencyclidine (PCP) toxicity. *Psychopharmacology Bulletin* 16:81–83.

Garey, R. E., McQuitty, S., Tootle, D., and Heath, R. G. (1980). The effects of apomorphine and Haldol on PCP-induced behavioral and motor abnormalities in the rat. *Life Sciences* 26:277–284.

Golden, N. L., Sokol, R. J., and Rubin, I. L. (1980). Angel dust: possible effects on the fetus. *Pediatrics* 65:18–20.

Greifenstein, F. E., De Vault, M., Yoshitake, J., and Gajewski, J. E. (1958). A study of a 1-aryl cyclo hexyl amine for anesthesia. *Anesthesia and Analgesia* 37:283–294.

Grove, V. E. (1979). Painless self-injury after ingestion of "angel dust." *Journal of the American Medical Association* 242:655.

Lerner, S. E., and Burns, R. S. (1978). Phencyclidine use among youth: history, epidemiology, and acute and chronic intoxication. In *Phencyclidine (PCP) Abuse: An Appraisal,* ed. R. C. Petersen and R. C.

Stillman, pp. 66–118. National Institute on Drug Abuse Research Monograph 21. Rockville, Md.: National Institute on Drug Abuse.

Luby, E. D., Cohen, B. D., Rosenbaum, G., Gottlieb, J. S., and Kelley, R. (1959). Study of a new schizophrenomimetic drug—Sernyl. *Archives of Neurology and Psychiatry* 81:363–369.

McCarron, M. M., Schulze, B. W., Thompson, G. A., Conder, M. C., and Goetz, W. A. (1981). Acute phencyclidine intoxication: incidence of clinical findings in 1,000 cases. *Annals of Emergency Medicine* 10:237–242.

Maddox, V. H. (1980). The discovery of phencyclidine. *Psychopharmacology Bulletin* 16:53–54.

Meibach, R. C., Glick, S. D., Cox, R., and Maayani, S. (1979). Localisation of phencyclidine-induced changes in brain energy metabolism. *Nature* 282:625–626.

Meltzer, H. Y., Sturgeon, R. D., Simonovic, M., and Fessler, R. G. (1980). Phencyclidine as an indirect dopamine agonist. *Psychopharmacology Bulletin* 16:62–65.

Menon, M. K., Clark, W. G., and Vivonia, C. (1980). Interaction between phencyclidine (PCP) and gaba-ergic drugs: clinical implications. *Pharmacology, Biochemistry and Behavior* 12:113–117.

Meyer, J. S., Greifenstein, F., and De Vault, M. (1959). A new drug causing symptoms of sensory deprivation. *Journal of Nervous and Mental Disease* 129:54–61.

Newmeyer, J. A. (1980). The epidemiology of PCP use in the late 1970s. *Journal of Psychedelic Drugs* 12:211–215.

Noguchi, T. T., and Nakamura, G. R. (1978). Phencyclidine-related deaths in Los Angeles county, 1976. *Journal of Forensic Science* 23:503–507.

Petersen, R. C., and Stillman, R. C. (1978). Phencyclidine: an overview. In *Phencyclidine (PCP) Abuse: An Appraisal*, ed. R. C. Petersen and R. C. Stillman, pp. 1–17. National Institute on Drug Abuse Research Monograph 21. Rockville, Md.: National Institute on Drug Abuse.

Rainey, J. M., and Crowder, M. K. (1975). Prolonged psychosis attributed to phencyclidine: report of three cases. *American Journal of Psychiatry* 132:1076–1078.

Rappolt, R. T., Gay, G. R., and Farris, R. D. (1979). Emergency management of acute phencyclidine intoxication. *Journal of the American College of Emergency Physicians* 8:68–76.

Rosen, A. (1979). Case report: symptomatic mania and phencyclidine abuse. *American Journal of Psychiatry* 136:118–119.

Showalter, G. V., and Thornton, W. E. (1977). Clinical pharmacology of phencyclidine toxicity. *American Journal of Psychiatry* 134:1234–1238.

Smith, D. E., and Wesson, D. R. (1980). PCP abuse: diagnostic and psychopharmacological treatment approaches. *Journal of Psychedelic Drugs* 12:293–299.

Snyder, S. H. (1980). Phencyclidine. *Nature* 285:355–356.

Tennant, F. S., Rawson, R. A., and McCann, M. (1981). Withdrawal from chronic PCP dependence with desipramine. *American Journal of Psychiatry* 138:845–847.

Ungerleider, J. T. (1980). PCP—a rational perspective. *Journal of Psychedelic Drugs* 12:191–194.

Walker, S. Yesavage, J. A., and Tinklenberg, J. R. (1981). Acute phencyclidine (PCP) intoxication: quantitative urine levels and clinical management. *American Journal of Psychiatry* 138:674–675.

Yago, K. B., Pitts, F. N., Burgoyne, R. W., Aniline, O., Yago, L. S., and Pitts, A. F. (1981). The urban epidemic of phencyclidine (PCP) use: clinical and laboratory evidence from a public psychiatric hospital emergency service. *Journal of Clinical Psychiatry* 42:193–196.

Zukin, S. R., and Zukin, S. (1980). [^{3}H]-phencyclidine binding to specific brain receptor sites. *Psychopharmacology Bulletin* 16:59–62.

CHAPTER 8

Benzodiazepine Withdrawal Syndrome

HANNES PETURSSON, M.D.
MALCOLM LADER, M.D.

The introduction into clinical practice of the benzodiazepine class of drugs, 20 years ago, marked the start of a new era in the treatment of anxiety. Being much safer and more effective than any previous anxiolytics, the benzodiazepines grew popular rapidly until they became among the most widely used of all drugs. This worldwide usage has actually diminished somewhat in the last few years, but health authorities and government agencies have expressed increasing concern about possible dependence and the potential incidence of withdrawal reactions. These qualms are fully justified. First, every previous antianxiety/sedative drug has sooner or later been found to induce dependence with a characteristic withdrawal syndrome, often preceded by the development of tolerance. Second, even though the literature up to now has generally showed little concern about the problem, recent investigations have suggested that the incidence of benzodiazepine withdrawal reactions is much greater than hitherto suspected. The history of drugs confirms that this is entirely consistent with the typical life cycle of sedative medicines. After introduction as major innovations, or after at least vast improvements on existing therapies, many years or even decades may elapse before these medicines' dependence liability is fully appreciated.

In this chapter we shall discuss the problem of benzodiazepine dependence, in particular the benzodiazepine withdrawal syndrome. It has become apparent that some of the current models of drug dependence are inappropriate to the study of benzodiazepine dependence. For example, the development of tolerance with dosage escalation and increased drug consumption is regarded as crucial to theories of drug dependence and withdrawal, and yet most patients who experience benzodiazepine withdrawal reactions have managed to stay within the therapeutically recommended dosage. Nevertheless, it is essential to examine this problem in the context of the currently accepted definitions of drug abuse and dependence (WHO 1974, p. 14):

[Drug dependence] a state, psychic and sometimes also physical, resulting from the interaction between a living organism and a drug, characterized by behavioural and other responses that always include a compulsion to take the drug on a continuous or a periodic basis in order to experience its psychic effects and sometimes to avoid the discomfort of its absence.

[Psychic dependence] a condition in which a drug produces a feeling of satisfaction and a psychic drive that require periodic or continuous administration of the drug to produce pleasure or to avoid discomfort.

[Physical dependence] an adaptive state that manifests itself by intense physical disturbances when the administration of the drug is suspended.

Drug abuse is persistent or sporadic excessive drug use inconsistent with or unrelated to medical practice. This description contains a value judgment and almost a moral pronouncement on the degree and type of drug use. For these reasons, it is simpler to confine medical terms to physical and psychic dependence and then to set the medical problem into the wider social context of drug abuse. For practical purposes, the prescriber should know (1) how assiduously the patient seeks the drug in question, (2) whether tolerance has developed as evidenced by escalation of dosage, and (3) whether a definable withdrawal syndrome supervenes when the drug is stopped.

Tolerance is of two major types, either or both of which may coexist with psychic or physical dependence. *Pharmacokinetic* or *metabolic tolerance* denotes the effect of prolonged drug exposure on its own pharmacokinetic properties, usually an increased rate of drug clearance. *Receptor-site tolerance,* on the other hand, implies adaptation and refers to the effect that the duration of the receptor's exposure to the drug may have on the physiological and clinical manifestations of the drug-receptor interaction.

Withdrawal syndrome occurs in drug-dependent people when the drug is withheld. It usually has both physical and psychological manifestations, which vary according to the drug on which dependence exists, length of usage, patient's previous personality, patient's expectations, and the like.

HISTORICAL ASPECTS

Psychotropic substances have been known and used for recreational and therapeutic purposes for thousands of years. In the 19th century, bromides were introduced as anticonvulsants and sedatives and were widely used. Their limited effectiveness, cumulative toxicity, and potential for abuse became apparent by the 1930s. Anesthetics, such as ether and chloroform, and sedatives, such as chloral hydrate and paraldehyde, were also developed in the 19th century. Chloral hydrate in more acceptable solid formulations still has some therapeutic usefulness, but paraldehyde is unpleasant to take, liable to be abused, and may induce psychotic states.

The last of the important sedatives discovered in the 19th century were the barbiturates. Many different compounds were introduced: ultrashort acting (e.g., anesthetic induction agents such as thiopental), short acting (e.g., secobarbital), medium acting (e.g., butobarbital), and long acting (e.g., phenobarbital). As with the bromides, over 50 years elapsed before the disadvantages of the barbiturates became fully appreciated. Such side effects as drowsiness, tolerance to therapeutic effects, dangers when taken in overdose, and physical and psychological dependence with consequent dangerous withdrawal syndromes led to a growing dissatisfaction with these drugs (DTB 1980).

Meprobamate was developed from mephenesin, a muscle relaxant, and was introduced as the first of the modern tranquilizers (Berger 1963). Unfortunately, its advantages over the barbiturates proved illusory. It was still dangerous in overdosage and likely to be associated with dependence. It is still used as a sedative and a muscle relaxant and finds its widest application in combination with an analgesic in the management of painful muscle and joint injuries. Tybamate is similar to meprobamate but is short acting, and its dependence-liability is believed to be low. Other nonbarbiturate hypnotics and sedatives were developed, including glutethimide, methylprylon, and ethchlorvynol. The eager acceptance of these drugs reflected growing dissatisfaction with the barbiturates, but these barbiturate substitutes also proved disappointing.

THE BENZODIAZEPINES

As with so many other psychotropic substances, the discovery of the benzodiazepines' tranquilizing effects was accidental (Ayd and Blackwell 1970). Appreciation of their unique properties led to the introduction of chlordiazepoxide in 1960 and diazepam three years later. Since then, well over a thousand benzodiazepines and related compounds have been synthesized, and nearly 30 different variants have been marketed in various parts of the world. The differences among the benzodiazepines are insubstantial and pertain mainly to their various pharmacokinetic properties.

Over the last two decades, the benzodiazepines have ousted their predecessors, the barbiturates, and have become among the most widely used of all prescribed drugs. Ayd and Blackwell (1970) estimated that during this time, about 500 million people have taken a benzodiazepine. Several surveys in different countries have suggested that about one in ten adult males and one in five adult females take tranquilizers or hypnotics, mainly benzodiazepines, at some time during each year. Of these people, between half and two-thirds take tranquilizers for at least a month at a time, and perhaps 2 percent of the adult population do so chronically throughout the year (Balter et al. 1974, Lader 1978). Diazepam is the most commonly used benzodiazepine and until recently accounted for about 4 percent of all prescriptions in the United Kingdom (Skegg et al. 1977). Finally, the benzodiazepines are the most common repeat prescriptions.

This extensive use of the benzodiazepines can be attributed both to their efficacy as anxiolytics, hypnotics, muscle relaxants, and anticonvulsants and to their high level of safety. More importantly, perhaps, the benzodiazepines have generally been regarded as having a low dependence–inducing potential, and this has encouraged further complacency regarding their widespread and chronic use. The relative scarcity of published evidence of clinical dependence and the low activity of benzodiazepines in animal models of dependence have been emphasized. Furthermore, most theories of drug dependence and withdrawal assume the onset of some form of tolerance that is easily detectable through an escalation of dosage and obvious signs of drug-seeking behavior. Most benzodiazepine-treated patients, however, remain within the therapeutically recommended dosage. Excessive doses when they do occur may be primarily a problem in those who also abuse other drugs and alcohol.

The peak of reporting of possible benzodiazepine dependence was between 1969 and 1973, that is, about ten years after their introduction. With the exception of the last two years, the numbers reported since then have been few. Although several hundred papers have documented cases of benzodiazepine dependence, the number of such reports is inconsequential compared with the wide and chronic usage of these drugs. The literature has been comprehensively reviewed by Marks (1978), Greenblatt and Shader (1978), Palmer (1978), Jepsen and Haastrup (1979), and Petursson and Lader (1981a). Marks (1978) reported that only 118 of these numerous publications contained fully verified cases of physical dependence with a definite withdrawal syndrome or carefully documented cases of psychological dependence.

It is difficult to reconcile these reviews with the more recent reports that claim that a substantial proportion of patients taking benzodiazepines do develop some form of dependence (Kemper et al. 1980, Petursson and Lader 1981b, Rickels 1981, Tyrer et al. 1981). The contradictions and opposing views expressed in the literature suggests that the problem of benzodiazepine dependence either is rare or is rarely recognized. One reason that signs of benzodiazepine dependence may be overlooked or misdiagnosed is because unlike withdrawal from opiates or alcohol, anxiety is the cardinal symptom of the benzodiazepine withdrawal syndrome. Furthermore, the temporal relationships of the respective syndromes are quite different because of pharmacokinetic differences. Also, the wide licit availability of the drugs renders superfluous any need for marked drug-seeking behavior. Nevertheless, published reports cannot be relied on as accurate or even approximate estimates, since many cases will not be reported. Furthermore, the best evidence for dependence-inducing properties is obtained by careful observation of withdrawal symptoms, and many patients may be reluctant to have their medication withdrawn because of previous unpleasant experiences when attempting themselves to lower the dose. This was apparent in Tyrer and associates' 1981 study in which only 40 out of 86 patients consented to withdrawal.

Some current models of drug dependence, withdrawal, and tolerance may be inappropriate for the study of benzodiazepine dependence. The multifactorial issue of benzodiazepine tolerance remains controversial. It is well known clinically and experimentally that tolerance to some of the effects of benzodiazepines can develop within 24 hours. Patients usually report that the initial sedation and drowsiness wear off after a week or so. It remains unclear whether tolerance to the anxiolytic effects also develops or whether patients continue to derive the same therapeutic benefits for many months or years. No doubt differences in personality also are important, in that only few long-term benzodiazepine-treated patients are likely to have "abuse-prone personalities." Most patients, therefore, are likely to comply with medical advice to stay within the prescribed dosage even if they become tolerant to the drugs' pharmacological effects.

BENZODIAZEPINE WITHDRAWAL SYNDROME

The fully developed benzodiazepine withdrawal syndrome includes severe sleep disturbance, irritability, increased tension and anxiety, panic attacks, hand tremor, profuse sweating, difficulty in concentration, dry retching and nausea, weight loss, palpitations, and muscular pains and stiffness. Instances are also reported of more serious developments such as seizures (Acuda and Muhangi 1979, Barten 1965, Bismuth et al. 1980, De Bard 1979, de la Fuente et al. 1980, Einarsson 1980, Fruensgaard 1976, Hollister et al. 1961, Howe 1980, Kemper et al. 1980, Khan et al. 1980, Le Bellec et al. 1980, Nerenz 1974, Rifkin et al. 1976, Vyas and Carney 1975), psychotic reactions (Allgulander and Borg 1978, Barten 1965, Bismuth et al. 1980, Darcy 1972, De Bard 1979, Dysken and Carlyle 1977, Floyd and Murphy 1976, Fruensgaard 1976, Fruensgaard and Vaag 1975, Haslerud and Heskestad 1981, Hollister et al. 1961, Kemper et al. 1980, Preskorn and Denner 1977), and even death (Relkin 1966).

During the last two years we have withdrawn 40 patients from long-term, therapeutic-dose benzodiazepine treatment and have recently reported our findings of withdrawal symptoms in the first 16 patients (Petursson and Lader 1981b). Their psychiatric diagnoses have been anxiety neurosis, or depression or personality disorder with anxiety, and none have been alcoholic or has abused other drugs. They all received benzodiazepines in therapeutic doses, i.e., within the manufacturer's recommended dose range, for at least 1 year (range: 1 to 20 years).

The withdrawal was gradual, double-blind, and placebo controlled. The patients were randomly allocated to two groups (A and B). Both groups continued with their drugs, full dose, for the first two weeks. Group A was then reduced to a half-dose for another 2 weeks before the medication was discontinued. Group B received the full dose of their medication for the first four weeks but were then withdrawn in the same manner as Group A was, i.e., two weeks later. During these phases, a placebo was substituted for the active drugs, and after withdrawal of the drugs, both groups continued on the placebo only for four and two weeks, respectively, followed by two weeks without any tablets or capsules. During the study period, which lasted ten weeks, patients were assessed at regular intervals of three, four, or seven days on a battery of clinical, physiological, and psychological variables.

All our patients, so far, have experienced some discernible withdrawal reactions, which were most pronounced three to seven days after finally stopping the medication. Anxiety rose sharply during the withdrawal, and to incipient panic in several patients, but usually subsided to pre-withdrawal levels over the next two to four weeks. Patients commonly experienced bodily symptoms of anxiety, such as a choking feeling, dry mouth, hot and cold feelings, legs like jelly, and so forth. Several became irritable, and a few complained of unpleasant feelings of depersonalization and derealization. All experienced significant sleep disturbance, sleeping only two to three hours per night during the first three to four days of drug withdrawal, but most returned to normal sleep patterns eight to ten days after discontinuation. Some experienced hand tremor and profuse perspiration; others had bad headaches and generalized aches and pains. More than half the patients lost their appetite and suffered from nausea, and a few reported vomiting in the mornings. Clinical depression was detected in some patients, but this was neither severe nor prolonged.

More importantly, as many as two-thirds of the individuals experienced mild to moderate perceptual disturbances. Some complained of intolerance to loud noises and bright lights, as well as numbness, paresthesia, unsteadiness, and a feeling of motion. Some patients complained of strange smells and a metallic taste; some chronic heavy smokers even had to give up their cigarettes temporarily. Fortunately, none of our patients developed withdrawal fits, except one patient who had previously attempted to withdraw abruptly. Two of our patients have experienced mild psychotic episodes of the paranoid type, and one described visual hallucinations.

Anxiety ratings rose as the drugs were discontinued but usually subsided to prewithdrawal levels over the next two to four weeks. This in itself suggests that the symptoms represent a true withdrawal syndrome and not a revival of the original anxiety symptoms. Furthermore, some of the symptoms were untypical of anxiety. The dysphoria was an amalgam of anxiety, depression, malaise, and depersonalization, and perceptual changes were common. Certain other symptoms, such as lack of coordination and unsteadiness, are not characteristic of anxiety. The dependence may have been psychological, although the placebo substitution makes this unlikely. Further support for a physical dependence is the fact that many patients had previously attempted to stop their medication and that their withdrawal symptoms were each time alleviated by reinstating the drug.

PATHOPHYSIOLOGY

Most theories of physical drug dependence postulate some form of central nervous system (CNS) counteradaptation to the actions of the drug of dependence. The withdrawal symptoms are, therefore, seen as rebound effects (rebound hyperexcitability) in the same physiological systems that were initially modified by the drug. Most of these theories assume that physical dependence is generally accompanied by tolerance and that the two phenomena wax and wane at about the same rate.

The benzodiazepines act primarily on subcortical structures such as the amygdala and hippocampus of the limbic system. Biochemical data indicate that inter alia the benzodiazepines indirectly potentiate and prolong the synaptic actions of GABA, an inhibitory neurotransmitter. The potent anticonvulsant effect of benzodiazepines is possibly due to their effect on GABA-ergic mechanisms. Furthermore, the benzodiazepines lower the turnover of both brain NA and 5-HT, perhaps through a primary action on GABA mechanisms. Tolerance tends to develop to the initial sedative effects of the benzodiazepines, perhaps mediated via an effect on NA mechanisms. The rebound phase, seen when animals are withdrawn from long-term benzodiazepine administration, consists of an enhanced release and decreased uptake of NA, DA, and 5-HT (Rastogi et al. 1978).

In humans, the neurochemical and physiological mechanisms underlying benzodiazepine withdrawal symptoms remain largely unknown. In our withdrawal studies the main physiological changes were marked reduction in EEG fast-wave activity (13.5 to 26.0 Hz) as the tranquilizers were withdrawn. This drug-related effect is the reverse of the increase normally seen following the administration of benzodiazepines. We also observed that auditory-evoked responses to auditory clicks increase over the same time, from very small prewithdrawal values to normal values. These effects may reflect psychological variables such as attention and arousal and could be regarded as objective indicators of the hypersensitivity reported by many patients.

Brown and colleagues (1978) reported a positive correlation between withdrawal symptoms and raised serum levels of growth hormone (GH) and cortisol. Our measures of 24-hour urinary excretion of MHPG, the noradrenaline metabolite, suggest that long-term benzodiazepine treatment is associated with reduced noradrenaline turnover, which reverts to normal following drug withdrawal (unpublished observation). But we have been unable to demonstrate an excessive "rebound" excretion of this metabolite during the withdrawal syndrome. These findings are interesting in view of the perceptual hypersensitivity experienced by our patients as well as their increased auditory-evoked responses. Animal studies so far suggest that changes in benzodiazepine receptors are insufficient to explain the development of tolerance and dependence following chronic treatment (Braestrup et al. 1979, Braestrup and Nielsen 1980, Möhler et al. 1978).

WITHDRAWAL AND TREATMENT

Although the extent of normal-dosage dependence remains unknown, the condition should be suspected when patients repeatedly try to wean themselves from their medication and restart the drug because of dysphoria, headache, perceptual hypersensitivity, or other symptoms unrelated to the initial anxiety syndrome. The same applies to any signs of active drug-seeking behavior, e.g., hoarding, future planning to ensure uninterrupted supply of benzodiazepines, registration with more than one doctor, importunate pleading, querulous whining, or threats in response to attempts to stop or curtail the prescriptions. Although less common, any signs of the development of tolerance and/or increase in dosage should alert the therapist to the possibility of dependence. Because of the unpredictable course of conditions such as anxiety, a trial of withdrawal is often justified in cases of prolonged benzodiazepine use, even in the absence of any signs of potential dependence.

Withdrawal can usually be carried out on an outpatient basis, but sometimes admission to hospital is indicated. Obviously, patients in the high-dose/long-term category or those who have previously experienced severe withdrawal reactions, such as psychosis or seizures, should be hospitalized for safe and successful withdrawal. Other factors to be considered are the patient's tolerance for subjective distress and methods of coping with this, e.g., self-medication with sedatives or misuse of alcohol. Adequate social support is important, and compliance is also affected by the therapist's attributes, whether he or she gains the cooperation of the patient and family, explains the possibility of withdrawal effects, and so on.

In our experience, outpatient withdrawal is safe in the majority of normal-dose patients, even in cases of prolonged treatment, although frequent medical supervision is required. Gradual reduction in dosage can usually be effected over a period of four weeks. Withdrawal symptoms may be related to the rate at which circulating benzodiazepines and their active metabolites are excreted and metabolized. Tyrer and associates (1981) suggested that if the drugs are reduced very gradually, the withdrawal symptoms may even be obviated. Hence, it may be beneficial to use a benzodiazepine with a long plasma half-life for effecting withdrawal in order to achieve a smoother fall in the bodily levels.

Assuming that some withdrawal symptoms may result from "neuro-chemical rebound," it is now essential to search for a nonbenzodiazepine tranquilizer that can be safely substituted during the withdrawal and that will not be cross-tolerant to the benzodiazepines. We have attempted to reduce the severity of the syndrome with oxypertine (Integrin®), a relatively specific catecholamine-depleting agent in low doses. Preliminary findings in a few patients given oxypertine 20 to 40 mg/day for four weeks, starting two weeks before the withdrawal, show that the drug may be useful during the withdrawal. No difficulties have been encountered in stopping it two weeks after discontinuing the benzodiazepines. A place-bo-controlled trial of oxypertine is currently in progress, as this drug seems more promising than do beta-adrenoceptor antagonists such as propranolol (Tyrer et al. 1981) or alpha-2 agonists such as clonidine.

At a one-year follow-up, about one-third of our patients were doing very well and have had minor or no problems since completing the withdrawal. Another third experience occasional episodes of anxiety and tension but are pleased to discover that they can manage without chronic sedative medication. Finally, a third of the patients are more or less chronically anxious and find it very difficult to stay off their drugs. In fact, most of them have recommended some form of anxiolytic medication. During the months following the withdrawal we have used general outpatient support and relaxation training, and three patients have started formal analytical psychotherapy. Another two patients have been treated with antidepressives.

PREVENTION

Generally, reducing the overall consumption of benzodiazepines should also reduce the dependence. Hence, prescriptions should be limited to valid clinical indications, the lowest therapeutically effective doses prescribed, and repeat prescriptions should be limited. The patient's circumstances need careful assessment before prescribing a benzodiazepine, and subsequently his or her condition should be regularly monitored, especially in cases with previous histories of alcohol or drug abuse.

The benzodiazepines are safe and effective in the short-term management of anxiety and insomnia. But because of unwanted effects and risk of dependence, long-term usage should be avoided wherever possible. Prolonged benzodiazepine treatment should never be stopped abruptly, because of potential withdrawal symptoms. Short-acting benzodiazepines are preferable in the treatment of insomnia that is not accompanied by anxiety. There is no good evidence that the anxiolytic effect of the drug lasts longer than four months.

SUMMARY

As with their predecessors, the benzodiazepines are fully capable of inducing both physical and psychological dependence. Human experimental studies confirm those in animals that definite dependence can be induced by giving high doses for a prolonged period. However, dependence on therapeutic doses can be demonstrated as a syndrome complex on withdrawal rather than as marked drug-seeking behavior.

The earlier literature on clinical dependence generally showed little concern, but most reports were on patients who had escalated their dosage. Our findings, however, like those of other recent reports, revealed that a substantial proportion of patients taking benzodiazepines in therapeutic doses do risk developing some form of dependence. Although severe withdrawal reactions, such as psychosis and seizures, are probably rare, a mild to moderately severe syndrome is commonly experienced on stopping long-term benzodiazepine treatment. The withdrawal symptoms include high levels of anxiety, irritability, weakness, bodily symptoms of anxiety, mild depression, disturbance of sleep and appetite with significant loss of weight, headache, generalized aches and pains, hand tremor and sweating, and—last but not least—perceptual disturbances. The demonstration of withdrawal problems in patients on normal, therapeutic doses and the psychological impairment associated with chronic sedative ingestion (McNair 1973) argue against regular daily medication for chronic anxiety. In view of the extremely wide usage of these drugs, large numbers of patients may be at risk, as perhaps 2 percent or so of the adult population take benzodiazepines chronically. Further studies are urgently needed of the incidence of withdrawal reactions and of tolerance and withdrawal mechanisms. Careful examinations of potentially useful treatment approaches to the withdrawal syndrome are also required.

REFERENCES

Acuda, S. W., and Muhangi, J. (1979). Diazepam addiction in Kenya. *East African Medical Journal* 56(2):76–79.

Allgulander, C., and Borg, S. (1978). Case report: a delirious abstinence syndrome associated with clorazepate (Tranxilen). *British Journal of Addiction* 76:175–177.

Ayd, F. J., and Blackwell, B., eds. (1970). *Discoveries in Biological Psychiatry*. Philadelphia: Lippincott.

Balter, M. B., Levine, J., and Manheimer, D. I., (1974). Cross-national study of the extent of anti-anxiety/sedative drug use. *New England Journal of Medicine* 290:769–774.

Barten, H. H. (1965). Toxic psychosis from transient dysmnestic syndrome following withdrawal from valium. *American Journal of Psychiatry* 121:1210–1211.

Berger, F. M. (1963). The similarities and differences between meprobamate and barbiturates. *Clinical Pharmacology and Therapeutics* 4:209–231.

Bismuth, C., Le Bellec, M., Dally, S., and Lagier, G. (1980). Dépendence physique aux benzodiazépines. *La Nouvelle Presse Médicale* 9(28):1941–1945.

Braestrup, C., and Nielsen, M. (1980). Benzodiazepine receptors. Arzneimittel Forschung. *Drug Research* 30(1):852–857.

Braestrup, C., Nielsen, M., and Squires, R. F. (1979). No changes in rat benzodiazepine receptors after withdrawal from continuous treatment with lorazepam and diazepam. *Life Sciences* 24:347–350.

Brown, W. A., Langhren, T. P., and Williams, B. W. (1978). Neuroendocrine correlates of clinical response during withdrawal from chlordiazepoxide. *Communications in Psychopharmacology* 2:251–254.

Darcy, L. (1972). Delirium tremens following withdrawal of nitrazepam. *Medical Journal of Australia* 2:450.

De Bard, M. L. (1979). Diazepam withdrawal syndrome: a case with psychosis, seizure and coma. *American Journal of Psychiatry* 136:104–105.

de la Fuente, J. R., Rosenbaum, A. H., Martin, H. R., and Niven, R. G. (1980). Lorazepam-related withdrawal seizures. *Mayo Clinic Proceedings* 55:190–192.

DTB (1980). Action from the CRM: barbiturates. *Drug and Therapeutics Bulletin* 18:9–11.

Dysken, M. W., and Carlyle, H. C. (1977). Diazepam withdrawal psychosis: a case report. *American Journal of Psychiatry* 134(5):573.

Einarsson, T. R. (1980). Lorazepam withdrawal seizures. *Lancet* 1:151.

Floyd, J. B., and Murphy, M. (1976). Hallucinations following withdrawal of Valium. *Journal of the Kentucky Medical Association* 74:549–550.

Fruensgaard, K. (1976). Withdrawal psychosis: a study of 30 consecutive cases. *Acta Psychiatrica Scandinavica* 53:105–118.

Fruensgaard, K., and Vaag, U. H. (1975). Abstinenspsykose efter nitrazepam. *Ugeskrift for Læger* 137:633–634.

Greenblatt, D. J., and Shader, R. I. (1978). Dependence, tolerance and addiction to benzodiazepines: clinical and pharmacokinetic considerations. *Drug Metabolism Reviews* 8(1):13–28.

Haslerud, J., and Heskestad, S. (1981). Abstinens og forvirringsreaksjoner etter Rohypnol-bruk. *Tidsskrift for den Norske Lægeforening* 101(1B):112.

Hollister, L. E., Motzenbecker, F. P., and Degan, R. O. (1961). Withdrawal reactions from chlordiazepoxide ("Librium"). *Psychopharmacologia* 2:63–68.

Howe, J. G. (1980). Lorazepam withdrawal seizures. *British Medical Journal* 1:1163–1164.

Jepsen, P. W., and Haastrup, S. (1979). Abstinensreaktioner efter benzodiazepines. *Ugeskrift for Læger* 141(17):1121–1125.

Kemper, N., Poser, W., and Poser, S. (1980). Benzodiazepin-Abhängigkeit. *Deutsche Medizinische Wochenschrift* 105(49):1707–1712.

Khan, A., Joyce, P., and Jones, A. V. (1980). Benzodiazepine withdrawal syndromes. *New Zealand Medical Journal* 92:94–96.

Lader, M. (1978). Benzodiazepines — the opium of the masses? *Neuroscience* 3:159–165.

Le Bellec, M., Bismuth, C., Lagier, G., and Dally, S. (1980). Syndrome de sévrage sévère après arrêt des benzodiazepines. *Thérapie* 35:113–118.

McNair, D. M. (1973). Antianxiety drugs and human performance. *Archives of General Psychiatry* 29:609–617.

Marks, J. (1978). *The Benzodiazepines. Use, Overuse, Misuse, Abuse.* Lancaster (England): MTP Press.

Möhler, H., Okada, T., and Enna, S. J. (1978). Benzodiazepine and neurotransmitter receptor binding in rat brain after chronic administration of diazepam or phenobarbital. *Brain Research* 156:391–395.

Nerenz, K. (1974). Ein Fall von Valium-Entzygsdelir mit Grandmal-aufällen. *Nervenarzt* 45:384–386.

Palmer, G. C. (1978). Use, overuse, misuse, and abuse of benzodiazepines. *Alabama Journal of Medical Science* 15(4):383–392.

Petursson, H., and Lader, M. H. (1981a). Benzodiazepine dependence. *British Journal of Addiction* 76:133–145.

———. (1981b). Withdrawal from long-term benzodiazepine treatment. *British Medical Journal* 283:643–645.

Preskorn, H., and Denner, J. (1977). Benzodiazepines and withdrawal psychosis. Report of three cases. *Journal of the American Medical Association* 231:36–39.

Rastogi, R. B., Lapierre, Y. D., and Singhal, R. L. (1978). Synaptosomal uptake of norepinephrine and 5-hydroxytryptamine and synthesis of catecholamines during benzodiazepine treatment. *Canadian Journal of Physiology and Pharmacology* 56:777–784.

Relkin, R. (1966). Death following withdrawal of diazepam. *New York State Journal of Medicine* 66:1770–1772.

Rickels, K. (1981). Benzodiazepines: use and misuse. In *Anxiety, New Research and Changing Concepts,* ed. D. F. Klein and J. G. Rabkin, pp. 1–26. New York: Raven Press.

Rifkin, A., Quitkin, F., and Klein, D. F. (1976). Withdrawal reaction to diazepam. *Journal of the American Medical Association* 236(19): 2172–2173.

Skegg, D. C. G., Doll, R., and Perry, J. (1977). Use of medicines in general practice. *British Medical Journal* 2:1561–1563.

Tyrer, P., Rutherford, D., and Huggett, T. (1981). Benzodiazepine withdrawal symptoms and propranolol. *Lancet* 1:520–522.

Vyas, I., and Carney, M. W. P. (1975). Diazepam withdrawal fits. *British Medical Journal* 4:44.

World Health Organization (WHO) Expert Committee on Drug Dependence (1974). 20th report. WHO technical report series no. 551.

CHAPTER 9

Cocaine: An Emerging Problem

EDWARD GOTTHEIL, M.D.
STEPHEN P. WEINSTEIN, PH.D.

Despite the burgeoning popularity of cocaine and an escalating number of popular articles and technical papers devoted to the problems of cocaine use and abuse, much is still not known, and what is known varies in reliability. Some information is based on controlled human experiments, some on animal studies, some from clinical observations, and much is myth that has evolved over time. This chapter will outline much of the available information, dispelling some myths and confirming others.

PREVALENCE

Twenty years ago there were about 10,000 cocaine users in the United States. Ten years ago there were about 100,000. Current estimates are that there are 10,000,000 users and another 5,000,000 experimenters. Some believe the true figures are twice as high (Demarest 1981). Surveys of high school seniors in 1975 and 1980 indicated that the proportion using cocaine in the last 12 (between 1979 and 1980) months had increased from 5.6 percent to about 12.4 percent, and the proportion believing that using cocaine once or twice could be harmful decreased from 43 to 31 percent (Johnston et al. 1980). From 1975 to 1980, the number of individuals seeking treatment for a cocaine abuse problem increased fivefold to 11,300; the number of emergency room admissions increased fourfold to 4,200; and the number of deaths increased fourfold to 250. The percentage of youths who indicated that they had tried cocaine doubled between 1976 and 1979, reaching 27.5 percent (Kotulak 1982).

Following the death of John Belushi in March 1982 Dr. Jack Durell, deputy director of the National Institute on Drug Abuse (NIDA), stated, "Cocaine usage has become epidemic. It is an exploding problem that has the potential for becoming a major health problem" (Kotulak 1982, p. A5) Cocaine is now the biggest producer of illicit income. Last year, street sales of cocaine reached an estimated $30 billion. This would rank it among the top ten U.S. companies in sales. Marijuana, the most widely used drug, accounted for some $24 billion (Demarest 1981).

THE SUBSTANCE

Cocaine is a naturally occurring stimulant drug which is extracted from the leaves of the coca plant *Erythroxylan coca* (Petersen 1977). (See Fig. 9-1). It is an alkaloid like caffeine, nicotine, or morphine (Van Dyke and Byck 1982).

The coca plant is found mainly along the Andes mountains in Peru and Bolivia but is now also grown in Colombia and parts of Argentina, Brazil, Mexico, the West Indies, and Ecuador. During the time of the Incas, production had spread to Panama and Chile and in the 19th century to Java, Ceylon, and Jamaica (Carroll 1977). Java is now reportedly the world's largest producer of coca leaves (Clark 1973).

The shrub, cultivated for convenient leaf picking, is kept pruned to a height of 3 to 6 feet, although it can reach a height of 6 to 8 feet. The leaves are elliptically shaped (1 to 4 inches long) and can be harvested several times a year (March, June, and November), since the plant is an evergreen. It produces cocaine for its full 40-year life span.

Soaking the remaining leaves in a solvent solution (e.g., kerosene) yields a pasty, coffee-colored residue which in turn is sold to illicit laboratories for further refining until the extract has been purified into a salt (90 to 100 percent pure) whose crystals appear as fine white flakes hav-

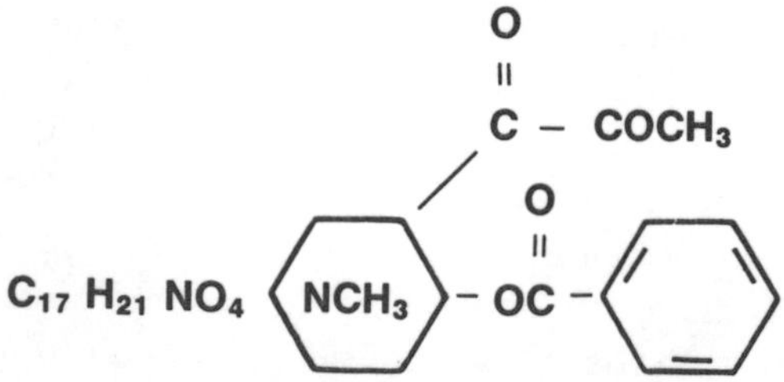

Figure 9-1. Cocaine

ing a powdery consistency. Cruder extractions by illicit laboratories will yield an extract of between 70 to 85 percent purity with nonalkaloid impurities (Gay et al. 1973, Hawks 1977).

Cocaine generally makes up between 0.65 and 1.2 percent of the dry weight of the coca leaf (Buck et al. 1968, Gay et al. 1973) but can range up to 1.8 percent (Van Dyke and Byck 1982).

HISTORICAL USAGE

It had been thought that the process of deriving cocaine from the chewing of coca leaves was developed by the Indians of the Andes mountains in about the 6th century, A.D. Cocaine was believed to have achieved its highest status around the 11th century under the rule of the Incas (Ashley 1975, Goodman and Gilman 1965; Petersen 1977a, 1977b). But recent archaeological findings indicate that experiences with cocaine were under way 5,000 years ago, well before the establishment of the Incan Empire (Van Dyke and Byck 1982), but its social or religious function at that time is not yet known.

The Bolivian and Peruvian Indians chewed coca leaves for a variety of religious, medicinal, and work-related reasons. The leaves took on special symbolic/religious significance under the Incas and became identified with the politically powerful as one of the prerogatives of rank. The myths of that time suggest that the drug was of divine origin and was passed on to the Incas as descendants of the gods. Its use was, therefore, a privilege. The coca leaves were considered to be precious, and their use was generally limited to the nobility and for religious ceremony (Eiswirth et al. 1972, Petersen 1977a, Van Dyke 1981).

By the end of the 15th century, coca plantations had become a state monopoly, and coca use was sharply restricted. Casual chewing was considered sacriligious and an affront to the nobility and religious elite. Coca was often used as a magical offering to the gods for safe passage on voyages, for continued health, or to restore health. Because of its energizing properties, it was also used by long-distance message carriers, and on occasion it was used to reward soldiers or workers who had completed a special project (Petersen 1977b, Van Dyke 1981, Van Dyke and Byck 1982).

With the decline of the Incan Empire during the 15th century and the granting of cultivation rights to privileged individuals, many of the restrictions concerning the planting and use of coca disappeared, and its availability became more and more widespread.

When Pizarro and the Spanish conquistadors established control of Peru in the 16th century, they had mixed feelings about the Indians' use of coca. The missionaries viewed it as a symbol of the devil's work and a barrier to religious conversion. But the Spanish entrepreneurs soon recognized that the coca habit was important to the health and motivation of the Indians and saw its utility in recruiting them to work in the mines and similar settings where conditions were brutal, labor arduous, and food limited. Economic considerations won out, and coca cultivation, distribution, and use were permitted and even encouraged. In 1569 Philip II of Spain legally declared coca necessary for the well-being of the Indians, while also urging the missionaries to end its use in native religious rituals (Petersen 1977b, Van Dyke and Byck 1982). In the 16th and 17th centuries the Spanish also reported on use of the leaves as an Indian folk remedy for various medical problems. Spanish physicians soon began advocating it as a cure for skin disorders, stomach problems, colds, asthma, rheumatism, headache, laryngitis, and toothaches (Petersen 1977b). Incan surgeons had used coca leaves as a local anesthetic for the practice of trephining, or neurosurgery designed to free evil spirits through holes in the skull (Hrdlicka 1939). In 1565, Nicholas Monardes published a glowing account of the effectiveness of coca in combating fatigue and hunger among the Indians. Other visitors to South America also returned with favorable accounts of the effects of chewing coca leaves.

The leaves were exported to Europe as botanical specimens in the 17th, 18th, and early 19th centuries. But the coca leaves did not retain their potency after drying and prolonged travel. Had they done so, the history of cocaine might have been similar to that of coffee or tobacco.

Europeans, therefore, never adopted the practice of chewing coca leaves, and thus coca became a true import only after the methodology for isolating the chemical constituents was developed during the 19th century. The cultural impact of cocaine therefore was molded by the attitudes and values of the late 19th century rather than the dominant influencers of the 16th century, which determined the patterns of tobacco and coffee use (Van Dyke and Byck 1982).

In 1859, the alkaloid was finally extracted from the coca leaf and named cocaine by Alfred Neiman, a Viennese biochemist (Clark 1973, Petersen 1977b, Van Dyke 1981). During that same year Dr. Paolo Mantegazza, who had lived for some time in the coca regions of South America, described the physiological and therapeutic effects of cocaine, rather lyrically endorsing its use:

I sneered at the poor mortals condemned to live in this valley of tears while I, carried on the winds of two leaves of coca, went flying through the spaces of 777,438 worlds, each more splendid than the one before. . . .

God is unjust because he made man incapable of sustaining the effect of coca all life long. I would rather have a life span of 10 years with coca, than one of 1,000,000 centuries without coca. (Andrews and Solomon 1975, p. 41)

Early in 1884, the young physician Sigmund Freud was looking for an area of scientific research in which he could develop a reputation and make a contribution. He had become interested in coca and cocaine through a series of enthusiastic articles appearing in 1880 in the *Therapeutic Gazette*, published in Detroit, Michigan, and he had also seen accounts of clinical observations of the effectiveness of cocaine in treating soldiers suffering from exhaustion and diarrhea, as reported by Dr. Theodor Aschenbrandt (Petersen 1977b). By April 30, 1884, Freud had ordered a supply of cocaine and experimented with it on himself. He was highly impressed with its positive effect on his mood and capacity for work. In May 1884 he began the unsuccessful cocaine treatment of his friend and colleague Ernst Von Fleischl-Marxow, a morphine addict. In July 1884 Freud's first paper on cocaine, "Über Coca," was published (Byck 1974).

In publishing "Über Coca," Freud established himself as a psychopharmacologist and an advocate of the therapeutic value of cocaine. He clearly described its effects on himself, particularly the euphoria and stimulation, sense of increased self-control, improved work capacity, and the disbelief that one is under the influence of a drug (Freud 1884):

Long-lasting, intensive mental or physical work can be performed without fatigue; it is an though the need for food and sleep, which otherwise makes itself felt peremptorily at certain times of the day, were completely banished. While the effects of cocaine last one can, if urged to do so, eat copiously and without revulsion; but one has the clear feeling that the meal was superfluous. Similarly, as the effect of coca declines it is possible to sleep on going to bed, but sleep can just as easily be omitted with no unpleasant consequences. During the first hours of the coca effect one cannot sleep, but this sleeplessness is in no way distressing.

I have tested this effect of coca, which wards off hunger, sleep, and fatigue and steels one to intellectual effort, some dozen times on myself. (Freud 1884, in Byck 1974, p. 60)

Freud overlooked reports of unfavorable effects of cocaine use and described its therapeutic uses as follows:

a) as a stimulant that would be valuable for psychiatrists;

b) for digestive disorders of the stomach — particularly for digestive relief after large meals;

c) in cachexia — to improve appetite and as a source of energy saving which could lower metabolism and combat wasting disease;

d) in treating alcohol and morphine addiction — as a temporary substitute for morphine or alcohol;

e) in asthma treatment — drawing an analogy from its reportedly favorable effects on mountain climbers;

f) as an aphrodisiac — citing reports of increased sexual capacity; and

g) as a local anesthetic — noting that its anesthetizing effect should be suitable for a number of applications. (Freud 1884, in Byck 1974, pp. 63–73)

This last use, as a local anesthetic, was developed in several experiments by a colleague of Freud's, Karl Koller, who applied it, under Freud's supervision, as a local anesthetic when eye surgery was performed by another cocaine experimenter, Leopold Königstein (Byck 1974). Koller eventually was recognized for the discovery, but Freud received little credit for his early suggestion of this valuable medical use.

Part of Freud's difficulty in establishing the credibility of his therapeutic applications was the debacle and ensuing critical outrage regarding his cocaine treatment of Fleischl's morphine addiction. Initially, the treatment with cocaine appeared to be succeeding; however, over time it became apparent that Fleischl was becoming increasingly dependent on the drug and was developing a full-blown cocaine psychosis. He began using increasing amounts of the drug, subcutaneously injecting up to a full gram per day. His symptomatology included insomnia, eccentric behavior, tactile hallucinations, and convulsions. These events, combined with a cocaine overdose death of one of his patients, led to very sharp attacks by the medical profession and ultimately to Freud's abandonment of his work with cocaine. Indeed, Albrecht Erlenmeyer, a German psychiatrist, accused Freud of unleashing the third scourge of humanity (after alcohol and the opiates) (Clark 1973, Petersen 1977b, Spotts and Shontz 1976, Van Dyke and Byck 1982).

In 1887 Freud published a defense of his work. He noted that the only people who became cocaine addicts were those who were already addicted to morphine and, also, that cocaine had differing effects on different individuals. Following that publication Freud gave up his work with cocaine (Spotts and Shontz 1976). By 1891 there were 200 reports of cocaine intoxication and 13 deaths attributed to the drug (Ashley 1975, Petersen 1977b).

Despite the growing concern of their European colleagues, many American physicians were still actively endorsing cocaine's use as a wonder drug. William Hammond, a former surgeon general of the United States, also advocated cocaine as a cure for morphine addiction, denied that it was habit forming, recommended it for a variety of mental and emotional disorders and was among the first to describe a dose-response curve for cocaine (Byck 1974).

In the mid-1880s William Halstead, the "father of modern surgery" developed the technique for nerve block anesthesia using cocaine and reported on over 1,000 operations using cocaine as a regional block. Unfortunately, Halstead had been experimenting on himself with cocaine and became heavily dependent on it. Reversing standard practice he began to use morphine to treat the dependence and subsequently became physically addicted to that drug. Despite a number of efforts to end his addiction, he remained morphine dependent for the remainder of his life (Byck 1974).

Americans soon recognized the commercial potential of this "miracle" drug. Between 1880 and 1914 cocaine became the basis of an explosion of patent medicines, tonics, soft drinks, ointments, suppositories, cigarettes, throat lozenges, and sprays, which allegedly could cure ailments ranging from alcoholism to colds, eczemas, corns, and venereal disease (Ashley 1975). Vin Mariani, a coca-based wine, was successfully developed and marketed by Angelo Mariani, a Corsican chemist. His wine was enthusiastically endorsed by illuminaries such as Anatole France, Henrik Ibsen, H. G. Wells, Jules Verne, Thomas Edison, and Auguste Rodin (Andrews and Solomon 1975). Coca-Cola, containing a cocaine extract of coca leaves, was introduced by A. A. Chandler in 1886 and became an instant success. It was advertised to cure headaches and relieve fatigue. By 1903 the cocaine extract had been removed, and the product was promoted as a soft drink. The flavoring, however, is still derived from decocainized coca leaves (Petersen 1977b).

Further popularization of cocaine stemmed from literature. Sir Arthur Conan Doyle, reportedly a cocaine abuser, had his hero detective, Sherlock Holmes, use cocaine regularly for mental stimulation (Clark

1973, Spotts and Shontz 1976). Robert Louis Stevenson, treated with cocaine for tuberculosis, supposedly wrote the initial draft of *Dr. Jekyll and Mr. Hyde* in three days during his treatment (Schultz 1971).

Accounts of cocainism, coca mania, and death resulting from continuous use of cocaine mounted. In the South the fear of cocaine-crazed blacks rebelling against segregation also grew, as did reports of cocaine's driving blacks to commit abnormal crimes (Ashley 1975). The combination of accurate documentation and popular myth began to sway public opinion against cocaine. The first federal effort to restrict cocaine use came in 1906 when the United States enacted the Pure Food and Drug Act, which required ingredient labeling on all over-the-counter preparations (Petersen 1977b, Spotts and Shontz 1976). State after state soon passed laws restricting or prohibiting the distribution of cocaine. Apparently cocaine was viewed as a greater threat than the opiates were. By 1914, 46 of the 48 states had passed legal restrictions on cocaine, whereas only 29 of the 48 had attempted to regulate the opiates (Ashley 1975). In 1914 Congress passed the Harrison Narcotic Tax Act, legally, albeit incorrectly, classifying cocaine as a narcotic. Individuals involved in the manufacture, importation, distribution, or dispensing of opium, coca, or their derivatives were required to register, pay taxes, and keep accurate records of the substances in their possession (Eiswirth et al. 1972). The use of cocaine was completely banned, although preparations containing small amounts of the opiates were permitted. Penalties in the form of fines and prison sentences were established and became more severe as controls on the narcotics (opium and cocaine) were tightened in subsequent amendments to the Harrison Act (Petersen 1977b).*

Synthetic and less toxic anesthetics were discovered, and cocaine's medical use declined markedly. In terms of general consumption, the change in cocaine's legal status and the subsequent decline in its availability removed it from public respectability. Cocaine drifted into the control of the anonymous underground. It became much more expensive, costing $30 per ounce in the 1920s compared with $10 per ounce before the Harrison Act. Its use was soon restricted to an even narrower stratum of society, remaining popular among members of the "bohemian set," such as jazz musicians, actors, actresses, and the wealthier (dealers) ghetto dwellers (Ashley 1975, Petersen 1977b, Spotts and Shontz 1976).

---

*In 1970 the Comprehensive Drug Abuse Prevention and Control Act replaced previous federal legislation. Cocaine was placed in Schedule II, the category for drugs with an acceptable medical use but with a high degree of abuse potential (Petersen 1977b).

By the 1930s the high cost of cocaine, combined with the availability of amphetamines, made cocaine use appear almost nonexistent. As late as 1960 the Federal Bureau of Narcotics reported seizing only 6 pounds of cocaine (436 pounds by 1971) (Petersen 1977b). But in the late 1960s and early 1970s cocaine was rediscovered, and its continued popularity had been ensured by the growing drug subculture, forever seeking involvement with a new status drug and looking for a better, safer high.

WHY ANOTHER WAVE OF COCAINE USE: THE USER'S CHANGING SOCIAL CHARACTERISTICS

There was relatively little reported use of cocaine between 1930 and 1965. During that period the artists, musicians, and actors of the bohemian subculture were the primary cocaine users. To that group were added heroin addicts, combining heroin with cocaine to form a "speedball" for a better high (Van Dyke 1981). Since 1965 the use of cocaine has inincreased markedly, along with the general increase in the social use of drugs. There is no one reason for the new wave of cocaine use. Its exotic history, high price, and rarity probably appeal to individuals who detour through the drug scene and yet emerge in respectable professions. Their affluence allows them access to cocaine, in turn making the drug fashionable and alluring (Van Dyke 1981). Therefore, cocaine has become a high-status drug, and the current users come more and more frequently from groups such as students, performers, athletes, as well as from such respectable, "straight" groups as businesspersons, lawyers, bankers, and the like. Cocaine is currently an emblem of wealth and status, the drug of choice for millions of upwardly mobile citizens. It is a beguiling drug that does not produce hangovers, lung cancer, holes in the arm, or burned-out brain cells, Instead, one takes a snort and, for about 30 minutes, has more drive, sparkle, and energy, without feeling drugged. During parties, cocaine enhances social interaction without the fear of adverse consequences. The individuals do not feel like addicts, as there is no apparent physical addiction. Cocaine is believed to be relatively risk-free and to have aphrodisiac properties. In the dating game, alcohol replaced candy, and now "nose candy" is replacing alcohol. A popular and flashy snorting technique is to sniff cocaine through rolled-up $100 bills.

The street names for cocaine reveal its status and anticipated effects: coke, snow, C, she, her, girl, white girl, lady, Connie, Bernice, Dama

Blanca, nose candy, blow, toot, leaf, flake breeze, Peruvian, heaven dust, heaven leaf, happy dust, happy trails, the star-spangled powder, the rich man's drug, the pimp's drug, and gold dust. It is described as the king, Cadillac, champagne, or caviar of drugs, though it costs more than any of these. It is about 70 times more costly than the finest beluga caviar. The current cost of gold is between $300 and $400 an ounce. But cocaine, at $100 a gram, is about $3,000 an ounce.

The effects of cocaine were described lyrically by Aleister Crowley in 1917:

The melancholy vanishes, the eyes shine, the wan mouth smiles. Almost manly vigor returns, or seems to return. At least faith, hope and love throng very eagerly to the dance; all that was lost is found. . . . To one the drug may bring liveliness, to another languor, to another creative force, to another tireless energy, to another glamor, and to yet another lust. But each in his way is happy. Think of it! . . . so simple and so transcendental! The man is happy. (Siegel 1977, p. 21)

Other reported subjective effects of cocaine include mood elevation to the point of euphoria, decrease in hunger, increases in energy and sociability, indifference to pain, and a marked decrease in fatigue. The user experiences a feeling of great muscular strength and increased mental capacity, leading to an overestimate of capabilities (Goodman and Gilman 1965, Siegel 1977).

Despite these glowing reports of cocaine's positive effects recent sharp increases in the dangerous patterns of intravenous injection, free basing (smoking cocaine paste), and combining cocaine with other drugs such as heroin, barbiturates, or quaaludes are clear indicators that cocaine use is far from being a benign problem (Siegel 1979, Van Dyke 1981).

THE PRODUCT, ADMINISTRATION, AND DOSAGE

PRODUCT

Cocaine, prepared in South America for export to the United States as a hydrochloride salt, is generally between 80 to 95 percent pure. It usually appears on import as either a translucent crystalline material (flake) or as small moderately transparent chunks (rock). Initial purchases in Boliva, Peru, or Colombia are generally in the 1 to 2 kilogram range.

Upon arrival in the United States it is quickly divided into lots of several ounces and sold. These ounces are then further reduced as the product passes through a variety of intermediaries, eventually being reduced to single grams or half-grams, known as spoons. During this reduction process the available product is frequently stretched by adding adulterants or short weighting. It would, therefore, be unusual for the product to reach the street at 90 percent purity (Hawks 1977).

Cocaine purchased in the street will probably have been adulterated with any of a variety of substances. These adulterants are designed either merely to expand the quantity and have no effect of their own (mannitol, lactose, glucose), to act as active substitutes (lidocaine, procaine, tetracaine), or to have a differential effect (heroin). If the original cocaine has been so diluted that it has no salable value, caffeine or amphetamines may be introduced for their stimulant effect (Hawks 1977). Drugs such as heroin and methamphetamine have also been sold as cocaine. The danger to the users is that they frequently cannot determine the amount or quality of the drug they are taking or estimate the effects of other chemically active adulterants (Eiswirth et al. 1972).

ADMINISTRATION AND DOSAGE

Intranasal. Snorting crystalline cocaine is the most common method of ingesting the drug. The material is chopped up with a razor blade into a fine powder, arranged in lines or columns, and then inhaled through one nostril while the other is held closed (Eiswirth et al. 1972, Siegel 1977).

In controlled-dose-effect studies with cocaine users, an intranasal dose of 10 mg could not be differentiated from a placebo, whereas doses of 25 and 100 mg produced euphoria. The physiological effects (increases in heart rate and blood pressure) both peaked at about 15 to 20 minutes after administration of the drug (Resnick et al. 1977). Van Dyke (1981) found that within a range of doses, higher levels produced higher peak plasma levels and more intense psychological effects. The reported pleasurable sensations are at their maximum for 15 to 20 minutes (Byck 1974, Eiswirth et al. 1972). Nasally ingested cocaine can be detected in the plasma within 3 minutes of ingestion and can persist in the plasma for a total of 4 to 6 hours (Van Dyke 1981).

Oral. Despite erroneous assumptions, particularly in the United States, the oral administration of cocaine is effective. Even though coca leaves were chewed in South America for at least 1,000 years, little was known about the effect of the small quantities of cocaine present in the leaves. In a series of experiments with native coca chewers, it was found that the same doses result in approximately the same plasma levels as achieved via the intranasal route. Absorption appears to take place through the oral mucosa and through the lower gastrointestinal tract after swallowing. Given cocaine in capsules, the plasma levels have taken longer to peak (50 to 90 minutes) than via the intranasal route (15 to 20 minutes). But the peak levels and psychological effects were similar for both means of ingestion (Van Dyke 1981).

Topical Anesthesia.   Cocaine's only concurrently recognized use in the United States is as a topical anesthetic in ear, nose, and throat surgery and in endoscopy of the upper gastrointestinal tract (Grinspoon and Bakalar 1979). It is used when both anesthesia and vasoconstriction are required (Barash 1977). Applied topically, cocaine combines the qualities of vasoconstriction, long duration of anesthesia, and relatively low toxicity in a way that no synthetic anesthetic has duplicated (Grinspoon and Bakalar 1979). Using a 4 percent solution, the latency is about 4 minutes; with a 10 percent solution, the latency drops to 2 minutes and the duration increases to over 30 minutes. The maximal concentration is 20 percent with a duration of 55 minutes, but with a greater toxicity risk (Smith 1973). Doses above 200 mg are not recommended, and reports of lethal doses range from 22 mg (submucosal injection) to 2,500 mg (subcutaneous injection) (Barash 1977). Further caution is indicated when other drugs are present, since cocaine's interaction with a wide variety of medications can be lethal. Care must be exercised in using cocaine with tricyclic antidepressants, methyldopa, reserpine, and the monoamine oxidase inhibitors (R. B. Smith 1973).

Intravenous.   "Shooting" cocaine intravenously produces an intense rush, a sense of exhilaration and euphoria, while abolishing feelings of hunger or fatigue. These feelings are accompanied by an overpowering desire to continue taking the drug (Eiswirth et al. 1972).

In controlled studies it was found that at 10 mg intravenous doses, the drug produced a pleasant high that lasted for 30 to 40 minutes. As the doses increased (up to 32 mg), the physiological and subjective changes also increased, and the effects began within a couple of minutes of injection and peaked within 5 to 10 minutes (Resnick et al. 1977). The intravenous injection of 8 to 16 mg of cocaine in a laboratory setting with volunteer subjects has also been found to produce subjective responses that are indistinguishable from 10 mg of intravenous dextroamphetamine (Fischman et al. 1976).

The let-down or depression that occurs after intravenous use is so sharp in contrast to the high that heavy users will continue regular use — often at 10-minute intervals to avoid the depressive symptoms (Eiswirth et al. 1972).

Most deaths from injecting cocaine intravenously generally are caused by respiratory collapse from using street-purchased cocaine. However, Allred and Ewer (1981) reported on the death of a man following the intravenous use of free-base cocaine. The patient they studied died of pulmonary edema; thus creating an additional area of concern for emergency room care.

Pulmonary.   For several years South American youths have smoked "pasta," a crude, pastelike derivative of coca leaves, which contains 40 to 85 percent cocaine sulfate and is mixed with tobacco or marijuana (Van Dyke 1981). There also have been reports of sharp increases in smoking free-base cocaine in the United States (Siegel 1979).

In an effort to obtain a "better" high and avoid the impurities of street cocaine, free basing has become popular among the more affluent users. It is expensive because substantial quantities of cocaine must be dissolved in an alkaline (basic) solution. The solution is boiled until a whitish lump, or free base, remains. Washing in a powerful solvent (ether) can further purify the product, and it is then smoked, either mixed with tobacco or in a water pipe. A highly concentrated dose thus is absorbed very quickly through the lungs (Demarest 1981).

With free-base smoking, plasma levels rise quickly to extremely high concentrations, often within 5 minutes of smoking. During this time, smokers report feeling relatively euphoric. But during the dysphoric stage (about 15 minutes after the cessation of smoking), the concentrations fall off sharply but remain relatively high (Van Dyke 1981). The pattern of an almost immediate euphoria followed by dysphoria and a strong desire to smoke again is characteristic of the free baser and leads to the consumption of large amounts of cocaine, frequently in a single smoking session which might last hours or days until the drug runs out. Experienced free basers report an awareness of the dysphoria as being an extremely unpleasant sensation that is overruled by the intense desire for the drug in an effort to achieve the initial euphoric high, a high that may never be achieved during any one smoking session, regardless of its length or the quantity of drug consumed.

In the more advanced stages of cocaine abuse, characterized by free basing and/or intravenous use, there is a tendency to mix in other drugs, generally either to intensify the high experience (amphetamine or heroin) or to calm down (alcohol, valium, quaalude, barbiturates) after a "run," thereby increasing both the immediate and long-term physical and psychological dangers.

COCAINE IN ANIMALS

In an effort to study and evaluate directly the effects of cocaine, a number of researchers have used the drug in controlled laboratory research. This vein of research could provide a working model for the exploration of cocaine's effects on humans.

PHYSIOLOGICAL EFFECTS

As a central nervous system (CNS) stimulant, the smallest measurable doses of cocaine produce increases in heart rate, respiratory rate, and pupil size in rats and monkeys. With higher doses, blood pressure increases, and with even higher doses, temperature also increases. Electroencephalographic activity is characterized by patterns indicating an arousal state, and with higher doses, grand mal convulsive patterns appear. At that point of imminent death the physical signs are those of a mixture of central nervous system stimulation, respiratory depression, and cardiovascular collapse. Death may be due to cardiovascular collapse, respiratory depression, or both (Woods 1977).

Even these physiological effects, including the lethal-dose level of cocaine, may be modified by environmental factors. For example, a greater proportion of mice will die, given the same sublethal dose of cocaine, if they are subjected to environmental stress such as being grouped together or administered electric shocks. In isolation the same dose level is not lethal to the mice (Lal and Chessick 1965).

STEREOTYPY

An unwarranted repetition of a series of responses (e.g., grooming a part of the body) can be induced by very large doses of cocaine. These doses are larger than those required to increase general activity. The effect has been observed in rats, cats, and dogs (Woods 1977). Using amphetamine (also a CNS stimulant) Randrup and Munkvad (1967) induced stereotyped behaviors in animal species, ranging from birds to primates. They suggested that the stereotyped response to amphetamine in animals is analogous to the stereotyped responses often seen in the human amphetamine psychoses. Cocaine, an even more power CNS stimulant, may produce similar effects.

AGGRESSION

In animal studies, cocaine by itself does not seem to increase general aggressiveness. However, in situations that provoke aggressive responding, cocaine may increase or decrease the response, depending on dose, species, and situation (Woods 1977).

LOCOMOTOR EFFECTS

Cocaine increases locomotion in mice, rats, and dogs. In the rhesus monkey, for example, one sees restlessness, increased activity, and increased sensitivity to environmental change (Woods 1977). Goodman and Gilman (1965) reported that after laboratory animals receive small amounts of cocaine, their locomotor activity is well coordinated, but with increased doses, their lower cortical motor centers are affected, causing tremors and convulsive movements. This effect may be the result of depressing inhibitory centers.

In attempting to learn how cocaine acts, a variety of drugs have been studied to determine their ability to modify cocaine's locomotor effect. Reserpine decreases the locomotor activity in mice, though it has the opposite effect with an amphetamine present (C. B. Smith 1963). Morphine decreases locomotion, whereas naltrexone, a narcotic-blocking agent, has no effect (Blumberg and Ikeda 1975). A number of agonists and antagonists of dopamine, norepinephrine, and serotonin have not been shown to have a uniform effect. At present, then, many interactions affecting locomotion have been noted, but they do not indicate any clear, simple neurochemical mechanism of action (Woods 1977).

COCAINE AS A REINFORCER

All animal species studied in operant behavior research (rats, dogs, baboons, monkeys) indicate a dose-dependent reinforcing effect of cocaine; i.e., they will increase or sustain the frequency of a response followed by cocaine delivery. For example, Siegel, Johanson, Brewster, and Jarvik (1976) found that when water-deprived rhesus monkeys were trained to smoke cocaine-dusted lettuce-leaf cigarettes for water, they would prefer the cocaine-based cigarettes to plain lettuce-leaf cigarettes.

Within a given range, response rates generally increase with increasing doses. For example, if an animal is conditioned to press a level to obtain a given dose and the dose is decreased, response rates will increase and continue to increase with decreasing doses to a point at which the dose has no discernible effect and then will drop off. Increasing the dose will then again increase response rates, up to some maximal rate above which the very high dose will yield a decreased response rate, possibly due to the drug's direct rate-decreasing effects (Woods 1977).

In these studies it was found necessary to restrict access to certain times of the day and to specify the number of injections, the dosage, or some combination in order to limit the total amount of cocaine intake (Woods 1977). For example, if not restricted, rhesus monkeys in long-term experiments will go through bouts of severe cocaine intoxication which may be manifested by profound to complete anorexia, restlessness, stereotyped movements, piloerection, tremor, and self-mutilation. The continuing CNS stimulation may produce grand mal convulsions and even death (Johanson et al. 1976). A bout may terminate in exhaustion, and then following a period of abstinence, another bout will occur. In the rhesus monkey, these cycles often produce death within a month, and occasionally in less than a week.

Rats trained to press a bar to obtain a drug would press the bar 250 times to obtain caffeine, 4,000 times to obtain heroin, and 10,000 times to obtain cocaine (Spotts and Shontz 1976). These findings, perhaps carried to an extreme, are not unlike the reports of free-base smokers, who will use as much drug as is available until they collapse from exhaustion; a pattern that if repeated over months and possibly years appears much like the pattern demonstrated by the rhesus monkeys studied by Johanson and associates (1976), with a very similar outcome.

COCAINE IN HUMANS

In humans, cocaine has a wide range of effects that contain an equally wide array of idiosyncratic, environmental, and social variables. Specific effects can vary with regard to setting (cocaine is often viewed as the special-occasion drug (Gay et al. 1973); individual psychological set (whether a fearful or an intrepid experimenter or a customary drug user); individual psychological state (happy, frightened, depressed, anxious); personal history and experience; chronic-versus-acute use; and method, dosage, and purpose of administration. Only a rather small percentage of these variables has been studied under laboratory conditions, and therefore, many of the reported effects are based on street hearsay and myth.

Cocaine's two major accepted pharmacological effects are as an effective, but potentially toxic, local or topical anesthetic and as one of the most powerful central nervous system stimulants known (Eiswirth et al. 1972). It is used medically and for social-recreational purposes and has acute, chronic, and toxic effects.

MEDICAL USE

In the United States, cocaine is now used only as a topical anesthetic in oral-pharyngeal surgery. Its efficacy, dosage, and toxicity were described earlier in this chapter. Until very recently, cocaine was the only local anesthetic that had a tendency to constrict blood vessels when applied topically. It had been the anesthetic of choice in eye surgery because it limited the flow of blood. But it has been found that the reduced flow can cause damage to the surface of the eye, and so its use is no longer recommended for eye surgery (Van Dyke and Byck 1982).

In Great Britain and Canada, (but not the United States), cocaine continues to be employed as an ingredient in Brompton's mixture, a preparation administered to relieve the pain of terminal cancer. The "cocktail" contains 10 mg of cocaine, 5 to 20 mg of morphine, and 2.5 mg of alcohol in a 20 ml solution with sugar syrup (Grinspoon and Bakalar 1979).

A clearer understanding of the psychoses could be obtained from studies of the affective changes resulting from high doses of cocaine (Grinspoon and Bakalar 1979, Post 1975).

Because of its toxicity and the availability of other effective pharmaceuticals, it is likely that medical research may be limited to studies of cocaine's effects as a drug of abuse or as a model for the investigation of psychoses.

SOCIAL-RECREATIONAL USE

Cocaine is widely available on the streets of most American cities. It can readily be purchased at a cost of $500 to $1,500 an ounce or for $60 to $100 a gram (Demarest 1981, Wesson and Smith 1977). Much of what is sold on the streets may not be cocaine at all or may be cocaine mixed with a variety of other substances (Eiswirth et al. 1972). It is used by seasoned drug users, as well as by middle-class professionals (Spotts and Shontz 1976, Wesson and Smith 1977). Cocaine can be chewed (as a coca leaf), used orally, snorted, injected intravenously, or smoked. The users' reports of the drug's effects vary with respect to the interactions of dose, adulterants, routes of administration, and a host of individual and environmental variables (Siegel 1977, Wesson and Smith 1977).

Siegel (1977), studying 85 volunteer social-recreational users, found that the use of cocaine might be periodically increased by some subjects under certain conditions. These situational variables might be efforts to increase work functioning, improve performance at play (sports or sex) or enhance mood during a period of depression. Other subjects might, at times, use cocaine on a daily basis or on a "binge" to relieve persistent problems or stress or to maintain a certain level of performance.

The combination of drug, individual, social, and environmental variables, as well as self-perceived circumstantial stressors and expected results from drug use, vastly complicate the determination of cocaine's effects on humans. The pattern of use from social-recreational to intense or compulsive use is reflected in the drug's acute and chronic effects.

ACUTE EFFECTS

As a central nervous system stimulant, cocaine has several distinct but interrelated effects. It is generally believed that cocaine stimulates the central nervous system from above. That is, the stimulation begins in the cortex and works downward to the lower brain centers (Clark 1973, Goodman and Gilman 1965, Spotts and Shontz 1976). The initial stage of cortical stimulation is marked by euphoria, garrulousness, excitement, and restlessness. The cocaine high is reportedly a vivid, sensation-enhancing experience (Demarest 1981). A lessened sense of fatigue may account for the heightened feeling of physical and mental powers reported by cocaine users (Clark 1973). As the dose increases, lower brain centers are stimulated, causing tremors and increased respiratory rates accompanied by decreased depth of respiration, emesis, and convulsions (Clark 1973, Spotts and Shontz 1976). The central stimulation is followed by depression, first of the higher cortical centers and then of the lower centers (Clark 1973). Theoretically, the subjective feelings of CNS depression, i.e., dysphoria, may explain the user's intense desire for more of the drug in order to regain the initial euphoria. Because the stimulation and depression cycles of the higher and lower brain centers do not take place at the same time, the subsequent doses could be ingested as the lower brain centers are being depressed and, eventually as the levels build, depressing these centers further and leading to an overdose reaction. As the levels increase, the medullary centers become depressed, resulting in apnea and death (Clark 1973).

Research by independent experimenters using different doses administered through either intranasal or intravenous methods has demonstrated that cocaine, even in relatively small doses, increases humans' heart rate and blood pressure (Fischman et al. 1976, Resnick et al. 1977). Cocaine affects the cardiovascular system by means of its ability to sensitize organs to the catecholamines, notably epinephrine, resulting in vasoconstriction and hypertension (Clark 1973, R. B. Smith 1973).

Cocaine reportedly can increase body temperature (Clark 1973, Spotts and Shontz 1976). According to Clark (1973), this effect is accomplished by increased muscle activity augmenting heat production, vasoconstriction lessening heat loss, and the direct action of raising the CNS thermostat. Resnick and colleagues (1977) did not verify this effect in their controlled study of different doses of cocaine administered by intranasal or intravenous routes. But three of cocaine's most popular street myths, i.e., initial euphoria, increased alertness, and appetite suppression, have been confirmed in laboratory studies of humans (Fischman et al. 1976, Resnick et al. 1977). Other reported effects, including heightened physical strength and mental capacity, creativity, sexual performance and libido, criminal activity, and aggressive behavior, either have to be studied in the laboratory or have not been formally verified (Byck and Van Dyke 1977).

CHRONIC EFFECTS

In 1917 Crowly described the effect of continued cocaine use;

But to one who abuses cocaine for his pleasure, nature soon speaks, and is not heard. The nerves weary of the constant stimulation; they need rest and food. There is a point at which the jaded horse no longer answers whip and spurs. He stumbles, falls a quivering heap, gasps out his life. . . . So perishes the slave of cocaine. With every nerve clamoring, all he can do is to renew the lash of the poison. The pharmaceutical effect is over; the toxic effect accumulates. The nerves become insane. The victim begins to have hallucinations . . . and alas! The power of the drug diminishes with fearful pace. The doses wax; the pleasures wane. Side-issues, invisible at first, arise; they are like devils with flaming pitchforks in their hands. (Siegel 1977, p. 122)

When used recreationally (less than two or three times per week), the severe pathological effects resulting from excessive daily use are not observed. Post (1975) suggested that the syndrome associated with chronic cocaine use is in fact a progression from euphoria to dysphoria to paranoid psychosis.

Increased anxiety, dysphoria, suspiciousness, disruption in eating and sleeping habits, weight loss, fatigue irritability, concentration difficulties, and psychological dependence are among the most commonly reported effects of regular, high-dose cocaine usage (Eiswirth et al. 1972, Goodman and Gilman 1965, Siegel 1977, Spotts and Shontz 1976, Van Dyke 1981). In addition, recent reports indicate that the lungs' monoxide-diffusing capacity may be sharply reduced following several months of free-base smoking (Weiss et al. 1981). Unlike the opiates or alcohol, cocaine does not produce a clear physical dependence, but symptoms such as anxiety and depression are commonly reported after the drug is withdrawn (Grinspoon and Bakalar 1979, Wesson and Smith 1977).

When chronically abused, a paranoid psychosis, almost indistinguishable from acute paranoid schizophrenia, is reported (Post 1975, Siegel 1977). The first hallucinatory symptoms to develop are tactile. The sensations of insects under the skin, or "cocaine bugs," are rather common characteristics of chronic use (Post 1975, Siegel 1977). Paranoid thinking and auditory, visual, and olfactory hallucinations come with continued use. Violent behavior may occur during the height of a cocaine psychosis (Post 1975, Spotts and Shontz 1976). But the diagnosis of psychosis is not clear, since other disturbances in thought, affect, and impulse control, with regressive behavior that characterizes psychoses, are not routinely present. In fact, the cocaine hallucinations often appear in the presence of clear mental ability (Siegel 1977). The hallucinations generally stop with the cessation of cocaine use (Post 1975) but may persist and require hospitalization and medication (Clark 1973, Wesson and Smith 1977).

TREATMENT

TOXICITY AND OVERDOSE

The symptoms of acute toxicity are related to central nervous system stimulation (Clark 1973). After a toxic dose, the individual is likely to be excited, restless, anxious, garrulous, and confused and may report a headache. Pulse is rapid, respiration irregular, and a chill may precede a temperature rise. Nausea, vomiting, and abdominal pain are common, and depression, delusion, seizure, unconsciousness, and death from respiratory failure may result (Clark 1973, Finkle and McCloskey 1977). High doses administered intravenously may result in almost immediate death from cardiotoxicity and cardiac arrest (Clark 1973).

Acute cocaine poisoning displays a very rapid onset of symptoms. Two-thirds of the 111 cocaine deaths studied by Finkle and McCloskey (1977) died within five hours, and one-third within one hour following ingestion of the drug. The route of administration was not a factor.

Treatment for acute toxicity consists of clearing the airway of any possible obstructions, supplying oxygen (if available), placing the patient in the Trendlenberg position (30° head down), to augment venous return to the heart and to prevent aspiration (Barash 1977). Convulsions, if present, should be treated with 25 to 50 mg of a short-acting barbiturate (pentobarbital). If the symptoms of acute anxiety, hypertension, and tachycardia are severe, treatment with 10 to 30 mg intravenous or intramuscular diazepam is recommended (Grinspoon and Bakalar 1979). If the symptoms (i.e., acute anxiety and depression with increased blood pressure and pulse rate) are less severe, treatment with oral diazepam (10 to 40 mg.) in repeated doses can be administered (Wesson and Smith 1977). Once cardiopulmonary function has been restored and stabilized, the prognosis for recovery is greatly increased, and within a few hours, life-threatening signs will disappear.

Cocaine is often used in conjunction with other drugs such as heroin, barbiturates, or alcohol, and it may be necessary to treat both the cocaine crisis and the sequelae of sudden withdrawal from a secondary but physically addictive substance (Wesson and Smith 1977).

THERAPEUTIC INTERVENTION

Although there is no apparent physical dependence, even with chronic excessive use, for many abusers the powerful psychological dependence and the concommitant euphoria and dysphoria cycles seem to be alleviated only by increasing the doses of cocaine. Soon the urge to continue increased doses may become an obsession, diverting people from normal pursuits into a complete preoccupation with the drug (Demarest 1981).

The obsessive reaction appears to be strongest among intravenous users or free-base smokers (Van Dyke and Byck 1982). Intranasal, recreational, irregular users may at various times lapse into a more regular pattern if the drug is available. When unavailable, they will be able to abstain, suffering few consequences (Van Dyke and Byck 1982).

Clark (1973) reviewed three suggested stages of treating chronic abusers. The first stage, detoxification, is essentially a medical problem which could require inpatient care for about one week. Reactions to the abrupt withdrawal of the stimulant drug may necessitate sedatives or phenothiazines. Sleepiness, severe depression, social withdrawal, and suicidal ideation characterize withdrawal (Clark 1973). Aside from withdrawal, psychiatric reactions to chronic use may range from acute anxiety to psychoses and require hospitalization and sedatives or phenothiazines. Repeated doses of Valium can be administered to relieve the anxiety and agitation. These doses can be increased or switched to major tranquilizers if the psychosis persists (Wesson and Smith 1977).

The second phase of treatment, initial abstinence, should be conducted on an outpatient basis over several months. Clark (1973) suggested continued frequent support in the context of intrapersonal and interpersonal exploration of the self without drugs. Essentially, this is the phase in which patients may, if they choose, engage in a meaningful psychotherapeutic relationship. But experience has shown that it is difficult to engage cocaine abusers in psychotherapy once the immediate medical crisis is past. The allure of the drug and the associated life-style, combined with a philosophical assumption that if they are "more careful next time, it won't happen again," often predominates. A group working in Aspen, Colorado, reported (*Time* 1982) success in overcoming patients' antitherapeutic destructive behavior by establishing a clearly explained self-designed blackmail contract at the point of intake, when the users are most desperate for help. If motivation should wane and cocaine use resume, the punishment is carried out.

The third phase of treatment is long-term aftercare. This phase begins once the patient demonstrates continuity and effective functioning. It has no particular time limit and is usually accomplished in regular, reinforcing group sessions (Clark 1973).

COCAINE TODAY

As this chapter demonstrates, there is much that remains to be learned about this almost mystically enticing drug. Although some of its physical effects are known, cocaine's effect on physical strength (its *raison d'être* for the Spaniards) and sexual function has not been adequately studied. Its impact on creative and intellectual capabilities has not been assessed. Many of the effects associated with toxicity, the development of severe psychological symptoms, and the reported depressions following chronic use need to be explored. Patterns of use, tolerance, dependence, and withdrawal, as well as the interaction of individuals and social variables, also require further study.

Cocaine retains its historical allure as a magical answer to the tedium, frustration, and physical and emotional pains of modern living. Today it is socially acceptable and very much in demand among members of the American middle class. Newspapers and magazines attest to the fact that as the market has grown, a viable, competitive, and all too frequently violent import and distribution industry has developed to meet that demand. But despite the recent negative press, those who use cocaine to escape the bad news of life are not very likely to be turned away by more bad news about their drug. Regulation and legal penalties have not had any discernible impact on current use and in fact have had the apparent effect of keeping both the price and the allure high.

We do know that cocaine can all too readily be abused. It has the ability to cause the dissipation of fortunes; the destruction of families; and the reduction of intelligent, highly functional human beings to obsessed, burned-out shells of themselves; and it can kill. More, much more, needs to be learned about this drug. Although cocaine has been around for a great many years, most of the research on it is recent. For many individuals, treatment has been found to be quite effective, especially if they are seen early in their stages of abuse. It is believed that as more experience is gained, more effective prevention and treatment techniques will be discovered.

REFERENCES

Allred, R. J., and Ewer, S. (1981). Fatal pulmonary edema following intravenous "free base" cocaine use. *Annals of Emergency Medicine* 10(8):441–442.

Andrews, G., and Solomon, D. (1975). *The Coca Leaf and Cocaine Papers*. New York: Harcourt Brace Jovanovich.

Ashley, R. (1975). *Cocaine: Its History, Uses, and Effects*. New York: St. Martin's Press.

Barash, P. G. (1977). Cocaine in clinical medicine. In *Cocaine: 1977*, ed. R. C. Petersen and R. C. Stillman, pp. 193–200. U. S. Dept. of HEW, PHS. Alcohol, Drug Abuse and Mental Health Administration, National Institute on Drug Abuse Research Monograph No. 13. Washington, D.C.: U.S. Government Printing Office.

Blumberg, H., and Ikeda, C. (1975). Naltrexone, morphine, and cocaine interactions in mice. *Pharmacologist* 17:206.

Buck, A. A., Sasaki, T. T., Hweitt, J., and Macrae, A. A. (1968). Coca chewing and health; and epidemiological study among residents of a Peruvian village. *American Journal of Epidemiology* 88:159–177.

Byck, R. (1974). *Cocaine Papers by Sigmund Freud*. New York: Stonehill.

Byck, R., and Van Dyke, C. (1977). What are the effects of cocaine in man? In *Cocaine: 1977*, ed. R. C. Petersen and R. C. Stillman, pp. 97–117. U.S. Dept. of HEW, PHS. Alcohol, Drug Abuse and Mental Health Administration, National Institute on Drug Abuse Research Monograph No. 13. Washington, D.C.: U.S. Government Printing Office.

Carroll, E. (1977). Coca: the plant and its use. In *Cocaine: 1977*, ed. R. C. Petersen and R. C. Stillman, pp. 35–45. U.S. Dept. of HEW, PHS. Alcohol, Drug Abuse and Mental Health Administration, National Institute on Drug Abuse Research Monograph No. 13. Washington, D.C.: U.S. Government Printing Office.

Clark, R. (1973). Cocaine. *Texas Medicine* 69:74–78.

Demarest, M. (1981). Cocaine: middle class high. *Time,* July 6, pp. 56–63.

Eiswirth, N. A., Smith, D. E., and Wesson, D. R. (1972). Current perspectives on cocaine use in America. *Journal of Psychedelic Drugs* 5: 153–157.

Finkle, B. S., and McCloskey, K. L. (1977). The forensic toxicology of cocaine. In *Cocaine: 1977,* ed. R. C. Petersen and R. C. Stillman, pp. 153–192. U.S. Dept. of HEW, PHS. Alcohol, Drug Abuse and Mental Health Administration, National Institute on Drug Abuse Research Monograph No. 13. Washington, D.C.: U.S. Government Printing Office.

Fischman, M. W., Schuster, C. R., Resnekov, L., Schick, J. F. E., Krasnegor, N. A., Fennel, W., and Freedman, D. X. (1976). Cardiovascular and subjective effects of intravenous cocaine administration in humans. *Archives of General Psychiatry* 33:983–989.

Freud, S. (1884). Über Coca. In *Cocaine Papers by Sigmund Freud,* ed. R. Byck (1974), pp. 48–73. New York: Stonehill.

Gay, G. R., Sheppard, C. W., Inaba, D. S., and Newmeyer, J. A. (1973). Cocaine perspective: gift from the sun god to the rich man's drug. *Drug Forum* 2:409–430.

Goodman, L. S., and Gilman, A. (1965). *The Pharmacological Basis of Therapeutics.* 3rd ed. New York: Macmillan.

Grinspoon, L., and Bakalar, J. B. (1979). Cocaine. In *Handbook on Drug Abuse,* ed. R. I. Dupont, A. Goldstein, J. O'Donnell, and B. Brown, pp. 241–247. U.S. Dept. of HEW and Office of Drug Abuse Policy, National Institute on Drug Abuse. Washington, D.C.: U.S. Government Printing Office.

Hawks, R. (1977). Cocaine: the material. In *Cocaine: 1977,* ed. R. C. Petersen and R. C. Stillman, pp. 47–61. U.S. Dept. of HEW, PHS. Alcohol, Drug Abuse and Mental Health Administration, National Institute on Drug Abuse Research Monograph No. 13. Washington, D.C.: U.S. Government Printing Office.

Hrdlicka, A. (1939). Trephination among prehistoric people. *Ciba Symposium* 1(6).

Johanson, C. E., Balster, R. L., and Bonese, K. (1976). Self administration of psychomotor stimulant drugs: the effects of unlimited access. *Pharmacology, Biochemistry and Behavior* 4:45–51.

Johnston, L. D., Bachman, J. G., and O'Malley, P. M. (1980). *Highlights from Student Drug Use in America 1975–1980.* U.S. Dept. of

Health and Human Services, PHS. Alcohol, Drug Abuse and Mental Health Administration, National Institute on Drug Abuse. Washington, D.C.: U.S. Government Printing Office.

Kotulak, R. (1982). Cocaine use spreading. *Philadelphia Inquirer,* March 28, p. A5.

Lal, H., and Chessick, R. D. (1965). Lethal effects of aggregation and electric shock in mice treated with cocaine. *Nature* 208:295–296.

Petersen, R. C. (1977a). Cocaine: an overview. In *Cocaine: 1977,* ed. R. C. Petersen and R. C. Stillman, pp. 5–15. U.S. Dept. of HEW, PHS. Alcohol, Drug Abuse and Mental Health Administration, National Institute on Drug Abuse Research Monograph No. 13. Washington, D.C.: U.S. Government Printing Office.

————. (1977b). History of cocaine. In *Cocaine: 1977,* ed. R. C. Petersen and R. C. Stillman, pp. 17–34. U.S. Dept. of HEW, PHS. Alcohol, Drug Abuse and Mental Health Administration, National Institute on Drug Abuse Research Monograph No. 13. Washington, D.C.: U.S. Government Printing Office.

Post, R. M. (1975). Cocaine psychoses: a continuum model. *American Journal of Psychiatry* 132(3):225–231.

Randrup, A., and Munkvad, I. (1967). Stereotyped activities produced by amphetamine in several animal species. *Psychopharmacologia* 11:300–310.

Resnick, R. B., Kestenbaum, R. S., and Schwartz, L. K. (1977). Acute systematic effects of cocaine in man: a controlled study by intranasal and intravenous routes. *Science* 195:696–698.

Schultz, M. G. (1971). The "strange case" of Robert Louis Stevenson. *Journal of the American Medical Association* 216:90–94.

Siegel, R. K. (1977). Cocaine: recreational use and intoxication. In *Cocaine: 1977,* ed. R. C. Petersen and R. C. Stillman, pp. 119–136. U.S. Dept. of HEW, PHS. Alcohol, Drug Abuse and Mental Health Administration, National Institute on Drug Abuse Research Monograph No. 13. Washington, D.C.: U.S. Government Printing Office.

————. (1979). Cocaine smoking. *New England Journal of Medicine* 300:373.

Siegel, R. K., Johanson, C. E., Brewster, J. M., and Jarvik, M. E. (1976). Cocaine self-administration in monkeys by chewing and smoking. *Pharmacology, Biochemistry, and Behavior* 4:461–467.

Smith, C. B. (1963). Enhancement by reserpine and alpha-methyl dopa of the effects of d-amphetamine upon the locomotor activity of mice. *Journal of Pharmacology and Experimental Therapeutics* 142:343–350.

Smith, R. B. (1973). Cocaine and catecholamine interaction: a review. *Archives of Otolaryngology* 98:139–141.

Spotts, J. V., and Shontz, F. C. (1976). *The Lifestyles of Nine American Cocaine Users: Trips to the Land of Cockaigne.* U.S. Dept. of HEW, PHS. Alcohol, Drug Abuse and Mental Health Administration, National Institute on Drug Abuse Research Issue No. 16. Washington, D.C.: U.S. Government Printing Office.

Time (1982) Kicking cocaine. April 12, pp. 51–52.

Van Dyke, C. (1981). Cocaine. In *Substance Abuse Clinical Problems and Perspectives,* ed. J. H. Lowinson and P. Ruiz, pp. 158–165. Baltimore: Williams & Wilkins.

Van Dyke, C., and Byck, R. (1982). Cocaine. *Scientific American* 246 (3):128–414.

Weiss, R. D., Goldenheim, P. D., Mirin, S. M., Hales, C. A., and Mendelson, J. H. (1981). Pulmonary dysfunction in cocaine smokers. *American Journal of Psychiatry* 138(8):1110–1112.

Wesson, D. R., and Smith, D. E. (1977). Cocaine: its use for central · nervous system stimulation including recreational and medical uses. In *Cocaine: 1977,* ed. R. C. Petersen and R. C. Stillman, pp. 137–152. U.S. Dept. of HEW, PHS. Alcohol, Drug Abuse and Mental Health Administration, National Institute on Drug Abuse Research Monograph No. 13. Washington, D.C.: U.S. Government Printing Office.

Woods, J. (1977). Behavioral effects of cocaine in animals. In *Cocaine: 1977,* ed. R. C. Petersen and R. C. Stillman, pp. 63–95. U.S. Dept. of HEW, PHS. Alcohol, Drug Abuse and Mental Health Administration, National Institute on Drug Abuse Research Monograph No. 13. Washington, D.C.: U.S. Government Printing Office.

PART IV

Psychiatric Syndromes Associated with Recent Medical Advances

. . . new diagnostic machines and new drugs to treat symptoms can sometimes leave untouched many of the complex, human needs of patients.

Cecil's Textbook of Medicine, Fred Plum, 1979

CHAPTER 10

Psychiatric Sequelae of Chronic Dialysis

WARREN R. PROCCI, M.D.

The development of maintenance hemodialysis has radically altered the treatment of chronic renal failure. Patients once consigned to the inevitability of almost certain death within a short period of time are now able to be kept alive for years, even indefinitely in some cases. It is a very dramatic treatment modality, and even the most medically sophisticated individual cannot fail to be impressed when viewing patients connected by tubes that carry their own blood to a very complex machine. Many observers have commented on this "umbilical" relationship with the machine, and this fact alone can probably account for much of psychiatrists long-standing interest in this treatment modality. Additionally, the concept of life "artificially" maintained by machine contributes to the psychiatric interest aroused by chronic dialysis.

Psychiatric papers on the effects of chronic dialysis began to appear almost immediately after its introduction into clinical practice. Early papers were, of necessity, anecdotal, descriptive, and almost always subjective. Over the years, psychiatric interventions into the effects of chronic dialysis have become much more refined and sophisticated, and the descriptions of psychiatric sequelae more detailed and reproducible.

This chapter will review some of the most common psychiatric sequelae of chronic dialysis, as well as some of the data concerning these sequelae. Since it has been estimated that nearly 2,000 studies have been done on the psychological, social, and treatment problems of patients with chronic renal failure (Blodgett 1981), this chapter can hardly be an exhaustive review. Rather, it is intended as only a brief overview of a complicated area.

UREMIC DELIRIUM

Uremic delirium is strictly not a complication of chronic dialysis per se, but since it is often part of the predialytic clinical course of the chronic dialysis patient, we shall discuss this condition. Stenbäch and Haapanen (1967) reported that nearly 40 percent of uremic patients developed a delirious condition.

CLINICAL FEATURES

Chronic renal failure is a complex illness with many different signs and symptoms, involving a multiplicity of organ systems and with a wide range of possible etiologies. The clinical features of uremia are highly variable because it can be influenced by so many factors.

Mental-status changes are frequent and have been recognized for many years (Baker and Knutson 1946). At this time, it is unclear whether this is a direct effect of one or more metabolic waste products on the tissue of the central nervous system or whether a psychogenically mediated reaction to the unpleasant and threatening presence of a serious chronic illness is responsible for the mental-status changes. Our focus will be more on the clinical features, and so we shall not discuss this question in detail. There is good evidence in the literature supporting organic factors in the production of at least some of the mental-status changes.

The early stage of chronic renal failure is frequently characterized by relatively nonspecific complaints of not feeling well. As the illness progresses, this becomes more pronounced, and lethargy, withdrawal, and apathy become prominent. In a formal mental-status examination, a psychiatrist might note signs of intellectual impairment, such as deficits in recent memory and impaired ability to perform routine calculations. Relatives might comment on emotional changes that they have noted in these patients, such as marked irritability. It is not unusual for these patients to be pleasant and cooperative one time but impatient and hostilely demanding shortly thereafter. This lability can cause significant problems in the management of these patients, since they can become angrily noncompliant regarding the stringent requirements of treating their chronic renal failure.For example, they may refuse to conform to their dietary restrictions, or they may fail to follow their prescribed drug regimen. But they rarely become intractable or uncontrollable at this stage. Careful psychological testing at this time usually reveals deficits in areas such as short-term memory and reaction time. Ginn and associates (1975) developed an excellent series of neurological and psychological probes for enumerating the central nervous system deficits produced by uremia.

They elegantly documented deficits in sustained attention and alertness, short-term memory, and reaction time. In general, psychiatric consultation is not requested at this early stage of renal failure.

As renal failure progresses to a severe and essentially irreversible state, these deficits become much more pervasive. Ultimately, a full-blown delirium can develop. In the predelirium stage, the patient's emotional symptoms often become much more marked, and an obvious depression, an angry paranoid state, or a sullen negativistic condition are but a few examples of the myriad of major personality disturbances that might appear (Baker and Knutson 1946). Quite obviously, these behaviors can be very irritating to family members as well as to medical care-givers. Psychiatric consultation may well be sought at this stage of the illness.

When a full delirium does develop, the signs and symptoms are, of course, legion, and the clinical picture in uremic deliria is similar to that of other deliria. Major deficits in orientation, short-term memory, and higher cortical functions are readily apparent. Delusions may be present, and vivid visual hallucinations are common. Auditory hallucinations may also be present. Uremic deliria vary considerably with regard to symptoms and course. Although there is generally a direct relationship between laboratory evidence of the uremia's severity and the presence of delirium (Stenbäch and Haapanen 1967), there can be a wide variation of clinical symptomatology among patients with similar laboratory values. Furthermore, in some cases, apparent improvement, as evidenced by decrements in laboratory indices of uremia, may be accompanied by either the worsening of an existing delirium or the introduction of a new delirium (Schreiner 1959). No doubt this reflects the complex effects of various metabolic waste products on the nervous system and the corresponding complexity of the nervous system's adaptive capacity.

Several investigators (Ginn et al. 1975, Kiley and Hines 1975, Tyler 1968) examined the electroencephalograms (EEGs) of patients with uremia and uremic delirium. They agreed that diffuse slowing with paroxysmal bursts of slow waves is the most common abnormality associated with uremia. They also agreed that the extent of this slowing can be correlated with the degree of uremia and that improvement of this abnormality routinely follows adequate dialysis.

The treatment of uremic delirium is similar to the treatment of any other delirium. Attempts must be made to orient the patient to his or her surroundings. Of course, the presence of familiar people and objects can be helpful. If the patient is sufficiently agitated and out of control, treatment with neuroleptic medication may be necessary. High-potency neuroleptics such as haloperidol or fluphenazine are probably preferable.

Dosage alterations in chronic renal failure are discussed later in this chapter. Ultimately, adequate dialysis should resolve the uremic deliria.

DIALYSIS DISEQUILIBRIUM SYNDROME

Dialysis disequilibrium syndrome characteristically occurs early in the dialysis treatment, often after the first few treatments. In general, it is most severe when plasma indices of uremia are highest and, therefore, the reduction in these values due to dialysis is at its maximum. At one time dialysis disequilibrium syndrome was referred to as the *reverse urea syndrome,* since it was thought to demonstrate that urea is removed more gradually from the cerebrospinal fluid (CSF) and from nervous tissue than it is from blood. This was postulated as creating an abnormal urea gradient with a resultant shift of fluid from blood to brain and therefore a relative cerebral edema. Though this may be a plausible explanation for the clinical picture, some data refute this hypothesis (Wakim 1969), and alternative hypotheses such as the presence of extreme hyperglycemia and hyperosmolality have been suggested (Rigg and Bercu 1967).

CLINICAL FEATURES

There are several possible manifestations of dialysis disequilibrium syndrome. The mildest form may be merely feelings of drowsiness and fatigue coupled with mild agitation and headache. More severe forms may be disorientation, memory deficits, and decrements in higher cortical functions. In its most severe form an agitated psychosis may be present, and seizures, coma, and death can occur in extreme cases. Signs of increased intracranial pressure such as nausea, vomiting, and papildema are observed in the most severe cases, as are headaches and blurred vision.

The progression to the more severe forms of this condition can be averted with proper treatment, which consists of more frequent but briefer dialysis (Rigg and Bercu 1967). The key, of course, is to attempt to reduce the absolute decrement in urea concentration so that serum osmolality is not changed so rapidly. It may be necessary to treat such patients with antipsychotic medication if a marked degree of psychotic behavior is present. Since seizures may occur with the more severe forms of this syndrome (Grushkin et al. 1972, Rigg and Bercu 1967), treatment with diphenylhydantoin, barbiturates, or diazepam may be necessary. For severe cases, some therapists recommend prophylactic use of these agents.

DIALYSIS DEMENTIA

Dialysis dementia is an interesting but unfortunately catastrophic complication of chronic dialysis. Because the first reports of this condition came from the University of Colorado dialysis group, the syndrome was given the name "Denver dialysis disease" (Alfrey et al. 1972, 1976). More recently this syndrome has been described by many other centers around the world (Elliott et al. 1978, Mahurkar et al. 1973, Rozas et al. 1978, Scheiber and Ziesat 1976), and so it is clearly not limited to one geographical area.

CLINICAL FEATURES

Dialysis dementia is a progressive encephalopathy that is ultimately fatal. It begins in a subacute fashion and, interestingly, usually only in those individuals who have been treated with chronic dialysis for at least several years (Burks et al. 1976, Chokroverty et al. 1976). The earliest sign, and therefore the one to which therapists must attend most carefully, is a disturbance in speech. Stuttering is usually the initial change, with dysarthia following. In more advanced stages of the illness, aphasic symptoms such as dysphasia and dyspraxia are observed. Often, it is the nursing staff who first become aware of the change in speech pattern. As the illness progresses, myoclonus is present. The syndrome is also characterized by a dementia similar in its mental-status changes to other dementing processes. Changes in orientation, recent memory, and higher cortical functioning can all be seen. Furthermore, there are behavioral and emotional disturbances, which may include personality changes, bizarre behavior, hallucinations, and delusions. Asterixis and seizures are late complications. There is currently no known effective treatment, and so coma and death are ultimately inevitable (Scheiber and Ziesat 1976). Since the neurological complications include seizures, it seemed logical to try anticonvulsant medication, and some optimistic reports suggested the efficacy of diazepam (Nadel and Wilson 1976). But more recent reports have not confirmed this, and diazepam appears to be useful on a temporary basis (Snider et al. 1979).

The EEG can be of some assistance in diagnosing this condition, as it characteristically contains a mild to moderate degree of slowing, as well as delta waves (Chokrovery et al. 1976). Postmortem pathological examination of brain and other nervous system tissue has failed to unearth any morphological correlate. This suggests some sort of metabolic abnormality or perhaps even a toxic condition (Chokroverty et al. 1976).

The etiology of the syndrome remains occult. Various etiologies have been postulated, including the sequelae of viral infection or trace metal abnormalities such as tin accumulation (Alfrey et al. 1972). Dopamine and asparagine deficiencies have also been considered. The latest thinking seems to have settled on aluminum as one of the strongest etiological culprits, and indeed, some evidence supports this (Vaisrub 1978). Early reports focused on the widespread use of aluminum hydroxide gels in the antacid preparations ubitquitously given to chronic dialysis patients (Alfrey et al. 1976). More recent reports have discarded this notion, and current theorizing suggests that the presence of aluminum in tap water, which is used in the dialysing medium, is responsible (Dunea et al. 1978, Rozas et al. 1978). There are data suggesting that use of aluminum-free water prevents the occurrence of this complication (Elliott et al. 1978, Rozas et al. 1978). Once this condition has developed, however, changing the water does not appear to be effective. It is intriguing to speculate on the possibility of renal transplantation as a treatment for this syndrome (Burks et al. 1976). There are available only limited data on this problem, though some evidence does suggest improvement in this condition following successful renal transplantation (Sullivan et al. 1977).

SUBDURAL HEMATOMA

Some reports have suggested that subdural hematoma is seen more often in patients on chronic hemodialysis (Leonard et al. 1969, Talalla et al. 1970). Whether or not this is so will require further study. Reportedly, the early symptoms of subdural hematoma in the chronic dialytic patient are nonspecific and include drowsiness, fatigue, lassitude, headache, and nausea. The typical focal signs of meningeal irritation and the deterioration of mental functioning come later. Since the early signs are similar to those of the dialysis disequilibrium syndrome, an accurate diagnosis can be difficult. Unfortunately, by the time the less-confusing symptoms of meningeal irritation are present, the condition usually has progressed substantially. If subdural hematoma is indeed a complication of chronic dialysis, it could be explained by the ubitquitous use of anticoagulants or the well-described bleeding tendency of uremia. Treatment, of course, is identical with that for subdural hematoma of other etiologies.

DEPRESSION

Probably the most common "psychiatric" complication of chronic dialysis is depression (Lefebvre et al. 1972, Levy 1981a). Though there are only a few studies of the incidence and/or prevalence of depression in this population, it is without question quite large. Probably at any given time, approximately 40 to 50 percent of a given chronic dialysis population will complain of depressed mood and will present signs and symptoms consistent with at least a moderate degree of depression, and 15 to 25 percent will describe and exhibit symptoms and signs of major depression (Bonney et al. 1978, Procci et al. 1981). Indeed, Reichman and Levy (1972) described depression as a typical stage through which all chronic patients pass as they adapt to maintenance hemodialysis.

The etiology of this depression is not clearly understood, but there are a myriad of psychological factors that could lead to a depressed mood. Chronic dialysis is a severe treatment regimen. It demands from the patient a great deal of time and sacrifice. There are strict dietary and fluid restrictions which many patients find intolerable (De-Nour and Czaczkes 1972; Procci 1978, 1981a, Winokur et al. 1973). Since food is a basic and primary reinforcer, many dialysis patients find it almost impossible to stick to the diet. Especially sensitive are those who have a paucity of resources and social supports, and so food then becomes an important alternative source of gratification.

Chronic dialysis is an extremely time-consuming treatment, requiring 15 to 20 hours or more per week for treatment and, if necessary, transportation to and from treatment. For many individuals, these time constraints preclude gainful employment. Numerous studies have demonstrated a high rate of job loss among chronic dialysis patients (De-Nour and Czaczkes 1976, Gutman and Amara 1978). Chronic dialysis is also extremely expensive. The current cost of a year's treatment is over $20,000 (Roberts et al. 1980). For all but a few rich patients, some form of insurance, usually a combination of private and governmental, is necessary. For many less-affluent patients, total dependency on governmental insurance in the form of Medicaid, Medicare, and the like is requisite. There is a certain paradox in the eligibility for such insurance coverage that stimulates nonemployment. If a wage earner's salary is above a certain minimal level, he or she is not eligible for governmental assistance. Rather than continuing to work, many dialysis patients will become unemployed in order to be relieved of the enormous cost of dialysis (Procci 1981b). Clearly, the life of the chronic dialysis patient is very difficult.

He or she may give up an important and gratifying role as an independent, wage-earning, self-sufficient member of his or her family and be relegated to a dependent, welfare-receiving, unemployed, and sick role. The high degree of depression present in this population is readily understandable.

CLINICAL FEATURES

Depression in the chronic dialysis patient is evidenced by many signs and symptoms, all varying in intensity. Typical depressive signs such as poor appetite, weight loss, fatigue, apathy, and sleep difficulty are common. But these are also features of the chronic illness state in general and uremia in particular so that diagnosis may be obscured and a careful differential diagnosis is essential (Wise 1974). Numerous writers have mentioned the omnipresence of denial in chronic dialysis patients as a prominent defense mechanism (Short and Wilson 1969). This can further cloud the diagnosis.

Some patients will not complain of feeling depressed but instead will act out their depression by not complying with one or more aspects of their treatment (Abram et al. 1971, De-Nour and Czaczkes 1972). Some patients will become angry, belligerent, and demanding with staff members. In extreme forms, patients will be uncooperative to the point of refusing to come for further dialysis. Overtly suicidal behavior is also observed. Abram and associates (1971) estimated that combining both overtly suicidal behavior with the more covert forms such as not coming for dialysis or engaging in food and fluid binges yields an overall suicide rate that is 100 to 400 times that of the general population, though some aspects of Abram's and colleagues' methodology have been criticized. A more recent study reported a suicide rate in dialysis patients 24 times that of the general population (Haenel et al. 1980). In any case, it is clear that there is an alarmingly high rate of overt and covert suicidal behavior in these patients.

There is at present no accepted treatment for the depression of chronic dialysis. Traditional psychotherapy is frequently offered but often resisted. When accepted, results have been far from desirable (De-Nour 1970). This is probably because such depressions are based in part on nearly insurmountable reality problems rather than on conflict as in neurotic depression, for which psychotherapy is more effective. Surprisingly, there are few data on the effect of antidepressant medication on chronic dialysis patients. Certain serious depressions with signs and symptoms similar to those seen in more classical major affective disorders may respond to antidepressant therapy. One report did describe some success in treating renal transplant recipients with tricyclic antidepressants (McCabe and Corry 1978). Further investigations of this issue are needed, as there are virtually no data on the effects on chronic dialysis patients of either the monoamine oxidase inhibitors or electroconvulsive therapy.

SEXUAL DYSFUNCTION

From the patient's point of view, sexual dysfunction is one of the most unpleasant of all the complications of chronic dialysis. Only in recent years has this problem come to the attention of nephrologists and psychiatrists. Levy's 1973 study was the first relatively large-scale effort to obtain information regarding sexual functioning in chronic renal failure. Since then there have been many studies that have investigated sexual functioning in the dialysis-patient population (Abram et al. 1975, Bommer et al. 1976, Chopp and Mendez 1978, De-Nour 1978, Milne et al. 1978, Procci et al. 1981, Salvatierra et al. 1975, Sherman 1975, Steele et al. 1976, Thurm 1975).

The problem of sexual dysfunction is complicated. Although the various studies have some discrepant results, they do agree on some points. Males report a decline in their interest in sex and also difficulties in obtaining and maintaining erections. More subtle complaints such as "lack of staying power" or the inability to obtain a second erection are also heard. Some data indicate that the problem worsens quite drastically with increasing age (Procci et al. 1981). Younger men seem better able to retain some of their sexual capacity than do older men for whom profound performance deficits are common. Exact figures are difficult to obtain, but it is probably safe to say that between 25 and 50 percent of males on chronic dialysis will suffer at least some degree of erectile failure, and of these approximately 10 to 20 percent suffer total impotence. The lower figures apply to younger men (age 20 to 40), and the higher figures apply to older men (40 to 60). Of course, this complication is most disturbing to those individuals whose interest in sex remains high, even though their performance capability declines.

In addition to these deficits in sexual performance, parallel research by endocrinologists has discovered profound hormonal abnormalities. Although there are some differences among the various investigators' results, several findings are similar. Testosterone levels are low (Chen et al. 1970, Guevara et al. 1969), and follicle-stimulating and luteinizing hormone levels are usually elevated (Lim and Fang 1976, Chen et al. 1970). More recent research has included prolactin measurements, and this hormone is usually elevated (Hagen et al. 1976). Unfortunately, the psychiatry and endocrine investigations have generally been performed by separate research teams, and so the relationship between the hormonal deficits and the sexual performance deficits is not well understood.

The etiology of male sexual dysfunction in end-stage renal disease has been vigorously debated (Levy 1981a). Proponents of a psychological etiology point to the high incidence of depression as well as to the demeaning aspects of chronic illness in general and maintenance hemodialysis in particular. The high rates of unemployment, the frequent need to accept welfare payment, the difficulties in rehabilitation, and the frequent role reversal all serve to deprive the male dialysis patient of his sense of masculinity and could conceivably contribute to psychogenic sexual dysfunction.

Proponents of an organic etiology cite profound hormonal deficits as a contributor, although as mentioned, few investigators have combined psychological and endocrinologic studies. Another possible etiology is neurologic. Extensive neuropathy is a common long-term complication of chronic renal failure, and the autonomic nervous system may well be affected. Indeed, there are data that correlate autonomic nervous system deficits with sexual performance deficits in chronic dialysis patients (Campese et al. in press). Several years ago, one research group presented interesting data concerning possible zinc deficiencies in impotent chronic dialysis patients (Antoniou et al. 1977). Placing zinc in the dialysis bath reportedly improved sexual performance. This is an intriguing idea, but so far this work has not been replicated, and so the possible role of zinc deficiency remains unclear. Finally, it is also conceivable that vascular deficits could be responsible, at least in some chronic dialysis patients.

With so many possible etiologies, it is obvious that the exact nature of this disturbance is obscure. Recently, several groups have advocated using nocturnal penile tumescence (NPT) as an aid in differentiating organic from psychogenic sexual disturbance (Fisher et al. 1979, Karacan et al. 1978, Wasserman et al. 1980). In a study of NPT in chronic dialysis, our research group at the University of Southern California (USC) found profound deficits in NPT in about 20 percent of males on chronic hemodialysis, and moderate deficits in about another 20 to 30 percent (Procci et al. 1981). Thus nearly 50 percent of males on chronic dialysis exhibited some degree of reduced NPT. In comparison, in a group of men with other chronic illnesses, NPT was not reduced. Also, the NPT deficit in chronic dialysis was more pronounced in older males (i.e., those 40 to 60 years old). Although this technique cannot definitively differentiate psychogenic from organic causes of erectile failure (Wasserman et al. 1980), it is certainly strongly suggestive. It appears that organic factors contribute to the etiology of at least some of the sexual dysfunctions in males treated with chronic hemodialysis. But the exact nature of the organic deficits is still unclear.

Females with chronic renal failure also have marked alterations in sexual functioning, but female sexual dysfunction has not received the same degree of attention as has male dysfunction. Women on chronic dialysis complain of their loss of interest in sexuality as well as their inability to experience sexual excitation. Many are anorgasmic.

Similar to the men, women also note hormonal deficits. Many have become anovulatory, and menses cease. Hyperprolactinemia is also present. Although there are reports of a few successful pregnancies among female dialysis patients, this is something of an exception, and many of these women are infertile, as are many of their male counterparts. The same argument exists concerning the etiology of female sexual dysfunction, i.e., psychogenic versus organic. Because women's sexual dysfunction has been studied less than male sexual dysfunction has, there are even fewer data on it. Furthermore, there is at present no way of differentiating organic from psychogenic sexual dysfunction in females, such as NPT provides for males.

Since the etiology remains obscure, there is no truly effective treatment for either male or female sexual dysfunction. Surprisingly, there are few data on possible ameliorative effects from the new behavior-oriented sex therapies that have evolved from Masters' and Johnson's pioneering work (Milne et al. 1978). As well, there are few data on hormonal treatments, though bromocriptine, a prolactin-lowering agent, could readily be given to patients with hyperprolactinemia, and the results studied. Several investigators have followed dialysis patients who are subsequently transplanted, and other investigators have compared dialysis patients with renal transplant recipients (Chopp and Mendez 1978, Levy 1973, Procci et al. 1978, Salvatierra et al. 1975). Basically, there appears to be at most only a mildly beneficial effect from renal transplantation. Relatively few patients seem to improve, many remain the same, and some actually worsen.

Since chronic illnesses are now receiving more attention, it is likely that this sexual dysfunction will be much more thoroughly investigated and ultimately better understood in the future.

PROBLEMS WITH REHABILITATION

Chronic dialysis is very expensive. The direct cost of dialytic treatment is only part of the cost of this illness and its treatment. Many patients are unable, or perhaps unwilling, to return to their jobs (Bonney et al. 1978, De-Nour and Czaczkes 1975), resulting in a serious loss of productivity.

As with many of the psychiatric sequelae of chronic dialysis, the problems of rehabilitation have only recently come to the attention of researchers. Most early research with chronic dialysis was necessarily concerned with the various technical aspects of dialytic treatment. Only in recent years, with the survival of chronic dialysis patients much improved, has it been possible to focus on the various psychiatric sequelae. Levy and Wynbrandt (1975) applied the concept of quality of life to the study of chronic dialysis patients. Essentially, they found that a majority of chronic dialysis patients felt that the quality of their lives had deteriorated since they had started maintenance hemodialysis. It seemed that the best one could hope for was stability of life or perhaps only a moderate decline. They noted that many of these patients did not return to work. In a study at USC, our group evaluated the concept of social disability among patients on maintenance hemodialysis (Procci 1981b). We found that a majority of chronic dialysis patients had great social disability consistent with a significant interference in their life-style. Furthermore we noted that this social disability tended to increase with the chronicity of dialysis. Those individuals with five or more years of dialysis suffered greater social disability than did the patients having started dialysis more recently. Finally, we found that approximately 60 percent of our sample had given up their jobs since beginning dialysis.

Certainly the expense of dialysis and the restrictiveness of the rules and regulations concerning the eligibility for receiving governmentally financed insurance do contribute to the high unemployment. In Scandinavia where eligibility for insurance to cover dialysis is independent of income, one group did not find high rates of unemployment in dialysis patients (Bergsten et al. 1977). Thus, some reform of these regulations should be considered. However, the problem with rehabilitation appears to go deeper. Many dialysis patients exhibit chronic states of apathy and demoralization, although they do not necessarily exhibit the classical signs of primary affective disorder. They lose interest in their typical day-to-day activities and seem to live a life built almost exclusively around the dialysis machine. Attempts to involve these patients not only in vocational but also in social rehabilitation often are resisted. Engel (1968) wrote extensively about a "giving up–given up" psychological state associated with a physiological state of conservation and/or withdrawal. In many respects some chronic dialysis patients fit this description.

This problem is compounded by the chronicity of dialytic treatment. It is, of course, a general principle of any rehabilitation effort that the longer a pathological condition exists with the individual remaining inactive, the more difficult it will be to motivate and propel him or her back into an active and productive life. Our own study did suggest that with increasing chronicity of dialysis, there is also increasing social disability (Procci 1981b). De-Nour and Czaczkes (1975) found that vocational rehabilitation improved during the first six months of chronic dialysis but after that remained stable, at best. This indicates that strong efforts toward maintaining employment as well as social activities should be undertaken early in the course of chronic renal failure, considerably earlier than the state of chronic dialysis by which time it may well be too late.

It is unlikely that traditional medical approaches will be able to offer much in the way of therapy for these problems, barring some dramatically new treatment technique that would drastically alter the course of chronic renal failure. Most likely, the interventions required to resolve problems with rehabilitation will need to come from other areas. No doubt, this kind of process is operative with other chronic illnesses as well. Indeed, the term *disease of medical progress* has been used to describe similar sequelae of other chronic illnesses in which individuals who would once have died are now able to live much longer but face a new set of problems that neither patient nor physician expected. These problems are likely to increase in the coming years as more chronically ill patients are able to live for longer periods of time.

ADAPTING TO CHRONIC DIALYSIS

The patient's response to chronic dialysis is not static. There are a series of relatively predictable stages through which many chronic dialysis patients progress, from the beginning of dialytic treatment until a state of relatively stable adjustment is attained. As with any generalized developmental sequence, there are many exceptions to these stages, though the following discussion is probably applicable to a majority of chronic dialytic patients.

Reichman and Levy (1972) investigated in detail the adaptation to chronic dialysis. Patients with end-stage renal failure who are in a predialytic condition are usually very ill. They are often fatigued and apathetic and show definite signs of major systemic illness. Since they are aware of their impending chronic dialysis, they generally experience some heightening of expectations as the dialytic treatments are commenced. Within a few weeks after the chronic dialysis has begun, there is a significant reduction in the levels of the various metabolic waste products in the sera of dialytic patients. This, combined with the novelty of the treatment and the inherent promise of a better life, stimulates in most patients a sense of increased emotional and physical well-being. Some feel hope, happiness, and sometimes outright euphoria. A few patients will even describe a sense of being reborn. The difficulties inherent in chronic dialysis, such as the pronounced dependency on the procedure and the various time and dietary restrictions, are usually either denied or minimized. This stage was dubbed the "honeymoon" by Reichman and Levy. It generally begins within one to three weeks after the onset of chronic dialysis, and in most cases it lasts anywhere from six weeks to six months.

But after practically every honeymoon, the lovers begin to see all their partner's blemishes, and the realization of being married to a fallible and imperfect partner becomes manifest. A similar process occurs with the chronic dialysis patient, and so a stage of disenchantment and discouragement begins. In some individuals it is gradual, but in others the onset may be abrupt. It may begin when the patient becomes aware that he or she will not be able to resume former activities. It also may begin when improvement in the patient's physical condition stops and a plateau is reached or even a decline starts. It must be remembered that chronic dialysis is by no means a curative treatment. The complications of end-stage renal disease, which are legion, continue despite the dialytic therapy. Hypertension, peripheral neuropathy, bone deterioration, and sexual dysfunction are but a few of the sequelae that may progress. Needless to say, this often leaves the dialysis patients with a feeling of futility and bitter disappointment. Such patients may feel that they have been duped into conforming to a constraining regimen that only gives them problems and does not stave off the long-term consequences of their illness. The patient's feelings of hope, contentment, and optimism, which developed during the honeymoon stage, erode in the realization of the limitations of chronic dialysis. This stage generally lasts anywhere from 3 to 12 months.

Unfortunately some individuals remain in chronic states of disenchantment and disappointment for the duration of their dialytic treatment. Although it is impossible to predict accurately and completely who will and will not adapt to chronic dialysis, there are some general findings.

Individuals who have shown flexibility in coping with previous stressors and individuals who have good interpersonal relationships are more likely to adapt successfully (Meldrum et al. 1968). De-Nour and Czaczkes (1975) reported that the patient's dependent needs (if low) and satisfaction with work (if high) are predictors of satisfactory adjustment. Surprisingly, intelligence and social class were not necessarily strong predictors of adaptation (Hagberg 1974, Winokur et al. 1973). In the past, when the number of dialytic machines was limited, physicians had the agonizing decision of choosing patients for dialysis (Abram and Wadlington 1968). Fortunately this is not the current situation, since there are enough machines to accommodate the population of chronic renal failure patients.

For the majority of dialysis patients, the stage of long-term adaptation is achieved, in which they realize that they must face a life governed by maintenance dialysis. Furthermore, they must accept the inherent limitations and learn to organize their lives so that they are neither dominated nor enslaved by dialysis. This is an ideal, however, and even the few who can achieve it usually do so only gradually. For these individuals the inevitable fluctuations in their physical health do not lead to disastrous consequences.

THE ACTING-OUT PATIENT

The acting-out patient represents a special problem in the chronic dialysis unit. The maintenance dialysis patient spends a great deal of time (at least 15 hours a week) with the same group of people, i.e., the dialysis nurses, the other dialysis patients, the nephrologists, and all the other members of the dialysis team. It is inevitable that patients will develop transference relationships with these other individuals, and thus the stage is set for acting out. This can occur in various forms, ranging from excessive dependent attachments to chronic unrelenting hostile attacks. Flirtatiousness may be seen, and it is not unusual for dialysis patients to date or seek to date nurses and vice versa. Dialysis patients will occasionally date one another, and in our unit at the LAC/USC Medical Center two chronic dialysis patients got married. Thus, the chronic dialysis unit is in many ways like an extended family or a small community.

In most cases this produces only minor problems, similar to those arising in any collection of diverse individuals who must spend time together. But major problems with the dialysis team's cohesiveness and morale can occur with the acting-out and manipulative patient. This is the kind of problem that calls for a well-organized liaison psychiatry service. Merely offering psychiatric consultation to the involved patient will result in an incomplete solution, since an entire system is involved. It may be more fruitful under such circumstances for the psychiatrist to attempt to meet with the dialysis team (Czaczkes and De-Nour 1978, De-Nour 1973). The task is to recognize not only that the patient is acting out but also that his or her behavior is affecting the functioning of the dialysis team. Ideally, the various team members will be able, with the assistance of the psychiatric consultant, to devise appropriate team strategies for dealing with these patients. When properly conducted, the liaison psychiatry approach can lead to enhanced team cohesiveness. There are also empirical data that suggest that better organized, more cohesive dialysis teams that have realistic expectations of their patients achieve better results with chronic dialysis patients in regard to both their physical and social rehabilitation (Czaczkes and De-Nour 1978).

THE DECISION TO WITHDRAW FROM CHRONIC DIALYSIS

The decision to withdraw from chronic dialysis is usually very unsettling for a chronic dialysis unit. There does exist a small number of patients who are unable to adjust to chronic dialysis. For them a serious attempt must be made to determine whether or not renal transplantation is a feasible alternative. There are some patients who though unable to tolerate the restrictions of dialysis, are quite able to handle a renal transplantation regimen. It must be understood that renal transplantation is no panacea. It presents different problems for successful adaptation, but some individuals who are unable to adapt to chronic dialysis can adapt reasonably well to renal transplantation and vice versa. Unfortunately there is very little available information that allows us to predict which patient will do well or poorly in these different treatment modalities (Kemph 1977). In any event, if transplantation is not a feasible alternative for the patient who just cannot adapt to chronic dialysis, he or she may request withdrawal from chronic dialysis.

In general it is probably wise to discuss this decision exhaustively with the patient and the key members of his or her family. They all must be prepared for the consequences that this decision entails. Death from uremia is very unpleasant, and the family must understand what is involved in caring for such an individual.

The decision can also have a profound effect on the dialysis team, especially if it is a patient for whom several staff members have strong feelings, either positive or negative. If the dialysis unit has a regular psychiatric consultant, he or she should probably meet with the dialysis team and allow them to air their feelings concerning the loss of one of their charges. The psychiatrist can be extremely helpful both in pointing out the patient's difficulties in adapting to chronic dialysis and in allowing the team members to discuss openly their feelings concerning chronic dialysis.

PSYCHOTROPIC DRUG USAGE

As this chapter demonstrated, chronic dialysis patients exhibit a wide range of psychopathologic signs, symptoms, and conditions, and it is inevitable that the psychiatric consultant will be asked about the various psychotropic medications. As a general principle, most of the drugs used to treat psychiatric illnesses are metabolized by the liver, and only inactive metabolities are then excreted by the kidneys (Bennet et al. 1971). This is usually the case for the phenothiazines and butrophenone neuroleptics, the tricyclic antidepressants, and the benzodiazipines. A recent report of several cases of major neurologic alterations in chronic dialysis patients treated with diazepam and flurazepam (Taclob and Needle 1976) substantiates the need for caution. But generally, chronic dialysis patients may use these medications in their usual therapeutic doses. Certainly these patients should be carefully watched for the development of untoward side effects. Common sense also dictates that such medications be introduced gradually and that the lowest effective dose to control the patient's symptoms be found. Since chronic dialysis patients often have complications of renal failure, such as hypertension, extra scrutiny and dosage alteration may be necessary.

A notable exception to this is lithium carbonate. Lithium is not metabolized but is excreted, almost entirely through the kidneys. In chronic renal failure, lithium accumulates rapidly in the blood, with resultant toxicity. Lithium therefore should not be used for patients with end-stage renal disease. In recent years, however, there have been reports of successfully treating manic-depressive chronic dialysis patients with oral lithium carbonate (Port et al. 1979, Procci 1977) The principle is simple. Dialysis removes lithium from the blood, but diseased kidneys do not. Between dialyses, therefore, whatever lithium is in the body will remain there, since there are no functional kidneys to remove it. But as long as it is known exactly how much lithium is removed from the blood by dialysis, an identical amount can be put back in. In theory, manic chronic dialysis patients can be adequately treated with as little as 300 to 600 mg of lithium carbonate following each dialysis (only three times a week in most cases), and this is indeed the case. In practice, it is feasible to treat chronic dialysis patients with lithium only when they can be psychiatrically evaluated and when there is ready access to a laboratory that can measure lithium levels (Port et al. 1979, Procci 1977). If these constraints are observed, lithium carbonate treatment can be used despite chronic renal failure and maintenance hemodialysis.

CONCLUSIONS

This chapter has given the reader only a superficial and bird's-eye view of a rather complicated issue. The sequelae of chronic dialysis are so numerous and so varied that a brief summary cannot really be satisfactory. As mentioned earlier, more than 2,000 studies have addressed various aspects of these sequelae (Blodgett 1981). The serious student of "psychonephrology," as Levy coined this area of inquiry (1981b), should make his or her own thorough review of this literature (Blodgett 1981, Czaczkes and De-Nour 1978, Levy 1974, 1981b). As greater attention is focused on chronic illness in general, we can expect that even more attention will be directed to the tribulations of chronic dialysis. One hopes that there will be some improvement in the still vaguely understood concept of quality of life for these patients.

We should note in concluding that chronic dialysis does *not* uniformly result in a bleak style of living. Some patients, albeit a minority, do well despite chronic dialysis and are able to maintain a reasonable facsimile of a normal life (Procci 1981b). Unfortunately, normality does not attract as much attention as pathology does, and so these patients have not been carefully investigated. Understanding how they are able to persevere may help in designing the novel kinds of interventions that will probably be necessary to enhance the life-style of chronic dialysis patients.

REFERENCES

Abram, H. S., Hester, L. R., Sheridan, W. F., and Epstein, G. M. (1975). Sexual functioning in patients with chronic renal failure. *Journal of Nervous and Mental Disease* 160:220–226.

Abram, H. S., Moore, G. I., and Westervelt, F. B., Jr. (1971). Suicidal behavior in chronic dialysis patients. *American Journal of Psychiatry* 127:1199–1204.

Abram, H. S., and Wadlington, W. (1968). Selection of patients for artificial and transplanted organs. *Annals of Internal Medicine* 69:615–620.

Alfrey, A. D., LeGrende, G. R., and Kaehny, W. D. (1976). The dialysis encephalopathy syndrome: possible aluminum intoxication. *New England Journal of Medicine* 294:184–188.

Alfrey, A. D., Mishell, J. M., Burks, J., Contiguglia, S. R., Rudolph, H., Lewin, E., and Holmes, J. H. (1972). Syndrome of dysprasiz and multifocal seizures associated with chronic hemodialysis. *Transactions of the American Society of Artifical Internal Organs* 18:257–261.

Antoniou, L. D., Shalhaub, R. J., Sudhakar, T., and Smith, J. C., Jr. (1977). Reversal of uremic impotence by zinc. *Lancet* 2:895–898.

Baker, A. B., and Knutson, J. (1946). Psychiatric aspects of uremia. *American Journal of Psychiatry* 102:683–687.

Bennet, W. M., Singer, I., Golper, T., Fey, P., and Coggins, C. J. (1971). Guidelines for drug therapy in renal failure. *Annals of Internal Medicine* 86:754–783.

Bergsten, E., Asaba, M., and Bergström, J. (1977). A study of patients on chronic hemodialysis. *Scandinavian Journal of Social Medicine* 11:1–31.

Blodgett, C. (1981). A selected review of the literature of adjustment to hemodialysis. *International Journal of Psychiatry in Medicine* 11:97–124.

Bommer, J., Tschope, W., Ritz, E., and Andrassy, K. (1976). Sexual behavior of hemodialysis patients. *Clinical Nephrology* 6:315–318.

Bonney, S., Finkelstein, F. O., Lytton, B., Schiff, M., and Steele, T. E. (1978). Treatment of end stage renal failure in a defined geographic area. *Archives of Internal Medicine* 138:1510–1513.

Burks, J. S., Alfrey, A. D., Huddlestone, J., Norenberg, M. D., and Lewin, E. (1976). A fatal encephalopathy in chronic hemodialysis patients. *Lancet* 1:764–768.

Campese, V. M., Procci, W. R., Levitan, D., Remoff, M. S., Goldstein, D. A., and Massry, S. G. (In press). Autonomic nervous system dysfunction and impotence in uremia. *American Journal of Nephrology*.

Chen, J. C., Vidt, D. G., Zorn, E. M., Hallberg, M. C., and Wieland, R. G. (1970). Pituitary-Leydig cell function in uremic males. *Journal of Clinical Endocrinology and Metabolism* 31:14–17.

Chokroverty, S., Bruetman, M. E., Berger, V., and Reyes, M. G. (1976). Progressive dialytic encephalopathy. *Journal of Neurology, Neurosurgery and Psychiatry* 39:411–419.

Chopp, R. T., and Mendez, R. (1978). Sexual function and hormonal abnormalities in uremic men on chronic dialysis and after renal transplantation. *Fertility and Sterility* 29:661–666.

Czaczkes, J. W., and De-Nour, A. K. (1978). *Chronic Hemodialysis as a Way of Life*. New York: Brunner/Mazel.

De-Nour, A. K. (1970). Psychotherapy with patients on chronic hemodialysis. *British Journal of Psychiatry* 116:207–215.

————. (1973). Role and reactions of psychiatrists in chronic hemodialysis programs. *International Journal of Psychiatry in Medicine* 4:63–76.

————. (1978). Hemodialysis: sexual functioning. *Psychosomatics* 19:229–235.

De-Nour, A. K., and Czaczkes, J. W. (1972). Personality factors in chronic hemodialysis patients causing noncompliance and medical regimen. *Psychosomatic Medicine* 34:333–344.

————. (1975). Personality factors influencing vocational rehabilitation. *Archives of General Psychiatry* 32:573–574.

————. (1976). The influence of patient's personality on adjustment to chronic dialysis: a predictive study. *Journal of Nervous and Mental Disease* 162:323–333.

Dunea, G., Mahurkar, S. D., Mamdani, B., and Smith, E. C. (1978). Role of aluminum in dialysis dementia. *Annals of Internal Medicine* 88:502–504.

Elliott, H. L., Dryburgh, F., Fill, G. S., Sabet, S., and Macdougall, A. I. (1978). Aluminum toxicity during regular hemodialysis. *British Medical Journal* 1:1101–1103.

Engel, G. L. (1968). A life setting conducive to illness. *Bulletin of the Menninger Clinic* 32:355–365.

Fisher, C., Schiavi, R. C., Edwards, A., Davis, D., Reitman, M., and Fine, J. (1979). Evaluation of nocturnal penile tumescence in the differential diagnosis of sexual impotence. *Archives of General Hospital Psychiatry* 36:431–437.

Ginn, H. E., Teschan, P. E., Walker, P. J., Bourne, J. R., Fristoe, M., Ward, J. W., McLain, L. W., Johnston, H. B., and Hamel, B. (1975). Neurotoxicity in uremia. *Kidney International* 7:5357–5360.

Grushkin, C. M., Korsch, B., and Fine, R. M. (1972). Hemodialysis in small children. *Journal of the American Medical Association* 221:869–873.

Guevara, A., Vidt, D., Hallbert, M. C., Zorn, E. M., Pohlman, C., and Weiland, R. G. (1969). Serum gonadotropin and testosterone levels in males undergoing intermittent hemodialysis. *Metabolism* 18:1062–1066.

Gutmann, R. A., and Amara, A. M. (1978). Outcome of therapy for end-stage uremia: an informed prediction of survival rate and degree of rehabilitation. *Postgraduate Medicine* 64:183–194.

Haenel, T., Brunner, F., and Battegay, R. (1980). Renal dialysis and suicide: occurence in Switzerland and Europe. *Comprehensive Psychiatry* 21:140–145.

Hagberg, B. A. (1974). A prospective study of patients in chronic hemodialysis. III. Predictive value of intelligence, cognitive deficit and ego defense structures in rehabilitation. *Journal of Psychosomatic Research* 18:151–160.

Hagen, C., Olgaard, K., McNeilly, A. S., and Fisher, R. (1976). Prolactin and the pituitary-gonadal axis in male uraemic patients on regular dialysis. *Acta Endocrinologica Copenhagen* 82:29–38.

Karacan, I., Sales, P. J., Ware, J. C., Deverent, B., Williams, R. L., Scott, F. B., Attia, S. L., and Beutter, L. E. (1978). Nocturnal penile tumescence and diagnosis in diabetic impotence. *American Journal of Psychiatry* 135:191–197.

Kemph, J. P. (1977). The kidney or the machine. *Journal of the American Medical Association* 237:2532.

Kiley, J., and Hines, O. (1975). Electroencephalographic evaluation of uremia. *Archives of Internal Medicine* 116:67–73.

Lefebvre, P., Nobert, A., and Crombez, J. C. (1972). Psychological and psychopathological reactions in relation to chronic hemodialysis. *Canadian Psychiatric Association Journal* 17:SS-9-SS-13.

Leonard, C. D., Weil, E., and Scribner, B. H. (1969). Subdural haematomas in patients undergoing hemodialysis. *Lancet* 2:239–240.

Levy, N. B. (1973). Sexual adjustment to maintenance hemodialysis and renal transplantation: national survey by questionnaire: preliminary report. *Transactions of the American Society of Artificial Internal Organs* 19:138–143.

————. (1974). *Living or Dying: Adaptation to Hemodialysis.* Springfield, Ill.: Charles C Thomas.

————. (1981a). Psychological reactions to machine dependency: hemodialysis. *Psychiatric Clinics of North America* 4:351–363.

————. (1981b). *Psychonephrology I: Psychological Factors in Hemodialysis and Transplantation.* New York: Plenum.

Levy, N. B., and Wynbrandt, G. D. (1975). The quality of life on maintenance hemodialysis. *Lancet* 1:1328–1330.

Lim, V. S., and Fang, V. S. (1976). Determination of plasma testosterone levels in uremic men with clomiphene citrate. *Journal of Clinical Endocrinology and Metabolism* 43:1370–1377.

McCabe, M. S., and Corry, R. J. (1978). Psychiatric illness and human renal transplantation. *Journal of Clinical Psychiatry* 39:393–400.

Mahurkar, S., Dhar, S. K., Salta, R., Meyers, L., Smith, E. C., and Dunea, G. (1973). Dialysis dementia. *Lancet* 1:1412–1415.

Meldrum, M. W., Wolfram, J. G., and Rubini, M. E. (1968). The impact of chronic hemodialysis upon the socioeconomics of a veteran patient group. *Journal of Chronic Disease* 21:37–52.

Milne, J. F., Golden, J. S., and Fibus, L. (1978). Sexual dysfunction in renal failure: a survey of chronic hemodialysis patients. *International Journal of Psychiatry in Medicine* 8:335–345.

Nadel, A. M., and Wilson, W. P. (1976). Dialysis encephalopathy: a possible seizure disorder. *Neurology* 26:1130–1134.

Port, F. .K., Knoll, P. D., and Rosenweig, J. (1979). Lithium therapy during maintenance hemodialysis. *Psychosomatics* 20:130–131.

Procci, W. R. (1977). Mania during maintenance hemodialysis successfully treated with oral lithium carbonate. *Journal of Nervous and Mental Disease*. 164:355–358.

———. (1978). Dietary abuse in maintenance hemodialysis patients. *Psychosomatics* 19:16–24.

———. (1981a). Psychological factors associated with severe abuse of the hemodialysis diet. *General Hospital Psychiatry* 3:111–118.

———. (1981b). Psychological disability during maintenance hemodialysis. *General Hospital Psychiatry* 3:24–31.

Procci, W. R., Goldstein, D. A., Adelstein, J., and Massry, S. G. (1981). Sexual dysfunction in the male patient with uremia: a reappraisal. *Kidney International* 19:317–323.

Procci, W. R., Hoffman, K. I., and Chatterjee, S. N. (1978). Sexual functioning of renal transplant recipients. *Journal of Nervous and Mental Disease* 166:402–407.

Reichman, F., and Levy, N. B. (1972). Problems in adaptation to maintenance hemodialysis. *Archives of Internal Medicine* 130:859–865.

Rigg, G. A., and Bercu, B. A. (1967). Hypoglycemia — a complication of hemodialysis. *New England Journal of Medicine* 277:1139–1140.

Roberts, S. D., Maxwell, D. R., and Gross, T. L. (1980). Cost-effective care of end-stage renal disease: a billion dollar question. *Annals of Internal Medicine* 92:243–248.

Rozas, V. V., Port, K. F., and Rutt, W. M. (1978). Progressive encephalopathy from dialysate aluminum. *Archives of Internal Medicine* 138:1375–1377.

Salvatierra, O., Fortmann, J. L., and Belzer, F. O. (1975). Sexual function in males before and after renal transplantation. *Urology* 5:64–66.

Scheiber, S. C., and Ziesat, H. (1976). Dementia dialytica: a new psychotic organic brain syndrome. *Comprehensive Psychiatry* 17:781–785.

Schreiner, G. E. (1959). Mental and personality changes in the uremic syndrome. *Medical Annals of the District of Columbia* 28:316–323.

Shea, E. J., Bogdan, D. F., Fromen, R. B., and Schreiner, G. E. (1965). Hemodialysis for chronic renal failure. IV. Psychological considerations. *Annals of Internal Medicine* 62:558–563.

Sherman, F. P. (1975). Impotence in patients with chronic renal failure on dialysis: its frequency and etiology. *Fertility and Sterility* 26:221–223.

Short, M. J., and Wilson, W. P. (1969). Roles of denial in chronic hemodialysis. *Archives of General Psychiatry* 20:433–437.

Snider, W. D., DeMaria, A. A., and Mann, J. D. (1979). Diazepam and dialysis encephalopathy. *Neurology* 29:414–415.

Steele, T. E., Finkelstein, S. M., and Finkelstein, F. O. (1976). Hemodialysis patients and spouses: marital discord, sexual problems, and depression. *Journal of Nervous and Mental Disease* 162:225–237.

Stenbäch, A., and Haapanen, E. (1967). Azotemia and psychosis: some observations on psychotic disturbances in patients with azotemia. *Acta Psychiatrica Scandinavica* 43(suppl.):30–38.

Sullivan, P. A., Muraghan, D. J., and Callaghan, N. (1977). Dialysis dementia: recovery after transplantation. *British Medical Journal* 2:740.

Taclob, L., and Needle, M. (1976). Drug-induced encephalopathy in patients on maintenance hemodialysis. *Lancet* 1:704–705.

Talalla, A., Hallbrook, M., Barbour, B. H., and Kurze, T. (1970). Subdural hematoma associated with long-term hemodialysis for chronic renal disease. *Journal of the American Medical Association* 212: 1847–1849.

Thurm, J. (1975). Sexual potency of patients on chronic hemodialysis. *Urology* 5:60–62.

Tyler, H. R. (1968). Neurologic disorder in renal failure. *American Journal of Medicine* 44:734–748.

Vaisrub, S. (1978). Dangerous waters. *Journal of American Medical Association* 240:1630.

Wakim, K. (1969). Predominance of hyponatremia over hypoosmolality in simulation of the dialysis disequilibrium syndrome. *Mayo Clinic Proceedings* 44:433–460.

Wasserman, M. D., Pollak, C. P., Spelman, A. J., and Weitzman, E. D. (1980). Theoretical and technical problems in the measurement of nocturnal penile tumescence for the differential diagnosis of impotence. *Psychosomatic Medicine* 42:575–585.

Winokur, M. Z., Czaczkes, J. W., and De-Nour, A. K. (1973). Intelligence and adjustment to chronic hemodialysis. *Journal of Psychosomatic Research* 17:29–34.

Wise, T. N. (1974). The pitfalls of diagnosing depression in chronic renal disease. *Psychosomatics* 15:83–84.

CHAPTER 11

Psychiatric Aspects of Surgery for Morbid Obesity

COLLEEN S. W. RAND, PH.D.
JOHN M. KULDAU, M.D.

Surgery for obesity is a radical treatment intended to produce weight loss in adults who cannot control their weight. It is offered as a last resort for morbidly obese adults whose health and functioning are severely compromised. These adults are at least 100 pounds or 100 percent overweight and are often much larger. They often are so heavy that they are literally physically disabled, and yet they cannot do the obvious on their own — permanently limit their caloric intake. Born with or acquiring the capacity to accumulate large amounts of fat and an ability to eat great quantities of food, surrounded by abundance, these adults gradually become immobilized by their weight. Relatively few elect surgery primarily for cosmetic reasons. Rather, most come because of major health problems and fear of a premature death.

On seeing a morbidly obese patient the outside observer is impressed with the massive amount of flesh carried on a normal human frame. Since most adults actively regulate their weight through diet and exercise, a typical reaction is, "How could this person let himself (or herself) get so fat?" The usual conclusion is that the enormous size must reflect some sort of major psychopathology. It thereby comes as somewhat of a surprise to many that morbidly obese patients do not consistently have psychiatric symptoms and that the majority are within the normal range on a large assortment of psychiatric test measures. Rather, they are deviant primarily in their ability to limit eating.

This chapter addresses the psychiatric adjustments of morbidly obese patients following surgery for obesity. First we shall present an overview of surgeries of obesity performed in the last ten years. Next we shall evaluate the preoperative psychiatric status of morbidly obese patients. Since the literature is limited, this section will also include data on obese adults. Finally, we shall describe the postoperative adjustment to weight reduction and other surgical sequelae.

SURGERY FOR OBESITY

Surgery for obesity is considered "developmental surgery"; that is, surgeons are still experimenting with procedures in order to develop an intervention that produces major permanent weight loss without excessive morbidity and mortality. There are more than ten different kinds of surgery for obesity, most of which can be divided into two categories: (1) surgeries that reduce the absorption of food eaten by shortening the small bowel and (2) surgeries that prevent excessive eating by reducing the stomach capacity. Other procedures include jaw wiring and vagotomy. Currently, surgeons at different centers disagree as to the best procedure, although the majority have discontinued the small bowel bypass because of the serious morbidity following the surgery.

SMALL INTESTINAL BYPASS

The first massive small bowel resections were performed on patients with gangrene in the majority of their intestine due to occlusion of the superior mesenteric artery. Marked weight loss occurred in those patients that survived (O'Leary 1976). In 1963, Payne, Dewind, and Commons described a trial of the jejunocolic shunt in an attempt to control morbid obesity through surgery. Major postoperative complications of diarrhea, electrolyte imbalance, and dehydration led to abandonment of this procedure in favor of the end-to-side jejunoileostomy (Payne and Dewind 1969). Variations of this procedure were developed in order to produce greater weight loss, e. g., Scott's and colleagues' (1973) end-to-end jejunoileostomy with the bypassed segment draining into the colon.

As longitudinal outcome data were published, some surgeons became increasingly cautious about performing the operation. For example, Halverson and associates (1978) reported that of the 100 morbidly obese patients studied prospectively, 58 percent experienced potentially life-threatening complications within 32 months after the jejunoileal bypass. The mortality rate was 5 percent; 17 percent underwent reversal and survived, producing a clear failure rate of 22 percent. Unfortunately, additional abnormalities related to malnutrition are still being discovered. Many surgeons have concluded that except under extenuating circumstances, the jejunoileal bypass is no longer an acceptable treatment for morbid obesity (Buckwalter 1978, Gold et al. 1982, Halverson et al. 1978). But other surgeons propose close postsurgical follow-up care and continue to perform the operation (Faloon et al. 1980, Gourlay and Reynolds 1978).

GASTRIC SURGERY

The gastric bypass was introduced by Mason and Ito in 1967. As its name implies, food cannot pass through part of the stomach. During surgery, the stomach is divided into a small upper pouch and a larger lower pouch. The small upper pouch is connected with the jejunum to reestablish continuity with the gastrointestinal tract. Progressive stretching of the upper pouch resulted in poor weight loss and necessitated further surgical innovation. The size of the upper pouch was reduced. Later modifications by Alden (1977) involved stapling rather than suturing the stomach. Griffen, Young, and Stevenson (1977) changed the early loop gastroenterostomy to a Roux-en-Y gastroenterostomy (see also Cegielski and Saporta 1981).

Gastroplasty, as an alternative to the gastric bypass, can also produce weight loss if an extremely small upper pouch (50 cc capacity) is created. The pouch is formed by placing a single or double row of staples across the stomach, leaving a small reinforced opening for food to pass from the upper to lower portions (Gomez 1980).

Recently, a technique of gastric wrapping was devised. The stomach is carefully stuffed into a preformed wrap made of Teflon, Dacron, or polypropylene mesh. The mesh wrap is intended to prevent stomach engorgement (Wilkinson and Peloso 1981), but it has proved difficult to keep the wrap securely in place.

The major concern with gastric surgeries is perforation of the upper or lower stomach, with subsequent peritonitis and death. As the techniques have improved, the rate of complications has fallen; currently between 7 and 25 percent of the patients have significant complications. Careful postsurgical management of eating and drinking is required to minimize vomiting and rupture of suture lines before they have healed (Buckwalter and Herbst 1980, Laws and Piantadosi 1981, Wilkinson and Peloso 1981). Peripheral neuropathy was recently reported as a rare but direct result of massive, rapid weight loss following gastric partitioning (Feit et al. 1982).

JAW WIRING

The high risk of operating on morbidly obese adults prompted some surgeons to try limiting food intake by wiring patients' jaws closed. The procedure, initially regarded as a safe, economical procedure, was largely abandoned because the patients could not maintain their weight loss once the wires were removed (Fordyce et al. 1979). Jaw wiring continues to be used occasionally as a preliminary treatment to produce weight loss before gastric surgery. A recent innovation may again popularize the procedure: successful weight loss maintenance has been reported in a pilot study for patients fitted with a snug nylon waist cord at the time their jaw wires were removed (Garrow and Gardiner 1981).

WHO ARE THE MORBIDLY OBESE?

DEFINITION

Although definitions of obesity vary, massive obesity is usually defined as being 100 pounds (45 kg) overweight and/or 100 percent over "ideal" body weight (Van Itallie and Kral 1981). There are no good statistics on the prevalence of massive obesity in the United States. The best estimates are that 1 percent or less of the adult population weighs more than 300 pounds. Most morbidly obese adults have a body fat content of 50 to 75 percent of their total body weight; normal weight adults range from 15 to 25 percent. The increased fat is thought to be distributed in an increased number of enlarged fat cells. The excess mortality associated with morbid obesity is caused primarily by higher rates of fatal coronary heart disease, stroke, and diabetes mellitus (Abraham and Johnson 1980, Van Itallie and Kral 1981).

ETIOLOGY

The etiology of obesity and morbid obesity is poorly understood. It is known that when people eat less, they lose weight, and conversely, when they eat more, they gain weight, all other factors held constant. But it is at best an oversimplification to explain obesity as the result of overeating. The underlying etiology of obesity is complex, including genetic, environmental, and sociobiological influences. The possibility of a viral etiology for some kinds of human obesity was suggested by the discovery of a viral-caused obesity syndrome in mice (Lyons et al. 1982). It is also unclear how many subtypes of obesity there are. For example, adults differ in their ability to gain weight when put on similar diets, indicating differences in metabolism of food or in hunger and satiety mechanisms (Booth et al. 1976, Mayer 1973, Monello et al. 1965, Sims et al. 1973), and they also differ markedly in their ability to lose weight on the same specified caloric amount (Garrow et al. 1978). The amount of fat included in diets directly influences how quickly weight can be gained (Sims et al. 1973), suggesting that either personal food preference or environmental availability of foods may facilitate obesity. The time distribution (i.e., frequency) of food intake also appears to affect weight gain (Hejda and Fábry 1964).

Defining and describing eating behaviors and their source and modifiability are important to both therapists and basic scientists, since changes in eating patterns over time (e.g., meal size and rate of eating) points to both psychosocial and biological causes (Meyer and Pudel 1972, Stunkard and Kaplan 1977). The practical implications of the relationship between obesity and eating patterns are underscored in the area of weight control. The main goal of behavior modification programs for weight control is to alter basic eating patterns so that less food will be consumed (Ferguson 1975).

There is much literature on the genetics of obesity (reviewed by Foch and McClearn 1980). The most carefully controlled work has been done with animals. Both farm and laboratory animals can be bred to increase the amounts of fatty tissue deposits. Syndromes of human obesity, such as the Laurence-Moon, Alstrom, and Prader-Labhart-Willi syndromes, have been associated with probable single-gene abnormalities. Twin studies, familial resemblance, and adoption studies all suggest an inheritable component of obesity, but one that is highly modifiable by the quality and quantities of food available and by exercise.

Morbidly obese patients come from homes where food is plentiful. Dietary histories indicate that preoperatively morbidly obese patients consume nearly 7,000 kcal per day. Direct observation of patients yields a somewhat lower figure (4,700 kcal per day; Bray et al. 1978). In our series of patients (n = 88; Kuldau and Rand 1980), 70 percent were markedly overweight by age 11, and only 15 percent became heavy as adults (i.e., 18 years or older). Most patients (60 percent) reported a gradual buildup of weight, with a few (10 percent) describing a history of weight plateaus and rises, a few (6 percent) relating large weight gain to pregnancies, a few (7 percent) reporting weight gains of 50 to 100 pounds in a few years, and the remainder (17 percent) having a history of enormous weight gains and losses (ups and downs of more than 50 pounds).

Morbidly obese patients also come from homes where there are other heavy people. Almost half (48 percent) of our patients had morbidly obese close blood relatives (compared with 18 percent in a comparison normal weight population), and 77 percent had heavy relatives (compared with 64 percent in the comparison sample; unpublished data).

PERSONALITY AND PSYCHIATRIC STATUS

Data on the personality characteristics and psychiatric status of morbidly obese adults are limited. With few exceptions, most data have been gathered in the context of treatment. Personality characteristics of obese adults, however, have been studied more extensively.

Underlying the research on personality differences between obese and normal-weight adults is the assumption that obesity is the symptom of an underlying personality disorder or psychiatric disturbance (Rand 1978). The basic premise is that all people need to exert the same amount of personal control in order to regulate their weight. The obese state, therefore, becomes an indication of the inadequacy of some personal control mechanism, and personality research becomes justified in trying to identify the deficit. Several thousand obese adults have been tested (Hällström and Noppa 1981, Moore et al. 1962). Obese and nonobese adults are similar on variables of tension-anxiety, nervous symptoms, depression, insomnia, psychoticism, and so forth. The few personality differences that have been documented are inconsistent from study to study. For example, in one study, obese adults were reported to be less stable than nonobese adults, and in another study no differences were observed (Hällström and Noppa 1981, Halmi et al. 1980).

There are many obese adults who are clearly neurotic, immature, or impulsive. The point is, however, that these personality characteristics occur with similar frequencies among both obese and nonobese populations. It has been much more fruitful to look for obese-nonobese differences in the areas of caloric consumption, exercise, and metabolism (Bray et al. 1978, Garrow et al. 1978, Kuldau et al. 1979).

From a psychiatric standpoint, despite careful study, only a minority of patients seeking bypass surgery have been considered to have diagnosable depression or neurotic syndromes. As a group, massively obese patients have been described as having "mild" personality disorders with traits of passive-dependence, passive-aggression, and emotional immaturity (Abram 1976; Hutzler et al. 1981). Considering that mild personality disorder is a vague diagnosis, it is difficult to assess its significance. Webb and colleagues (1976) reported that the obese patients presenting themselves for the operative procedure (n = 70) were clinically more normal than were a matched comparison group of psychiatric clinic patients (n = 32). Similar results were obtained by Wise (1979): responses of ileo-bypass candidates (n = 24) were compared with those of psychiatric outpatients using the SC1-90 and a semistructured interview. Bypass candidates had less symptomatology on all dimensions except somatic complaints.

In our study of married morbidly obese surgical candidates and married nonobese comparison adults, both groups scored within the "normal" range on the Health Opinion Survey, a scale measuring psychoneuroticism, and were statistically comparable (Rand et al. 1982, Warheit et al. 1976).

WHY DO MORBIDLY OBESE ADULTS ELECT SURGERY FOR OBESITY?

Simply put, for many there is no apparent alternative offering a reasonable hope of relief from the medical and psychosocial consequences of being morbidly obese. Continuing weight gain, major physical health problems, social isolation, shame, inability to maintain personal cleanliness, and employment difficulties motivate massively obese persons to seek surgery. In general, other kinds of treatments designed to produce weight loss achieve results that are neither impressive nor sustained (Jeffrey et al. 1978, Quaade 1979). Most morbidly obese patients have tried repeatedly to lose weight. Many have successfully lost tens of pounds but have been unable to maintain the weight loss. With a fear of ever-continuing weight gain and increasing disability, patients inquire about surgery with the renewed hope of obtaining a "cure" for their obesity.

INDICATIONS FOR SURGERY

The criteria for accepting an applicant for surgery for obesity vary among centers. No absolute set of indications has been established. Usually the patient must weigh 45.2 kg (100 pounds), or 100 percent, more than ideal weight, as predicted from insurance tables with height and sex corrections, although this limitation is sometimes lowered in special circumstances. Some surgeons require the presence of medical complications of obesity, though others do not. Most require evidence that the obesity is long standing (two to five years) and that conservative treatment has been tried (Bray and Benefield 1977, Laws and Piantadosi 1981, O'Leary 1976, Woodward et al. 1975). The potential risks and benefits to the patients and their families are emphasized, and an informed consent is required.

Contraindications to surgery vary according to the kind of surgery planned. General contraindications include strong ambivalence in the patient about the operation, progressive myocardial disease, and severe psychiatric distress (e.g., acute psychosis, alcoholism). Because of the necessity for postoperative compliance with food restrictions and drug supplements (in the case of the jejunoileal bypass), psychiatrists are often asked to help assess emotional stability, life-style, and ability to carry out the expected postoperative requirements. In his summary Solow (1977) justifiably argued against premature use of psychosocial screening criteria while knowledge is still so limited.

We found data on the psychosocial adjustment of patients following the intestinal bypass operation on approximately 260 of the more than 6,000 operations reported in the literature (Iber and Cooper 1977, Phillips 1978) and on even fewer (n = approximately 100) on patients receiving gastric surgeries (Halmi et al. 1980a, Halmi et al. 1980b, Saltzstein and Gutmann 1980). This is a very small number, considering that a major desired outcome is improved psychosocial adjustment.

The available psychiatric reports indicate a mixed outcome. A few researchers were more impressed with the psychiatric morbidity associated with the procedure, but most emphasized the improved psychosocial adjustments of their patients (compare, for example, Solow et al. 1974 with Winklemann 1975). The operation's psychiatric outcomes seem to depend on several factors: the aspect of psychosocial behavior being evaluated, the length of time after the operation the evaluation is made, physiological complications of the operations, and the patient's preoperative psychiatric status.

PSYCHIATRIC AND PSYCHOSOCIAL SEQUELAE TO SURGERY

Most studies of psychosocial aspects of surgery for obesity are retrospective and report on small numbers of patients. The literature to date may be summarized as follows:

DEPRESSION AND OTHER PSYCHIATRIC SYMPTOMATOLOGY

Surgery for obesity often leads to improved psychological functioning. Solow and associates (1974) reported that weight loss reduced the patients' sense of entrapment, helplessness, and failure. Decreases in depression and improvements in self-esteem were directly proportional to weight loss (Solow 1977). Some researchers found that bypass patients frequently experience some depression, especially during the first six postoperative months (e.g., Kalucy and Crisp 1974, Rigden and Hagen

1976). This period of emotional upheaval has been thought to be related to the physical discomforts (e.g., diarrhea, vomiting) associated with the operation (Crisp et al. 1977, Rigden and Hagen 1976).

Some patients may be adversely emotionally affected by the metabolic deficiencies associated with the jejunoileal bypass (Bech and Hey 1979). Additionally, weight loss with its associated state of starvation can produce emotional changes (Stunkard and Rush 1974).

In assessing the psychiatric sequelae to surgery, the patients' emotional reactions during their previous efforts to lose weight by dieting should be compared with their emotional reactions following surgery. Halmi and colleagues (1980b) discovered far fewer untoward emotional reactions and a greater incidence of positive emotions for both jejunoileal bypass and gastric bypass patients following surgery than during dietary treatment.

Gastric bypass and partition surgeries have been expected to produce substantial emotional distress. The logic is that since eating is used by most morbidly obese patients as a means of coping with stress, the drastic restriction of eating will lead to emotional upheaval. In our series, one-year postoperative gastric partition patients reported being angry and depressed because they could not eat, as well as relieved and joyful. But most were able to adjust to the restricted eating.

Six to 24 months following surgery, Halmi and associates (1980a) interviewed 80 morbidly obese patients who underwent gastric bypass operations. The third *Diagnostic and Statistical Manual of Mental Disorder* (DSM-III) criteria were used to make psychiatric diagnoses. Thirty-eight patients had an Axis I clinical psychiatric diagnosis, with depressive disorders occurring most frequently (28.7 percent). All of the patients identified as being depressed had their affective disorder before surgery. Halmi and colleagues concluded that there was no evidence of an increased prevalence of major psychiatric disorder in this postoperative group of morbidly obese adults.

Patients with a preoperative history of successful coping under stress experienced fewer psychiatric problems than did those with a premorbid history of psychiatric problems (e.g., Kuldau and Rand 1980, Saltzstein and Gutmann 1980, Wise 1976, Wittkower 1971). In addition, those patients who elected the operation for medical rather than psychosocial reasons had fewer psychiatric problems (Weiss 1974). Some, albeit a minority, had serious psychiatric problems (e.g., Abram et al. 1976, Kalucy and Crisp 1974). In general, medical complications following surgery have not been associated with increased psychiatric symptoms unless the patient also had clinically significant preoperative symptoms (Saltzstein and Gutmann 1980).

SOCIAL RELATIONSHIPS

There can be a general improvement in social relationships and sexual functioning following the bypass operation (Castelnuovo-Tedesco and Schiebel 1976, Crisp et al. 1977, Kalucy and Crisp 1974, Rand et al. 1982, Rigden and Hagen 1976, Solow 1977, Solow et al. 1974, Solow 1977; Wittkower 1971). But some patients experience greater social uneasiness, since they no longer use eating to allay anxiety in social situations (Kalucy and Crisp 1974). Other patients become more realistic in appraising their social abilities with their weight loss (Solow 1977, Weiss 1974). For some patients, becoming more assertive and socially effective after their operation resulted in increased interpersonal strain (Castelnuovo-Tedesco and Schiebel 1976, Crisp et al. 1977).

Our one-year follow-up data on 80 morbidly obese patients receiving the jejunoileal bypass (Kuldau and Rand 1980) are consistent with the above findings. Patients no longer avoided going out because they were embarrased about their size, and they showed a dramatic increase in their participation in sports, dancing, and organized group activities. Over half (61 percent) reported that others found it easier to relate to them (unpublished data).

Whenever one person in an intimate group undergoes a major personal change, other interpersonal adjustments can be expected. In this context, marital relationships between the patient and his or her spouse often had to change in order to accommodate the patient's increased social and physical energies. Frequently, patients reported that these adjustments led to improved marital relationships (Crisp et al. 1977; Rand et al. 1982). Half (50 percent) of our patients increased their activities with their spouse outside the home, with most of the others (47 percent) reporting no change. The incidence of marital harmony in the three years following surgery for couples remaining married rose to the same level as that of normal-weight comparison adults. Morbidly obese patients had a higher preoperative divorce rate, which remained higher, particularly among patients reporting marital difficulties before surgery. In a few cases in our series and others, freedom from excessive weight precipitated marital problems (Crisp et al. 1977, Neill et al. 1978). But generally, most patients' marriages improved.

Enjoyment of sexual relationships increased following surgery. Most patients (63 percent) reported that their sex life was much better and made comments like, "My weight got in the way before. Now it's wonderful to be so close." Twenty-three percent of the patients reported that their sex life was unchanged, and the remaining 14 percent found that it had worsened. This latter group included one patient who became widowed, two who became separated from their spouse, and one who was having many marital problems (Rand et al. 1982).

BODY IMAGE AND SELF-ESTEEM

Weight loss from surgery is associated with a marked improvement in appearance and body image (Abram et al. 1976, Castelnuovo-Tedesco and Schiebel 1976, Harris and Frame 1968, Kalucy and Crisp 1974, Ridgen and Hagen 1976, Solow et al. 1974). Although negative self-evaluations are common, they do not seem to be nearly as distressful as those associated with the original obesity (Crisp et al. 1977, Stunkard and Mendelson 1967). Self-esteem also improves after surgery (Abram et al. 1976). Interestingly, improvement in body image is reported to occur soon after surgery, within the first six months (Rigden and Hagen 1976), even though most patients are still massively obese.

In our series (unpublished data), 70 percent of the patients felt more self-confident by the end of the first postoperative year. Only 20 percent continued to be bothered when children or adults ridiculed their size (compared with 86 percent preoperatively), even though almost all patients (92 percent) felt that they were still heavy. Of the patients who avoided looking in their mirror before surgery (n = 45), 67 percent no longer did so. In fact, most patients (70 percent) looked at themselves in a full-length mirror several times a week. Almost all patients (89 percent) celebrated losing weight by purchasing clothing and found that getting properly fitting clothes was much easier. Improvements in self-esteem and greater acceptance of body image have been attributed to the changes in assessment of personal efficacy and of lessening entrapment (Solow et al. 1976).

WORK AND PRODUCTIVE ACTIVITY

A general improvement in job adjustment and competence has been reported (Castelnuovo-Tedesco and Schiebel 1976). Solow's (1977) prospective study found that of 29 patients, 22 made vocational gains; 10 previously unemployable patients found jobs or started school after surgery; 6 previously employed patients definitely improved their job performance; 6 reported somewhat improved job performance; 2 employed and 4 unemployed patients experienced no change; and 1 patient was unable to return to work because of insignificant weight loss and disabling side effects. Crisp, Kalucy, Pilkington, and Gazet (1977) found that younger patients with fewer accumulated physical and psychosocial disabilities were more likely to begin or return earlier to work.

In our series, the majority (82 percent) of patients employed before surgery returned to work by three months following surgery, with the remaining patients at work by six months. Sixty-five percent of the home-makers (n = 20) were more able to cope with their homemaking tasks at the one-year postoperative interview than they had been before surgery; 10 percent reported decreased ability. The patients' comments suggest that some of the improvements at work and home were directly related to the physical effect of having less weight to carry. Greater self-confidence and willingness to cope with demands also improved some patients' work performance.

EATING BEHAVIORS AND PATTERNS

Eating behaviors and patterns are, as mentioned earlier, a crucial area of study, in that social and biological factors come together not only in producing the obesity but also in mediating the outcome of obesity surgery. Although rectal tenderness secondary to the diarrhea following intestinal bypass surgery undoubtedly serves to decrease eating in some patients, it seems clear that alterations of some more fundamental physiological mechanisms controlling hunger and satiety are involved. Stunkard (1959, 1976) identified two kinds of eating patterns exhibited by some obese persons: the night-eating syndrome and binge eating (bulimia). Reactive hyperphagia, continual eating, and absence of hunger and/or satiety sensations have also been associated with being obese and with episodes of weight gain (e.g., Meyer and Pudel 1972, Monello et al. 1965, Rand and Stunkard 1977). All of these unusual eating patterns have characteristics suggesting a strong biological component. In fact, the use of animal models for biological bases of eating and satiety behaviors has become an active research area (Gibbs and Smith 1977, Stricker 1978, Stunkard 1980).

Data documenting food regulation and eating patterns of the massively obese are sketchy (e.g., Stunkard 1976). Partial normalization typically occurs after the jejunoileal bypass operation (Mills and Stunkard 1976). Patients have been observed to consume substantially fewer calories six months after jejunoileostomy, compared with the preoperative period: 3,400 kcal per day compared with 4,800 kcal per day (Bray et al. 1978). Meal times are more normal, and the amounts eaten at meals and between meals are reduced. At six months, patients crave sweets and other foods less and are more sensitive to feelings of satiety (Bray et al. 1979). Decreases in the total amount of food consumed, in reactive hyperphagia, and in binge eating are common (Abram et al. 1976, Brewer et al. 1974, Castelnuove-Tedesco and Schiebel 1976, Crisp et al. 1977, Kuldau and

Rand 1980, Mills and Stunkard 1976). Several patients experienced a loss of excitement associated with eating behaviors, which led to fewer binges, less night eating, less difficulty stopping eating, reduced craving of sweets, less eaten at meals, and less food consumption in general (Mills and Stunkard 1976). It has been hypothesized that specific metabolic changes produced by the bypass are partially responsible for the normalization of eating behaviors (Bray et al. 1979, Kissileff et al. 1979, Robinson et al. 1979).

There are no observational data on changes in eating behaviors of morbidly obese patients following gastric surgery. Success of the surgery depends on decreased caloric consumption. Failure to lose adequate weight is attributed to frequent consumption of high caloric soft food and liquids, stretching of the stomach pouch by ingesting progressively larger amounts, or rupture of suture lines. Following surgery, patients typically feel full with very small servings and free from constant hunger and craving (Saltzstein and Gutmann 1980). Postsurgical guidelines usually include an instruction to chew each mouthful of food 20 times (i.e., very thoroughly). Thorough mastication is necessary to prevent vomiting and blockage of the small stomach food-passage opening. Most patients claim that one or two experiences with vomiting is all they need before they comply with this instruction, although a few continue to overeat and vomit. The implied eating-behavior changes that accompany successful weight loss include decreased rate of eating, smaller portions consumed, and increased chewing of food (Halverson and Koehler 1981).

DISCUSSION

The major concern of postsurgical psychiatric adjustment is that an emotional crisis will be precipitated by surgery, subsequent weight loss, and a new shape. If morbid obesity is viewed as a symptom of major personality disturbance, removal both of eating as gratification and of a protective shape should lead to significant negative psychiatric sequelae. However, most patients do not experience an emotional crisis following surgery. Successful treatment of the presenting complaint (morbid obesity) is sufficient to facilitate their social reintegration.

Individual patients do, on occasion, require postoperative psychiatric care. By and large, these patients are symptomatic *before* surgery, and arrangements are made preoperatively for follow-up care in psychiatric outpatient clinics. There are also a few patients whose psychiatric status worsens following surgery. In our series, most of these patients were reacting to major life stresses (e.g., a son refusing to have needed heart-valve surgery). Occasionally a patient will respond neurotically to a new challenge (e.g., a patient became exceedingly anxious in crowds after returning to college; Kuldau and Rand 1980). But in the literature reviewed above, we found no evidence of systematic symptom substitution, emotional regression, or other kinds of personality disintegration as a result of surgery (Nurnberger and Hingtgen [1973] discuss the issue of symptom substitution).

Absence of clinically significant psychopathology following surgery is not the same as absence of emotional turbulence during the postsurgical period. Patients must incorporate the impact of surgery, weight loss, and a new shape into their identity and future plans. Changing one's personal framework of "being, doing, and becoming" requires effort and often produces stress. For example, greater physical mobility and increase in social activities can be difficult when significant others prefer the status quo or when a new repertoire of social behaviors must be learned.

Solow (1977) hypothesized that the length of time elapsed following surgery influences the kinds of psychosocial adjustments and stresses experienced. During the first six postoperative months, the predominant stresses are those associated with recovery from surgery, surgical morbidity, and adjustment to dietary restrictions and regulations. During the second postsurgical year, the central stresses are often those of personal identity and interpersonal relationships. Frequently, a new equilibration is not achieved until the third postsurgical year. Solow noted that generally positive reports of outcomes from surgery are usually based on longer follow-up periods than are studies emphasizing psychiatric morbidity.

Following surgery, amidst the postoperative stresses, patients are enjoying positive events. A patient can be distressed about a medical problem yet be delighted about losing weight and becoming increasingly physically mobile. Patients are not unidimensional—improvement in one area is appreciated, and problems in other areas are a concern. Even within a single area of functioning there can be mixed emotional reactions: gastric-partition patients often express both frustration and relief regarding their inability to eat as they did before surgery.

Despite a progression of stresses, our data and those of others suggest that most patients unequivocally consider the operation to be "worth it" *if* they lose weight. The personal changes associated with becoming less heavy must be exceptionally rewarding. Virtually no patient has requested that the operation be reversed for personal reasons, and patients typically refuse medically imperative reversals unless they can be assured that they can have the "other obesity surgery." From the patient's perspective, negative personal (psychiatric, medical) and interpersonal sequalae are balanced by the chance to lead a more active, normal life. Crisp and colleagues generalized that patients at the two-year post-operative evaluation were "sadder and wiser, but on the whole satisfied and more fulfilled" (1977, p. 118). With major weight loss, patients can and are willing to enter into the regular routines, hassles, and pleasures of living. Both normal and neurotic morbidly obese patients share the benefits of successful weight loss in similar ways. The management of neurotic patients, then, must take into account that which is chronically neurotic and that which is simply expected, given weight change.

REFERENCES

Abraham, S., and Johnson, C. L. (1980). Prevalence of severe obesity in adults in the United States. *American Journal of Clinical Nutrition* 33:364-369.

Abram, H. S., Meixel, S. A., Webb, W. W., and Scott, H. W. (1976). Psychological adaptation to jejunoileal bypass for morbid obesity. *Journal of Nervous and Mental Diseases* 162(3):151-157.

Alden, J. F. (1977). Gastric and jejunoileal bypass. *Archives of Surgery* 112:799-806.

Bech, P., and Hey, H. (1979). Depression or asthenia related to metabolic disturbances in obese patients after intestinal bypass surgery. *Acta Psychiatrica Scandinavica* 59:462-470.

Booth, D. A., Toates, F. M., and Platt, S. V. (1976). Control system for hunger and its implications in animals and man. In *Hunger: Basic Mechanisms and Clinical Implications,* ed. D. Novin, W. Wyricka, and G. Bray, pp. 127-143. New York: Raven Press.

Bray, G. A., and Benfield, J. R. (1977). Intestinal bypass for obesity: a summary and perspective. *American Journal of Clinical Nutrition* 30:121-127.

Bray, G. A., Dahms, W. T., Atkinson, R. L., Mena, I., Taylor, I., Rodin, J., Schwartz, A., and Frame, C. (1979). The control of food intake: effects of dieting and intestinal bypass. *Surgical Clinics of North America* 59(6):1043-1054.

Bray, G. A., Zachary, B. A., Dahms, W. T., Atkinson, R. L., and Oddie, T. H. (1978). Eating patterns of massively obese individuals. *Journal of the American Dietetic Association* 72:24-27.

Brewer, C., White, H., and Baddeley, M. (1974). Beneficial effects of jejeunoileostomy on compulsive eating and associated psychiatric symptoms. *British Medical Journal* 4:314–316.

Buckwalter, J. A. (1978). Clinical trial of surgery for morbid obesity. *Southern Medical Journal* 71(11):1370–1371.

Buckwalter, J. A., and Herbst, C. A. (1980). Complications of gastric bypass for morbid obesity. *American Journal of Surgery* 139(1):55–60.

Castelnuovo-Tedesco, P., and Schiebel, D. (1976). Studies of superobesity: II. Psychiatric appraisal of jejunoileal bypass surgery. *American Journal of Psychiatry* 131(1):26–31.

Cegielski, M. M., and Saporta, J. A., Sr. (1981). Surgical treatment of morbid obesity: an update. *Obesity/Bariatric Medicine* 10(2):44–47.

Crisp, A. H., Kalucy, R. S., Pilkington, T. R. E., and Gazet, J-C. (1977). Some psychosocial consequences of ileojejunal bypass surgery. *American Journal of Clinical Nutrition* 30:109–120.

Faloon, W. W., Flood, M. S., Aresty, S., and Sherman, D. C. (1980). Assessment of jejunoileostomy for obesity—some observations since 1976. *American Journal of Clinical Nutrition* 33:431–439.

Feit, H., Glasberg, M., Ireton, C., Rosenberg, R. N., and Thal, E. (1982). Peripheral neuropathy and starvation after gastric partitioning for morbid obesity. *Annals of Internal Medicine* 96:453–455.

Ferguson, J. M. (1975). *Learning to Eat Right: Behavior Modification for Weight Control*. Palo Alto, Calif.: Bull.

Foch, T. T., and McClearn, G. E. (1980). Genetics, body weight, and obesity. In *Obesity*, ed. A. J. Stunkard, pp. 48–71. Philadelphia: Saunders.

Fordyce, G. C., Garrow, J. S., Kark, A. E., and Stalley, S. F. (1979). Jaw wiring and gastric bypass in the treatment of severe obesity. *Obesity/Bariatric Medicine* 8(1):14–17.

Garrow, J. S., Durrant, M. L., Mann, S., Stalley, S. F., and Warwick, P. M. (1978). Factors determining weight loss in obese patients in a metabolic ward. *International Journal of Obesity* 2(4):441–447.

Garrow, J. S., and Gardiner, G. T. (1981). Maintenance of weight loss in obese patients after jaw wiring. *British Medical Journal* 282(6267):858–860.

Gibbs, J., and Smith, G. P. (1977). Cholecystokinin and satiety in rats and rhesus monkeys. *American Journal of Clinical Nutrition* 30:758–761.

Gold, J. M., O'Leary, J. P., Alexander, R. W., and Cerda, J. J. (1982). Liver failure after obesity bypass: the natural history of hepatic function and morphology following takedown of jejunoileal bypass for liver failure. *Obesity and Bariatric Medicine* 11(2):47–53.

Gomez, C. A. (1980). Gastroplasty in the surgical treatment of morbid obesity. *American Journal of Clinical Nutrition* 33:406–415.

Gourlay, R. H., and Reynolds, C. (1978). Complications of surgery for morbid obesity. *American Journal of Surgery* 136:54–60.

Griffen, W. O., Young, V. L., and Stevenson, C. C. (1977). A prospective comparison of gastric and jejunoileal bypass procedures for morbid obesity. *American Surgeons* 186:500–509.

Hällström, T., and Noppa, H. (1981). Obesity in women in relation to mental illness, social factors and personality traits. *Journal of Psychosomatic Research* 25(2):75.

Halmi, K. A., Long, M., Stunkard, A. J., and Mason, E. (1980a). Psychiatric diagnosis of morbidly obese gastric bypass patients. *American Journal of Psychiatry* 137(4):470–472.

Halmi, K. A., Stunkard, A. J., and Mason E. E. (1980b). Emotional responses to weight reduction by three methods: gastric bypass, jejunoileal bypass, diet. *American Journal of Clinical Nutrition* 33:446–451.

Halverson, J. D., and Koehler, R. E. (1981). Gastric bypass: analysis of weight loss and factors determining success. *Surgery* 90(3):446–455.

Halverson, J. D., Wise, L., Wazna, M. F., and Ballinger, W. F. (1978). Jejunoileal bypass for morbid obesity—a critical appraisal. *American Journal of Medicine* 64:461–475.

Harris, J., and Frame, B. (1968). A psychiatric study of patients undergoing intestinal bypass for treatment of intractable obesity. Paper presented at the 124th annual meeting of the American Psychiatric Association, Boston. Reported by Solow, C. (1977). Psychosocial aspects of intestinal bypass surgery for massive obesity, current status. *American Journal of Clinical Nutrition* 30:103–108.

Hejda, S., and Fábry, P. (1964). Frequency of food intake in relation to some parameters of the nutritional status. *Nutritio et Dieta* 6:216–228.

Hutzler, J. C., Keen, J., Molinari, V., and Carey, L. (1981). Superobesity: a psychiatric profile of patients electing gastric stapling for the treatment of morbid obesity. *Journal of Clinical Psychiatry* 42(12):458–462.

Iber, F. L., and Cooper M. (1977). Jejunoileal bypass for the treatment of massive obesity. Prevalency, morbidity, and short- and long-term consequences. *American Journal of Clinical Nutrition* 30:4.

Jeffrey, R. W., Wing, R. R., and Stunkard, A. J. (1978). Behavioral treatment of obesity—state of art 1976. *Behavioral Therapy* 9(2):189.

Kalucy, R. S., and Crisp, A. H. (1974). Some psychological and social implications of massive obesity. A study of some psychosocial accompaniments of major fat loss occurring without dietary restriction in massively obese patients. *Journal of Psychosomatic Research* 18:465-473.

Kissileff, H. R., Nakashima, R. K., and Stunkard, A. J. (1979). Effects of jejunoileal bypass on meal patterns in genetically obese and lean rats. *American Journal of Physiology* 237(3):R217-R224.

Kuldau, J. M., Barnard, G., Kreutziger, S., and Rand, C. S. W. (1979). Psychosocial effects of jejunoileal bypass for obesity: six-month follow-up. *Psychosomatics* 20(7):462-472.

Kuldau, J. M., and Rand, C. S. W. (1980). Jejunoileal bypass for obesity: general and psychiatric outcome after one year. *Psychosomatics* 21(2):534-539.

Laws, H. L., and Piantadosi, S. (1981). Superior gastric reduction procedure for morbid obesity—a prospective randomized trial. *Annuals of Surgery* 193(3):334-336.

Lyons, M. J., Faust, J. M., Hemmes, R. B., Buskirk, D. R., Hirsch, J., and Zabriski, J. B. (1982). A virally induced obesity syndrome in mice. *Science* 216:82-85.

Mason, E. E., and Ito, C. (1967). Gastric bypass in obesity. *Surgical Clinics of North America* 47:1345-1349.

Mayer, J. (1973). Physiology of hunger and satiety: regulation of food intake. In *Modern Nutrition in Health and Disease, Dietotherapy*, ed. R. S. Goodhart, and M. E. Shils, pp. 474-492. Philadelphia: Lea and Febiger.

Meyer, J-E., and Pudel, V. (1972). Experimental studies on food-intake in obese and normal weight subjects. *Journal of Psychosomatic Research* 16:305-308.

Mills, M. J., and Stunkard, A. J. (1976). Behavioral changes following surgery for obesity. *American Journal of Psychiatry* 133(5):527-531.

Monello, L. F., Seltzer, C. C., and Mayer, J. (1965). Hunger and satiety sensations in men, women, boys and girls: a preliminary report. *Annuals of the New York Academy of Science* 131(1):593-602.

Moore, M. E., Stunkard, A., and Srole, L. (1962). Obesity, social class and mental illness. *Journal of the American Medical Association* 181:962-966.

Neill, J. R., Marshall, J. R., and Yale, C. E. (1978). Marital changes after intestinal bypass surgery. *Journal of the American Medical Association* 240(5):447-450.

Nurnberger, J. I., and Hingtgen, J. N. (1973). Is symptom substitution an important issue in behavior therapy. *Biological Psychiatry* 7(3):221-236.

O'Leary, J. P. (1976). An appraisal of the status of small bowel bypass in the treatment of morbid obesity. *Clinics in Endocrinology and Metabolism* 5(2):481-502.

Payne, J. H., and DeWind, C. T. (1969). Surgical treatment of obesity. *American Journal of Surgery* 113:141-147.

Payne, J. H., DeWind, C. T., and Commons, R. R. (1963). Metabolic observations in patients with jejunocolic shunts. *American Journal of Surgery* 106:273-289.

Phillips, R. B. (1978). Small intestinal bypass for the treatment of morbid obesity. *Surgery, Gynecology and Obstetrics* 146(3):455.

Quaade, F. (1979). Jejunoileal bypass for morbid obesity: a bibliographic study and randomized clinical trial. *Surgical Clinics of North America* 59(6):1055-1069.

Rand, C. S. W. (1978). Treatment of obese patients in psychoanalysis. *Psychiatric Clinics of North America* 1(4):661-671.

Rand, C. S. W., Kuldau, J. M., and Robbins, L. (1982). Surgery for obesity and marriage quality. *Journal of the American Medical Association* 247(10):1419-1422.

Rand, C. S. W., and Stunkard, A. J. (1977). Psychoanalysis and obesity. *Journal of the American Academy of Psychoanalysis* 5(4):459-497.

Rigden, S. R., and Hagen, D. Q. (1976). Psychiatric aspects for intestinal bypass surgery for obesity. *American Family Physician* 13(5):68-71.

Robinson, R. G., Folstein, M. F., and McHugh, P. R. (1979). Reduced caloric intake following small bowel bypass surgery: a systematic study of possible causes. *Psychological Medicine* 9:37-53.

Saltzstein, E. C., and Gutmann, M. C. (1980). Gastric bypass for morbid obesity — preoperative and postoperative evaluation of patients. *Archives of Surgery* 115:21-28.

Scott, H. W., Dean, R., Shull, H. D., Abram, H. S., Webb, W., Younger, R. K., and Brill, A. B. (1973). New considerations in the use of jejunoileal bypass in patients. *Annals of Surgery* 177:723-735.

Sims, E. A. H., Danforth, E., Jr., Horton, E. S., Bray, G. A., Glennon, J. A., and Salans, L. B. (1973). Endocrine and metabolic effects of experimental obesity in man. *Recent Progress in Hormone Research* 29:457-496.

Solhaug, J. H., and Bassoe, H. H. (1979). Jejunoileal bypass operation for the treatment of morbid obesity — short- and long-term consequences analyzed in a follow-up study of 36 patients. *Scandinavian Journal of Gastroenterology* 14(5):535-543.

Solow, C. (1977). Psychosocial aspects of intestinal bypass surgery for massive obesity: current status. *American Journal of Clinical Nutrition* 30:103–108.

Solow, C., Silberfarb, P. M., and Swift, K. (1974). Psychosocial effects of intestinal bypass surgery for severe obesity. *New England Journal of Medicine* 290(6):300–304.

Stricker, E. M. (1978). Hyperphagia. *New England Journal of Medicine* 298:1010–1013.

Stunkard, A. J. (1959). Eating patterns and obesity. *Psychiatric Quarterly* 33:284–295.

———. (1976). *The Pain of Obesity.* Palo Alto, Calif.: Bull.

———. (1980). *Obesity.* Philadelphia: Saunders.

Stunkard, A. J., and Kaplan, D. (1977). Eating in public places: a review of reports of the direct observation of eating behaviors. *International Journal of Obesity* 1:89–101.

Stunkard, A. J., and Mendelson, M. (1967). Obesity and the body image. I. Characteristics of disturbances in the body image of some obese persons. *American Journal of Psychiatry* 123(10):1296–1300.

Stunkard, A. J., and Rush, J. (1974). Dieting and depression reexamined: a critical review of reports of untoward responses during weight reduction of obesity. *Annals of Internal Medicine* 81:526–533.

Van Itallie, T. B., and Kral, J. G. (1981). The dilemma of morbid obesity. *Journal of the American Medical Association* 246(9):999–1003.

Warheit, G. J., Holzer, C. E. III, Bell, R. A., and Arey, S. A. (1976). Sex, marital status and mental health: a reappraisal. *Social Forces* 55(2):459–470.

Webb, W. W., Phares, R., Abram, H. S., Meixel, S. A., Scott, H. W., and Gerdes, J. T. (1976). Jejunoileal bypass procedures in morbid obesity: preoperative psychological findings. *Journal of Clinical Psychology* 32(1):82–85.

Weiss, L. (1974). Predicting postoperative psychopathological reactions in intestinal bypass candidates. *Obesity/Bariatric Medicine* 3(5):168–172.

Wilkinson, L. H., and Peloso, O. A. (1981). Gastric (reservoir) reduction for morbid obesity. *Archives of Surgery* 116:602.

Winklemann, E. I., Schumacher, O. P., Hermann, R. E., Esselstyn, C. B., and Schwartz, R. A. (1975). Study raises question about jejunoileal bypass. *Journal of the American Medical Association* 231(2):126.

Wise, T. N. (1976). Adverse psychologic reactions to ileal bypass surgery. *Southern Medical Journal* 69(12):1533–1535.

_____. (1978). Massive obesity and sexual activity. *Medical Aspects of Human Sexuality* 12(1):7-23.

_____. (1979). Psychological profiles of candidates seeking surgical correction for obesity. *Obesity* 8:83-86.

Wittkower, E. D. (1971). Some selected psychosomatic problems of current interest. *Psychosomatics* 7:21-29.

Woodward, E. R., Payne, J. H., Salmon, P. A., and O'Leary, J. P. (1975). Morbid obesity. *Archives of Surgery* 110:1440-1445.

CHAPTER 12

Psychological Aspects of Transplantation Medicine

LYNNA M. LESKO, M.D., PH.D.
DAVID R. HAWKINS, M.D.

Man has been fascinated with the transplantation of organs or body parts for hundreds of years. Ancient mythology speaks of the chimera, with its lion's head and serpent's tail, and the two-headed dogs. Probably one of the earliest examples of clinical transplantation is the medieval story of St. Cosmos and St. Damien. In the earliest example of a team approach, one, a surgeon, and the other, a physician, amputated the gangrenous leg of a white Roman patient and grafted in its place a leg from a recently deceased Ethiopian Moor. Their miraculous operation overcame immunological problems unresolvable until current transplant medicine. In the past 20 years there have been major advances in organ transplantation in the treatment of many physiological and metabolic abnormalities which have helped make this medieval third-century legend an actual event. Today, transplantation is rapidly changing from a controversial research procedure into a standard therapeutic modality, which has followed progress in the fields of supportive and intensive care, immunosuppressive protocols, and histocompatability typing.

Although the transplantation of organs has required certain knowledge to become possible and hence is a technique dependent on research, its realization has had, as Moore asserted, a "remarkable impact . . . on physiology, immunogenetics, autoimmunity, epidemiology, thanatology, neoplasia, psychiatry, ethics, the law, and society itself" (F. D. Moore, p. 359). Each new advance and each new organ, which we term the transplant, brings new life to some individual, but also major, often intriguing new problems for the care-givers.

The transplantation process starts with the patient's agonizing decision to undergo a new and generally experimental treatment that may be fatal or to choose symptomatic treatment and face a definitely shortened life. No other procedure in medicine or surgery confronts the patient and his or her family with comparable emotional stress. A major research question is what leads patients to decide to accept or reject innovative treatments. The difficult decision of whether to accept the procedure is followed by the necessary commitment to the physiological demands of the protocol. There are also the specific psychological difficulties, such as proximity of death, changed family relationships, body-image changes, changes in self-reliance and dependency, and finally readjusting to appropriate life.

What has been the impact of the transplantation process on psychiatry? First, psychiatrists are asked to join the team required to carry out these complex new procedures. There, their role is to deal directly with the psychological problems of patient and donor, helping each utilize his or her coping skills most effectively. Psychiatrists also must treat psychiatric abnormalities that have been created by these procedures. Also, as a member of the team it is the psychiatrist's task to help plan procedures and to help the staff deal with the complex and often painful feelings stirred up in those undertaking these procedures. Here again is an opportunity to learn more about the functioning of small groups engaged in a complex and difficult task. Second, and probably in the long run the most important outcome, is that we have been challenged or given the opportunity, depending on one's point of view, to learn new things about humans' coping mechanisms in response to major stress. Situations have now been created that heretofore existed only in fantasy. Studying patients going through these new complicated, painful, life-threatening procedures, which often lead to major changes in body image and at times permit essentially a rebirth, can give us new understanding of basic emotional coping mechanisms, both when the brain is functioning adequately physiologically and when its function is compromised metabolically.

Our review of the psychological aspects of transplantation medicine addresses five major areas: (1) the principles that apply to the history and state of the art of transplant medicine, (2) the psychological management of the transplant patient and donor, (3) the psychological effects of treatment, (4) the diagnosis and management of psychiatric syndromes that complicate the course of transplantation and convalescence, and (5) the role of the consultation-liaison psychiatrist as part of the transplant team.

HISTORICAL PERSPECTIVE

Ever since the first attempts in the early 1950s, by Murray, Merrill, and Hume in Boston and Hamburger in Paris, to transplant human kidneys, it has been obvious that transplantation medicine would become a new and exciting clinical specialty. The years between 1963 and 1966 were a time of unlimited optimism, and in 1966–1967 the Transplant Society was founded. Transplantation as an alternative but experimental treatment for deficiencies of numerous vital organs was widespread by that time. Renal transplantation research comprises the largest part of the current work, followed by heart, bone marrow, liver, and pancreas research. The history and present status of transplantation medicine are briefly reviewed below.

KIDNEY TRANSPLANTATION

The first attempt at inserting an artificial kidney was made in 1913 by Abel, Rountree, and Turner (Merrill 1981). Their network of semipermeable tubes was perfected in dogs, to be used to treat salicylate intoxication in humans. In the next 30 years there were many unsuccessful attempts to bring this laboratory apparatus into clinical use. Koeff perfected his dialysis device in the early 1940s, and by May 1948 Peter Bent Brigham Hospital in Boston had dialyzed the first patient for two and a half hours. From that year until the 1980s there have been thousands of patients maintained on kidney dialysis. In 1979, 3,700 of the 45,000 hemodialysis patients in the United States underwent the transplantation of a kidney. Twelve hundred of these organs were from family members and 2,500 from cadaver donors (Stewart 1981).

Merrill (1979), one of the pioneers in the field, wrote a brief but fascinating account of this landmark surgical procedure (the first of which opened the doors to a whole host of other organ transplants). The stage was set for renal transplantation by Nobel prize winners Medawar and Burnett, whose experiments demonstrated how tolerance of skin grafts could be produced in mice by injecting spleen cells from the potential donor mouse into neonatal or fetal mice (Billingham et al. 1955).

In the 1940s, Hamburger, in the United States, and Hume, in France, tried to transplant kidneys in the laboratory, using antihistamines and the newly available corticosteroids to prevent rejection. In the later part of that decade Kiss, in Paris, transplanted a few human kidneys taking advantage of an unlimited cadaver supply from French prisoners executed by guillotine. None of these was successful. The development of the artificial kidney by Kolff in the later 1940s provided an effective way of maintaining end-stage uremic patients and thus the impetus to perfect the transplantation of kidneys. In 1952 Hume transplanted a human kidney to the thigh of a patient, affixing it to the femoral blood vessels. A skin ureterostomy enabled urine from the transplanted organ to be collected. Investigators were hopeful that this thigh transplant would prevent the extensive trauma of retroperitoneal surgery (Hume et al. 1955). Seventeen such "kidney in a thigh pouch" were performed, and to everyone's surprise these organs functioned better than did the experimental dog models. One patient actually left the hospital to live a normal but restricted life for six months.

In 1952, the first transplant from a living donor to a recipient was performed in Paris by Hamburger. The graft from the patient's mother developed normal function within 36 hours and successfully maintained this function for 13 days before failing. At this time retroperitoneal surgery now seemed feasible, but the immunological problems posed insurmountable problems. In December 1954, Murray, in Boston, performed the first successful kidney transplant between identical twins (Murray et al. 1976). The transplanted healthy kidney functioned immediately in the uremic twin, and he left the hospital three weeks later with normal renal function reversing his malignant hypertension. Although he developed recurrent nephritis in his transplanted kidney, he lived successfully for 7 years and eventually died of a myocardial infarction at age 29.

It became obvious that if one were to begin successfully transplanting kidneys from unrelated donors, immunosuppression of the recipient would have to be improved. But immunosuppression in the early 1960s by means of total body irradiation proved nonspecific and unpredictable. The advent of drug-induced immunological tolerance in 1959 provided a key to the success of future transplantation. In April 1962, a drug-treated recipient of a cadaver kidney survived for over a year, the world's first real survivor (Merrill et al. 1963).

The National Kidney Registry has compiled data on over 20,000 transplantations to date. Current 1-and 4-year survival rates for transplant recipients of cadaver donor organs are 75 percent and 50 to 60 percent, respectively. Patients receiving related living donor organs have better survival rates of 95 percent for one year and 90 percent for four years.*

---

*F. Stewart, personal communication, 1981.

CARDIAC TRANSPLANTATION

Heterotopic cardiac transplants in animals were first performed in 1905 by Alexis Carrel and Charles Guthrie at the University of Chicago. Contraction in donor animal hearts was noted for as long as a few hours. But it was not until December 1967 that Christiaan Barnard performed the first human cardiac homograft in Cape Town, South Africa. The following year Norman Shumway carried out the first cardiac retransplant at Stanford University. The initial enthusiasm waned, but in 1978–1980 there was a renewed interest in cardiac transplantation as an effective management of irreversible end-stage heart disease.

The major centers for cardiac transplantation are (1) Stanford University, Palo Alto, California; (2) Groote Shur Hospital, Cape Town, South Africa; (3) Hôpital de la Pitie, Paris; (4) the Medical College of Virginia and (5) Columbia-Presbyterian Hospital, New York (in order of number transplantations performed). As of August 1978, 406 transplants had been performed on 395 patients, of whom 100 were still alive. Interestingly, one-quarter of these transplants were carried out in 1968 (Griepp 1979).

Only patients who have American Heart Association Class IV end-stage or terminal heart disease, with no realistic hope for recovery, are selected for transplantation. Indications for surgery include end-stage coronary artery disease, idiopathic cardiomyopathy, valve disease with cardiomyopathy and occasionally posttraumatic aneurysm, congenital heart disease, and cardiac tumor (Oyer et al. 1981). Potential recipients are usually very ill, and 90 percent die within three months after selection if an appropriate donor organ is not found. According to Shumway and Stinton (1979), it is reasonable to expect 65 percent of patients to survive for one year after transplantation and 50 percent to survive for five years. Rehabilitation or quality of life after transplantation is difficult to define and evaluate, but a reasonable estimate is that 85 percent of patients are considered rehabilitated in the most general terms of resuming activities and returning to work.

BONE MARROW TRANSPLANTATION

Bone marrow transplantation is the treatment of choice for (1) "severe" aplastic anemia, immundeficiency disease, some congenital hematological disorders such as Fanconi's anemia, Wiskott-Aldrich syndrome, and radiation accidents; (2) experimental therapy for acute and chronic leukemias, solid malignant neoplasms that are particularly sensitive to radiotherapy; and (3) possibly malignant genetic disorders of the bone marrow such as thalassemia and sickle cell anemia (Storb 1981). The centers for bone marrow transplantation are few—Fred Hutchinson Cancer Research Center in Seattle, M.D. Anderson Cancer Center in Houston, John Hopkins University in Baltimore, and Memorial Sloan-Kettering Cancer Center in New York City, to name the largest.

The mortality in severe cases of aplastic anemia treated with conventional therapy is 75 to 90 percent; most patients die within six months of diagnosis. This type of transplantation has become a promising therapeutic modality, since 50 percent of aplastic patients survive for one to six years with complete hematologic restoration (Borten and Rimm 1976). Graft rejection is the usual cause of high mortality.

The past ten years have witnessed major advances in the treatment of childhood acute lymphocytic leukemias, resulting in better prognosis and longer survival. Unfortunately, this has not been the case for adults with acute leukemia. Complete remissions after conventional induction and consolidation chemotherapy are achieved in 50 to 80 percent of adult patients. But after relapse, long-term remissions are not usually possible with currently available chemotherapy. Consequently, the median survival of adult leukemics is 12 to 20 months. Current studies imply that leukemics should be transplanted in remission rather than in relapse and that patients grafted in their second or third remission have a higher incidence of their leukemia recurring. About 60 percent of adult leukemics transplanted in Seattle are alive in unmaintained remission with a marrow graft having functioned for between 27 and 48 months (Thomas 1979a, 1979b). Bone marrow transplantation, once considered a research endeavor for terminally ill patients, seems to be developing into a reasonable therapeutic option.

PANCREATIC TRANSPLANTATION

Total pancreas and islet-cell transplantations are still very much in their infancy as treatments for diabetes. By 1980 there had been 73 attempts in 68 patients at islet-cell autotransplantation (Sutherland et al. 1981). Total pancreas transplantation is clearly more efficient than islet-cell transplantation is and is being tried again now that there is a new pancreatic transplant technique that eliminates the exocrine function of the organ by injection of neoprene into the pancreatic duct, thus obtaining a pure endocrine pancreatic segment. The total world experience in total pancreas transplantations between 1966 and 1980 was 110 transplants in 104 patients. Since 1978, both Sutherland (Sutherland et al. 1981) in Minneapolis and Traeger (Traeger et al. 1980) in Lyons, France, have been performing "segmental" pancreas transplantations which allows the transplant to come from a living family donor. Sutherland (Sutherland et al. 1981) has 11 patients alive, 3 of whom were cured of diabetes, out of 13 who received transplants. Traeger (Traeger et al. 1980) has 15 patients in his recent transplant group, with 10 survivors and graft survival ranging from 1 to 650 days; 4 are currently at more than 150, 435, and 650 days. The pancreatic graft survival is longer in (1) patients who have renal insufficiency and subsequent dialysis and (2) patients in whom both the kidney and pancreas are transplanted simultaneously or successively. Currently, it is very risky to treat patients who are at an early stage of diabetic degenerative complications, because transplant survival is still chancy and medical treatment is usually highly effective (Traeger et al. 1980).

LIVER TRANSPLANTATION

Orthotopic liver transplantation requires the removal of the diseased native organ and its replacement with a cadaver graft. The first liver transplants were performed in 1963 in Denver and Boston, and it was not until 1968 that a patient survived for more than one year. Success was due to the perseverance and meticulous surgical techniques of Starzl (Starzl et al. 1979, 1981), in Denver, and Calne (Calne and Williams 1979), in England. Candidates for liver transplantation include any patient with chronic end-stage liver disease who is less than 45 to 50 years old, who neither is infected nor has metastatic malignancies, and whose prognosis is hopeless unless surgery is performed (Calne and Williams 1979). Diagnoses include chronic proaggressive hepatitis, primary and secondary biliary cirrhosis, Budd-Chiari syndrome, and occasionally hepatoma. By July 1977, the liver transplant registry had recorded 259 orthotopic transplants. Between 1967 and 1976 the Denver group alone had transplanted 111 recipients; 25 percent survived for at least one year, and 12 percent are still living, four and a half to ten and a half years later. A second Denver series of 30 patients was compiled between 1976 and 1978, with 50 percent of the patients surviving at least one year and 43 percent surviving two and a half to four years (Starzl et al. 1981). Better biliary tract reconstruction, diagnosis of improved post-operative dysfunction, and new advances in immunosuppression have increased survival rates. By 1980, the Denver team had added 30 more patients to their registry.

MORAL AND ETHICAL ISSUES

Organ transplantation involves many difficult and complex moral, ethical, and psychological issues (Allgower and Gruber 1970, Levine et al. 1975, Murray 1979, Paton 1971, Reeves 1969, Siemsen et al. 1978). Transplantation, especially of bone marrow, is being presented as a treatment option to patients at earlier stages of their disease, and therefore it has become even more important to evaluate the attendant moral and ethical issues. The issues associated with transplantation are not new and involve questions about the definition of death; the quality of life; the allocation of a scarce resource, the donor organ; the institution of research protocols; the problems of treatment choice, informed consent, and competency; the rights of minors; the welfare of the individual and society; and the selection of decision makers. Organs appropriate for transplantation usually come from young people dying suddenly from accidents, cerebral injury, or tumor or infarction (living related donors can also be a source for bone marrow and kidney transplants). Therefore, the interpretation and meaning of death become important, and the definition of death has resulted in stringent requirements for brain death. Public attention and opinion have become concerned with the protection of the donor with irreversible brain damage rather than the living healthy donor or even the recipient.

Determining how therapeutic and/or how experimental an innovative treatment is poses many questions. Currently, physicians disagree on the experimental-versus-routine and conventional quality of transplantation. Organ donation between twins, has moved out of the experimental realm to almost the therapeutic realm, and bone marrow transplantation is felt to be the treatment of choice for severe aplastic anemia. The physician is obliged to protect the recipient. This dilemma of providing therapeutic but innovative and experimental care put a halt to cardiac transplantation in the early 1970s, since mortality was too high, and death came too soon.

Today, organ transplantation is still more an experimental procedure than an established treatment, and it is offered only to terminally ill patients. This raises the ethical question of whether informed, voluntary consent is truly informed and truly voluntary. The transplant physician, of course, does not know all of the answers to questions about discomfort, risks, dangers, and prognosis. The ability of the patient to understand the protocol is quite different from the competency of the physician. Norman Shummay, a prominent cardiac surgeon, stated, "When you get a very sick patient . . . , to the doctor, it may be a clinical trial, but to that patient, it is very definitely therapy" (Fox 1970, p. 413).

How many medical professionals and how much money and time should be involved in hemodialysis and transplantation are ethical questions. Even though donor organs are scare and the quality of rehabilitation after transplantation is questionable, renal transplantation at least allows the patient freedom from dialysis and is less costly than long-term hemodialysis. According to the Council on Scientific Affairs, "The extra cost of surgery is offset by dialysis savings within 18 months after transplantation" (Council on Scientific Affairs 1981). We have only briefly touched on a few of the medical and ethical issues related to transplant medicine. Much of the literature pertains to dialysis and kidney transplants but can be applied to other transplant settings. Rene Fox has written extensively on this subject, and her 1970 article is a broad-based reference with which the interested reader may start.

STAGES OF THE TRANSPLANTATION PROTOCOL

Each transplantation process — whether kidney, cardiac, bone marrow, liver, or pancreas — can be divided into several stages, which encompass both medical and surgical management, each accompanied by a particular emotional tone. Brown and Kelly (1976) described the course and experience of patients undergoing bone marrow transplantation according to the stages through which a transplant patient proceeds. We have been able to translate these stages to other protocols.

The *decision to accept* the transplantation procedure is often made against a background of chronic illness and organ failure. There may be months or even years of feeling sick and tired and relying on drugs and equipment (dialysis for the renal patient, cardiac drugs for the heart patient, and chemotherapy for the cancer patient). The fear of death and the prospects of hope are always present. The decision to accept often must be made many miles from the transplant center and often must be made quickly, owing to organ availability or urgent medical recommendations. Patients with severe aplastic anemia usually develop their condition suddenly, and so their decision-making process turns into an emergent medical necessity. They are often unfamiliar with chronic illness and begin the transplant procedure without much experience as patients. Their decision to accept or reject the transplant recommendation is always preceded by the stress of batteries of physiological tests and tissue typing of family members (when living family donors are used for kidney, bone marrow, pancreas transplants).

The *medical evaluation and preparation* may take place on an outpatient basis and then be continued at the transplant center. Physiological tests continue. A psychiatric assessment should be undertaken simultaneously to evaluate the patients' (1) personality and past history, (2) social support, and (3) mechanisms by which they have coped with previous illness.

Waiting may be difficult and prolonged if cadaver organs are used (liver, heart, and some kidney transplants).

The few days or hours before the actual transplant require more tests, immunosuppression (drugs and multiple blood transfusions for graft enhancement), and *preparation for surgery*. The recipient may be prepared within hours if cadaver organs are used. If family members are used as donors, then the preparation may be extended over a few days and be less hurried. In the case of bone marrow transplantation, patients must enter a sterile isolation room to avoid infection and undergo a 10-day pretransplant conditioning period of immunosuppressive drugs and total body irradiation. Hickman or Broviac catheters are surgically placed for hyperalimentation. For these patients this conditioning regimen is a point of no return, for unlike kidney or pancreas transplantation, there is no dialysis or insulin to fall back on once the procedure has begun.

The *transplant day* itself is brief compared with the convalescent period. It is paradoxically uncomplicated and undramatic for the bone marrow transplant patients, involving only an infusion of several packets of concentrated bone marrow. For other patients it may involve long and complicated abdominal or thoracic surgery. In the cases of cardiac and liver transplantation, there is the chance of immediate death caused by a nonfunctioning organ. A living family donor must undergo major surgery, possibly for the first time.

The *convalescence* period is punctuated by the spector of transplant rejection, continuation of immunosuppressive drugs, and the possibility of infection. A waiting period for marrow engraftment and the reaction of graft-versus-host disease (a turning of the transplant against the recipient) are unique to transplantation of bone marrow.

Preparation for discharge is begun after the transplanted organ is functioning adequately (one to three months after transplant) and concern for infection is low. The patients show a heightened interest in the real world and attempt to "pick up their lives" where they left off sometime before their illness started. As the patients begin learning self-care outside the hospital (Hickman line care, regimens of medications), their excitement over their anticipated discharge is mixed with their fear of leaving the security of the transplant unit.

Adaptation outside the hospital is long and protracted. Weekly visits to the transplant clinic (twice-weekly visits for cardiac transplant patients) for surveillance cultures and metabolic checks are routine for at least the first few months. As the time following transplantation increases, patients turn their concerns from organ rejection to life as survivors. Rehabilitation is often as much a psychological as a medical process.

PSYCHOLOGICAL CARE OF THE PATIENT

Patients for whom transplantation of an organ is recommended display the range of psychological character structures. Most fall within the range of normality and have no major psychiatric disease or personality disorder. Some of the more severely disturbed are deemed not suitable for the rigors of the transplantation procedures, but today the psychological abnormality must be profound for transplantation to be absolutely rejected. There is no particular personality type seen among transplant patients, and they use various coping mechanisms to deal with the stresses encountered. Common sense suggests that patients who already have a poor psychological adjustment or psychiatric illness are more at risk for psychological distress or abnormality related to the transplant. But we have noticed that some fairly disturbed individuals seem to handle the procedure well, whereas others, without obvious difficulty, experience considerable distress.

Even though we have emphasized the wide range of patients' adaptive techniques, there are some problems and ways of dealing with them common to each transplant procedure. Each stage of organ transplantation tends to be characterized by a particular emotional tone with identifiable difficulties. The *pretransplant* stage is generally one of hopefulness in which patients deny their fears. Usually there is considerable anxiety; frustration runs high when there is a long, uncertain waiting period for a suitable donor. The *transplant stage* proper is predominated by fears of surgery and sterile isolation; the patients must also deal with unpleasant side effects of immunosuppressant drugs. Fear of surgery seems to lead to an increased preoccupation with questions about why they are ill. Their explanations range from "deserving" their illness to being the strongest in the family and therefore the best able to cope with illness. In the former instance, the disease is perceived as a punishment and is related to real or fantasized guilt over past misdeeds, which in turn may be real or imagined. Current guilt is a prominent feature of this period. Patients are concerned with all the worry they are causing their families. They feel that they may be taking unfair advantage of the donors, who frequently are siblings and often perceived as sacrificing themselves. And at times the patients worry that the transplantation may ultimately cause the donor's demise. The *posttransplant state* is characterized by rapid fluctuations in the patient's physical condition, usually matched by swings between hope and despair, security and anxiety. Control over one's physical and psychological condition is of paramount importance, but later these preoccupations are overtaken by conflicts of whether or not to leave the protected environment.

PSYCHOLOGICAL THEMES

Rebirth and Body Image.   Investigators have noted recurring psychological themes expressed by transplant recipients. Abram emphasized (1) the effects of transplant on the personality structure and (2) themes of rebirth (Abram 1970, 1978). Fantasies that one may become a different person are common after receiving an organ from another person. A young male recipient on our bone marrow transplant unit hoped he would acquire with the transplanted marrow some of his donor brother's athletic skills and good looks. His mother added, on the transplantation day, that she hoped her recipient son would acquire the donor son's even-tempered personality. Abram reported a patient who had been a "Grand Dragon in the Klu Klux Klan" and then became an active member of the National Association for the Advancement of Colored People after receiving a kidney from a black donor (Abram 1972, 1978).

Psychological conflicts regarding sexual identity may come to the forefront after surgery and are particularly likely if the organ is from a donor of the opposite sex. Male patients have voiced concern after transplantation that they may have acquired some feminine characteristics, and some have been noted to sit down while urinating if their kidney donor was a female. Female recipients have had reciprocal concerns. Basch (1973) reported the case of a young male patient who became panic stricken after learning his kidney was donated by a male homosexual. When patients learn that they have received their respective transplanted organs from the same donor (usually a cadaver) they often consider themselves "transplant twins." Schowalter (1970) described a symbiotic relationship between two adolescent girls who received transplants from the same donor and who became excessively concerned about what happened to each other. Abram (1972) compared acquiring a kidney from a cadaver with adopting a baby. The mother of the adopted child must remain anonymous to the new adopting parents, just as the name, source, and history of the cadaver kidney donor are unknown to the kidney recipient.

Often after a transplant, the patient recipient expresses a feeling of being reborn or of having a "new lease on life" or "a second chance" (Cramond et al. 1967a, Crombez and Lefebvre 1972, Kemph 1966). This is particularly true after cardiac transplantation (Abram 1970, Lunde 1969). Hackett (1972) described a "Lazarus" syndrome in patients who survive a cardiac arrest. This life-extending view has received much attention on our bone marrow transplant unit. Often such an attitude is initiated by members of the staff who now have a ritual on the day of their transplant, in which patients receive a birthday card and cake with candles.

There is much talk by staff, patients, and families about this "special" birthday party. One aplastic anemia patient subsequently celebrated her birthday on the "new day" after her second bone marrow transplant and made an effort to spend that day visiting a bone marrow patient currently on the unit. One patient planned his wedding on the first anniversary of his transplant.

Integration of the New Organ.   The ability to transplant a living structure from one human being into another presents psychological problems never before faced by human beings (Freebury 1974). Until this new procedure, surgery either repaired the structure or organ or removed it. In the latter instance, the patient experienced a loss and had to go through a process of mourning the lost organ. Now with transplantation, the recipient must integrate a new living part into his or her body, an event heretofore impossible except in fantasy. There is some analogy with the growth of the fetus in the mother's body. That event, however, is a common ingredient of human experience. Moreover, the fetus is a creation of the mother along with her partner, not something belonging to another person and then given to the recipient. Transplantation is life extending and necessitates the recipient to integrate a new foreign part or object.

Castelnuevo (1973, 1978), who studied these problems extensively, stated that the psychological integration of the new organ into the body scheme of the recipient takes some time and may not occur smoothly. Muslin (1971) was the first to discuss the process of assimilation of a new transplanted organ, which is initially a foreign object, in terms of the ego's integration of a new object. This process of integration involves incorporation, introjection, and identification. Muslin conceptualized "three stages of internalization" or "psychological passage" which he maintained began with a "foreign body stage," in which the transplanted organ is "new, separate or sticking out." The recipient is the new organ's caretaker and feels protective of his or her "new baby." The second stage, according to Muslin, is one of "partial incorporation," when the patient begins to talk less about the organ's newness. The final stage, or "complete incorporation," is characterized by "a lack of awareness of the new organ unless the patient is asked about it" (p. 1185). Muslin viewed this process as universal, though empirical studies have yet to demonstrate that.

Basch also discussed the intrapsychic integration of kidney grafts and hypothesized that assimilation of the kidney does not take place in stages, but rather there is a specific style of integration peculiar to each patient and his particular intrapsychic mechanisms. "This assimilation is affected not only by the patient's pre-operative ego functioning and object relations, particularly if there is a live donor, but also by the specific transplantation experience and other reality factors" (1973, p. 378).

Viederman (1974b) emphasized the difficulty that the psychic apparatus has in integrating experiences that are drastically new or different from past experiences, stating that transplantation surgery is a dramatic new realm of human experience. Viederman also pointed out that whenever there is a need to integrate such a new experience, the ego inevitably attempts to "search for meaning." He asserted that "the degree of comfort and safety which a person will experience in accepting a transplanted organ will depend on the quality of his relationship with the donor, both real and fantasized" (p. 285). The degree to which the transplant is a "hostile introject" or a "benevolent introject" will be of great importance, and Viederman postulated that the fear of loss is likely to be most intense when the transplanted organ is seen as a hostile introject. A benevolent introject will lead to "a positive change in the self concept" (p. 285). He presented cases illustrating the activation of both such introjects. Viederman noted that there are many patients for whom there is little conflict and in whom it is difficult to evaluate the nature of the intrapsychic equilibrium. In some instances there seemed to be actual identification with the object or part object, and this seems particularly to be the case when the transplantation has been from a donor of the opposite sex.

We have found that patients undergoing bone marrow transplantation have had little difficulty in "assimilating" their new organ. This almost certainly is related to the difference in psychological meaning when one inherits a solid organ, as compared with bone marrow, which is fluid and actually becomes regenerated by the donor himself or herself. The actual transplant experience is perceived by the recipient as being no different from a blood transfusion, and it does not require the major surgical procedures that are part of the transplantation of other organs. Individuals do not really think of bone marrow as a true organ. Solid organs may be viewed more as objects with all their donor-associated characteristics. We have not documented any fantasy in our patients about such assimilation. Indeed, the received bone marrow transplant would have to *assimilate* the immunosuppressed host rather than the reverse. Even during graft-versus-host disease, no patient has stated, "The graft is destroying or rejecting me." To date our patient population has been small, and it may be that later, others, particularly if they are more sophisticated and truly understand the immunological aspects of graft-versus-host disease, will reveal such thoughts.

Rejection of the New Organ.   Several researchers have reported that a recipient's death or acute organ rejection has occurred after some paramount loss or disintegration of a close interpersonal relationship (Basch 1973, Tourkow 1974, Viederman 1975). Eisendrath (1969) observed that 8 out of 11 patients who died following renal transplantation had experienced a loss, abandonment by family, extreme pessimism, or unusual panic far above and beyond those patients who had survived. This has led to questions about the relationship between a patient's psychological state and the viability of the transplanted organ. Animal studies have documented the suggested role of the central nervous system in the control of immunogenesis (Salomon and Amkraut 1970). One can infer that a patient's immunological balance might be influenced by emotional factors. It is interesting to postulate a relationship between the psychological conflicts of transplant patients and the biological processes of rejection and/or graft-versus-host disease. In 1975 Viederman examined such an interplay between psychic and somatic factors in the rejection of a transplanted kidney in a young patient. This patient reacted to his father's death "with an incomplete mourning response and had coped with the loss through identification and search for surrogate father figures" (p. 957). The death of such a parental figure immediately preceded his admission for rejection of his transplanted kidney and development of a peptic ulcer. Viederman saw a causal relationship between a somatic event (kidney rejection) and a psychic antecedent. Such relationships are still theoretical and anecdotal but warrant serious study.

TRANSPLANTATION AND COPING MECHANISMS

The question of transplantation surgery arises only in patients who already are dealing with a severe, chronic, usually life-threatening disease. They, therefore, are subject to all of the difficulties inherent in this situation and also the added issues already mentioned that go with acquiring a donated organ. As Viederman pointed out, "Any person confronted with hospitalization for serious disease will be forced to relinquish much of his autonomy, his independent judgment and his control over his own body" (1974a, p. 68). The patient's (1) ability to delegate much of his or her own control and authority to others and (2) capacity to establish a close trusting relationship with the staff will most likely influence his or her emotional reaction to care and subsequent compliance to treatment. Viederman suggested that this type of coping strategy, a transition from independence and autonomy to complete dependency, is a regression psychodynamically and closely related to the mother-child dyad.

We find it useful to conceptualize the patient's task of adjusting as one that requires coping mechanisms, psychological techniques used consciously and unconsciously by the patient to master or adapt to the environment. In this situation the major environmental problems are those brought on by the transplantation procedure. Obviously many of the techniques, such as repression, reaction formation, regression, displacement, projection, and rationalization, which are generally known as ego defenses, are among the coping mechanisms. Even though they are used to repress stressful impulses and anxiety, they may also be used successfully by patients to master their transplant environment.

Hamburg and associates (1953) and Visotsky and associates (1961) used the concept of coping behavior to study patients with life-threatening crises requiring extensive medical care and long-term hospitalization; more specifically they focused on patients with severe burns and with poliomyelitis. As Visotsky and colleagues pointed out, it is appropriate to notice and study the variety of behavior patterns, and they can be conceived of as serving one or more of the following: keeping distress within manageable limits, mobilizing hope, maintaining a sense of personal warmth, restoring relations with signifcant other people, and enhancing prospects for recovery, increasing the likelihood of working out a favorable out-of-hospital situation. Clearly, the principles of these studies can be appropriately applied to a transplant patient. Adler (1972) studied in depth the coping mechanisms of one patient, Miss R, through the course of her kidney transplantation. Miss R's major adaptations were regression, rationalization, repression, and displacement. These had assisted her in coping with fears and anxieties and helped maintain an equilibrium in the face of the "emotional onslaught" of surgery.

The prolongation of life not only adds time but also raises the question as to the quality of the life that is prolonged. To the fear that their lives will be shortened, patients with chronic disease who are undergoing transplantation now have to face another fear: "Will this new life or extended life be acceptable?" This dilemma was discussed by Beard (1969) in "Fear of Death and Fear of Life." Christopherson and Gonda (1973) considered grief as a mechanism for coping and found that it is a universal phenomenon in patients with end-stage renal failure, even when they opt for renal transplantation. These patients are forced to grieve not only for the loss of a friend and loss of control over a signficant bodily function but also for the loss of their own lives. Thus, whenever transplant patients face the possibility of their own death within a certain length of time, they begin their anticipatory grieving.

The view of transplantation as perceived by care-givers may not be entirely consonant with that of the recipient of a transplanted organ. Often the patient seems to have exchanged one set of problems for another. Calland (1972) wrote from the vantage point of a physician who also had been a dialysis and transplant patient. After a renal transplant the patient is "free from the machines, tubes, dialysis supplies, dietary fluid and travel restrictions, anemia, the mess of cleaning up after a run and all the shunt or fistual problems that plague the patient on hemodialysis" (p. 334). But in addition to basic anxieties, "they carry the constant burdens of fear of rejection and of the primary complications of immunosuppressive therapy; cushingoid faces, infections, cancer, diabetes, capillary fragility, osteoporosis, glaucoma, cataracts and acne" (p. 334). Calland appropriately asked, "Is transplantation 'the true answer' for all patients?" Transplantation may be considered by care-givers "the solution or cure" to chronic illness; however some recipients regard it as palliative and far from liberation. It must be pointed out, however, that Calland was speaking from the perspective of one who had had five renal transplantations. Certainly the experience of many patients with various transplants has been, on the whole, a very good one.

Lefebvre and Crombez (1981) discussed an interesting phenomenon they saw in their renal transplant recipients toward the end of their hospitalization. Many of their patients had become relatively disillusioned, which they termed "the one day at a time" syndrome. The patients often said, "I don't look beyond tomorrow" or "I aim only at short-term goals." This appears to be an adaptation or defensive attitude. Lefebvre and Crombez feel that this attitude can sometimes have a progressive, adaptive and life-enhancing impact, although at other times it may result in negative, life-constricting, and regressive behavior. The former attitude they view as a progressive hypomanic defense whereby anxiety and depression concerning the transplant are present and conscious but generally manageable. The latter attitude they view as a regressive megalomanic defense whereby anxiety is denied.

The coping mechanisms in these patients are an exciting and challenging research area for psychiatrists. The field is still new and complex enough so that there are almost certainly general principles still to be learned. It is important, however, to underscore the necessity to understand each patient as an individual and to ascertain what his or her previous coping mechanisms were. Though psychiatric abnormalities are occasionally seen in patients undergoing transplantation, for the most part the therapist's task is to understand the types of problems faced by these patients and their typical ways of adjusting or maladjusting. It then becomes the therapist's job to help make the adjustment as effective as possible and to minimize the degree of suffering.

PSYCHIATRIC SYNDROMES IN THE COURSE OF TRANSPLANTATION

Several important psychiatric problems may develop in the course of transplantation. Patients may experience emotional disturbances such as anxiety, agitation, depression, suicide, impotence, and noncompliance. Concurrent psychiatric illness may also complicate the transplant.

EMOTIONAL DISTURBANCES RELATED TO ILLNESS AND TRANSPLANTATION

Some patients, because of their character structure and methods of coping, are unable to adapt to illness, transplantation, or convalescence and rehabilitation. Their altered behavior may take the form of excessive manipulation, hostile attitudes, increased and regressive dependency, and excessive demands for attention. This maladaptive behavior may compromise care and adversely affect results, since transplantation requires a high level of participation and cooperation. Maladaptive behavior requires attention from and management by all team members.

There is a high incidence among transplant recipients of psychiatric problems after surgery, among which depression and anxiety are by far the most common. In 1971, Penn and colleagues reported that 32 percent of 292 kidney transplant recipients had postoperative emotional difficulties (mainly anxiety reactions and depression) and that 7 recipients eventually committed suicide. A little more than one-third of these patients with postoperative problems had previously had psychiatric symptoms (depression, immature personality disorder, organic brain syndrome). Penn and colleagues added that at some stage, practically all patients experienced episodes of anxiety and/or depression secondary to a complication, a painful treatment, drug therapy, fear of death, or an unresolved grief reaction to the loss of organs. In their patients, depression was often transient and cleared once the complication was satisfactorily treated. Depression and anxiety were found both before and after surgery in the hepatic transplant patients, but Penn and associates noted that it was difficult to evaluate these patients because of common pretransplant encephalopathy and decreased postoperative survival.

It has been difficult to evaluate the prevalence of anxiety and depression in renal transplant recipients, since many of the earlier researchers did not distinguish the etiology of these reactions (physiologic versus psychologic) or indicate the transplant milieu (donation by cadaver or living relative). In 1966, Kemph noted only occasional hysteria, phobia, confusion, anxiety, and psychosis, and these were usually transient. Colomb and Hamburger (1967) reported 1 case of depression and 8 cases of "overt or partially concealed" anxiety in 44 kidney recipients. Short and Harris (1969) observed severe psychotic depressions in 2 of their 19 recipients. In 1969, Ferris wrote that out of 54 kidney recipients, (1) 55 percent of those receiving transplants from living related donors had some type of psychiatric complication (depression and psychosis); (2) 31 percent of those receiving transplanted cadaver organs developed anxiety and depression; and (3) 100 percent of the patients receiving multiple cadaver organs or receiving living relatives' organs that failed and were subsequently retransplanted with cadaver organs developed severe anxiety depression and psychosis secondary to multiple rejection. Abram (1972) observed that 23 percent of renal transplant recipients had after surgery moderate psychiatric complications and evidence of psychosocial upheaval and that 26 percent were unable or unwilling to return to work.

Several investigators have studied the quality of life of children and adolescents who chose transplantation to manage their end-stage renal failure. Korsch and associates (1973), Lilly and associates (1971), and Bernstein (1971) all found that major psychiatric disturbances were uncommon in children treated by transplantation. They did note, as others have, that life was considered fearful and constricted, and its quality was compromised. Poznanski and colleagues (1978) interviewed children and adolescents two to ten years after their transplants and discovered that 61 percent of patients made periodic depressive statements. Fifty percent were functioning at school and on jobs. The other 50 percent were depressed and not functioning; two adolescent boys from this group had made several suicide attempts. This latter group was notable because they all had decreased renal functions, episodes of rejection, or retransplantation.

Chapman and Cox (1977) studied anxiety, pain, and depression in 67 abdominal surgery patients, i.e., kidney transplant donors, kidney transplant recipients, and a general surgery group, at three different times (the day before surgery, the day after, and three days after). Renal donors and recipients showed more extreme responses to pain than did general surgical patients, who showed the least amount of change in state anxiety. Chapman and Cox concluded that "the meaning attached to the stress of surgery significantly affects the subjective state surrounding the operation (p. 7).

There has been much less written about depression and anxiety during heart transplantation. In 1969 Lunde noted that after cardiac transplantation 1 out of 9 patients developed a depression, 2 had minor mood and cognitive alterations, and 3 developed a psychosis. Christopherson and colleagues (1976) felt there was definite therapeutic usefulness in cardiac transplantation, since 91 percent of 54 patients were successfully rehabilitated six months after surgery, only 7 percent sustained substantial physical diabilities, and 2 percent were psychiatrically disabled with grave marital problems.

Because there has been so little written about depression and anxiety after surgery in heart transplant patients, it seems reasonable to refer to some of the earlier work in the 1960s on psychiatric problems in open-heart surgery patients (Abram 1965, Kornfield et al. 1965) and to make some general inferences. Kimball (1969) studied patients before open-heart surgery and divided them into categories of "adjusted, symbiotic, anxious and depressed" on the basis of factors identified in a presurgery interview. He stated that "patients manifesting considerable pre-operative anxiety or depression have a greater chance of not surviving surgery and a greater morbidity after surgery than other patients. . . . For others the operation threatens to upset the balance that the disease has come to hold in their adjustment to life, and for this group there is a higher incidence of morbidity as well as a failure to realize an improvement in their life adjustment following surgery" (p.358). Possibly this information may be valuable in predicting the postoperative course and outcome following cardiac transplant.

Extreme depression and anxiety may lead to suicide in transplant recipients. Suicide is particularly common in renal transplant patients (Colomb and Hamburger 1967, Dubovsky and Penn 1980) and may even take the subtle form of noncompliance, i.e., discontinuation of medication or diet. Abram (Abram 1970, 1978) collected statistics on suicidal behavior in chronic dialysis patients from over 201 centers. Of 3,478 patients, 20 successfully committed suicide (overdoses, cutting shunts), 17 made unsuccessful attempts, 117 died from unwillingness or inability to follow the protocol, and 22 withdrew from the dialysis programs. In addition there 107 "accidents." Forty-two deaths (20 actual suicides, 22 withdrawals) out of 3,478 or 1.21 percent, is much higher than the suicide rate in the normal population (1/10,000 or 0.01 percent). If one included those 117 who could not follow the dialysis protocol, the figure would be even higher at 4.6 percent.

Sexual dysfunction is common with chronic renal failure (De-Nour 1978, G. L. Moore 1976), occurring in 50 to 80 percent of male dialysands (Abram 1978). Decreased sexual functioning may be proportional to the degree of depression and the patient's self-image when it is clear that there are no organic causes (Dubovsky and Penn 1980). Women are less likely to experience loss of sexual function and are capable of producing offspring (Korsch et al. 1980). But they do worry about the cosmetic toll on their bodies (G. L. Moore 1976). Impotence is found in 22 to 43 percent of male kidney transplant patients (Abram 1978, Levy 1973, Salvatierra et al. 1975). To these researchers' knowledge there have been no reports of this phenomenon in other organ recipients. Organic etiologies, such as the side effects of steroids and antihypertensive drugs, poor graft function, decreased hormones and tracemetals, decreased penile blood flow, and nerve supply problems secondary to transplant surgery, have been implicated. But as Dubovsky and Penn found (1980), anxiety, depression, and poor self-image clearly contribute to posttransplant sexual dysfunction. Male kidney transplant patients have often (1) been concerned with adapting to illness-prone roles that they consider female, (2) fantasized about a possible transplanted organ from a female donor, (3) felt that transplantation is a form of castration, or (4) feared that intercourse would damage their new transplanted organ. Dubovsky and Penn concluded that sexual potency was not often improved by reducing steroids and antihypertensive drugs. Many feel that sexual dysfunction therapy is not used extensively enough in these patients.

It is well known that much of the renal dialysis population is noncompliant from time to time (Armstrong 1978). Unfortunately this noncompliance can carry lethal consequences and may contribute to the high number of patient suicides. There have been a number of reports in the renal transplantation literature concerning noncompliance as an explanation of graft failure following surgery. Uehling and colleagues (1976) documented eight instances of adult renal transplant patients' not taking immunosuppressive drugs. Korsch and associates (1978) noted that 14 patients (13 were adolescent, of whom 12 were girls) interrupted immunosuppressive treatment following kidney transplantation; 6 later lost their allografts; and 8 developed impaired renal function. Noncompliance was suspected when cushingoid symptoms diminished and changes in renal function occurred. Dubvosky and Penn (1980) believe that kidney recipients fail to comply because they (1) dislike the side effects of corticosteroid, (2) deny the severity of their condition, (3) become disappointed and frustrated that surgery does not magically change their life, or (4) feel that surgery has actually resulted in a cure and that they no longer need medication. Finally, a few fail to comply as a way of expressing anger at their condition and taking ultimate control. Some patients distrust their physicians and stop medication or feel that no matter what they do, nothing will be successful. On our bone marrow transplant unit we have found little steroid-related noncompliance; however many of our young transplants fail to follow the dietary and alcohol consumption restrictions necessary for graft-versus-host disease control. One patient insisted on resuming a natural megavitamin regimen which contained possibly toxic quantities of fat-soluble vitamins. Noncompliance should be met with an attempt to understand the patient's motivations, to respect for his or her wish for control, and to avoid a physician-patient power struggle.

CONCURRENT PSYCHIATRIC ILLNESS

Any transplant recipient who has had a history of previous psychiatric illness may exacerbate or resume his or her symptoms during the course of transplantation. Major psychiatric syndromes, such as bipolar affective illness, schizophrenia, and psychotic depression, require psychiatric consultation and psychopharmacological managment. They may compromise the transplant recipient and endanger his or her cooperation and compliance. The use of psychopharmacologic active drugs in their treatment will be discussed below.

PSYCHOPHARMACOLOGIC DRUG USE

The liaison psychiatrist and transplant team should always use caution in prescribing psychotropic drugs for a transplant patient, since they often mask the symptoms of altered mental status that accompany a developing organic brain syndrome. These drugs should be used only after the etiology of a mental symptom is clear.

The treatment of kidney transplant recipients with pharmacologic agents require special attention to two factors that make these patients quite different from others: (1) dialyzable medications will be removed via hemodialysis and be reduced below therapeutic levels; (2) since renal patients have no or little usable kidney function, medications removed solely by the kidney accumulate in toxic levels (Levy 1981b). Fortunately, neuroleptics, minor tranquilizers, and antidepressants belong to neither group and thus may be given at near comparable doses to those given patients with normal kidney function (Basch 1980, Bennett et al. 1980). Lithium is excreted solely by the kidneys and is freely dialyzed. It should be avoided in patients with moderate to severe reduction of glomerular filtration rate. For manic-depressive patients it should be administered after dialysis, and serum levels should be closely monitored. Abram

(1978) found that dialysis patients respond poorly to antidepressants, and consequently uses them only in cases of severe depression and chronic insomnia. He emphasized that transient anxiety states and psychotic episodes usually respond to diazepam and neuroleptics, respectively. Cardiac and bone marrow transplant recipients are somewhat easier to treat with psychotropic medication unless, of course, they have accompanying renal insufficiency.

Sleep may be assisted by the benzodiazepines. Diazepam (Valium®) may be used for anxiety and uncomfortable diagnostic procedures. It is slowly metabolized by the liver, and accumulation of active breakdown products may occur over several days. This may be especially troublesome for any transplant patient who has compromised liver function. A shorter-acting antianxiety drug such as oxazepam (Serax®) may be preferred. The benzodiazepine derivative, flurazepam (Dalmane®), does not depress respiration, has no effect on rapid eye movement sleep and thus, for sleep, has an advantage over barbiturates. Barbiturates have no use in transplant medicine other than as antiepileptics. A patient who becomes irrational, agitated, or violent may be successfully treated, without complications, by neuroleptics.

PSYCHOLOGICAL EFFECTS OF TREATMENT

As already mentioned, organ transplantation demands an extraordinarily high level of commitment and cooperation from the recipients. Increased cooperation by the patient goes hand in hand with increased knowledge about the illness. Thus it is important for patients to have (1) a careful and accurate description of the protocol and its desired response and (2) information about the treatment's side effects that must be tolerated in order to achieve the desired response. Understanding that a side effect of treatment *may* occur may make it easier to accept and tolerate if it does. It was often (mistakenly so) felt that if patients were told of possible side effects, they were more likely to complain and develop them (Holland 1977). The therapist and transplant team should be familiar with the effects of transplant treatment on psychologic function and use that knowledge to assess the patient.

MEDICATION

Many medications used in the transplantation protocol may be associated with neuropsychiatric side effects. Such psychiatric symptoms are distressing, and so patients are reluctant to disclose them. Not all psychiatric symptoms are drug induced; some are caused by an underlying reaction to the transplant itself. Therefore, it is wise for the therapist to be familiar with those drugs that frequently lead to psychiatric complications, so that he or she may help the team distinguish between those problems caused by drugs and those caused by functional issues. A number of cardiovascular drugs that have been associated with psychiatric sequelae (Erman and Guggenheim 1981, Klerman 1981) are often used in kidney and heart transplant patients: *Lidocaine*, used as an antiarrhythmic agent in coronary-care units, can result in excitement, apprehension, agitation, restlessness, and depression, if used in high doses. Toxic levels of *digitalis* may precipitate a psychoticlike state with disorientation, hallucinations, delusions, agitation, and irritability; yellow vision can be an indicator of toxic levels. Depression may develop after long-term high dose usage. Antihypertensives, such as *reserpine* (Serpasil®) have often been associated with depression, lethargy, mild changes in mood, and loss of libido. This affective change may be due to depletion of brain stores of several neurotransmitters. *Guanethidine* (Ismilin®) may produce depression, lassitude, and inhibition of ejaculation, and long-term use of propranalol (Inderal®) may cause nightmares, insomnia, impotence, lassitude, hallucinations, and depression (Kathol et al. 1980, Opie 1980). *Methyldopa* (Aldomet®), another antihypertensive drug, is associated with depression and may lead to other side effects such as lethargy, drowsiness, nightmares, and confusion (McCabe and Corry 1978). Like reserpine, methyldopa is thought to cause depression by decreasing neurotransmitters. *Hydralazine* (Apresoline®), *Clonidine* (Catapress®), and *Prazosin* (Minipress®), have also been associated with depression and impotence.

Corticosteroids are universally employed in high doses as immunosuppressive agents to prevent posttransplant organ rejection. In chronic administration they produce cushingoid symptoms of moon faces, acne, hyperphagia, obesity, insomnia, diabetes, cataracts, muscle atrophy, and stunted growth in children (Fine et al. 1979). They may produce a variety of psychiatric symptoms such as euphoria, hypomania, lability of affect, depression, and psychosis (Carpenter et al. 1972). These disturbances are usually dose dependent but may occur at any dosage or especially on abrupt change or withdrawal of medication. Psychotic reactions are best treated by lowering or withdrawing the steroid; this discontinuation of steroid must be weighed against its therapeutic immunosuppressive benefit. At times neuroleptic treatment in moderate dosage is necessary. For kidney transplant patients, the most frequent neurologic complications result from immunosuppressive drugs. Depressing immunologic systems makes the transplant patient highly susceptible to fungal (aspergillosis) infections. Fungal brain abscesses often cause delirium, seizures, and headaches. Fifteen percent of all renal transplant patients exhibit central nervous system (CNS) fungal infections at autopsy.

Transplant patients may develop ulcers secondary to the stress of transplantation and immunosuppressive drugs. *Cimetidine* (Tagamet®), on H$_2$ (histamine) receptor antagonist, has been often used to treat such ulcer disease. The incidence of psychological side effects such as confusion, depression, and paranoid psychosis is common with this drug and greatly increased in the presence of coexistent metabolic disturbances, cerebral impairment, preexisting psychiatric illness, high dosage, and advanced age (Weddington 1982).

Chemotherapeutic agents such as cytoxan and methyltrexate are used in the bone marrow transplant procedure, at sublethal doses for marrow suppression and subsequent immunosuppression. Fatigue, weakness, nausea, and vomiting are significant neuropsychiatric side effects of cytoxan (Holland 1977), which is thought to activate the chemoreceptor trigger zone (CRTZ) situated around the fourth ventricle. Antiemetic agents such as phenothiazines, especially prochlorperazine (Compazine®), act in diminishing impulses from the CRTZ and should be started about six to eight hours before the patient receives chemotherapy. Tetrahydrocannabinol (Δ^9-THC), the active component of marijuana, has strong antiemetic effects and is becoming widely used clinically on an experimental basis. Methotrexate does not cross the blood-brain barrier, but when given intrathecally for prophylactic measures against CNS leukemia may produce a leukoencephalopathy with focal signs of meningeal irritation, paraparesis, and mental confusion.

TRANSPLANT SURGERY

Two decades have passed since human kidney transplantation began as an experimental procedure to aid end-stage renal failure patients; it is now widely accepted as an established therapeutic modality. However, the surgery itself is not without vascular, gastrointestinal, colonic, pancreatic, and hepatic complications (Lee et al. 1978). Kidney transplant patients are at higher risk for neoplastic problems (lymphoma is 30 times higher, and reticular cell sarcoma is 35 times higher in these patients than in the normal population). Neoplasms appear early, on the average of 34 months after transplantation. Involvement is characteristically in the CNS, with most of the neoplasms confined to the brain. These, of course, can lead to organic brain syndromes with fluctuating delirium, personality and behavior changes, and depression. Immunosuppressive therapy may contribute to the increased incidence of these de novo neoplasms.

Disturbed calcium metabolism with secondary hyperparathyroidism is common in chronic renal failure and hemodialysis. Hypercalcemia and secondary hyperparathyroidism after successful renal homotransplant were documented in 3 to 70 percent of recipients (Lee et al. 1978). Hypercalcemia can appear three days after transplant and persist up to 12 months; such changes in serum calcium can result in fluctuations of mental status. Hyperparathyroidism and hypomagnesemia are frequently associated with an increased risk of affective disorders (Klerman 1981).

Psychosis is a frequent, serious, postoperative complication in cardiac transplant recipients. Lunde (1969) reported that three out of nine heart transplants performed at Stanford University in 1968 were associated with postoperative psychosis. Two of the three developed a psychosis secondary to hepatic failure and organic brain syndrome. The third patient developed an extensive delusion system in which he believed the nurses were trying to kill him with various immunosuppressive drugs. There was concern about treating such patients with chlorpromazine because the transplanted heart is denervated. It was felt that the lowered peripheral vascular resistance seen with phenothiazines might be exaggerated in a patient with a denervated heart. Fortunately, this was not the case. Current practice indicates haloperidol (Haldol®) as the drug of choice, owing to its few cardiovascular side effects.

TOTAL BODY IRRADIATION

Irradiation may be used alone or in combination with immunosuppressive drugs and chemotherapy in several organ transplant procedures. Patients who choose bone marrow transplantation receive before surgery immunologically and hematopoietically lethal doses of total body irradiation (TBI). TBI is given in the range of 800 to 1,300 rads, usually divided into twelve treatments. The effects of this irradiation on the central nervous system may lead to transient or delayed neuropsychological sequelae. Total and half-body irradiation was studied by Gottshalk and colleagues (Gottshalk et al. 1969) in 16 advanced-cancer patients whose emotional and cognitive functions were monitored. Immediate impairment of intellectual function, even though persisting for only a day, was indicated by Gottshalk's highly sensitive instrument of psychological state based on content; no impairment was found using the more commonly used Reitan Battery. TBI can be used in combination with chemotherapy, and data from a report by Meadows and associates (1981) suggest that children who get intrathecal cranial irradiation and methotrexate often develop mild learning and intellectual disabilities. Mild, unrecognized delirium may be caused by radiation rather than solely by stress or chemotherapeutic agents. Santos and Kaiser (1981) believe that there could be a more rational basis, than is now used, for the timing and dosing of total body irradiation with the choice of chemotherapy.

GERM-FREE ENVIRONMENTS

Optimal care for some types of organ transplantation requires germ-free environments. Currently, reverse isolation (requiring staff and visitors to use cap, mask, gown, gloves, booties) is used more often than sterile laminar airflow rooms. Although therapeutically useful to decrease the risk of infection after surgery and bone marrow suppression, this environment requires prolonged physical isolation of the patient from staff and family.

The initial psychological interest in bone marrow transplantation was connected with the possible harmful effects of sensory deprivation precipitated by such germ-free environments. Holland and colleagues (1977) carried out the first major systematic study of cancer patients treated in isolation. Using a nurses' rating scale of patients' daily behavior, psychological state, and mood, they studied 50 leukemics undergoing chemotherapy in germ-free laminar airflow rooms. They found that the patients adapted well to their protected environment and ironically complained of overstimulation, along with the lack of physical touching. A survey of cancer centers using germ-free isolation (Kellerman et al. 1977) indicated that children adapt better to isolation and have fewer psychological reactions. Finally, patients are able to withstand the emotional stress of germ-free isolation, and their behavioral changes are related to the severity of their illness rather than to the isolation itself (Gordon 1975, Holland 1977, Lesko et al. 1983).

GRAFT-VERSUS-HOST DISEASE

Engraftment of donor bone marrow in the recipient is a sign of success, but it sometimes paradoxically brings with it the life-threatening problem of graft-versus-host disease (GVHD). When competent lymphoid cells are transferred from a donor to a recipient who is incapable of rejecting them, the grafted cells survive, giving themselves time to recognize the host antigens and react immunologically against them. Such a "turning of the transplanted organ against the recipient" is unique to bone marrow transplantation. Approximately 50 percent of recipients develop mild to moderate GVHD, which is fatal in 20 percent of patients. GVHD has manifestations similar to an acute immune disease: enteritis, serositis, malar erythema, depigmentation skin eruptions, polymositis, and increased liver enzymes (Storb et al. 1981). Because most autoimmune diseases, such as lupus erythematosis, produce a transient vasculitis of the brain, it is important to monitor GVHD patients for mild or sub-clinical mental changes indicative of CNS involvement. There is a strong likelihood of mild cerebral dysfunction related to GVHD.

HICKMAN LINE CATHETERIZATION AND TOTAL PARENTERAL NUTRITION

Total parenteral nutrition (TPN) was introduced by Dudrick and col-leagues in 1968. The continuous infusion of a hypertonic solution of protein hydrolysates, glucose, vitamins, minerals, and lipids requires an indwell-ing catheter in the large vessels and right atrium; it is used for congenital anomalies of the gut, short-bowel syndrome, inflammatory bowel disease, hepatic and renal disease, treatment of neoplastic disease, and severe burns. Theoretically, patients may be maintained indefinitely on TPN, and it is currently being used extensively in bone marrow transplant pa-tients for nutrition (the catheter is also used as a route for blood products, immunosuppressive drugs, and other medication). Patients stop TPN but their Hickman/Broviac lines stay in place for up to 100 days after transplantation.

Complications of TPN (Ota et al. 1978) include osmotic diuresis with hyperosmolar dehydration and metabolic disorders such as hypo- and hyperglycemia, hyponatremia, hypophosphatemia, hypokalemia, hypomagnesia, and prerenal azotemia, all of which can result in a meta-bolic-organic brain syndrome. Total parenteral nutrition and Hickman line catheterization have resulted in profound anxiety, depression, fear, and negative body image, as noted by Price and Levine (1977), and Malcolm and associates (1980). Adjustment problems of transplant pa-tients include (1) the temporary loss of basic functions such as eating, controlling one's own nutrition, and mobility; (2) a high level of technical self-care and catheter maintenance; and (3) partial dependence on nursing care, which later creates a period of separation anxiety at time of discharge. ("Is it a lifeline or a chain?")

There is a growing interest in the relationship of nutritional status to neurotransmitter synthesis and subsequent changes in behavior and mood (Curzor 1978, Monckeberg 1971). Changes in precursor avail-ability may affect the metabolism and synthesis of brain neurotransmitters, and one may therefore postulate nutritionally caused behavioral distur-bances. Alterations in vitamin (especially B-family) and tryptophan meta-bolism are other possible causes for small alterations in mood.

DIALYSIS

By virtue of the progression of their chronic disease or by its treatment (i.e., dialysis), renal transplant recipients may be susceptible to fluctuations in intellectual and cognitive functioning, affect, and behavior. But with the advent of hemo- or peritoneal dialysis, at least part-time reversal of the uremic syndrome is possible. There is, however, a variety of pathological conditions that may alter cerebral function secondary to dialysis (Marshall 1979, Rasken and Fishman 1976, Stewart and Stewart 1979). Dialysis disequilibrium syndrome (Tyler 1965), dialysis dementia (Weddington 1978), Wernicke's encephalopathy (Fares 1972), and subdural hematoma (Leonard et al. 1969, Talalla et al. 1970) are a few. Between 1965 and 1975, 31 percent of the deaths in the dialysis series at Denver were related to a new, progressively fatal neurological syndrome (Burks et al. 1976), which was first reported in 1972 by Alfrey and colleagues (1972). In 1973 Mahurkar and colleagues (1973) introduced the term *dialysis dementia.*

ROLE OF THE LIAISON PSYCHIATRIST

The liaison psychiatrist working with the transplant team is responsible for the recipient, donor, family, and staff (Levy 1981b). Each of these responsibilities will be discussed below.

RECIPIENT

Most patients accepted into a transplant program are evaluated by a team of physicians, specialists (hematologist, oncologist, transplant surgeon), and a psychiatrist. Abram (1969, 1978a), one of the first psychiatrists to work with a transplant team, believed that patients should be rejected for dialysis treatment on medical (including psychiatric) grounds only. He named the absolute psychiatric contraindications as being (1) present and previous psychosis (unrelated to uremia), in which the patient would not be able to follow through with treatment because of impaired-reality testing, and (2) severe mental retardation, which might prevent the patient from understanding what was required. Today, each transplant team sets its own criteria for accepting or rejecting a prospective recipient, and usually there are very few restrictions, even psychological ones. Many bone marrow transplant teams do carefully screen potential donors. Full cooperation from the donor must be guaranteed,

since after the recipient is given lethal doses of irradiation and chemotherapy, there is "no going back." Patients with preexisting bipolar affective disorder have been maintained on lithium during bone marrow
transplantation,* and in our bone marrow unit we transplanted a mildly
retarded 18-year-old without psychological complications.

Once the liaison psychiatrist has assisted the transplant team in selecting the patient, he or she is ready to focus attention on patient care. One
of the psychiatrist's tasks is to predict the prospective recipient's emotional
response to receiving an organ and his or her ability to follow protocol.
In assessing the recipient's personality structure, particular attention is
paid to responses to past emotionally stressful experiences. Information
gathered about the strengths and weaknesses of the patient's coping skills
is used in his or her care and management. The recipient's expectations
of transplantation and fantasies with regard to the new organ are also
watched. The team should understand (1) the meaning that the physical
illness or impairment has to each patient's needs and life-style, (2) the
envisioned threat with which the patient is trying to cope, and most importantly, (3) the type of defensive and adaptive styles (behavior) that
may help or hinder the patient's cooperation and recovery.

The liaison psychiatrist must forgo or bend many of the usual rules
that apply in a psychotherapeutic session. For example, Patenaude and
associates (1979) have asserted that patients are not seen for the full
50-minute hour on the bone marrow transplantation unit. Flexibility is
mandatory in carrying out one's work, and often large blocks of time are
used to see a family member or patient. Sleep, meals, medical treatments,
daily hygiene schedules, Hickman line care, and patient discomfort often
necessitate return visits. A patient who is talkative one day may be very
ill or delirious another, emphasizing possible rapid changes in the patient's mental status. It is important for the psychiatrist to feel comfortable conducting a brief session gowned in mask, surgical gown, boots,
gloves, and protective hat if a patient is in a germ-free room. All patients
in the bone marrow transplant units are in semisterile or germ-free rooms
and require a nurse's constant attendance.

Often the liaison psychiatrist will be asked to assist the rest of the team
in managing side effects from various drugs. As mentioned above, steroids
used to prevent rejection can cause affective disturbances. Many of the
renal and cardiac patients require reserpine, guanethidine, digoxin, and
propranolol, all of which sometimes cause psychological disturbances.
Psychoses after transplantation are rare and usually secondary to or-

---

*N. Straker, personal communication, 1980.

ganic brain syndrome. The most common psychiatric problems seen in transplant patients usually are in the patient's medical condition (complications such as rejection and infection). According to Dubovsky and Penn (1980), postoperative depression is particularly likely if the patient's expectations before surgery were unduly high. During the first week, the psychiatrist can monitor these feelings and should help the recipients discuss their (1) feelings of guilt over taking the donor's organ and making him or her temporarily ill, (2) fears that the new organ will not function, and (3) anger at the staff in reaction to dependency problems. These sessions allow the patients to express their feelings freely and to understand their shifting moods of anxiety, depression, and guilt.

Transplantation does not guarantee full restoration of normal or before-illness health, and thus the transplant recipient requires considerable support from the psychiatrist throughout discharge and convalescence. As the discharge draws near, the patient changes his or her psychological set and must contend with separation from the staff or unit and with feelings of protracted dependency on them. He or she often begins work too soon, works too hard, and becomes exhausted or, conversely, does far too little. During clinic visits the psychiatrist should continue to see the patient and help him or her struggle to adjust to a different life-style outside the transplant unit. The psychiatrist and team also need to support the patient through expected periods of organ rejection and subsequent hospitalizations.

THE LIVING RELATED DONOR

Understandably, there is usually only little psychological attention paid to the healthy donor. But in fact there are often serious problems for the living relative donor that are multidetermined and at times complex. They may provide the seed for future psychological morbidity or lead to difficulties in interpersonal relationships between the donor and the recipient or other members of the family.

Some psychiatrists like Cramond and his colleagues (Cramond 1968, 1971; Cramond et al. 1967a, 1967b) recommend universal and careful psychiatric screening of the donors, whereas others, like Eisendrath and his associates (1969), recommend eliminating it except under unusual circumstances such as when the surgeon is in doubt. Cramond suggests that if a potential donor is rejected on psychological grounds, he or she not be told the true reason. Abram (Abram 1969) agreed with Eisendrath and pointed out that just as the therapist cannot predict which patient will adjust well or poorly to dialysis, the therapist also cannot predict the donor's reaction. There are some therapists, according to Abram, who wish to eliminate the use of living donor organs because of inherent psychological conflicts between donor and recipient. Some of the issues that the therapist should be concerned about in working with a donor are (1) psychological stability, (2) degree of ambivalence, (3) possible family pressure for donation ("ostracized family members who are often 'black sheep' try to redeem themselves by giving a lifesaving organ" [Abram 1978a, p. 373]), (4) motivation for the donation, and (5) personality structure (for hospital management of the donor).

Very little has been written about heart transplant donors and their families, and there are many differences between heart and kidney donation. The removal of a kidney from an unrelated cadaver donor is not as emotionally charged as is the removal of a heart. Clearly, the heart has more symbolic significance than does the kidney, and the cessation of heart function is viewed by many family members as a sign of death. Heart donation requires attention to be shifted from the motives and psychological reactions of the donor to those of the family, which finally decides on the donation. Christopherson and Lunde (1971) observed that family motivation for donorship can be divided into four categories: (1) a family history of heart disease or future cardiac problems; (2) family's academic or medical sophistication: science would benefit rather than themselves personally; (3) donor's own desire to donate; and (4) unsophisticated families trying to make meaning out of a traumatic and totally unexpected death. Donor family responses in this study ranged from requests for no contact with the transplant team to anger because they were not involved. Meetings between donor and recipient families are infrequent but have been arranged. For 20 to 21 donor families, involvement and interest in the transplant decreased sharply after four to six weeks. Christopherson and Lunde found that this period of time corresponded to the length of time in Lindemann's acute grief syndrome (Lindemann 1944). The therapist can be instrumental in assisting families during and after donation.

The transplantation of a segment of pancreas or a kidney is quite different from the transplantation of bone marrow. In the former instances, the donor loses an organ, or part of one, and in the latter he or she donates a body product that is easily regenerated within a few weeks. The psychiatrist should prepare the kidney donor for surgery by helping him or her to understand that the loss of an organ will probably not physiologically affect his or her future. Each donor has his or her own needs, motivation, and altruistic feelings. Both Kemph and Cramond described the ambivalent "dependency which develops between donor and recipient." This is exemplified in the donor's being involved in the loss of the kidney and its fate and the recipient feeling beholden to the family member who donates (Cramond 1971, Kemph 1971).

Fellner and Marshall (1968), in studying 12 kidney donors, discovered to their surprise that the decision-making process did not occur as the result of an extended period of deliberation and evaluation; rather, it was "an instantaneous and irrational response." However, they still regarded the act of donation as positive, with few donors having any regrets. They went on to study donor selection (Fellner 1971) and identified three subsystems within the process of donor self-selection: (1) "medical selection" involves HLA blood typing and other histocompatability tests; (2)"donor self-selection" is made by a potential donor without deliberation and without consulting spouses; (3) "the family subsystem" of donor selection is usually governed by family dynamics. Fellner observed that "the family system of donor selection is clearly at its most efficient level very early in the selection process and works primarily in the direction of excluding some family members from participation. Once the potential donors are known and made available to the renal team, the power of the family system to influence the medical selection process diminishes greatly."

Kemph (1971), a pioneer in the psychological management of kidney donors and recipients, recommended that the psychiatrist's attention be focused on the donor after surgery while the nursing staff, team, and family are attending the recipient. As the attention shifts from donor to recipient, depression in the donor is often likely. He or she mourns the loss of body part and resents those who suggested participation. The donor feels sick and weak when only yesterday he or she was well. According to Kemph, most donors recover psychologically, but their recovery is often hastened when one has the "opportunity to achieve catharsis of underlying feelings" and fantasies. In summary, the liaison psychiatrist may be asked to perform three tasks for the organ donor: (1) assist the team in screening and selecting the donor; (2) preparing the donor for surgery; and (3) attending to donor's concerns, feelings, and fantasies after surgery.

FAMILY

Transplantation is difficult for the rest of the family as well as for the recipients and donors. The numerous repeated stresses and disappointments of chronic chemotherapy or hemodialysis, along with uncertainty about the future are shared by parents, siblings, children, and spouses. These worries are aggravated by the fact that the procedure itself is still experimental. The decision for transplantation may be more difficult when children are the patients. Patenaude and associates (1979) found that even the most untroubled families suffer from the pressures of chronic illness, the transplant procedure, and dislocation from home and friends. Some families must travel thousands of miles to a specialized unit. Families must set up a new home away from home and periodically take their other children out of school. Even if the transplant center is in the same area or city, the dislocation can be considerable. Most units encourage families to participate actively in caring for the patient, which may require all-day trips to the unit. Each family brings to the transplantation procedure its own marital conflicts, financial problems, school problems, and psychological concerns of the children.

The liaison psychiatrist can assist families with (1) rearranging their life-styles, e.g., dislocation from friends and home and relocation to the transplant center; (2) managing preexisting family or marital problems; (3) coping with the strain of having the wage earner ill over a long period of time or the mother-figure incapacitated; (4) airing concerns about donor selection (selection of a living donor establishes new and sometimes difficult relationships among siblings and family members); and (5) dealing with signs of organ rejection and/or a transition into some terminal phase.

On many transplant services, psychiatrist, social worker, and nurse meet weekly with the families of bone marrow transplant recipients. One mother asked for advice about how to tell her four young children that their father was dying. Later she needed help in comforting her 4-year-old who believed that "daddy died because he came home for her birthday party and caught a bad germ." Another mother needed assistance in allowing her teenage son independence and control over his Hickman line care, eventual discharge to home, and the subsequent changes in his convalescent life-style and relationship with girlfriend. The wife of one leukemic who had died during the procedure frequently visits and discusses her return to work and feelings of guilt and joy in developing new friendships. Another patient's young wife felt isolated and alone when trying to share hospital and home responsibilities with her mother-in-law. Our transplant team and others have recognized that a patient's positive response to treatment and hospital can be completely undone if the patient returns to an unstable marital or family situation.

TEAM AND STAFF

The fourth area in which the psychiatrist may be of use is in helping the other members of the transplant team to cope with the psychologically stressful tasks they must perform. Chronic medical care such as hemodialysis and chemotherapy not only is stressful for patients and families but also makes many demands on staff members. These demands are continued when the patient and team decide on transplantation. The transplant team works with the patient and family intensively for long periods of time, and consequently, an unusual sense of intimacy develops. Each staff member, of course, has his or her own feelings about and countertransference to the patient. Because of this intimacy the staff may (1) become overprotective and possessive of their patients, especially when they are transferred to step-down units; (2) become angry themselves when a transplant patient does not return to a productive life-style or dies in spite of their efforts; (3) develop hostility toward patients who consider withdrawing from chemotherapy, dialysis, or transplant protocol, if the quality of life available to them is not sufficient (McKegney and Lange 1971); (4) take on parental or spousal responsibilities when caring for their patients, which may become overstimulating for the patients. The staff members can be made aware of these emotional reactions and be helped to handle these and other situations more appropriately.

Regular staff meetings with a psychiatrist usually center on patient management, ethical decision-making processes, and improved communications with patients and families. The psychiatrist may often interpret for the staff a patient's anger and maladaptive behavior. Sometimes interstaff conflicts are introduced, and the psychiatrist must balance the roles of team participant and team consultant with that of staff psychotherapist. In the latter situation in which the psychiatrist's own stance may approach that of a psychotherapist, it is important not to define himself or herself as such or permit the others to do so. When individuals in the team show major distress it should be referred to another psychiatrist for consultation. In unusual cases of group problems, a consultant skilled in group therapy may be brought in. Using psychotherapeutic knowledge and skills but avoiding the full-scale psychotherapeutic position requires fine judgment and balance by the liaison psychiatrist.

Bloom summarized the function of the liaison psychiatrist as "witness, bystander," and "translator" of emotional events. He or she is a "catalyst in promoting the best and most adaptive ways of interpersonal functioning" (1981, p. 51). As a participant observer, one can be a catalyst for growth among team members. Patenaude (Patenaude et al. 1979), a liaison psychiatrist on a pediatric bone marrow unit, views her role as a "lightening rod." The pressure of a psychological-minded team member legitimizes certain topics that would otherwise be discussed less often or not at all.

In summary, the role of a psychiatrist on a transplantation team includes: (1) assisting the team in predicting the psychological implications and effects of the organ transplant on the donor, family, and recipient; (2) determining a patient's coping style, predicting his or her emotional response, and therefore preventing the development of complicated and severe emotional disturbances; (3) supporting patient and family throughout the preparation, transplant, and convalescent period; (4) helping the team in the psychological management of the patient during treatment; and (5) providing psychotherapy and medication when serious disturbances develop.

SUMMARY

One of the most exciting events in modern biomedical science is organ transplantation. At present, transplantation is changing from an innovative and controversial research procedure to a standard therapeutic modality. Each new advance in the field prolongs the lives of chronically ill patients and also creates new problems for the patients' care-givers. There has also been an impact on psychiatry, as psychiatrists have been challenged and given an opportunity to learn new things about patients' responses to illness and stress in a novel situation (once only possible in fantasy). Also with this challenge in mind, psychiatrists are being asked to become members of a complex group—the transplant team.

We surveyed the psychological aspects of transplant medicine, comparing and contrasting different transplant procedures. We reviewed the history of organ transplantation as well as the ensuing ethical issues. Each transplantation process, whether kidney, heart, bone marrow, liver, or pancreas, can be divided into several stages, which we described, along with their accompanying emotional tones. In providing psychological care for transplant recipients, donors, and families, care-givers must be familiar with psychological themes such as rebirth, integration, and rejection of a new organ and body image, and the patient's mechanisms of coping with the extreme stress of such protocols. Transplantation, with its medication, surgery, total body irradiation, germ-free environments, graft-versus-host disease, Hickman/Broviac line catheterization, and/or total parenteral nutrition and dialysis, can precipitate psychological effects or be associated with neuropsychiatric sequelae. In response to transplant illness, patients may also develop emotional disturbances, such as anxiety, agitation, depression, suicide, impotence, and noncompliance. We discussed these reactions and guidelines for managing the transplant patient with previous or concurrent psychiatric illness. Finally, the liaison psychiatrist's role as a team member and his or her responsibilities to recipient, donor, and family, were outlined. We hope that this brief chapter will help familiarize the therapist with this psychologically intriguing field, from both a historical and a state-of-the-art perspective, and will provide a departure point for future reading, study, and patient care.

REFERENCES

Abram, H. S. (1965). Adaptation to open-heart surgery: a psychiatrist study of response to the threat of death. *American Journal of Psychiatry* 122:659–668.

———. (1969). The psychiatrist, the treatment of chronic renal failure and the prolongation of life II. *American Journal of Psychiatry* 126:157–167.

———. (1970). Psychological reaction to cardiac operations: an historical perspective. *Psychiatry in Medicine* 1:227–294.

———. (1972). The psychiatrist, the treatment of chronic renal failure and the prolongation of life III. *American Journal of Psychiatry* 128:1534–1539.

———. (1978a). Renal transplantation. In *Massachusetts General Hospital Handbook of General Hospital Psychiatry*, ed. T. P. Hackett and N. H. Cassen, pp. 365–379. St. Louis: C. V. Mosby.

———. (1978b). Repetitive dialysis. In *Massachusetts General Hospital Handbook of General Hospital Psychiatry*, ed T. P. Hackett and N. H. Cassen, pp. 342–365. St. Louis: C. V. Mosby.

Abram, H. S., Moore, G. L., and Westervelt, F. B. (1970). Suicidal behavior in chronic dialysis patients. Paper presented at the 123rd Annual Meeting of the American Psychiatric Association, May.

Adler, M. L. (1972). Kidney transplantation and coping mechanisms. *Psychosomatics* 13:337–341.

Alfrey, A. D., Mishell, J. M., Burks, J. S., Contiguglia, S. R., Rudolph, H., Lewin, E., and Holmes, J. H. (1972). Syndrome of dyspraxia and multifocal seizures associated with chronic hemodialysis. *Transactions of the American Society of Artificial Internal Organs* 18:257–267.

Allgower, M., and Gruber, V. F. (1970). Ethical problems of organ transplantation. *Progress in Surgery* 8:1–13.

Armstrong, S. H. (1978). Psychological maladjustment in renal dialysis patients. *Psychosomatics* 19 (3):169–171.

Basch, S. H. (1973). The intrapsychic integration of a new organ. *Psychoanalytic Quarterly* 42:364–384.

_____. (1980). Emotional dehiscence after successful renal transplantation. *Kidney International* 17:388–396.

Beard, B. H. (1969). Fear of death and fear of life. *Archives of General Psychiatry* 21:373–380.

Bennett, W. M., Muther, R. A., Parker, R. A., Feig, P., Morrison, G., Golpert, T., and Singer, I. (1980). Drug therapy in renal failure: dosing guidelines for adults, part II: sedatives, hypnotics, tranquilizers. *Annals of Internal Medicine* 93:286–325.

Bernstein, D. (1971). After transplantation — the child's emotional reactions. *American Journal of Psychiatry* 127:1189–1193.

Billingham, R. E., Brent, L., and Medawar, P. B. (1955). Acquired tolerance of tissue hemografts. *Annals of the New York Academy of Science* 59:409–415.

Bloom, V. (1981). Functions of a liaison psychiatrist in a kidney center: personal reflections. *Dialysis and Transplantation* 10 (1):51–55.

Borten, M. M., and Rimm, A. A. (1976). Bone marrow transplantation from histocompatible allogenic donors for aplastic anemia. *Journal of the American Medical Association*, pp. 1131–1135.

Brown, H. N., and Kelly, M. J. (1976). Stages of bone marrow transplantation: a psychiatric perspective. *Psychosomatic Medicine* 38 (6):439–446.

Burks, J. S., Alfrey, A. D., Huddlestone, J., et al. (1976). A fatal encephalopathy in chronic haemodialysis patients. *Lancet* 1:764–768.

Calland, C. H. (1972). Iatrogenic problems in end stage renal failure. *New England Journal of Medicine* 287 (7):334–336.

Calne, R. Y., and Williams, R. (1979). Liver transplantation. *Current Problems in Surgery* 16 (1):3–44.

Carpenter, W. T., Strauss, J. S., and Bunney, W. E. (1972). The psychobiology of cortisol metabolism; clinical and theoretical implications. In *Psychiatric Complications of Medical Drugs*, ed. R. I. Shader, pp. 49–73. New York: Raven Press.

Castelnuovo-Tedesco, P. (1973). Organ transplant, body image, psychosis. *Psychoanalytic Quarterly* 42:349–362.

_____. (1978). Ego vicissitudes in response to replacement or loss of body parts. *Psychoanalytic Quarterly* 47:381–397.

Chapman, C. R., and Cox, G. B. (1977). Anxiety, pain and depression surrounding elective surgery: a multivariate comparison of abdominal surgery patients with kidney donors and recipients. *Journal of Psychosomatic Research* 21:7–15.

Christopherson, L. K., and Gonda, T. A. (1973). Patterns of grief: end-stage renal failure and kidney transplantation. *Transplantation Proceedings* 5:1051–1057.

Christopherson, L. K., Griepp, R. B., and Stinson, E. B. (1976). Rehabilitation after cardiac transplantation. *Journal of the American Medical Association* 236(18):2082–2084.

Christopherson, L. K., and Lunde, D. T. (1971). Heart transplant donors and their families. *Seminars in Psychiatry* 3(1):26–35.

Colomb, B., and Hamburger, J. (1967). Psychological and moral problems of renal transplantation. In *Psychological Aspects of Surgery*, vol. 4, ed. H. S. Abram, pp. 157–177. Boston: Little, Brown.

Council on Scientific Affairs (1981). Organ donor recruitments. *Journal of the American Medical Association* 246(19):2157.

Cramond, W. A. (1967). Renal homotransplantation — some observations on recipients and donors. *British Journal of Psychiatry* 113:1223–1230.

———. (1968). Medical, moral, and legal aspects of organ transplantation and long term resuscitative measures: psychological, social and community aspects. *Medical Journal of Australia*, pp. 622–627.

———. (1971). Renal transplantations — experiences with recipients and donors. *Seminars in Psychiatry* 3(1):116–132.

Cramond, W. A., Court, J. H., Higgins, B. A., Knight, P. R., and Lawrence, J. R. (1967a). Psychological screening of potential donors in a renal homotransplantation programme. *British Journal of Psychiatry* 113:1213–1221.

Cramond, W. A., Knight, P. R., and Lawrence, J. R. (1967b). The psychiatric contribution to a renal unit undertaking chronic hemodialysis and renal homotransplantation. *British Journal of Psychiatry* 113:1201–1212.

Crombez, J. C., and Lefebvre, P. (1972). The behavioral responses of renal transplant patients as seen through their fantasy life. *Canadian Psychiatric Association Journal* 17:19–23.

Curzor, G. (1978). Influence of nutritional state on transmitter synthesis. *Proceedings Nutrition Society* 37:155–157.

De-Nour, A. K. (1978). Hemodialysis: sexual functioning. *Psychosomatics* 19(4):229–235.

Dubovsky, S. L., and Penn, I. (1980). Psychiatric considerations in a renal transplant surgery. *Psychosomatics* 21(6):481–490.

Dudrick, S. J., Wilmore, D. W., Vars, H. M., and Rhodes, J. E. (1968). Long term parenteral nutrition with growth development, and positive nitrogen balance. *Surgery* 64:134–142.

Eisendrath, R. M. (1969). The role of grief and fear in the death of kidney transplant patients. *American Journal of Psychiatry* 126:381-387.

Eisendrath, R. M., Guttman, R. D., and Murray, J. E. (1969). Psychological consideration in the selection of kidney transplant donors. *Surgical Gynecology Obstetrics* 129:243-248.

Erman, M. K., and Guggenheim, F. G. (1981). Psychiatric side effects of commonly used drugs. *Drug Therapy*, pp. 55-64.

Fares, A. A. (1972). Wernecke's encephalopathy in uremia. *Neurology* 22:1293-1297.

Fellner, C. H. (1971). Selection of living kidney donors and the problem of informed consent. *Seminars in Psychiatry* 3(1):79-85.

Fellner, C. H., and Marshall, J. R. (1968). Twelve kidney donors. *Journal of the American Medical Association* 206(12):2703-2707.

Ferris, G. N. (1969). Psychiatric considerations in patients receiving cadoveric renal transplants. *Southern Medical Journal* 62:1482-1484.

Fine, R. N., Malekzadeh, M. H., Pennisi, A. J., Henger, R. B., Uittenbogaart, C. H., Negrete, V. F., and Korsch, B. M. (1979). Long term results of renal transplantation in children. *Pediatrics* 61(4): 641-650.

Fox, R. C. (1970). A sociological perspective on organ transplantation and hemodialysis. *Annals of the New York Academy of Science* 169(2):406-428.

Freebury, D. R. (1974). The psychological implications of organ transplantation: a selective review. *Canadian Psychiatric Association Journal* 19:593-597.

Gordon, A. M. (1975). Psychological adaptation to isolator therapy in acute leukemia. *Psychotherapeutics Psychosomatics* 26:132-139.

Gottshalk, L., Kunkel, R., Wohl, T. Soenger, E., and Winget, C. (1969). Total and half body irradiation: effect on cognitive & emotional processes. *Archives of General Psychiatry* 21:574-580.

Griepp, R. B. (1979). A decade of human heart transplantation. *Transplantation Proceedings* 11(1):285-292.

Hackett, T. P. (1972). The Lazarus complex revisited. *Annals of Internal Medicine* 76:135-136.

Hamburg, P. A., Hamburg, B., and DeGonza, S. (1953). Adaptive problems and mechanisms in severely burned patients. *Psychiatry* 16:1-20.

Holland, J. (1977). Psychological aspects of oncology. *Medical Clinics of North America* 61(4):737-748.

Holland, J., Plumb, M., Yates, J., Harris, S., Tuttolomondo, A., Holmes, J., and Holland, J. (1977). Psychological response of patients with acute leukemia to germ free environments. *Cancer* 40:871–879.

Hume, D. M., Merrell, J. P., Miller, B. F., and Thorn, G. W. (1955). Experience with renal homo-transplantation in the human report of 9 cases. *Journal of Clinical Investigation* 34:327–382.

Kathol, R., Noyes, R., Slymen, D. J., Crowe, R. R., Clancy, J., and Kerber, R. E. (1980). Propranolol in chronic anxiety disorders. *Archives of General Psychiatry* 37:1361–1365.

Kellerman, J., Rigler, D., and Siegel, S. (1977). The psychological effects of isolation in protected environments. *American Journal of Psychiatry* 134(5):563–565.

Kemph, J. P. (1966). Renal failure, artificial kidney and kidney transplantation. *American Journal of Psychiatry* 122:1270–1274.

––––––. (1971). Psychotherapy with donors and recipients of kidney transplants. *Psychiatry* 3(1):145–158.

Kimball, C. P. (1969). Psychological responses to the experience of open heart surgery. *American Journal of Psychiatry* 126(3):348–359.

Klerman, G. L. (1981). Depression in the medically ill. *Psychiatric Clinics of North America* 4(2):301–318.

Knight, J. A. (1980–1981). The liaison psychiatrist in kidney transplantation. *International Journal of Psychiatry in Medicine* 10(3):221–233.

Kornfeld, D. S., Zimberg, S., and Malm, J. R. (1965). Psychiatric complications of open heart surgery. *New England Journal of Medicine* 273:287–292.

Korsch, B. M., Fine, R. N., and Negrete, V. F. (1978). Non-compliance in children with renal transplants. *Pediatrics* 61(6):872–876.

Korsch, B. M., Klein, V. D., Negrete, V. F., Henderson, D. J., and Fine, R. N. (1980). Physical and psychological follow-up on off-spring of renal allograft recipients. *Pediatrics* 65(2):275–283.

Korsch, B. M., Negrete, V. F., Gardner, J. E., Weinstock, C. L., Mercer, A. S., Grushkin, C. M., and Fine, R. N. (1973). Kidney transplantation in children: psychological follow-up on children and family. *Journal of Pediatrics* 83:399–408.

Lee, H. M., Madgo, G. E., Mendez-Picon, G., and Chatterjee, S. N. (1978). Surgical complications in renal transplant recipients. *Surgical Clinics of North America* 58(2):285–304.

Lefebvre, P., and Crombez, J. C. (1981). The "one day at a time" syndrome in post transplant evolution. *Canadian Journal of Psychiatry* 25:319–324.

Leonard, C. D., Weil, E., and Schribner, B. H. (1969). Subdural hematoma in patients undergoing hemodialysis. *Lancet* 2:239–240.

Lesko, L., Kern, J., and Hawkins, D. R., (1983). Psychological aspects of patients to germ-free environments. A critical review of the literature and patient management. *Medical and Pediatric Oncology*, in press.

Levine, M. D., Cametta, B. M., Nathan, D., and Curran, W. J. (1975). The medical ethics of bone marrow transplantation in childhood. *Journal of Pediatrics* 86(1):145–150.

Levy, N. B. (1973). Sexual adjustment to maintenance hemodialysis and renal transplantation: national survey by questionniare: preliminary report. *Transactions of the American Society of Artificial Internal Organs* 19:138–143.

———. (1981a). Psychological reactions to machine dependency: hemodialysis. *Psychiatric Clinics of North America* 4(2):351–365.

———. (1981b). *Psychonephrology I: Psychological Factors in Hemodialysis and Transplantation.* New York: Plenum.

Lilly, J., Giles, G., Hurwitz, R., Schroter, G., Takogi, H., Gray, S., Penn, I., Halgrimson, C. G., and Strazl, T. E. (1971). Renal homotransplantation in pediatric patients. *Pediatrics* 47:548–557.

Lindemann, E. (1944). Symptomatology and management of acute grief. *American Journal of Psychiatry* 101:141–148.

Lunde, D. T. (1969). Psychiatric complications of heart transplants. *American Journal of Psychiatry* 126(3):369–373.

McCabe, M. S., and Corry, R. J. (1978). Psychiatric illness and human renal transplantation. *Journal of Clinical Psychiatry* 39(5):393–400.

McKegney, F. P., and Lange, P. (1971). The decision to no longer live on chronic hemodialysis. *American Journal of Psychiatry* 128:3.

Mahurkar, S. D., Dhar, S. K., Salta, R., Meyers Jr., L., Smith, E. C., and Dunea, G. (1973). Dialysis dementia. *Lancet* 1:1412–1415.

Malcolm, R., Robson, J., Vanderveen, T. W., and Mahlen, P. (1980). Psychosocial aspects of total parenteral nutrition. *Psychosomatics* 21(2):115–123.

Marshall, J. R. (1979). Neuropsychiatric aspects of renal failure. *Journal of Clinical Psychiatry* 40:81–85.

Meadows, A., Gordon, J., Littman, K., Glaser, J., and Fergusson, J. (1981). Pattern of cognitive dysfunctions in children with acute lymphocytic leukemia treated with cranial radiation. ASCO Abstract A:C-222.

Merrill, J. P. (1979). A historical perspective of renal transplantation. *Proceedings of the Clinical Dialysis Transplant Forum* 9:221–225.

————. (1981). Early days of the artificial kidney and transplantation. *Transplantation Proceedings* 13(1) (suppl.):4–8.

Merrill, J. P., Murray, J. E., Takacs, F. J., Hager, E. B., Wilson, R. E., and Dammin, G. J. (1963). Successful transplantation of a human cadaver kidney. *Journal of the American Medical Association* 185: 347–353.

Monckeberg, F. (1971). Malnutrition and mental behavior. *Nutritional Review* 27(191):1429–1433.

Moore, F. D. (1980). Transplantation—a perspective. *Transplantation Proceedings* 12(4):539–550.

Moore, G. L. (1976). Psychiatric aspects of chronic renal disease. *Postgraduate Medicine* 60:140–146.

Murray, J. E. (1979). Ethics in transplantation. *Transplantation Proceedings* 11(1):1145–1148.

Murray, J. E., Tilney, N. L., and Wilson, R. E. (1976). Renal transplantation: a twenty-five year experience. *Annals of Surgery* 184(5):565–573.

Muslin, H. L. (1971). On acquiring a kidney. *American Journal of Psychiatry* 127(9):1185–1188.

Opie, L. (1980). Beta blocking agents. *Lancet* 2:428–429.

Ota, D. M., Imbembo, A. L., and Zuidema, G. D. (1978). Total parenteral nutrition. *Surgery* 83:503–520.

Oyer, P. E., Stinson, E. B., Reitz, B. A., Bieber, C. P., Jamieson, S. W., and Shumway, N. E. (1981). Cardiac transplantation. *Transplantation Proceedings* 13(1):199–206.

Patenaude, A. F., Szymanski, L., and Rappeport, J. (1979). Psychological cases of bone marrow transplantation in children. *American Journal of Orthopsychiatry* 49(3):409–422.

Paton, A. (1971). Life and death: moral and ethical aspects of transplantation. *Seminars in Psychiatry* 3(1):161–168.

Penn, I., Bunch, D., Olenik, D., and Abounda, G. (1971). Psychiatric experience with patients receiving renal and hepatic transplants. In *Psychiatric Aspects of Organ Transplantation*, ed. P. Castelnuovo-Tedesco, pp. 133–144. New York: Grune & Stratton.

Poznanski, E. O., Miller, E., Salguero, C., and Kelsh, R. (1978). Quality of life for long term survivors of end stage renal disease. *Journal of the American Medical Association* 239(22):2343–2347.

Price, B., and Levine, E. (1977). Permanent total parenteral nutrition: psychological and social responses of the early stages. *Journal of Parenteral Enteral Nutrition* 1:24-28.

Rasken, N. H., and Fishman, R. A. (1976). Neurological disorders in renal failure. *New England Journal of Medicine* 294:204-209.

Reeves, R. B. (1969). The ethics of cardiac transplantation in man. *Bulletin of the New York Academy of Medicine* 45(5):404-411.

Salomon, G. S., and Amkraut, A. A. (1970). Emotions, stress and immunity. *Frontiers of Radiation Therapy and Oncology* 7:84-96.

Salvatierra, O., Fortman, J. L., and Belzer, F. D. (1975). Sexual function in males before and after renal transplantation. *Urology* 5:64-66.

Santos, G., and Kaiser, H. (1981). Current states of autologous marrow transplantation. In *Cancer Achievements: Challenges and Prospects*, vol. 2, ed. J. H. Burchenal and H. Oettgen, pp. 673-682. New York: Grune & Stratton.

Schowalter, J. E. (1970). Multiple organ transplantation and the creation of surgical siblings. *Pediatrics* 46(4):576-580.

Short, M. J., and Harris, N. L. (1969). Psychiatric observations of renal homotransplantation. *Southern Medical Journal* 62:1479-1482.

Shumway, N. E., and Stinton, E. B. (1979). Two decades of experimental and clinical orthotopic hemotransplantation of heart. *Perspectives in Biology and Medicine* 2:S81-S88.

Siemsen, A. W., Beauchamp, T. L., Hopper, S., and Robertson, J. A. (1978). Medical, moral and legal aspects of renal replacement therapy (part II). *Proceedings of the Clinical Dialysis Transplant Forum* 8:35-48.

Starzl, T. E., Iwatsuki, S., Klintmalm, G., Schroter, G. P. J., Weil, R., Koep, L. J., and Porter, K. A. (1981). Liver transplantation, 1980, with particular reference to cyclosporin -A. *Transplantation Proceedings* 13(1):281-285.

Starzl, T. E., Koep, L. J., Halgrinson, L. G., Hood, J., Schroter, G. P. J., Porter, K. A., and Weil, R., (1979). Liver transplantation, 1978. *Transplantation Proceedings* 11(1):240-246.

Stewart, R. M., and Stewart, R. S. (1979). Neuropsychiatric aspects of chronic renal disease. *Psychosomatics* 20(8):524-531.

Storb, R. (1981). Bone marrow transplantation for the treatment of hematologic malignancy and of aplastic anemia. *Transplantation Proceedings* 13(1):221-225.

Storb, R., Atkinson, K., et al. (1981). Graft-versus-host disease, immunologic reconstruction and graft host tolerance in marrow recipients. In *Cancer Achievements: Challenges and Prospects for the 1980s,* ed.

J. H. Burchenal and H. Oettgen, pp. 639–648. New York: Grune & Stratton.

Sutherland, D. E. R., Goetz, F. C., and Najarian, J. S. (1981). Review of world's experience with pancreas and islet transplantation and results of intraperitoneal segmental pancreas transplantation from related and cadaver donors at Minnesota. *Transplantation Proceedings* 13(1):291–297.

Talalla, A., Hallbrook, H., Barbaur, B. H., et al. (1970). Subdural hematoma associated with long term hemodialysis for chronic renal disease. *Journal of the American Medical Association* 212:1847–1849.

Thomas, E. D., Buckner, C. D., Clift, R. A., et al. (1979a). Marrow transplantation for acute nonlymphoblastic leukemia in first remission. *New England Journal of Medicine* 301:597–599.

Thomas, E. D., Sanders, J. E., Flournoy, N., et. al. (1979b). Marrow transplantation for patients with acute lymphoblastic leukemia in remission. *Blood* 54:468–476.

Tourkow, L. (1974). Psychic consequences of loss and replacement of body parts. *Journal of the American Psychoanalytic Association* 22:170–181.

Traeger, J., Dubernard, J. M., Touraine, J. L., and Malik, M. C. (1980). Selection of the diabetic patient for segemental pancreatic transplantation. *Transplantation Proceedings* 12(4):5–7.

Tyler, H. R. (1965). Neurological complications of dialysis transplantation and other forms of treatment in chronic uremia. *Neurology* 12:1081–1088.

Uehling, D. T., Hussey, J. L., Weinstein, A. B., Wank, R., and Bach, F. H. (1976). Cessation of immunosuppression after renal transplantation. *Surgery* 79:278–282.

Viederman, M. (1974a). Adaptive and maladaptive regression in hemodialysis. *Psychiatry* 37:68–77.

———. (1974b). The search for meaning in renal transplantation. *Psychiatry* 37:283–289.

———. (1975). Psychogenic factors in kidney transplant rejection: a case study. *American Journal of Psychiatry* 132(9):957–959.

Visotsky, H. M., Hamburg, D. A., Gross, M. E., and Levovitz, B. Z. (1961). Coping behavior under extreme stress. *Archives of General Psychiatry* 5:423–448.

Wardle, E. N. (1973). Dialysis dementia. *Lancet* 2:47.

Weddington, W. W. (1978). Dementia dialytica. *Psychosomatics* 19(6):367–370.

Weddington, W. W., Muelling, A. E., and Moosa, H. H. (1982). Adverse neuropsychiatric reactions to cimetidine. *Psychosomatics* 23(1):49–53.

PART V

Syndromes Updated

Men make their own history, but they do not make it just as they please; they do not make it under circumstances chosen by themselves, but under circumstances directly found, given and transmitted from the past.

The Eighteenth Brumaire of Louis Bonaparte, Karl Marx, 1852

CHAPTER 13

Neuroleptic-induced Tardive Dyskinesia

DILIP V. JESTE, M.D.
RICHARD JED WYATT, M.D.

HISTORICAL BACKGROUND

It took five years after the initial use of chlorpromazine as a neuroleptic before tardive dyskinesia appeared in the literature. Schoenecker (1957) is generally given the credit for first reporting neuroleptic-induced tardive dyskinesia. His case descriptions suggest reversible tardive dyskinesia in three of his four patients, according to his article entitled "A Peculiar Syndrome in Oral Region as a Result of the Administration of Megaphen." (A brand name for chlorpromazine.)

Sigwald and his colleagues (1959) in Paris first described in detail the tardive dyskinesia syndrome. They divided neuroleptic-induced dyskinesias into three subtypes: (1) acute dyskinesias that occur early in the course of treatment with piperazine phenothiazines and that show rapid improvement; (2) subacute dyskinesias that become manifest later in the course of neuroleptic treatment and that are not related to the type of neuroleptic and disappear within one or two weeks of discontinuing neuroleptics; and (3) chronic dyskinesias that are much less common but pose a serious problem because of their tendency to continue long after withdrawal of medication.

Uhrbrand and Faurbye (1960) in Denmark published the first epidemiological survey of "reversible and irreversible dyskinesias after treatment with perphenazine, chlorpromazine, reserpine and electroconvulsive therapy." They concluded that prolonged use of neuroleptics was likely to induce dyskinesias, especially in the elderly and those with brain damage, and that these dyskinesias tended to be irreversible in certain cases. Walter Kruse (1960) was the first American psychiatrist to report tardive dyskinesia. He described three patients with phenothiazine-induced abnormal involuntary movements that did not respond to antiparkinsonian medication and were still present long after the neuroleptics were discontinued. Since the mid-1960s there has been a progressive increase in case reports, as well as epidemiologic studies of tardive dyskinesia.

Tardive dyskinesia may be defined as a syndrome consisting of abnormal stereotyped involuntary movements—usually, but not always, of the choreoathetoid type, principally affecting the mouth, face, limbs, and trunk—and occurring relatively late in the course of drug treatment and in the etiology of which the drug treatment is necessary. One criticism of the concept of tardive dyskinesia is that dyskinesia frequently occurs spontaneously among chronic psychiatric patients. Similar movement disorders were also described in psychiatric patients long before neuroleptics were introduced into psychiatry (Garber 1979). We therefore looked at studies before and after neuroleptic use (Jeste and Wyatt 1981a).

PRENEUROLEPTIC STUDIES

There were few formal studies of abnormal involuntary movements in psychiatric patients before 1955. Kraepelin (1919) referred to a number of bodily symptoms of schizophrenia, such as wrinkling of the forehead; distortion of the corners of the mouth; irregular movements of the tongue and lips; twisting of the eyes, opening them wide and shutting them tight; grimacing; nystagmus; smacking and clicking with the tongue; sudden sighing; laughing; clearing the throat; fine twitching of lips; tremor of outstretched fingers; and sprawling, irregular movements called *athetoid ataxia*. Kraepelin also stated that the appearance of abnormal involuntary movements was a sign of poor prognosis, indicating a loss of volitional control, and heralded the onset of "incurable terminal states."

There are several differences between Kraepelin's description and the characteristics of tardive dyskinesia. Although some of the movements described by Kraepelin resemble those of tardive dyskinesia—e.g., smacking of the lips and choreoathetoid movements of extremities—others such as nystagmus, laughing, or tremors of outstretched hands are not a part of the tardive dyskinesia syndrome. It is apparent that the characteristic symptom complex of tardive dyskinesia was not prevalent among mental hospital patients in Kraepelin's days. Also, the abnormal involuntary movements in Kraepelin's patients occurred in poor prognosis, late-stage schizophrenics. In contrast, tardive dyskinesia has been reported in schizophrenic outpatients and inpatients with neurotic and affective disorders who have received neuroleptics.

Mettler and Crandell (1959) conducted a study of neurologic disorders at a state hospital in 1955 — before neuroleptics had been introduced into general use. They found that only 0.5 percent of the total hospital population had chorea or athetosis.

POSTNEUROLEPTIC STUDIES

We found 12 major studies comparing the prevalence of dyskinesia among neuroleptic-treated and nonneuroleptic-treated patients (Jeste and Wyatt 1981a). Ten of these 12 studies found a much higher prevalence of dyskinesia among neuroleptic-treated than among nonneuroleptic-treated patients.

When all 12 studies are considered together, the overall prevalence of dyskinesia is three and a quarter times greater in the neuroleptic-treated group (19.2 percent) than in the nondrug-treated group of patients (5.9 percent). According to neurologists like Baker (1969) and Altrocchi (1972), spontaneous orofacial dyskinesia not secondary to a known neurologic disease is rare. Kline (1968) initially questioned the existence of neuroleptic-induced persistent tardive dyskinesia but later concluded (Simpson and Kline 1976) that it is common enough to make it "a matter of extreme importance."

PREVALENCE AMONG CHRONIC PSYCHIATRIC INPATIENTS

There are many reports on the prevalence of tardive dyskinesia among hospitalized patients. These studies differ in their methodology. In order to get a reliable estimate of the prevalence of tardive dyskinesia, we selected those studies that met certain minimum requirements: (1) publication in recognized scientific journals or books in English or German, (2) some description of the original patient population that was screened for tardive dyskinesia, (3) study involving at least 50 patients in the total population, and (4) an apparently valid diagnosis of tardive dyskinesia based on the investigators' clinical examination.

The most reliable estimate of the current prevalence of tardive dyskinesia among chronically ill, neuroleptic-treated patients in psychiatric hospitals is 25 percent. This is an overall figure, and so the actual prevalence in different subpopulations may vary. For example, geriatric inpatient units are likely to have a prevalence exceeding 25 percent, and younger patients should have a lower proportion of cases with dyskinesia. Tardive dyskinesia is reversible in a little over one-third of all cases. The prevalence of persistent tardive dyskinesia among chronic inpatients would therefore be about 17 percent.

The risk of persistent tardive dyskinesia attributable to neuroleptics can be calculated by subtracting the prevalence of persistent dyskinesia in the nonneuroleptic-treated population from the prevalence of persistent dyskinesia in the neuroleptic-treated population. The mean prevalence of dyskinesia among nonneuroleptic-treated psychiatric inpatients is 5.9 percent. Assuming that, like many other conditions, the symptoms are reversible in one-third of the cases, the prevalence of nonneuroleptic-induced persistent dyskinesia among psychiatric inpatients would be about 4 percent. Subtracting this figure from the 17 percent prevalence of persistent dyskinesia among neuroleptic-treated patients would give a 13 percent risk of developing persistent dyskinesia attributable to neuroleptics (Jeste and Wyatt 1982).

MANIFESTATIONS: A TOPOGRAPHICAL CLASSIFICATION

Below is a classification of the various manifestations of tardive dyskinesia according to their localization. The dyskinetic manifestations may be unilateral or bilateral. Even when bilateral, they may be asymmetrical in intensity, being more pronounced on one side than on the other.

1. Mouth, face, and pharynx
   A. Tongue
      a. Fine vermicular contractions or tremor of intrinsic muscles of the tongue inside the oral cavity.
      b. Gross movements of (the extrinsic muscles of) the tongue inside the oral cavity. The bonbon sign refers to tongue movements producing a bulge in the cheek.
      c. Protrusion of the tongue outside the oral cavity. This may be a repetitive, short-duration protrusion or a more prolonged one.
   B. Jaw
      a. Vertical movements — repeated clenching of teeth and biting, opening, and closing of mouth.
      b. Horizontal movements from side to side.
      c. Combined or complex movements — chewing.
   C. Lips
      a. Lower lip-pouting.

      b. Both lips — clicking and smacking (sudden and audible parting of lips), puckering (as if a purse string running through the lips were pulled), and licking and sucking movements.

    D. Other facial muscles

      a. Eyes, eyelids, and eyebrows — blinking, blepharospasm (twitching or spasmodic contraction of orbicularis oculi), and lifting of eyebrows.

      b. Cheeks — retraction of angle of mouth, grimacing, puffing of cheeks, and sucking movement.

      c. Forehead — frowning.

    E. Pharynx and larynx

      a. Grunting and other similar sounds.

      b. Palatal dyskinesia.

2. Extremities

    A. Upper extremities

      a. Choreiform movements of arm and forehead.

      b. Athetoid movements of forearm, hand, and fingers.

      c. Choreoathetoid movements involving a part of or the entire upper extremity.

      d. Ballistic movements of arms.

    B. Lower extremities

      a. Toes — horizontal (spreading of toes), vertical (retroflexion), and combined movements. Occasionally, athetoid (slow, wavelike) movements of toes.

      b. Foot and ankle — stamping movements, inversion and eversion of foot, and lateral oscillations of ankle.

      c. Leg and knee — stamping of leg and lateral movements of knee.

      d. Entire lower extremity — stamping, shifting of weight from one extremity to the other, restlessness, and fidgety movements. Rarely, sudden ballistic movements.

3. Trunk and axial muscles

    A. Trunk

      a. Rocking, oscillatory, or twisting movements.

      b. Respiratory irregularities and gastrointestinal symptoms such as retching and vomiting due to dyskinesias of diaphram, intercostal, and abdominal muscles.

B. Neck and shoulder girdle

    a. Anterioposterior (nodding), lateral, or rotatory movements.

    b. Movements resembling torsion dystonias (torticollis).

    c. Raising or shrugging of shoulders.

C. Pelvic girdle

    a. Movements resembling torsion dystonias (tortipelvis).

    b. Twisting or undulating movements seen on lying down, standing, or walking.

    c. Gait disturbance — ataxic, broad-based, or spastic gaits.

DIAGNOSTIC CRITERIA

For clinical, research, medical, and legal purposes, it is necessary to have operational criteria for diagnosing neuroleptic-induced tardive dyskinesia. The following are criteria that we have found helpful (Jeste and Wyatt 1982):

PHENOMENOLOGY

1. Nature of the abnormal movements: dyskinesia may be defined as choreiform (i.e., nonrepetitive, rapid, jerky, quasi-purposive movements) or athetoid (i.e., continuous, slow, sinuous, purposeless movements) or rhythmic abnormal involuntary movements in certain areas of the body that are reduced by voluntary movements of the affected parts and are increased by voluntary movements of the unaffected parts.

2. Other characteristics: the abnormal movements are aggravated by stress and reduced when the person is relaxed. They may be temporarily controlled by volitional effort. The movements are absent during sleep.

3. Specific localization of neuroleptic-induced tardive dyskinesia: one or more areas, involving the tongue, jaw, and extremities, are affected in most cases.

4. Movements to exclude: tremors, myoclonus, mannerisms, compulsions, and akathisia are not a part of the dyskinesia syndrome, but some of these involuntary movements may coexist with dyskinesias.

HISTORY

1. Duration of dyskinesia: the movement disorder should be present for more than two weeks before tardive dyskinesia can be diagnosed.

2. Neuroleptic treatment: the patient should have a history of treatment with neuroleptics for at least three months, with the total amount exceeding 100 g equivalent of chlorpromazine.

3. Onset of dyskinesia: the same movements should not have been present before treatment with neuroleptics. The dyskinesia should have appeared either while the patient was on neuroleptics or within a month of neuroleptic withdrawal.

TREATMENT RESPONSE

1. Antiparkinsonian agents have no effect on or even aggravate tardive dyskinesia.

2. Increasing the dose of a neuroleptic, changing to a multiple daily dose administration, or switching to a different neuroleptic usually reduces the dyskinesia's intensity. Dose reduction or withdrawal of neuroleptics tends to worsen the symptoms, at least temporarily.

3. Catecholaminergic agents such as L-dopa and amphetamines aggravate tardive dyskinesia.

CONDITIONS TO RULE OUT AS THE PRIMARY CAUSE OF DYSKINESIA

Ill-fitting dentures, use of drugs like L-dopa or amphetamines, Huntington's disease, Wilson's disease, and Sydenham's chorea are among the major causes of movement disorders similar to neuroleptic-induced tardive dyskinesia (Granacher 1981). But the mere presence of such conditions does not necessarily exclude a diagnosis of neuroleptic-induced dyskinesia. It is necessary, however, to determine that these other conditions are not primarily responsible for the patient's dyskinesia.

EARLY DIAGNOSIS

Any patient who has been on neuroleptics for at least several months may be at risk for developing tardive dyskinesia. When such a patient begins to exhibit any abnormal involuntary movements of face, mouth, or limbs that were not present earlier, a possibility of dyskinesia may be considered. Facial tics, abnormal jaw movements, fine wormlike movements of the intrinsic muscles of the tongue inside the mouth, or mild choreoathetoid movements of the fingers or hands are probably some of the early signs of tardive dyskinesia. Aggravation of symptoms on neuroleptic dose reduction, suppression on increasing the dose, and nonresponse to anti-parkinsonian medications may be used to support the diagnosis of tardive dyskinesia.

COURSE

In the absence of a definitive treatment for tardive dyskinesia, the course of dyskinesia needs to be studied against the background of neuroleptic therapy. Most studies show that the continued administration (for months) of neuroleptics to patients with dyskinesia results in a temporary suppression of symptoms but produces neither cure nor aggravation of dyskinesia. Withdrawal of neuroleptics has been found to reverse dyskinesia in a little over one-third of the dyskinetic patients. Thus, both reversible and persistent tardive dyskinesias are apparent. A third subtype is the intermittent dyskinesia.

REVERSIBLE DYSKINESIA

In 33.5 percent of patients, symptoms remitted within three months of neuroleptic discontinuation. Only 5 percent of the remaining patients experienced reversal of dyskinesia more than three months after the drugs were stopped (Jeste and Wyatt 1982). It is quite likely that some of the patients who respond to a variety of nonspecific treatments have reversible dyskinesia.

INTERMITTENT DYSKINESIA

We have observed some patients who have had remissions and relapses of dyskinesia during the course of stable neuroleptic therapy. There was no obvious association between the appearance or disappearance of dyskinesia and the patient's clinical status or therapeutic alteration. Gardos and associates (1977) described patients whose dyskinesia underwent "very extensive fluctuations" in severity over time. It remains to be seen whether patients with intermittent dyskinesia eventually develop persistent tardive dyskinesia.

Cutler and colleagues (1981) reported the occurrence of "state-dependent dyskinesia" in two rapidly cycling manic-depressive patients. The two patients, a 57-year-old woman and a 58-year-old man, had significantly greater dyskinesia during depression than during mania, over several cycles. Tardive dyskinesia was most severe during the period of "switch" from mania into depression.

PERSISTENT DYSKINESIA

Persistent dyskinesia is a serious complication of long-term neuroleptic treatment, since it does not respond to neuroleptic withdrawal or to most other available treatments. Although there have been relatively few studies on the course of dyskinesia over long periods in such subjects, the general impression is that there is often no marked improvement in the symptoms' severity.

In the majority of patients with persistent tardive dyskinesia, the symptoms remain fairly stable over a long period of time, although some fluctuations in severity do occur. We should add that "persistent" does not always mean "irreversible."

ETIOLOGY

Tardive dyskinesia results from long-term treatment with neuroleptics. Only some patients so treated develop tardive dyskinesia. Variables related to both the drug treatment and the individual patients contribute to the etiology of this disorder.

PATIENT-RELATED VARIABLES

The prevalence of tardive dyskinesia is three times greater in patients over 40 than it is in patients under 40. Demars (1966) and Simpson and associates (1978) also found that the mean age of their dyskinesia patients was significantly older than that of patients without dyskinesia. Jus and colleagues (1976) reported that age at onset of treatment was the most significant variable distinguishing the two groups. Our own study (Jeste et al. 1982a) corroborated the significant association between dyskinesia and older age at onset of the treatment. It is also possible that older individuals develop tardive dyskinesia with smaller total amounts and shorter duration of neuroleptic treatment, as compared with younger patients.

Age is also related to the localization and reversibility of tardive dyskinesia. Crane (1968a) noted that choreiform limb dyskinesia was significantly more common than orofacial movements in patients under 40. In older patients, oral dyskinesia was slightly (but not significantly) more common. Bell and Smith (1978) also found a higher prevalence of total body dyskinesia in elderly subjects. Reversible dyskinesia is generally seen more in younger patients.

Elderly persons usually have an increased susceptibility to adverse drug effects. Peripheral or pharmacokinetic mechanisms—absorption, metabolism, and excretion of drugs—are often altered and result in their increased accumulation in the elderly. Several studies (Jeste and Wyatt 1982) found a tendency for greater serum-neuroleptic concentrations in older patients, as compared with younger subjects.

In regard to central mechanisms, Weiss and associates (1979) and Makman and associates (1979) presented biochemical evidence for selective decreases in the number of biogenic receptors as well as in the receptor capacity to develop supersensitivity with aging in animals. Schocken and Roth (1977) reported a reduction in humans in the number of β-adrenergic receptors with age. It is possible that the neuronal damage in the nigrostriatal system of the aged may involve alteration of presynaptic mechanisms (e.g., diminished reuptake and/or metabolism of catecholamines) which may lead to the development of tardive dyskinesia. Interestingly, Tanner and Domino (1977) reported enhanced effects in aged gerbils of d-amphetamine (with predominantly presynaptic action), but not of apomorphine (presumed to be a postsynaptic dopamine receptor agonist).

Various physical diseases (e.g., arteriosclerosis) accompanying old age may, in unknown ways, predispose to tardive dyskinesia. Also, the elderly subjects are likely to receive drugs, such as anticholinergic and antihistaminic agents, that may cause dyskinesia. The aged might be getting higher doses of a neuroleptic because they do not understand the directions for taking the medicine. Local factors like ill-fitting dentures may also contribute to oral dyskinesia.

The overall mean prevalence of dyskinesia is about 36 percent higher in women than in men. Smith and associates (1978) observed among inpatients a linear increase in the prevalence of dyskinesia with age in women, whereas men had a curvilinear relationship. In a study of outpatients, Smith and associates (1979) found a linear increase in the prevalance of dyskinesia with age in both genders, although the positive relationship with age was somewhat attenuated among older men. It is not clear whether any observed differences in the prevalence of dyskinesia in the two genders are a result of possible biological characteristics of the genders (such as brain neurotransmitter concentrations or the role of hormones) or merely reflect differences in treatment. For example, Degkwitz and Wenzel (1967) found that women were treated with higher doses of more potent neuroleptics and also received antiparkinsonian medications more often than men did. Jones and Hunter (1969) and Simpson and colleagues (1978) noticed that the duration of neuroleptic treatment was significantly longer in female patients than in male patients.

Tardive dyskinesia occurs in some patients who have had relatively brief or low-dose neuroleptic treatment. This indicates the likelihood of a constitutional predisposition to tardive dyskinesia. The nature of the presumed constitutional predisposition to tardive dyskinesia is uncertain.

We found significantly lower platelet and lymphocyte monoamine oxidase and higher plasma dopamine-beta-hydroxylase activities and higher serum-neuroleptic levels in elderly patients with tardive dyskinesia, as compared with controls matched for age, gender, primary psychiatric illness, hospitalization, and length of neuroleptic treatment (Jeste et al. 1981, 1982). It is tempting to suggest that certain disturbances in central dopaminergic and noradrenergic functions and in the peripheral metabolism of neuroleptics might increase susceptibility to neuroleptic-induced tardive dyskinesia, at least in a proportion of patients.

Myrianthopoulos and associates (1962) conducted a survey to determine hereditary susceptibility to neuroleptic-induced parkinsonism. Their results suggested a possibility of genetic predisposition to neuroleptic-induced parkinsonism.

So far, the possibility of hereditary susceptibility to tardive dyskinesia has been studied little. Dr. Jacob Brody of the National Institutes of Health in Bethesda, Maryland, studied six pairs of twin patients (four monozygotic and two dizygotic) on long-term high-dose phenothiazine treatment. He found that the specific type of neurologic side effect was not determined genetically, since the identical twins appeared to develop distinctly different patterns of reaction (personal communication from Dr. Brody).

Some researchers have found a much higher percentage of edentulous patients in the tardive dyskinesia group, as compared with non-dyskinetic patients. Sutcher and associates (1971) proposed that the loss of teeth (as well as the rich supply of nerve endings within them) or inadequate dental-oral prosthesis might result in confusing proprioceptive input from the stomatognatic system into the thalamus and the extrapyramidal system. The consequent oral dyskinesia represents searching movements of the buccolingual masticatory muscles to find clues to orient the mandible and oral structures in space. Brandon and colleagues (1971), however, noted that ill-fitting dentures did not necessarily contribute to the development of orofacial dyskinesia but were often a consequence of the dyskinesia.

Dyskinesia has been observed not only among schizophrenic patients but also among neurotic patients, patients with psychosomatic disorders, and those with major affective disorders who have received long-term neuroleptic treatment. If the overall prevalence of tardive dyskinesia is highest among chronic schizophrenics, it is mainly because that group is most likely to have been treated with neuroleptics, in higher doses and for prolonged periods.

Crane (1972) suggested that tardive dyskinesia was more likely to develop in patients with neuroleptic-induced parkinsonism than in subjects not exhibiting that side effect. There is, however, no satisfactory evidence to support the notion that the occurrence of neuroleptic-induced parkinsonism in patients indicates their increased susceptibility to tardive dyskinesia.

Tardive dyskinesia is a side effect of long-term treatment with neuroleptics. We would, therefore, expect a history of significantly longer neuroleptic therapy in patients with dyskinesia than in nondyskinetic patients. On analyzing the data with discriminant function analysis, Gardos and associates (1977) and Jeste and associates (1979) found that duration of neuroleptic treatment was a significant discriminator between dyskinetic and nondyskinetic patients. In a cross-cultural comparison of psychiatric inpatients from Turkey and the United States, Crane (1968a) observed a markedly higher prevalence of tardive dyskinesia in the American patients, who had received neuroleptics for a much longer period than the Turkish subjects had. Yet a number of investigators have reported no significant positive relationship between tardive dyskinesia and length of neuroleptic administration (Jeste and Wyatt 1982). It seems, therefore, that the length of neuroleptic administration is an important variable, although not the only one, in determining the prevalence of tardive dyskinesia. The interaction of the treatment length and other variables such as constitutional predisposition may be more crucial than the duration of drug per se.

Jus and colleagues (1976) concluded that the prevalence of dyskinesia was not related to the mean monthly amount or mean standard deviation of the monthly amount of neuroleptics. Some, but not all, researchers found a significant positive association between the total amount of neuroleptics ingested and the prevalance of tardive dyskinesia. Most investigators found that the prevalence or severity of tardive dyskinesia was not related to the current daily dose of neuroleptics.

A number of investigators reported that the prevalence of tardive dyskinesia could not be correlated with the use of any specific neuroleptics. Some investigators believe that tardive dyskinesia is rare when certain neuroleptics like reserpine, clozapine, or thioridazine are used, but there is no strong clinical basis to support this belief.

Recently, there have been several articles indicating that the use of depot fluphenazine may be associated with a particularly high prevalence of tardive dyskinesia. Gardos and associates (1977) found that the total amount of long-acting fluphenazine was fourth among five variables that significantly discriminated between the dyskinesia and nondyskinesia groups. Smith and colleagues (1978) also noted a positive correlation between fluphenazine intake and dyskinesia score. Among schizophrenic outpatients, Chouinard and colleagues (1979) found that the prevalence of tardive dyskinesia was positively correlated with five variables, including a history of fluphenazine treatment. In a prospective study on the incidence of tardive dyskinesia, Gibson (1978) followed 374 outpatients receiving intramuscular depot fluphenazine or flupentixol. Over a three-year follow-up period, the proportion of patients with tardive dyskinesia jumped from 8 to 22 percent, although in three-fourths of the cases the symptoms of dyskinesia were mild.

Methdological problems and population differences make it difficult to interpret definitively those studies suggesting that depot fluphenazine, more than other neuroleptics, may be associated with a significantly higher prevalence of tardive dyskinesia. To summarize, if given for a sufficient length of time to susceptible individuals, all neuroleptics probably have a similar propensity to produce tardive dyskinesia.

Since persistent tardive dyskinesia results from the long-term administration of neuroleptics, it is logical to expect that frequent and prolonged interruptions in drug treatment would reduce the incidence of dyskinesia (Ayd 1970, Crane 1972). Degkwitz (1969) reported that persistent dyskinesia occurred more frequently in patients who had a history of frequent interruptions in treatment. Crane (1974) observed that the dyskinesia and nondyskinesia groups did not differ from each other in continuity of drug regimens (defined as taking the medication at least 90 percent of the time).

We (Jeste et al. 1979) studied three groups of patients, those with persistent dyskinesia, those with reversible dyskinesia, and those with no dyskinesia. The persistent dyskinesia group had significantly more drug-free periods of two months each and significantly more drug-free time since onset of neuroleptic treatment than did the groups with reversible dyskinesia and no dyskinesia.

It is possible that frequent and prolonged interruptions in long-term neuroleptic therapy may increase the likelihood of persistent dyskinesia in patients who are otherwise predisposed (for unknown reasons) to develop tardive dyskinesia. A possible neurophysiologic basis for this suggestion is indicated in the phenomenon of "kindling." Goddard (1972) and Post and Kopanda (1976) discovered that repeated intermittent administration of electrical or chemical (e.g., cocaine, lidocaine, fluoroethyl, pentylenetetrazol) stimulation results in sensitization or kindling. But on the other hand, continuous or massed stimulation retards kindling and produces tolerance.

In summary, the contribution of drug interruptions to the prevention of persistent tardive dyskinesia is, at best, uncertain. Prolonged and lengthy drug-free periods have not been found to reduce the chances of developing persistent tardive dyskinesia.

Kiloh and associates (1973) and Klawans (1973) were probably the first to name antiparkinsonian drugs as causal agents in tardive dyskinesia. We (Jeste and Wyatt 1982) found nine epidemiological studies in which a possible relationship between the use of antiparkinsonian agents and the prevalence of tardive dyskinesia was explored. It is quite striking that only one of these studies (Perris et al. 1979) found a significant association between the two. Thus, the published data offer little support to the assertion that antiparkinsonian drugs significantly increase the prevalence of tardive dyskinesia.

Early reports (e.g., Hunter et al. 1964, Uhrbrand and Faurbye 1960) indicated that tardive dyskinesia patients had received not only long-term neuroleptic treatment but also physical treatments such as electroconvulsive therapy (ECT) and leucotomy. This raised the possibility that these somatic therapies might precipitate tardive dyskinesia by causing brain damage. Yet, a literature review indicates that there is little satisfactory evidence to implicate physical treatments like ECT, leucotomy, and insulin coma in the etiology of tardive dyskinesia. It is also notable that dyskinesia was not reported as a complication of these treatments before the entry of neuroleptics into psychiatry, although somatic therapies had been a common treatment of psychiatric patients since the late 1930s.

PATHOPHYSIOLOGY

Supersensitivity of nigrostriatal postsynaptic dopamine receptors is usually believed to be responsible for neuroleptic-induced tardive dyskinesia. This hypothesis is based on pharmacologic data, similarity with L-dopa-induced dyskinesia, and animal studies. Yet, a critical examination of the available data merely indicates that tardive dyskinesia is associated with catecholaminergic hyperactivity. Postsynaptic dopamine receptor supersensitivity is probably a normal consequence of neuroleptic treatment and does not explain why tardive dyskinesia develops in only some patients. We tested the dopamine supersensitivity hypothesis of tardive dyskinesia in several ways: (1) examining the relationship of tardive dyskinesia to old age and to a history of neuroleptic-induced parkinsonism, (2) CSF studies, and (3) challenges with dopamine agonists. Our findings did not confirm postsynaptic dopamine-receptor supersensitivity in tardive dyskinesia (Jeste and Wyatt 1981b).

We found that a large subgroup of tardive dyskinesia patients is characterized by several peripheral indices of increased catecholaminergic — especially noradrenergic activity — e.g., high plasma dopamine-beta-hydroxylase (DBH) activity, low platelet monamine-oxidase activity, and elevated plasma renin activity. Follow-up studies over periods of 12 months and longer show that these biochemical parameters remain relatively stable in patients with persistent tardive dyskinesia. Available data indicate that these biochemical characteristics are not a result of the physical manifestations of tardive dyskinesia. Preliminary studies show that a reduction in DBH activity with a DBH inhibitor, disulfiram, is accompanied by improvement in tardive dyskinesia.

We also studied serum-neuroleptic concentrations in different groups of patients. We found that serum-neuroleptic concentrations are much higher in the elderly than in younger patients and that they tend to be significantly elevated in a small subgroup of dyskinetic patients (Jeste et al. 1981, 1982b). It is tempting to speculate that high neuroleptic concentrations in the tissues might be one of the risk factors for the development of tardive dyskinesia, at least in a small subgroup of patients.

TREATMENT

The possible treatments for tardive dyskinesia can be divided into a number of classes.

Neuroleptics.   It is ironic and intriguing that neuroleptics are the most effective agents for suppressing the symptoms of dyskinesia, but the use of neuroleptics as a treatment for tardive dyskinesia is controversial. The first article on the treatment of dyskinesia with a neuroleptic appeared in 1961 (Brandrup 1961). Since then, about 50 reports on the treatment of dyskinesia with neuroleptics have been published. Of the patients treated with neuroleptics, 67.4 percent had significant improvement in their dyskinesia. Neuroleptics as a group proved to be more effective than any other major treatment for suppressing the symptoms of tardive dyskinesia (Jeste and Wyatt 1982).

Some investigators have reported specific antidyskinetic action for individual neuroleptics. Duvoisin (1972) suggested that reserpine was unique in that it was the only effective neuroleptic that was not also a cause of persistent dyskinesia. In a crossover trial of three neuroleptics,

Gerlach and Simmelsgaard (1978) found that haloperidol had significantly greater antidyskinetic effects than did thioridazine and clozapine. Clozapine has often been touted as a "revolutionary" neuroleptic in that it (presumably) does not owe its neuroleptic action to dopamine blockade or dopamine depletion. Simpson and Varga (1974) discovered that clozapine was devoid of extrapyramidal side effects.

An overview of the studies with neuroleptics did not support the superiority of any neuroleptic over others in the treatment of tardive dyskinesia. The proportion of patients improved with commonly tried neuroleptics ranges from 62 percent (thiopropazate) to 79 percent (haloperidol); the figures for reserpine and tetrabenazine are 64 percent and 68.4 percent, respectively.

These studies are important for understanding both the beneficial and the harmful effects of long-term administration of neuroleptics in patients with tardive dyskinesia. There are no standard definitions of "long-term" and "short-term" studies. We arbitrarily defined long-term studies as those in which neuroleptics were administered for more than two months; the remaining studies were classified as short-term ones. Excluding the 12 studies in which either the length of treatment was not mentioned or the results were not given in terms of numbers of patients improved or unimproved, we found 13 long-term studies and 21 short-term ones. Of the 117 patients who were given neuroleptics for more than two months, 76.6 percent improved, and 60.9 percent of the 95 patients treated for shorter periods improved. Thus, it appears that the overall efficacy of neuroleptics may not decrease with continued administration. Although Kazamatsuri and colleagues (1973) and Gibson (1978) reported that some of their patients seemed to develop tolerance to the antidyskinetic effects of neuroleptics, most other investigators did not notice significant development of tolerance.

The improvement in dyskinesia produced by neuroleptics is essentially symptomatic. Therefore, discontinuing their use even after prolonged administration has usually resulted in a recurrence of dyskinetic symptoms. (A possible exception to this is the study by Jus and associates [1979], discussed below, which used a "desensitization" technique.) The symptoms may be severe for one or two weeks following neuroleptic withdrawal but then return to their pretreatment intensity. There is no clinical evidence that treatment with neuroleptics for several months results in a further improvement or worsening of dyskinesia. Obviously, more work on this issue is necessary before we can reach definite conclusions. The available data suggest, however, that treatment of tardive dyskinesia with neuroleptics for months produces symptomatic masking of dyskinesia and that subsequent drug withdrawal leads to a return of the dyskinesia to its pretreatment intensity.

Jeste and associates (1977) found that dividing the total daily dose of a neuroleptic into four equal doses (four-times-a-day administration) was significantly more effective in suppressing dyskinesia than once-a-day administration of the total dose. Our subsequent experience confirmed this observation in some patients. Maintaining a fairly stable concentration of neuroleptics in serum (and brain?) over a 24-hour period (by giving multiple daily doses) might be presumed to result in a fairly steady blockage of dopamine receptors and, therefore, a constant suppression or masking of dyskinetic symptoms. As well, neuroleptics should be used in the lowest effective doses.

Because tardive dyskinesia is supposed to result from the supersensitivity of dopamine receptors, Jus and colleagues (1979) postulated that the desensitization of those receptors might provide a basis for a definitive treatment of that disorder. They conducted a four-year trial in which neuroleptics and antiparkinsonian agents were slowly but progressively reduced, and reserpine and/or haloperidol were administered in small, slowly increasing and then decreasing doses. Of the 62 patients treated, 40 showed significant improvement. In 26 patients, the improvement persisted after reserpine and/or haloperidol were withdrawn, until the end of the study. Eighteen patients had a relapse of dyskinetic symptoms following reserpine and haloperidol withdrawal; reinstitution of those drugs in the same small doses produced improvement again. The overall results of this study are encouraging. An alternative explanation for the results could be that the patients who improved had reversible dyskinesia, whereas those who did not improve had persistent dyskinesia.

Other Dopamine Antagonists.   The use of nonneuroleptic dopamine antagonists in treating tardive dyskinesia is of both clinical and theoretical interest. Unfortunately, the number of such drugs is small, and the mechanism of action of some of them is controversial.

Nonneuroleptic dopamine antagonists have been found to be useful in about one-half of patients with tardive dyskinesia treated for a few days to a few weeks. There is, however, no evidence that these drugs act specifically on dyskinesia or that they are beneficial over long periods of time.

Cholinergic Drugs.   In the 1970s, *deanol* (2-dimethylaminoethanol) was probably the single most extensively tried drug in the treatment of tardive dyskinesia. Between 1974 and 1979 over 30 reports on the use of deanol in tardive dyskinesia were published. Yet, the value of deanol in this condition continues to be uncertain. Out of a total of 222 patients treated with deanol, only 35.4 percent were reported to have improved.

Physotigmine is a cholinesterase inhibitor that is generally administered parenterally (intramuscularly or intravenously). Its effects are relatively short lasting. In the studies of physostigmine in the treatment of tardive dyskinesia, 60.3 percent of the total of 58 patients given physostigmine improved. The drug was usually administered on a single occasion, and its effects were observed for two to 24 hours.

Choline is a naturally occurring precursor of acetylcholine. Choline is normally present in certain foods like soybeans, liver, fish, meat, eggs, and products containing lecithin. The brain cannot synthesize choline. The main source of brain choline is free choline taken up from the bloodstream at the blood-brain barrier. Choline chloride is bitter tasting and produces a body odor that is best described as "dead fish." This odor is presumed to be caused by trimethylamine, a metabolite of choline formed in the gut. Cholinergic reactions like lacrimation, blurred vision, anorexia, and diarrhea may occur. Tamminga and associates (1980) reported depression severe enough to warrant discontinuation of medication in two of their four patients on choline; depression remitted on discontinuing choline. Thus, the use of choline on a routine clinical basis is inconvenient and unpleasant and may cause major side effects. Of the total 34 patients treated with choline, 47.1 percent showed improvement. The clinical improvement could not be correlated with an increase in plasma choline.

Lecithin is the naturally occurring source of dietary choline. Lecithin is phosphatidylcholine, which is metabolized to choline in the intestine and liver. There have been only a few published studies — a majority of which were nonblind — on the value of lecithin in treating tardive dyskinesia. Although the initial results are encouraging, the number of patients treated has been small, and so the role of lecithin in the treatment of dyskinesia should be considered experimental. The inconvenience of administering bulky amounts of this chemical every day and the possiblity of cholinergic side effects and other untoward reactions like depression should also be borne in mind.

GABA'ergic Drugs.   Benzodiazepines (e.g., diazepam) are the most commonly prescribed GABA'ergic drugs in psychiatry. They are classified as sedatives, and their anxiolytic, anticonvulsant, and muscle-relaxant actions are of considerable clinical value.

Of the 15 studies we reviewed, 13 studies classified the patients as both improved and unimproved. Most of the studies done were relatively short term. The overall weighted mean rate with benzodiazepines was 69.4 percent, whereas that with the presumptively more specific GABA'-ergic drug, sodium valproate, was only 49.1 percent (Jeste and Wyatt 1982).

Several researchers have reported side effects with GABA'ergic drugs. Singh and associates (1980) noted major behavior problems in one of the three patients treated with diazepam. Sedman (1976) encountered a high incidence of side effects with clonazepam, including drowsiness that sometimes progressed to confusion and ataxia, especially in elderly subjects. Tamminga and colleagues (1979) found a five-day trial of muscimol useful in patients with tardive dyskinesia but added that this drug would be of little value because of its behavioral side effects, such as worsening of psychosis.

Dopaminergic Drugs.   Most of the dopaminergic drugs have no effect on or worsen tardive dyskinesia. A different approach to the treatment of tardive dyskinesia with L-dopa was suggested by Alpert and Friedhoff (1980). It is based on a theory that temporarily increasing dopamine levels by treatment with L-dopa would reduce dopamine-receptor supersensitivity. Experiments by Friedhoff and Alpert (1978) indicated that a combination of L-dopa and carbidopa reversed the manifestations of haloperidol-induced dopamine-receptor supersensitivity in rats. In their clinical trial, Alpert and Friedhoff (1980) found improvement in three of their patients treated with L-dopa. Two other patients had to be taken off the drug because of side effects such as a grand mal seizure and allergic rash, and two more patients showed no signs of adaptation to L-dopa during a week of treatment at the maximal dose before they were removed from the study for administrative reasons. The theory of receptor-sensitivity modification by L-dopa administration is attractive; however, the incidence of various side effects (including worsening of psychosis) with L-dopa is rather high. Hence, further experimental work is necessary before this approach can be recommended for routine clinical use.

Anticholinergic Drugs.   Anticholinergic drugs like trihexyphenidyl are useful in treating neuroleptic-induced parkinsonism. Some clinicians tend to prescribe these drugs routinely in combination with neuroleptics. Hence, the number of patients with tardive dyskinesia who have received antiparkinsonian medication at one time or another is quite large. There is a consensus among some clinicians and investigators that anticholinergic agents are of limited benefit in treating tardive dyskinesia.

Miscellaneous Drugs.   For various reasons, a number of miscellaneous drugs have been tried in the treatment of tardive dyskinesia. *Fusaric acid* is an inhibitor of dopamine-beta-hydroxylase (DBH) and reduces noradrenaline synthesis. Its effects on brain dopamine and serotonin concentrations are variable. Viukari and Linnoila (1977) found significant improvement in tardive dyskinesia with fusaric acid treatment. This report assumes added significance in view of our finding (Jeste et al. 1981, 1982a) of high-plasma DBH in patients with tardive dyskinesia. Another DBH inhibitor, disulfirm, was successfully tried in patients with L-dopa induced dyskinesia (Birket-Smith and Andersen 1973) and deserves careful experimental study in tardive dyskinesia. Of course, it is too early to recommend fusaric acid or disulfiram for clinical use as antidyskinetic agents. *Propranolol* is specific β-adrenergic receptor blocker. Bacher and Lewis (1980) found that low doses of propranolol were useful in significantly reducing dyskinesia in seven out of their ten patients. This finding is consistent with the possibility of noradrenergic hyperactivity in tardive dyskinesia.

Most of the other miscellaneous drugs have not been found to be of significant value in treating tardive dyskinesia. The combined overall rate of improvement with these drugs in 38 percent. Further studies on certain types of drugs, e.g., DBH inhibitors or β-adrenergic receptor blockers may be of interest.

Neuroleptic Withdrawal.   Neuroleptic withdrawal usually results in an initial aggravation of dyskinesia which reaches its peak intensity within one to two weeks (Crane et al. 1969, Jeste et al. 1979). The dyskinesia then becomes less severe and either continues to lessen and then disappear (within three months in 33.5 percent and after three months in another 3 percent of patients) or persists at a plateau of severity (in the remaining 63.5 percent of patients).

Withdrawal of neuroleptics results in remission of dyskinesia in a little over one-third of all patients. In most of these patients (with reversible dyskinesia), the symptoms remit within three months of discontinuation of the drugs. Old age and brain damage have been found to be associated with persistent dyskinesia (Smith and Baldessarini 1980).

Nondrug Treatments.   A number of psychological, surgical, electrical, dental, and other treatments have been tried in individual cases.

Dental or denture problems may be caused by abnormal involuntary movements of tongue, jaw, and lips or may make such movements worse. Using well-fitting dentures may help such patients. The abnormal movements in tardive dyskinesia can be controlled voluntarily by many patients, using biofeedback, although for only brief periods of time. This fact and reports of the successful use of biofeedback in certain other movement disorders prompted Albanese and Gaarder (1977) to try using biofeedback in two patients with oral dyskinesia. Ten sessions of electromyographic feedback to the masseter muscles resulted in symptom relief in both patients, who were well motivated for the treatment. The value of other nondrug treatments for tardive dyskinesia is questionable.

SUMMARY

Neuroleptic-induced tardive dyskinesia is a serious iatrogenic disorder. Since neuroleptics are still the most effective treatment for chronic schizophrenia and certain other neuropsychiatric disorders, the use of neuroleptics should not be banned. There is, however, a need to restrict these drugs to specific indications, such as those recommended in the recent American Psychiatric Association Task Force Report on tardive dyskinesia (Baldessarini et al. 1980), and to prescribe them in the lowest effective doses. Further research on pathophysiology, identification of risk factors, and prevention and management of tardive dyskinesia are necessary.

NOTE

This chapter was written by the authors in their personal capacity and does not necessarily reflect the views of the National Institute of Mental Health.

REFERENCES

Albanese, H., and Gaarder, K. (1977). Biofeedback treatment of tardive dyskinesia—two case reports. *American Journal of Psychiatry* 134:1149–1150.

Alpert, M., and Friedhoff, A. J. (1980). Clinical application of receptor modification. In *Tardive Dyskinesia—Research and Treatment*, ed. W. E. Fann, R. C. Smith, and D. F. Domino, pp. 471–473. New York: SP Medical and Scientific Books.

Altrocchi, P. H. (1972). Spontaneous oral-facial dyskinesia. *Archives of Neurology* 26:506–512.

Ayd, F. J., Jr. (1970). Prevention of recurrence (maintenance therapy). In *Clinical Handbook of Psychopharmacology*, ed. A. DiMascio and R. I. Shader, pp. 279–310. New York: Science House.

Bacher, N. M., and Lewis, H. A. (1980). Low-dose propranolol in tardive dyskinesia. *American Journal of Psychiatry* 137:495–497.

Baker, A. B. (1969). Discussion. In *Psychotropic Drugs and Dysfunctions of the Basal Ganglia,* ed. G. E. Crane and R. Gardner, Jr., pp. 28–29. Publication 1938. Washington, D.C.: American Psychiatric Association.

Baldessarini, R. J., Cole, J. O., Davis, J. M., Gardos, G., Preskorn, S. H., Simpson, G. M., and Tarsy, D. (1980). *Tardive Dyskinesia: Task Force Report.* Washington, D.C.: American Psychiatric Association.

Bell, R. C. H., and Smith, R. C. (1978). Tardive dyskinesia: characterization and prevalence in a state-wide system. *Journal of Clinical Psychiatry* 39:39–47.

Birket-Smith, E., and Andersen, J. V. (1973). Abnormal involuntary movements induced by anticholinergic therapy. *Acta Neurologica Scandinavica* 50:801–811.

Brandon, S., McClelland, H. A., and Protheroe, C. (1971). A study of facial dyskinesia in a mental hospital population. *British Journal of Psychiatry* 118:171–184.

Brandrup, E. (1961). Tetrabenazine treatment in persisting dyskinesia caused by psychopharmaca. *American Journal of Psychiatry* 118:551–552.

Chouinard, G., Annable, L., Ross-Chouinard, A., and Nestoros, J. N. (1979). Factors related to tardive dyskinesia. *American Journal of Psychiatry* 136:79–83.

Crane, G. D., Ruiz, P., Kernohan, W. J., Wilson, W., and Royalty, N. (1969). Effects of drug withdrawal on tardive dyskinesia. *Activitas Nervosa Superior* 11:30–35.

Crane, G. E. (1968a). Dyskinesia and neuroleptics. *Archives of General Psychiatry* 19:700–703.

————. (1968b). Tardive dyskinesia in schizophrenic patients treated with psychotropic drugs. *Agressologie* 9:209–218.

————. (1972). Pseudoparkinsonism and tardive dyskinesia. *American Journal of Psychiatry* 127:143–146.

————. (1974). Factors predisposing to drug-induced neuroleptic effects. In *The Phenothiazines and Structurally Related Drugs,* ed. C. J. Carr and E. Usdin, pp. 269–279. New York: Raven Press.

Cutler, N. R., Post, R. M., Rey, A. C., and Bunney, W. E. (1981).

Depression-dependent dyskinesias in two cases of manic-depressive illness. *New England Journal of Medicine* 304:1088-1099.

Degkwitz, R. (1969). Extrapyramidal motor disorders following long-term treatment with neuroleptic drugs. In *Psychotropic Drugs and Dysfunctions of the Basal Ganglia*, ed. G. E. Crane and B. Gardner, pp. 22-32. Publication 1938. Washington, D.C.: U.S. Public Health Service.

Degkwitz, R., and Wenzel, W. (1967). Persistent extrapyramidal side effects after long-term application of neuroleptics. In *Neuropsychopharmacology*, ed. H. Brill, pp. 608-615. Amsterdam: Excerpta Medica Foundation.

Demars, J. C. A. (1966). Neuromuscular effects of long-term phenothiazine medication, electroconvulsive therapy and leucotomy. *Journal of Nervous and Mental Disease* 143:73-79.

Duvoisin, R. C. (1972). Reserpine for tardive dyskinesia (cont.). *New England Journal of Medicine* 286:611.

Friedhoff, A. J., and Alpert, M. (1978). Receptor sensitivity modification as a potential treatment. In *Psychopharmacology—A Generation of Progress*, ed. M. A. Lipton, A. DiMascio, and K. F. Killam, pp. 797-802. New York: Raven Press.

Garber, R. S. (1979). Tardive dyskinesia (letter to editor). *Psychiatric News*, May 4, p. 2.

Gardos, G., Cole, J. O., and La Brie, R. A. (1977). Drug variables in the etiology of tardive dyskinesia—application of discriminant function analysis. *Progress in Neuropsychopharmacology* 1:147-154.

Gerlach, J., and Simmelsgaard, H. (1978). Tardive dyskinesia during and following treatment with haloperidol, haloperidol plus biperiden, thioridazine, and clozapine. *Psychopharmacology* 59:105-112.

Gibson, A. C. (1978). Depot injection and tardive dyskinesia. *British Journal of Psychiatry* 132:361-365.

Goddard, G. V. (1972). Long-term alterations following amygdala stimulation. In *The Neurobiology of the Amygdala*, ed. S. Eleftheriou, pp. 581-596. New York: Plenum.

Granacher, R. P., Jr. (1981). Differential diagnosis of tardive dyskinesia: an overview. *American Journal of Psychiatry* 138:1288-1297.

Hunter, R., Earl, C. J., and Thornicroff, S. (1964). An apparently irreversible syndrome of abnormal movements following phenothiazine medication. *Proceedings of the Royal Society of Medicine* 57:758-762.

Itoh, H., and Yagi, G. (1979). Reversibility of tardive dyskinesia. *Folia Psychiatrica et Neurologica Japonica* 33:43-54.

Jeste, D. V., DeLisi, L. E., Zalcman, S., Wise, C. D., Phelps, B. H.,

Rosenblatt, J. E., Potkin, G. S., Bridge, T. P., and Wyatt, R. J. (1981). A biochemical study of tardive dyskinesia in young male patients. *Psychiatry Research* 4:327–331.

Jeste, D. V., Kleinman, J. E., Potkin, S. G., Luchins, D. J., and Wienberger, D. (1982a). Ex uno mutli: subtyping the schizophrenic syndrome. *Biological Psychiatry* 17:199–222.

Jeste, D. V., Linnoila, M., Wagner, R. L., and Wyatt, R. J. (1982b). Serum neuroleptic concentrations and tardive dyskinesia. *Psychopharmacology* 76:377–380.

Jeste, D. V., Olgiati, S. O., and Ghali, A. Y. (1977). Masking of tardive dyskinesia with four-times-a-day administration of chlorpromazine. *Diseases of the Nervous System* 38:755–758.

Jeste, D. V., Potkin, S. G., Sinha, S., Feder, S. L., and Wyatt, R. J. (1979). Tardive dyskinesia—reversible and persistent. *Archives of General Psychiatry* 36:585–590.

Jeste, D. V., and Wyatt, R. J. (1981a). Changing epidemiology of tardive dyskinesia: an overview. *American Journal of Psychiatry* 138: 207–209.

Jeste, D. V., and Wyatt, R. J. (1981b). Dogma disputed: is tardive dyskinesia due to postsynaptic dopamine receptor supersensitivity? *Journal of Clinical Psychiatry* 42:455–457.

Jeste, D. V., and Wyatt, R. J. (1982). *Understanding and Treating Tardive Dyskinesia.* New York: Guilford Press.

Jones, M., and Hunter, R. (1969). Abnormal movements in patients with chronic psychiatric illness. In *Psychotropic Drugs and Dysfunctions of the Basal Ganglia*, ed. G. E. Crane and R. Gardner, Jr., pp. 53–65.

Jus, A., Jus, K., and Fontaine, P. (1979). Long-term treatment of tardive dyskinesia. *Journal of Clinical Psychiatry* 40:72–77.

Jus, A., Pineau, R., Lachance, R., Pelchat, G., Jus, K., Pires, P., and Villeneuve, R. (1976). Epidemiology of tardive dyskinesia: part II. *Diseases of the Nervous System* 37:257–261.

Kazamatsuri, H., Chien, C., and Cole, J. O. (1972). Therapeutic approaches to tardive dyskinesia. *Archives of General Psychiatry* 27:491–499.

————. (1973). Long-term treatment of tardive diskinesia with haloperidol and tetrabenazine. *American Journal of Psychiatry* 130:479–483.

Kiloh, L. G., Sydney-Smith, J., and Williams, S. E. (1973). Antiparkinsonian drugs as causal agents in tardive dyskinesia. *Medical Journal of Australia* 2:591–593.

Klawans, J. L., Jr. (1973). The pharmacology of tardive dyskinesia. *American Journal of Psychiatry* 130:82–86.

Kline, N. S. (1968). On the rarity of "irreversible" oral dyskinesia following phenothiazines. *American Journal of Psychiatry* 124:48–54.

Kraepelin, E. (1919). *Dementia Praecox and Paraphrenia*. Trans. R. M. Barclay and G. M. Robertson. New York: Robert E. Krieger, 1971.

Kruse, W. (1960). Persistent muscular restlessness after phenothiazine treatment: report of three cases. *American Journal of Psychiatry* 117:152–153.

Makman, M. H., Ahn, H. S., Thal, L. J., Sharpless, N. S., Dvorkin, B., Horowitz, S. G., and Rosenfeld, M. (1979). Aging and monoamine receptors in brain. *Federation Proceedings* 38:1922–1926.

Mettler, F. A., and Crandell, A. (1959). Neurologic disorders in psychiatric institutions. *Journal of Nervous and Mental Disease* 128:148–159.

Myrianthopoulos, N. C., Kurland, A. A., and Kurland, L. T. (1962). Hereditary predisposition in drug-induced parkinsonism. *Archives of Neurology* 6:19–23.

Perris, C., Dimitrijevic, P., Jacobsson, L., Paulsson, P., Rapp, W., and Froberg, H. (1979). Tardive dyskinesia in psychiatric patients treated with neuroleptics. *British Journal of Psychiatry* 135:509–514.

Post, R. M., and Kopanda, R. T. (1976). Cocaine, kindling and psychosis. *American Journal of Psychiatry* 183:627–634.

Schocken, D. D., and Roth, G. S. (1977). Reduced β-adrenergic receptor concentration in aging man. *Nature* 27:856–858.

Schoenecker, M. (1957). Ein eigentmliches syndrom im oralen bereich bei megaphenapplikation. *Nervenarzt* 28:35.

Sedman, G. (1976). Clonazepam in the treatment of tardive oral dyskinesia. *British Medical Journal* 2:583.

Sigwald, J., Couttier, D. Raymondeaud, C., and Piot, C. (1959). Quatre cas de dyskinesie facio-bucco-lingui-masticatrice à evolution prolonǵee secondare à un traitment par les neuroleptiques. *Revue of Neurologique* 100:751–755.

Simpson, G. M., and Kline, N. S. (1976). Tardive dyskinesia: manifestations, incidence, etiology and treatment. In *The Basal Ganglia*, ed. M. D. Yahr, pp. 427–432. New York: Raven Press.

Simpson, G. M., and Varga, E. (1974). Clozapine—a new antipsychotic agent. *Current Therapeutic Research* 16:679–686.

Simpson, G. M., Varga, E., Lee, J. H., and Zoubok, B. (1978). Tardive dyskinesia and psychotropic drug history. *Psychopharmacology* 58:117–124.

Singh, M. M., Nasrallah, H. A., and Lal, H. (1980). Treatment of tardive dyskinesia with diazepam: indirect evidence for the involvement of limbic, possibly GABA'ergic mechanisms. *Brain Research Bulletin* 5:673–680.

Smith, J. M., and Baldessarini, R. J. (1980). Changes in prevalence, severity and recovery in tardive dyskinesia with age. *Archives of General Psychiatry* 37:1368–1373.

Smith, J. M., Kucharski, L. T., Oswald, W. T., and Waterman, L. J. (1979). A systematic investigation of tardive dyskinesia in inpatients. *American Journal of Psychiatry* 136:918–922.

Smith, J. M., Oswald, W. T., Kucharski, L. T., and Waterman, L. J. (1978). Tardive dyskinesia: age and sex differences in hospitalized schizophrenics. *Psychopharmacology* 58:207–211.

Sutcher, H. D., Underwood, R. B., Beatly, R. A., et al. (1971). Orofacial dyskinesia: a dental dimension. *Journal of the American Medical Association* 216:1459–1463.

Tamminga, C. A., Crayton, J. W., and Chase, T. N. (1979). Improvement in tardive dyskinesia after muscimol therapy. *Archives of General Psychiatry* 36:595–598.

Tamminga, C. A., Smith, R. C., and Davis, J. M. (1980). The effects of cholinergic drugs on the involuntary movements of tardive dyskinesia. In *Tardive Dyskinesia — Research and Treatment*, ed. W. E. Fann, R. C. Smith, J. M. Davis, and E. F. Domino, pp. 411–418. New York: SP Medical and Scientific Books.

Tanner, R. H., and Domino, E. F. (1977). Exaggerated response to d-amphetamine in geriatric gerbils. *Journal of Gerontology* 23:165–173.

Uhrbrand, I., and Faurbye, A. (1960). Reversible and irreversible dyskinesia after treatment with perphenazine, chlorpromazine, reserpine and electroconvulsive therapy. *Psychopharmacology* 1:408–418.

Viukari, M., and Linnoila, M. (1977). Effect of fusaric acid on tardive dyskinesia and mental state in psychogeriatric patients. *Acta Psychiatrica Scandinavica* 56:57–61.

Weiss, G., Greenberg, L., and Cantor, E. (1979). Age-related alterations in the development of adrenergic denervation supersensitivity. *Federation Proceedings* 38:1915–1921.

SAVINGS CERTIFICATE

psychology today

UP TO 51% OFF!

Now you can save up to 51% on a subscription to
PSYCHOLOGY TODAY.

Choose Your Savings

Yes ☐ Two years of Psychology Today (24 issues) for $22.97. I save 51%!

Yes ☐ One year of Psychology Today for $12.97. I save 45%!

Savings based on the annual newsstand cover price of $23.40.

54M11

Name _____

Address _____

City _____ State _____ Zip _____

Please allow 4-6 weeks for delivery of your first issue. Basic subscription price $15.99.

CHAPTER 14

Multiple Personality

D. WILFRED ABSE, M.D.

The most important, and perhaps the most permanent part of Pierre Janet's (1907) work in abnormal psychology, was his remarkable series of studies on the dissociations of hysteria, especially those massive dissociations that become manifest as somnambulisms, fugues, and multiple personalities. Alongside Janet's studies are those of Morton Prince (1957). The deeper nature of these older studies has so far been inadequately recognized by psychoanalysts. Some, however, are now focusing on pathological splitting, sometimes writing as if they had discovered the phenomenon for the first time (Kernberg 1975).

The third *Diagnostic and Statistical Manual of Mental Disorders* (1980) (DSM-III) with which we are presently burdened, gives the following criteria for multiple personality:

A. The existence within the individual of two or more distinct personalities, each of which is dominant at a particular time.

B. The personality that is dominant at any particular time determines the individual's behavior.

C. Each individual personality is complex and integrated with its own unique behavior patterns and social relationships. (1980, p. 259)

The first two statements are obvious, and the third reeks with redundancy. The word integration, when better used with reference to multiple personality, surely indicates that the partial manifest personalities are not integrated adequately with one another and into the personality as a whole.

In regard to differential diagnosis, presumably in order to achieve brevity, the remarks in the DSM-III oversimplify at the expense of conformity to the facts:

Psychogenic Fugue and Psychogenic Amnesia may be confused with Multiple Personality, but do not present its characteristic repeated shifts of identity and usually are limited to a single, brief episode. Also, in both Psychogenic Amnesia and Psychogenic Fugue, awareness of the original personality is absent. Complex social activities, memories, behavior patterns, and friendships are not present in Psychogenic Amnesia and are uncommon in Psychogenic Fugue. (1980, p. 258)

Of course, "awareness of the original personality" is in fact just as often absent in multiple personality, part of the dynamics of which is rooted in memory dysfunction (amnesic disorder). Besides, fugue or other alterations of consciousness and amnesia are often preludes to the full development of multiple personality and are characteristic of that disorder. As for the psychotic disorders that the DSM-III distinguishes from multiple personality, often the division of the self is part of a defensive effort to avoid the more drastic regressive molecular disintegration of schizophrenia, a defense that sometimes fails, as we shall show here.

In 1891, George M. Beard wrote a series of essays in the *New York Medical Record* in which he introduced the term *border-liners* and applied it to "that large class of nervous persons, sometimes hypochondriacal, sometimes neurasthenic, sometimes hysterical, sometimes epileptic, sometimes inebriate, sometimes several of these united" who, he wrote further, "are almost insane at times and yet may never become insane, though sometimes they may cross the borderline." He pointed out, too, that such patients sometimes raise questions before they are over the line, such questions as whether sequestration and observation, and "even a measure of restraint," away from home and friends, may be required to prevent a tragic outcome. Whichever one of the complex current definitions is applied to this "class of nervous persons" by those who have rediscovered it, it is certain that multiple personality belongs to it. The DSM-III states, very conservatively, "Child abuse and other forms of severe emotional trauma may be predisposing factors" (1980, p. 258). I have never found severe psychic trauma to be absent in such cases. Another predisposing factor may be sought in a schizoid biotype of the sort developed by the Italian school of anthropology more than 80 years ago and later by Kretschmer and by Sheldon and his collaborators. Certainly when adequate family and hereditary histories are taken in cases of multiple personality, a constitutional basis appears probable. It is not, of course, sufficient merely to state, as the DSM-III does, that "psychosocial stress most often precipitates the transition from one personality to another" (1980, p. 258).

Rather, it is necessary to probe the factors of motivation involved in transition.

Jeanne Lampl-De Groot (1981) recently reminded us of certain necessary considerations concerning human development and its relation to multiple personality. Progression in development, she asserted, is not an ever-ongoing process for the child. It alternates with regressive attitudes. Some residues of each developmental phase are preserved in the psychic depths. "These remnants are," she wrote, "the constituents of the multiple personality of human beings." She gave a few examples of the more adaptive utilization of something normatively like multiple personality:

(1) A mother, nursing her baby, is able to revive the experiential world of her own infancy, so that her empathy is enhanced with benefit to her own well-being and for the baby's basic trust.

(2) An adult playing with a toddler returns in some measure to his own state of mind as a toddler thus being able to respect the toddler's needs for autonomy and for closeness (refueling).

(3) A teacher who switches sometimes from his adult attitude to the still retained facets of his own latency or puberty will promote his pupils' capacity for and wish to learn. Here too flexibility is an essential condition for optimal functioning. (1981, p. 620)

Lampl-De Groot recognized that in its most flagrant forms, with which we are concerned here, multiple personality proper is the expression of severe psychopathology. These flagrant forms show a lack of flexibility in the encounter with situations that generate the reemergence of early unresolved and traumatic conflicts. Here molar splitting has become a more fixed pattern, one that may prevent, at any rate temporarily and sometimes permanently, the personality's molecular disintegration. Not only has the patient lost the flexibility of switching from one facet of his or her personality to another; he or she also becomes altogether immersed in one when the other now confronts him or her with an unbearable strain. In multiple personality proper, the patient switches from one fixed pattern of personality, comprising a gestalt in its own right, to another without later adequate progressive integration of these patterns. Moreover, he or she is lost episodically in an alternate identity in a way that crosses the border into delusions, a false current notion of the self, so that his or her conscious experience is very different from the normative flexible exhibition of different facets of personality as these occur interactionally with different other people. This existential difference is underestimated in Lampl-De Groot's notes. The victim of multiple personality is periodically obliged to desert completely his or her usual identity.

But there is a condition that hovers between the complete desertion of one identity for another and one that is so common that it is apt to be taken too much for granted, namely, the gross change in personality that often occurs in episodic alcoholism. In a literary fictional model of alternating personality, Robert Louis Stevenson's *Dr. Jekyll and Mr. Hyde* (1886), a chemical agent periodically transforms Dr. Jekyll into Mr. Hyde. Who can doubt that this was partly based on Stevenson's observations of alcohol abuse? The fictional model accurately portrays a kind of superego cleavage, a strict internal regulation, resulting in a commonplace respectability being replaced following chemical imbibition by a permissive maladjustment that allows sadistic behavior to emerge.

BRIEF HISTORICAL NOTES

Dual personality was frequently reported in the 19th-century medical literature on both sides of the Atlantic. French psychiatrists described a number of instances. In the later decades of the 19th century, as a result of using hypnosis, they sometimes uncovered otherwise "latent" personalities, which their experience with spontaneously occurring dual personalities in some other victims of hysterical neurosis had given them grounds for suspecting. These psychiatrists found levels of personality beneath the personality of waking life, and so they devised methods to permit these latent personalities to come upon the stage of consciousness and action, pushing aside the usual self. For some time toward the turn of the century, alternating personalities were discussed as a dramatic expression of multiple selves occupying the same human body.

Notable among the many spontaneously occurring dual personalities recorded was the case of Félida X reported by Étienne Eugène Azam (1887). His account was published with an introduction by Jean-Martin Charcot, the pioneer of the diagnosis and treatment of hysteria in our era of modern neurology and medicine. Charcot was especially interested in what Azam described as *une condition séconde* ("a second psychic state") as evinced in the shifts of consciousness displayed by Félida. Later, Breuer and Freud were impressed with the phrase *une condition séconde*, much used by Charcot, in regard to hypnoid states and to the immanence of mental conflict in human development and existence, as Freud later elaborated.

Félida was a troubled young woman who had exhibited hysterical symptoms since puberty. One day she fainted, went into a brief lethargy, and then became happy and assertive, grateful for having lost her feeling of sadness, which she recalled. After a few hours she had a similar episode (of fainting and lethargy) which resulted in the return of her subdued personality. Once, while in her second personality, she gave herself to her lover and became pregnant. When her drab personality returned, she was bewildered and unable to grasp what was happening as her pregnancy advanced and became obvious. But soon she appeared once more in her happy personality and apologized to Azam for having caused him embarrassment in her ignorant confusion.

Félida X illustrates that switching follows a short time of clouding of consciousness and that sometimes one personality is amnesic for the other, whereas the second is aware of the experiences of the first. In another type of double personality, the two alternating personalities maintain complete independence of each other with no linkage through memory. In the case of Félida, then, her drab, usual personality knew nothing and remembered nothing of the personality that emerged following a transitional hypnoid state, but this newly emerging identity knew about herself and of Félida's usual more constricted mental condition. Both Janet (1907) and Ellenberger (1970) later identified Félida's second condition as providing a short-lived opportunity for her to be healthier, in contrast with the usual judgment we all make concerning Stevenson's fictional model of Dr. Jekyll becoming diseased and depraved in the person of Mr. Hyde.

The case of Félida also exemplifies the more common successive partial personality type, rather than the rare simultaneous type, usually less clearly demarcated, anyway. Morselli (1944–1945), using drugs, felt himself merging with a wild beast, like the lycanthrope of legend, and sometimes found it difficult to disengage his usual self.

In hypnotic treatment of cases of dual personality, it was found that sometimes a third personality emerged. Thus Janet (1889, p. 318), working with Lucie, came upon both Leona and Rose, as they identified themselves, in the course of his experimental work. He noted that "once baptised, the unconscious personality is more clear and definite; it shows its psychological traits more clearly." Personality clusters may exhibit sharp boundaries, but there are grounds for believing that iatrogenic suggestion, perhaps unconscious, tends to promote the proliferation of additional personalities in the hysterical patient whose psychic organization is susceptible to such cleavage. The case published as that of *Sybil* (Schreiber 1973) is one of a woman possessed by 16 different personalities, some of which seemed to have come about from iatrogenic suggestion in the course of therapeutic interaction that dealt with highly dramatized decomposition products.

In connection with the description of hypnoid states by Breuer and Freud (1885), it should be mentioned that hysterical borderliners are especially apt to experience marked alteration in the symbolizing, integrative, and adaptive functioning of the ego, to an extent that goes far beyond the usual or normative diurnal fluctuations. The fugue state is one of a variety of hypnoid states (Abse 1966) and one that represents part of an attempt at flight from a currently frustrating life situation. Fugue is always related to a wish fantasy, which includes feelings of well-being that dominate consciousness, replacing an awareness of frustration as well as a sense of ill-being. In fugue, such consciousness is characterized by vague ideation, restricted in its association and suffused with strong pleasurable affect. Sometimes such a fugue state is a prelude to the emergence of a second personality.

William James (1896) discussed the case of a New England clergyman, Ansel Bourne, who lived for two months as another person. He disappeared after a visit to the bank in a little Rhode Island town. Two weeks later a stranger, "Mr. Brown," appeared in a Pennsylvania village, set up a shop, and proceeded to live quietly and normally in his new community. James (1950) told the story of this man's awakening one day in his real personality, aghast and bewildered at finding himself in a strange environment in which he had been successfully operating as a shopkeeper, and having no recollection of his former life. Mitchell (1922), writing of the relationship between multiple personality and fugue, noted that Bourne's last memories of the events preceding his fugue "were, however, recovered during hypnosis, and the revelation so obtained of his frame of mind at the beginning of his fugue indicated he wanted to get away somewhere — he didn't know where — and have a rest."

Fugue is typically precipitated by a need to escape from some intolerable pressure. In clinical practice, the intolerable situation is often enough the accumulation of hostile feelings toward a spouse that cannot be expressed by the repressive-masochistic type of personality involved in marital tension. Thus there is the purpose of avoiding the turmoil of interpersonal conflict and being aggressive. In such a case as Ansel Bourne's, the dissociated personality is acting out a wish fantasy in which feelings of pleasure and satisfaction replace the misery of a disturbed marital situation. The fugue, and the subsequent assumption of another identity, made it possible to file away this misery for a time.

Two points are important in a consideration of such a case as Ansel Bourne's. Unlike the contrast in the case of Félida X, the dissociated personality of the shopkeeper was not remarkably different from that of the clergyman — he remained orderly and responsible within strict limits — but in this flight he avoided fight, *thus ensuring the continuation of his core personality.* A relatively peaceful solution was thus ushered in by fugue. This differs from that invariably involved in the somnambulistic hypnoid state, in which the critical emotional turmoil comes vividly to mind in the struggle to alter and master it, as I previously noted (1966). Moreover, in this case, the mental splitting enabled the reverend gentleman to avoid fracturing his image of himself in many important respects, whereas in other cases to be discussed below, the motivational factor is even more intense, inasmuch as ego feeling is altogether threatened by schizophrenic disorganization, and so an alternate superego-ego organization, vastly different, becomes the lesser of two evils.

Ellenberger (1972), analyzing, with the help of two other documents he discovered, Breuer's (1895) original report of Anna O, highlighted the desperate struggle for a consolidated identity represented in this woman's celebrated illness. Ellenberger showed that her illness could be partly understood as a creation of her "mythopoeic unconscious," a creation that Breuer, as an unconscious collaborator, unwittingly encouraged. Ellenberger compared Anna O's (Bertha Pappenheim's) experience with Dr. Breuer with that of Fredericke Hauffer's experience with Dr. Kerner, who reported on his patient in his monograph *The Seeress of Prevorst* (1829). (This was actually the first recorded study in the field of dynamic psychiatry to be devoted to an individual patient.) The development of the seeress under Kerner's observation is a paradigm of the psychotherapeutic situation of therapist and hysterical personality. It was out of such a situation that Bertha Pappenheim succeeded in becoming a pioneer of social work and fighter for women's rights.

As Breuer described her situation in one of the documents unearthed by Ellenberger, Anna O's personality at one phase of her illness was split into one conscious person, normal but sad, and another who was morbid, uncouth, and agitated and who spoke in an agrammatical jargon derived from four different languages. In a later phase, the sick and normal personalities coexisted, but in a different time frame — the sicker personality living one year before the healthier one. Since Anna O's mother kept a diary of her illness, Breuer was able to ascertain that the events she hallucinated day by day had actually occurred one year earlier. She sometimes shifted spontaneously from the correctly time-oriented normal personality to the other, and Breuer could also provoke the shift by showing her an orange. He had, from time to time, given her food and drink, including orange juice, and the orange apparently symbolized the everflowing breast by means of which she could be soothed and calmed. Although Félida X's personality switches were accompanied by a contrast in mood, the boundaries of Anna O's partial personality system were not so clearly demarcated. It is noteworthy that her experience with Breuer, who for two years listened to her and cared for her, ultimately helped integrate her personality in such a way that she became, in turn, able to listen to and care for the mentally disturbed. Although the famous abreactions in the course of Anna O's therapeutic interaction were doubtless important to the cure of many of her symptoms, it seems likely that profound processes of identification were at work not only then but also in her later career.

THE PSYCHOTIC BREAKPOINT AND RESTITUTION

Typical of many multiple personalities in my experience is the following vignette. This patient was first encountered in the Dorothea Dix State Hospital in Raleigh, North Carolina, in a consultation to be followed by a teaching session. Her physicians included a senior psychiatrist and several residents in training. One of the residents gave an account of her history before the interview, reading from the chart. The young woman had been in the hospital for three months. On admission she had been paranoid and hallucinating and had been unable to give a coherent account of herself. She believed that she had been attacked by evil spirits; the threatening voices that she periodically heard made her feel that she continued to need protection from further attacks. From the medical notes it was apparent that she had improved in the hospital, following psychotropic medication within a therapeutic milieu of considerable friendly support, so that she was now able to discuss more realistically her situation and problems and to conduct herself appropriately, including participating in adjunctive therapeutic activities within the hospital. The history was of a well-adjusted, physically attractive young girl brought up as a fundamentalist Christian. She had done well academically in school and college and had been a very obedient do-gooder who had consistently pleased her parents. While at college she had become friendly with a young man who led her into social activities with a group whose general behavior included dancing and singing and rebellious political discussions. The college was not far from her home. Soon she ceased to visit home frequently, and this led to a disturbance in the family. At this point in her history she "mysteriously disappeared." In fact, she went to New York and found a job as a shop assistant. During this time in New York, she had assumed another name and another personality and had forgotten about her home and background in North Carolina. In New York, she was vivacious and hedonistic, finding work as a model to support herself. She had numerous unstable heterosexual relationships there. Then one such friendship became more sustained. During the course of this developing relationship, the young man discussed living together. At this point, she became panic stricken and confused and soon was hallucinating, and so she was taken to the hospital. There, after some weeks, she recovered in the person of her previous personality. She went back to her family in North Carolina. Soon the secondary personality again took possession of her. She left her family and took a job in a larger city in North Carolina where she again became heavily involved with a young man and again decompensated, leading to her present hospital treatment. Now in the interview, she was the modest, staid, and obedient self who knew of her other self only through hearsay.

THE PATIENT'S EXPERIENCE

In writing about hysteria generally, Pierre Janet (1907) repeatedly used the phrase "a malady of the personal synthesis," and this is starkly exhibited in cases of multiple personality. Below is an excerpt from a recent evaluative dialogue with another young woman. This patient, interviewed in a state hospital in Virginia, had imbibed a whole bottle of chloral hydrate immediately before her admission. During the interview it became clear that it was "Olympia" who had swallowed the overdose of hypnotic medication.

Dr. A: I gather Ronnie got his car stuck in the mud, became angry, and told you to leave, and you've been upset since.

Pt: Olympia took my clothes out of the drawer and threw them on the floor and turned the bed upside down.

Dr. A: Olympia?

Pt: She is another person. She wants to die because Daddy beat her up so much and raped her when she was 10 years old.

Dr. A: But Olympia is you, or part of you?

Pt: He used to beat me up all the time. One time he took a belt and put it around my neck and swung me around the room and then let go and bam! I was on the floor. One time I tried to stab him, and I knocked him down and broke his rib. He was a terrible man. He was an alcoholic; all of this is his fault. He made me like this and I hate being like this. I'm getting better, though. I'm not getting upset as I did. Olympia has come out only twice since February. They say she came out screaming in the shower. I

don't remember that. Then another night she came out and turned over all the furniture. Nothing was standing except the TV
set. She had set my clothes on fire and I had them on. That's
what they told me. But I didn't do it. Olympia did. I didn't
because I don't want to die. I like living. I have Holly around,
too. She's funny.

Dr. A: Holly?

Pt: Yeah. She's funny. She came out one night and performed for
everybody, and it was fun. I knew what she was doing 'cause she
let me see it, you know. She acted like a fool, running around,
and laughed and sang songs.

Dr. A: Like a fool—you mean like a clown?

Pt: Yeah. She's been pretty smart.

Dr. A: I see. Why does she call herself Holly?

Pt: I don't know. I remember being conceived.

Dr. A: Conceived?

Pt: Yeah.

Dr. A: How do you mean?

Pt. Before I was a baby in Mama's stomach. Oh, I was waiting on
the waiting line where little babies were.

Dr. A: Yes?

Pt: . . . and I knew what my life was going to be through the whole
time I lived, and I didn't want to go into this life.

Dr. A: You didn't want to come in?

Pt: Uh, uh. I wanted to go in for another family, but they wouldn't
let me, whoever created us. I don't know if there's a God or not. I
think we're created by other beings.

Dr. A: I see. And you mean these other beings had you in the lineup
for this particular family.

Pt: Yeah. I didn't like it.

Dr. A: And you wanted to get into another family. Where was your
home?

Pt: Chicago.

Dr. A: All these terrible things happened there?

Pt: Yes. And he died there, after I left.

Dr. A: How old are you?

Pt: Twenty-two. I've been sick for ten years, but I was well for five of
them.

Dr. A: How is that?

Pt: I felt well for five years when I was worshipping Satan and taking
drugs, [ages] 16 to 21. I could have been the queen of the cult.

Dr. A: The queen of the cult?

Pt: He promised to get me into a good life. I worshiped him for two
years, and I could have been the queen of the cult. They liked me

because I see auras and things like that. I hate to be punished for
things. When I die, I'll probably go to hell. God doesn't like me.

Dr. A: Is that why you turned to Satan?

Pt.: Yes. He always causes bad luck for me.

Dr. A: Who caused bad luck?

Pt: God. I invited Him to my house one day, and He was perhaps too
stuck up to come. He should have come. I got the right to know what
He looks like. He thinks He can ruin me, and I don't even know Him.
Sometimes I think He is a figment of people's imagination. They just
got to have something to lean on. So they lean on . . .

Dr. A. (interrputing): Don't you think that applies to Satan, that he could
be a figment of people's imagination?

Pt: He was real. I saw him really. In another person's body.

Dr. A: Whose body?

Pt: Greg's.

DEFINITIONAL CONFUSION

Alan Krohn (1978) wrote extensively on the importance of the ego in
defining hysteria. As Knight (1953) and Reichard (1956) previously
pointed out, the capacity for integration and the vulnerability to regression
depend not only on the libidinal fixations, which may be multiple, but
also on the strength of ego functioning. Reichard (1956), in reexamining
Freud's and Breuer's early work on hysteria (1893–1895), showed that
the patients were by no means a homogeneous group, inasmuch as two
of the five were suffering from psychotic disturbances at the time of treatment. She proposed the differentiation of hysteria from other related disorders through more adequate assessment of ego functions.

Glover (1932) earlier insisted that besides the usual descriptive standard, a standard based on the historical modification of ego structure needs
also to be taken into account in classifying mental disorders. He felt that
diagnostic evaluation should be based on three sorts of criteria: the descriptive, the developmental, and reality testing. As I previously elaborated
(1966), such evaluation also usefully includes study of the repertoire of
exhibited ego defenses. In regard to the ego defenses, one must distinguish
molar dissociation from molecular disintegration, in addition to studying
ego defenses other than dissociation. The following case, which shows
beginning molecular disintegration, is readily distinguished from the
molar dissociation that was illustrated here in cases of multiple personality.
This case therefore passes into the diagnostic category of schizophrenia.

A 33-year-old divorced woman was interviewed in the Dorothea Dix State Hospital in Raleigh, North Carolina. The patient appeared pale and undernourished. Her facial expression was blank (poker faced), and she spoke in a monotonous voice without adequate affective expression. She was disoriented as to time and person but not as to place. She stated that she felt that her soul was, with difficulty, trying to hold her body together. But there were many souls, some of which she feared were escaping her. In the event of this happening, she felt that she would break into pieces. Some of these souls were against her, whereas some were nice and struggled against the others. Her body, she felt, had been severely punished without reason, and one soul had been murdered. She spoke then of a "Theresa" who tried to get inside her and with her eyes to teach her body to put her mouth to her vagina or rectum. At one time Theresa was taken out, but she had remained a nuisance, sometimes getting back in. One time her rectum was lanced to get her out. At this time, the patient interrupted her conversation with me to talk to a soul, which she instructed to keep her rectum free from saliva and to hold her together from right to left. The patient then went on to discuss disconnectedly her feeling that she had left parts of herself all along the way from New York to California. She spoke again, more connectedly, about her mother-in-law who, she thought, was responsible for sexual perversions and for killing the president. She described her mother-in-law as a "sexual maniac," saying that she kept trying to put her vagina into the mouth of one of her souls (at this point slapping the right buttock, as if to locate the soul involved). Further conversation with this patient led to her talking about her father. She stated that her father's first body was attempting to put its penis into one soul's mouth, and this was terrible. She then related her difficulty with her saliva, stating that she felt her mouth and rectum should be dry and that she had to spit out all her saliva. She continued to insist that her mother-in-law had killed the president, and when amplification of this was requested, she explained that she had killed Franklin D. Roosevelt by cutting his main artery. She further explained that her mother-in-law had killed all presidents who were not elected and that she had informed the doctors how to put the artery back together. On request, the patient gave her married name but stated that her present self or body was different, again giving her single name at the end of interview.

This interview represents most of the content of the patient's remarks but gives only a hint of the more formal elements involved in her efforts at communication. In fact, the patient exhibited considerable difficulty with abstract thinking. Neologisms were common, blocking was evident from time to time, and her attention could not be focused for the purpose of history taking. Any attempt at anamnesis resulted in apparently irrelevant replies, and tangentially she would discuss the ideas outlined above; she was then encouraged to do this.

It is apparent that the patient was communicating her inner perception of a disintegrating personality process. She remarked (1) that her soul was, with difficulty, trying to hold her body together, (2) that in the event of some souls escaping she would break into pieces, (3) that she felt that she had left parts of herself all the way from New York to California, and (4) that she had informed the doctors (i.e., she knew) how to put the artery back together.

These statements expressed her experience of threatened and actual disintegration as well as her attempts to resist the process. Destructive impulses were partly projected onto her mother-in-law, and then, as reported in the last remark, she obtained delusional satisfaction that she knew better than the doctors did about how to make the repair. Her delusions also revealed her experience of an internal drama of struggling souls.

In commenting on this case (which I have previously and more amply discussed [1966]), Volkan (1976) noted that what the patient described is not only in the ordinary sense "symbolic," for what is described not only stands for other representations but is also something(s) that the patient had *become*. This also occurs in those cases of multiple personality that successfully resist the molecular disintegration of schizophrenia. Moreover, in multiple personality proper, there is also a basic weakness of ego boundaries, and so ego feeling becomes excessively heavily invested in one or another past identification with distortion of reality. Regression to primary identification, to that sort of identification that preceded the formation of ego boundaries, occurs in vulnerable people under conditions of arousal of strong emotion, and in this respect multiple personality has a feature in common with schizophrenia. I have discussed elsewhere (1971) the contribution of disordered metaphoric symbolism to acataphasia in schizophrenia and its relationship to delusional identity. Volkan stated, "In one sense the analyst is fortunate when a severely regressed patient communicates, even when the communication is so primitive that the patient becomes what he inwardly perceives his psychic state to be. This process provides disclosure of the nature of such manifestations as 'fragmented islands'. By using such terminology as 'primitive ego nuclei' we can put these structures in perspective and assess the advance of the therapeutic process." (1976, p. 7).

Krohn (1978) found that the essential differences between the hysteric and the schizophrenic are the hysteric's access to intact — though infantile —

mental representations of objects, the ego's capacity to use fantasies of such objects, and the ego's capacity to maintain commerce with the environment, "all of which are weak or non-existent in the psychotically regressed." Multiple personality, inasmuch as it shares these features with hysteria (and is also distinguished from schizophrenia by molar or block dissociation rather than molecular disintegration), comes under the category that I termed *hysteriform* (1966) and that Easser and Lesser (1965) designated *hysteroid*. Hysteriform conditions are those that somewhat resemble hysteria but differ in that they sometimes present transitions from hysteria to psychotic disturbances (e.g., hypnoid alterations of consciousness such as fugue and somnambulism) and evince the phenomenon of large units of experience (memories and fantasies) being sequestrated from other large units of experience (molar dissociation), though in themselves these large units remain intact. Krohn stated:

Though there are exceptions (Marmor 1953, Wittels 1931), there is a consensus that "hysteria" and "hysterical personality" be reserved for relatively mild or moderate forms of neurotic and/or character disturbance, characterized by a relatively intact ego, mild to moderate incapacity to handle life responsibilities, and phallic oedipal (as opposed to pregenital) levels of fixation. The recent contribution on the borderline personality strongly suggests that such terms as "hysteroid" (Easser and Lesser 1965) and "hysteriform" (Abse 1966) be discarded, and that such patients be considered as borderline personalities. (1978, pp. 125–126)

My opinion is that these terms are better retained, as they show the relationship to "hysteria" yet sufficiently modify the designation to indicate that much that was subsumed traditionally under the term of hysteria both long before Janet's and Freud's work and later now needs further discrimination.

It is pertinent here to call attention to the Oedipus legend. The same Oedipus who killed his father and married his mother began life by being exposed on a mountain, deprived of maternal care. Although the final stages of the Oedipus drama are more representative of one broad category of hysterical character disorder and neurosis, one generally accessible to psychoanalysis of relatively limited duration, there is a second broad category for which the beginnings of the legend are more parabolic. This second broad category contains those with pronounced oral character traits, undergirded sometimes by more severe narcissistic ego disorder. Within the gamut of such hysteriform borderliners are found those that develop multiple personality as an attempted defense against schizophrenic loss of ego feeling with molecular disintegration.

It is remarkable to what extent the phenomena of multiple personality are misperceived, sometimes regarded as fraudulent and sometimes receiving supernaturalistic explanations. Misperceptions are not confined to the lay public. Thus one authoritative source (Hill et al. 1979, p. 224) blandly asserted, "There is no relationship between multiple personality and schizophrenia"!

SOME RECENT STUDIES

A case that was recently studied from a psychological viewpoint by Ludwig, Brandsina, Wilbur, Bendfeldt, and Jameson (1972), is that of Jonah, 27 years old, who came to hospital complaining of severe headaches often followed by amnesia. Observation first revealed striking alternations of personality on different days and, later, four relatively stable personality structures. Jonah, the primary personality and designated "the square," was overanxious, shy and retiring, polite and passive, and highly conventional, unaware of the secondary personalities. Sammy, "the mediator," took over when Jonah needed legal aid. He first emerged at age 6 when Jonah's mother stabbed his stepfather, whereupon Sammy succeeded in persuading his parents never again to fight in front of the children, a reform that assuaged in some degree the fright that Jonah had experienced. King Young, "the lover," emerged soon afterward in response to Jonah's mother's dressing him in girl's clothing—King Young thereafter looked to Jonah's masculine sexual interests whenever they were threatened. Usoffa Abdulla, "the warrior," was a cold, belligerent, and angry partial-personality system, who emerged at about age 9 following a fracas when a gang of white boys beat up the timid black Jonah. Whenever there was a physical threat Usoffa was apt to emerge, and he would fling caution to the winds and fight viciously and relentlessly.

The psychological studies showed that the four personalities tested quite differently on all measures that were related to emotionally laden topics but scored similarly on tests relatively free of emotion or interpersonal conflict, such as intelligence and vocabulary tests. In this case, it was very clear that the split-off personalities had important protective and defensive roles to ensure the continued existence of the terror-stricken

Jonah, who, however, without considerable psychological help could not change himself sufficiently to absorb and integrate the other fragments of himself. These facets of himself were necessary for the survival and growth of his individuality as a man in a stressful, complex, and often hostile world.

Congdon, Hain, and Stevenson (1961) also supplemented clinical observation in the psychotherapeutic process with psychological tests in the case of a dual personality, a 23-year-old housewife, alternating from Betty to Elizabeth, and Elizabeth to Betty. Elizabeth began as an imaginary playmate in Betty's childhood. The Rorschach inkblot test showed that Betty, the primary personality, had a general personality structure strongly suggestive of hysteria, but with much effort deployed to control emotion, and a strong emphasis on adapting through conformity to social convention (compare Jonah). Elizabeth showed much less control and a lack of social conscience and constraint. Despite these contrasts, other responses to Rorschach testing showed similarities. The contrasts were also evident on sentence-completion tests. Betty showed overly strong needs to be good, passive, and compliant, whereas Elizabeth exhibited a need for rebellion and independence. Betty valued being good, which Elizabeth found to be a bore. Betty's associations in the word-association test predominantly revolved around phobias and affects of fear and disgust. She exhibited major conflicts in sexual and social areas. Elizabeth's associations were frequently diametrically opposite. In contrast with Betty's frequent associations of "filthy," "dirty," "frightening," and "sickening," Elizabeth gave hedonistic associations such as "pleasure" and "happiness." When away from sensitive topics, especially sex, Betty and Elizabeth showed similar associations. These contrasting and alternating personalities, as I discussed previously (1966), consisted of two ego-superego organizations, partly dissociated from each other and partly overlapping.

Earlier in 1957, Thigpen and Cleckley wrote *The Three Faces of Eve*, the subject of which had been studied by Osgood and Luria using the semantic differential. Later, Osgood, Luria, Jeans, and Smith (1976) studied the three faces of another subject, Evelyn, using the same method. In both of these cases a blind analysis of their personalities revealed their important differences, that is, without any access to the clinical phenomena. In 1975, the original Eve revealed her identity as Mrs. Chris Sizemore, a fourth and further integrated self, through interviews with journalists, corroborating the usefulness of her earlier psychotherapy with Thigpen and Cleckley in beginning a more adequate process of individuation.

INTERMITTENT AND SUSTAINED ALTERATIONS OF CONSCIOUSNESS

In fugue, as we noted, there is a purpose in what seems aimless wandering. Hazy thought processes quite dissociated from the residual personality are sometimes geared to the special purpose of setting the stage for the emergence of an alternate ego-superego organization. Fugue is but one of a variety of different hypnoid states (see Abse 1966, chap. 8). The dissociated personality, which may later emerge more starkly, in fugue is acting out a wish fantasy, and the consciousness is temporarily suffused with feelings of well-being; these replace the consciousness of frustration and the feelings of ill-being that preceded the fugue. This contrasts with the somnambulistic hypnoid states in which the painful past experience of stress is evoked in vivid imagery in an effort to alter and master it.

An example of a somnambulistic state is well illustrated in the case of Iréne, described by Janet in 1907. Iréne repeatedly rehearsed the death of her mother, experienced under especially stressful condtions. In her usual condition following the demise of her mother, she forgot not only all she had dramatized in the repeated somnambulisms but also the dire events themselves: " 'I know very well my mother is dead', she stated, 'since I have been told so several times, because I see her no more and because I am in mourning, but I really feel astonished at it. When did she die?'"

Hypnoid alterations of consciousness often occur in persons whose habitual cognitive style is global, relatively diffuse, and impressionistic — the hysterical style of mentation described by David Shapiro (1965). Thus when such people are involved in marital conflict, they are apt to escape into diminished awareness without adequate self-observation, and this may permit an unacknowledged part of the self to emerge into consciousness. Breuer and Freud (1895) pointed out the importance of hypnoid states from which most major and complex hysterias arise, noting that Moebius "had already said the same thing in 1890." Moebius (1894) wrote:

The necessary condition for the pathogenic operation of ideas is, on the one hand, an innate — that is, hysterical — disposition, and, on the other, a special frame of mind. It must resemble a state of hypnosis; it must correspond to some kind of vacancy of consciousness in which an emerging idea meets with no resistance from any other — in which, so to speak, the field is clear for the first comer. We know that a state of this kind can be brought about not only by hypnotism but by emotional shock (fright, anger, etc.) and by exhausting factors (sleeplessness, hunger, and so on). (p. 17)

Certainly a hypnoid state that comprises a suspension of reflective self-representations often precedes the switch to a very different personality or to a restricted core, as we adumbrated above.

Roy Schafer (1968) noted that "young children and those adults whose ego development has been restricted may be said to have, at best, weak and inconsistently maintained reflective self-representations" (p. 104). For Schafer, a "reflective self-representation" is the mental presentation of oneself as the thinker of the thought, the feeler of the feeling, and the source of the impulse to action. He stated: "In order for what is thought to be taken uncritically as an actuality, the reflective self-representations must be suspended. Their suspension may be brief or long-lasting. . . . The thinker vanishes but the thought remains — now as an event, a thing, a concrete external reality, for there is no thinker to know it for what it is. . . . It is of the essence of primary process ideation not to state or imply reflective self-representations." (p. 92).

Important to understanding the variety of hypnoid states, as I previously considered (1966), are the criteria advanced by Rapaport (1951) in defining the varieties of thought organization that characterize different states of consciousness: the use of visual imagery; the use of verbalization; the awareness of awareness; explicitness or implicitness; differentiation; and the recruitment of connotative enrichment by means of condensation, displacement, and symbolism.

TRAUMATIC EARLY EXPERIENCE AND FOCAL ATTENTION

The genetic importance of early traumatic experience constitutes the common background of cases of multiple personality. The now well-known case of Sybil (Schreiber 1973) is paradigmatic in this respect. Sybil's mother was afflicted with a psychotic character disorder and behaved cruelly toward her daughter. Schreiber wrote:

In early 1957, the analysis unfolded a drama of cruelty, secret rituals, punishments and atrocities inflicted by Hattie on Sybil. Dr. Wilbur became concerned that the taproot of Sybil's dissociation into multiple selves was a large, complicated capture-control-imprisonment-torture theme that pervaded the drama. One escape door after another from cruelty had been closed, and for Sybil, who was a battered child four decades before the battered child syndrome was medically identified, there had been no way out. (p. 158)

In order to set a flexible and optimal distance from another person in adult life, according to the time and nature of the interpersonal relationships, one must early achieve what Mahler and colleagues (1975) called *psychological birth*. According to Margaret Mahler, the process of separation and individuation is concentrated in the first two and a half years of life. She concurred with earlier analytic views, including, notably, Trigant Burrow's (1964), of the importance of the early infant-mother relationship in respect to its providing a foundation for a sound sense of identity — or failing to do so. The infant is not at first aware of the mother, then during a period of symbiosis, he or she sees her as part of himself or herself, the "mothering half" of the symbiotic dyad. Later the infant comes to a terrifying awareness of the mother's separateness and in the "rapprochement crisis" experiences intense feelings of ambivalence. The infant longs to return to the comfort of symbiosis and yet wants to strengthen a tenuous, emerging sense of self. He or she wishes to be more independent but is fearful of a greater vulnerability. Severe schizoid problems that loom in the background of cases of multiple personality are the result of unresolved and still intensely cathected conflicts originating in this early period. Because of the nature of the mothering, the symbiotic phase becomes dyssymbiotic, inasmuch as it has become an impediment to growth. In later childhood there are, characteristically, superadded sexually traumatic experiences. Multiple discrete formations of personality can be understood partly as attempts to master successive traumatic situations in which elements of the growing self were impounded.

The language we use to describe and understand multiple personality is based on the analogy of physical force causing the segmental fragmentation of a shaped material object. It is, for the most part, a useful analogy, inasmuch as there are psychic traumas and psychic shapes. Between the times of definitive fracture are intermittent phases of alteration of consciousness, the hypnoid states, as detailed in my *Hysteria and Related Mental Disorders* (1966).

The capacity for focal attention as it develops is linked to the emergence of reality testing. This development during infancy and childhood is complex. Ernest G. Schachtel, in *Metamorphosis* (1959), found:

It is a change from (1) a diffuse total awareness of well- or ill-being, in which at first there is no distinction between the infant and the environment, through (2) a diffuse, more or less global awareness of an impinging environment to (3) a state in which distinct needs and feelings become increasingly differentiated and discrete objects emerge from the environment. Ultimately, these objects are conceived by the child to have an existence of their own that continues even when the object does not impinge on the child's receptors. (p. 253)

The earlier states of consciousness adumbrated by Schachtel are regressively revived in the retreat from separation-individuation under traumatic stress before molar dissociation becomes established.

CONCLUSION

In this brief review of aspects of multiple personality, we must again emphasize that nature does not always draw sharp boundaries. In a hospital admission psychiatric interview of a 25-year-old man in a profound depression, I mentioned to him the remarkable impression that he spoke with two voices. The contours of intonation of these two voices were actually quite distinct. In one, he spoke in a firm, deep bass, in the other in a bleating, whining falsetto. His history included his being beaten by his alcoholic father until he was 15½. Then one evening, after coming home drunk, his father proceeded, as was his wont, to beat up his wife. The patient intervened, and in the ensuing struggle with the ataxic father, two of the father's ribs were broken. The father never tried to beat the patient thereafter. As he recounted his biography, the patient's voice changed back and forth for each side of the historical caesura, and in due course, I pointed this out. The patient stated that he was conforming to his changes of mood and that he and others had sometimes remarked on the considerable change in his voice. He acknowledged that he felt differently at these different times. He worked as a medical technician in the emergency room of a large general hospital, assisting in the necessary surgery. At his work he had always felt masterful, as at some other times. On the other hand, there were times that he felt helpless and hopeless, which was when the falsetto voice emerged. But in this case, the patient did not see this as different personalities but, rather, as changes in himself. Discussion of this, however, was rewarding in subsequent psychotherapy as the patient became aware of the deeper significance of his shifting ego states.

Finally, from the above considerations it should be clear that multiple personality disorder with its etiology in psychic traumas is, from one viewpoint, usually neglected or related to narcissistic personality disorder, since the splitting and active dissociation of mutually contradictory self and object representations are central defensive mechanisms of both. As pointed out by Akhtar and Thomson (this volume, chap. 2), there is greater cohesion of the self and less risk of regressive fragmentation in those labeled narcissistic personaltiy disorder.

REFERENCES

Abse, D. W. (1966). *Hysteria and Related Mental Disorders*. Bristol (England): John Wright.

———. (1971). *Speech and Reason*. Charlottesville: University Press of Virginia.

Azam, E. (1887). *Hypnotisme, Double Conscience et Altération de la Personalité*. Paris: J.B. Ballière.

Beard, G. M. (1891). On border-liners. *New York Medical Record*.

Breuer, J. and Freud, S. (1895). Studies on hysteria. *Standard Edition* 2.

Burrow, T. (1964). *Preconscious Foundations of Human Experience*, ed. W. E. Galt. New York: Basic Books.

Congdon, M. A., Hain, J., and Stevenson, I. (1961). A case of multiple personality illustrating the transition from role-playing. *Journal of Nervous and Mental Disease* 132:497.

Diagnostic and Statistical Manual of Mental Disorders. (1980). 3rd ed. Washington, D.C.: American Psychiatric Association.

Easser, S., and Lesser, B. (1965). Hysterical personality: re-evaluation. *Psychoanalytic Quarterly* 34:390–405.

Ellenberger, H. F. (1970). *The Discovery of the Unconscious*. New York: Basic Books.

———. (1972). The story of Anna O: a critical review with new data. *Journal of the History of Behavioral Science* 8:267–279.

Glover, E. (1932). A psychoanalytic approach to the classification of mental disorders. *Journal of Mental Science* 78:810–825.

Hill, P., Murray, R., and Thorley, A., eds. (1979). *Essentials of Post-Graduate Psychiatry*. London: Academic Press.

James, W. (1950). *The Principles of Psychology*. 1st ed., 1890. New York: Dover.

Janet, P. (1889). *L'Automatisme Psychologique*. Paris: Alcan.

──────. (1907). *The Major Symptoms of Hysteria*. New York: Macmillan.

Kernberg, O. F. (1975). *Borderline Conditions and Pathological Narcissism*. New York: Jason Aronson.

Kerner, J. (1829). *Die Seherin von Prevorst*. Stuttgart-Tübingen: Cotta.

Knight, R. P. (1953). Borderline states. *Bulletin of the Menninger Clinic* 17:1–12.

Krohn, A. (1978). *Hysteria: The Elusive Neurosis*. New York: International Universities Press.

Lampl-De Groot, J. (1981). Notes on "multiple personality." *Psychoanalytic Quarterly* 50(4):620.

Ludwig, A. M., Brandsina, J. M., Wilbur, C. B., Bendfeldt, F., and Jameson, D. H. (1972). The objective study of a multiple personality or are four heads better than one? *Archives of General Psychiatry* 26:298–310.

Mahler, M. S., Pine, F., and Bergman, A. (1975). *The Psychological Birth of the Human Infant*. New York: Basic Books.

Marmor, J. (1953). Orality in the Hysterical Personality. *Journal of the American Psychoanalytic Association* 1:656–675.

Mitchell, T. W. (1922). *Medical Psychology and Physical Research*. London: Methuen.

Moebius, P. (1894). Über astasie-abasie. *Neurologische Beitrage* 1.

Morselli, G. E. (1944–1945). Mescalina e schizophrenia. *Revista de Psicologia* 40–41:1–23.

Osgood, C. E., Luria, Z., Jeans, R. F., and Smith, S. W. (1976). The three faces of Evelyn. *Journal of Abnormal Psychology* 85:247–286.

Prince, M. (1957). *The Dissociation of a Personality*. 1st ed., 1905. New York: Meridian.

Rapaport, D., ed. (1951). *Organization and Pathology of Thought*. New York: Columbia University Press.

Reichard, S. (1956). A re-examination of *Studies in Hysteria*. *Psychoanalytic Quarterly* 25:155–177.

Schachtel, E. G. (1959). *Metamorphosis*. New York: Basic Books.

Schafer, R. (1968). *Aspects of Internalization*. New York: International University Press.

Schreiber, F. R. (1973). *Sybil*. Chicago: Henry Regnery.

Shapiro, D. (1965). *Neurotic Styles*. New York: Basic Books.

Stevenson, R. L. (1886). *The Strange Case of Dr. Jekyll and Mr. Hyde*. London: Longmans.

Thigpen, C. H., and Cleckley, H. (1957). *The Three Faces of Eve*. New York: McGraw-Hill.

Volkan, V. D. (1976). *Primitive Internalized Object Relations*. New York: International Universities Press.

Wittels, F. (1931). Der hysterische charakter. *Psychoanalytische Bewegung* 3:138–165.

Epilogue

New opinions are always suspected, and usually opposed,
without any reason but because they are not already common.

An Essay Concerning Human Understanding, John Locke, 1690

Rare and Unclassifiable Psychiatric Syndromes

DILIP RAMCHANDANI, M.D.

"A syndrome is a disorder characterized by a group of signs and symptoms that appear collectively and in consistent relation to one another" (American Heritage Dictionary 1980, p. 1305). Over a period of time a syndrome may become established, be forgotten, or be assimilated in a newer, broader entity. The reasons for this are manifold. Some deviant or disordered behaviors are offshoots of the prevailing sociocultural environment (Meth 1974), the political milieu, or the turbulence of an era. But the particular mix of environmental variables and developmental universals that evolves into a syndrome is not clearly understood.

This chapter will describe a number of unusual syndromes that have appeared in the psychiatric literature over the last two decades. The compilation can be viewed as an addendum to an earlier listing of "rare and unclassifiable" (Arieti and Bemporad 1974) diagnostic entities, i.e., various syndromes that were either not well understood or not well established. Unusual, unclassifiable, and topical conditions always pose problems in terms of theory and, as Arieti and Bemporad pointed out, prove stimulating in the long run.

MOTORCYCLE SYNDROME

Nine young men who were involved in motorcycle accidents sought intensive psychotherapy following the accidents. An in-depth study of these men (Nicholi 1970) revealed some common features:

1. Unusual preoccupation with motorcycles. Daydreaming and vivid fantasies evoked by the distant sound of motorcycles.

Repeated dreams involving motorcycles, either pleasurable or terrifying.

2. Accident proneness dating back to childhood.

3. Persistent, conscious, and unconscious fears of bodily injury.

4. Distant, conflict-ridden relationship with a critical father and strong identification with the mother, who was seen as inadequate as themselves.

5. Little physical or intellectual activity, except motorcycle riding.

6. Fear of and counterphobic involvement with aggressive women. Sexual difficulties, lack of gratification, or intense homosexual concerns, despite promiscuity.

7. Sleeping difficulties, drug and alcohol abuse, aimless wandering, impulsivity, and defective self-image.

Motorcycle accidents are a leading cause of death among young men. The motorcycle serves as an extension of what the patient considers his masculine self and is like an emotional prosthesis. When the patient feels weak, the motorcycle gives him a sense of strength; when he feels passive, it gives him a sense of doing something; and when he feels effeminate, it gives him a feeling of virility. The motorcycle, therefore, may have here a positive adaptive function, but it also evokes an acute sense of potential danger. Fears of castration and going blind are often present in these men. They also recall early difficulties with loss of control, and memories of their inability to express anger, especially toward their fathers. Often the motorcycle is purchased against the father's wish. A specific ego defect, therefore, forms the core of the motorcycle syndrome. The motorcycle has a special symbolic meaning, and its positive adaptive function is accompanied by a defensive use. These men pass time performing an unconstructive activity. A loud, noisy, breathtaking ride may relieve their apprehension of examinations but helps little in preparing for them. The conscious awareness of the potential dangers only lessens such men's control of the cycle which in turn serves as a vehicle for acting out unconscious conflicts.

This syndrome is especially significant in view of the motorcycle's association with youth gangs and the fear of them, as well as urban violence in general.

PRESIDENTIAL ASSASSINATION SYNDROME

Assassinations and attempts on the lives of public figures have always evoked shock and outrage, and the controversy surrounding the successful insanity plea by John Hinckley is still simmering. Following the assassination of President John F. Kennedy, a group of patients who had been commited to a federal facility for threatening the life of the president of the United States was studied. The results then were tested for their applicability to Kennedy's assassin, Lee Harvey Oswald, and the actual assassination. The conclusions (Rothstein 1964) suggested the existence of a psychopathological continuum, of which Hinckley and Oswald represent the extreme.

The life histories of 11 male patients were found to have some common features:

1. Maternal deprivation during these men's formative years is almost universal, and there is evidence of great rage against women.

2. These men have significant identity confusion and often use aliases.

3. Unsatisfactory mothering was coupled with the absence of an adequate father, which led to defective masculine identification, and indeed, homosexual overtones are prominent.

4. In adolescence, these men rejected their families and sought a larger organization such as the military, prison, or even a psychiatric institution.

5. If this did not help, they often allied themselves with socialistic or ultraconservative societies and ideals.

6. These men's repeated failures and disappointments mobilized tremendous rage, which was displaced onto powerful political, social, or religious figures, who then became the targets of assassination threats or attempts.

Rothstein (1966) compared these conclusions with the details of Oswald's life history, a summary of which follows:

Oswald's father died several months before his birth. Oswald's mother was reported to be a manipulative, attention seeking, and seductive woman who appeared to have tenuous hold on reality during the trial. She was reported to have had difficulties in meeting the emotional needs of her children. She had bathed all her children until age 11 when "they got a little too old for her to look at." Oswald shared her bed until a fairly advanced age. Once, when he was in his early teens, she insisted that Oswald be examined to assure the intactness of his genitalia, and she appeared almost disappointed that he was found to be normal. At age 13 he was evaluated for behavioral difficulties and hospitalized for a time with the diagnosis of schizoid personality disorder. At age 17 Oswald quit school to join the military, where he related poorly to authorities and was court-martialed twice and subsequently discharged. He was extremely resentful of this and even wrote threatening letters to the secretary of defense. Later he defected to the Soviet Union, where he met and married his wife. Shortly after the wedding he returned to the United States with her. Their relationship was stormy and characterized by her tendency to ridicule and deprive him, particularly sexually. At the time of the assassination, she had given birth to a child and was living with a friend. The separation was at her insistence. In fact, Oswald had repeatedly pleaded with her to return to him.

The underlying theme here appears to be a struggle between the wish for a bountiful mother and the fear of a rejecting mother.* The rejection of family during adolescence and enlistment into the military or some other organization appear to serve a dual purpose of providing the patient with much-needed external controls and removing him from free access to the opposite sex. The bountiful mother who will assume total care of him is, of course, not to be found. Therefore the patient sets himself up for eventual disenchantment. The president or the pope is attacked because he is seen as the rejecting mother. Understandably, the responses expected from this powerful figure are both help and punishment. Even a death sentence, to these individuals, may represent an oceanic reunion with the mother, rather than a castrative retaliation.

---

*There is an interesting dynamic revelation in the film *Taxi Driver* in which an assassination attempt is followed by the rescue of a teenage prostitute ("bad" mother) in a regressive and restitutive attempt. Hinckley's struggle reached a natural climax when he attempted to kill President Ronald Reagan (rejecting, bad mother) in order to prove his love for (or gain the love of) actress Jodie Foster (bountiful, good mother)

PHAEDRA COMPLEX

Legend has it that Phaedra married King Theseus whose son, Hippolytus, was a handsome athlete who scorned women. Nonetheless, young Phaedra was attracted to Hippolytus. But when made aware of this, he cursed Phaedra, who committed suicide and left a note accusing Hippolytus of having violated her. Theseus banished his son, who later met with a violent death. Too late, Theseus learned of his son's innocence and killed himself, thus completing the tragedy.

The parent-stepchild attraction can become a disruptive force within the family triad, as described by Messer (1969) in an interesting case history and discussion. A synopsis of the case follows:

Mrs. R., a 37-year-old housewife, was admitted to a medical ward for multiple physical complaints. An extensive work-up did not yield any clues about her malady. Out of desperation a psychiatrist was consulted. An interview with the patient revealed that she was married to her second husband, from whom she had grown apart over the years. She said that lately they had been arguing a great deal, especially about her 18-year-old daughter from her first marriage who lived with the couple. Her husband had been complaining that the daughter was too wanton in her ways and needed more discipline. The daughter had been dating, and the patient's husband was particularly critical of this behavior. Mrs. R. felt that his surveillance of her daughter's activities was excessive, and she resented the fact that he was so preoccupied with her daughter's affairs and paid scant attention to the patient. In a subsequent family meeting it was obvious that the relationship between the stepfather and daughter was overtly seductive. They bickered constantly with each other while the patient sat neglected and listened. Moreover, they both joined in condemning the patient for her sickness and neediness.

In the course of normal psychosexual development, a young child's flirtation and romantic involvement with the parent of the opposite sex culminates in the youngster's growing up and seeking heterosexual relationships outside the family. Deprivation of the love of the opposite-sex parent — the incest taboo, is absolute, though this may not be so in stepfamilies in which the incest taboo may be subtly weakened between the parents and stepchildren. For example, the children's calling their step-parents by their first names is not unusual. The dilution of the taboo may be traced to the difficulty in accepting the stepparent or stepchild. Lack of harmony in the mother-father relationship in such instances is usually an effect rather than a cause. Although no tragedy ensued in the case described above, the morbidity was a result of the patient feeling neglected by her husband and angry at both him and her daughter. This syndrome becomes significant in view of the increasing incidence of divorce and remarriage.

DYSMORPHOPHOBIA

Dysmorphophobia, a term first coined by Morselli (1886), is the subjective feeling of ugliness in a person of normal appearance (Andreasen and Bardach 1977). Much has been written about this condition, but it has eluded the recognition it deserves, partly because it has been thought to be a nonspecific symptom that can occur in illnesses ranging from personality disorder to severe depression and schizophrenia (Hay 1970). Dysmorphophobia can certainly be a harbinger of schizophrenia (Fenichel 1945), or it may even be delusional, in which case the term *monosymptomatic hypochondriacal psychosis* is applied (Riding and Munro 1975). There is a case to be made, however, for considering dysmorphophobia as a distinct entity in a large number of patients who show certain special features (Andreasen and Bardach 1977).

Such patients typically seek elective cosmetic surgery for the deformity they feel saddled with, and they may never see a psychiatrist at all. The onset of the feeling of deformity is sudden and is often the result of an innocuous remark or experience. The patients are usually young adults who may show a mixture of obsessional, schizoid, and narcissistic traits. There is generally no evidence of an overt thought disorder. The patients may have magical expectations about what might be achieved from the corrective surgery that they seek. Indeed, certain transsexuals seeking surgery may have similar expectations. The feeling of deformity may pertain to any of the body parts, such as penis, breasts, chin, nose, extremities, lines under eyes, mouth, and smile (Hay 1970). One of Hay's patients presented as follows:

A 23-year-old painter complained about the appearance of his mouth and requested cosmetic surgery. When he was 17 and dressed to go out one evening, his younger sister commented that he looked nice but that he had a small mouth. This comment triggered much rumination. He studied himself in a mirror, began to compare himself with other people, and became increasingly preoccupied. He was self-conscious and embarrassed to meet people, especially girls, and in a few years became virtually a recluse. He bought a camera and tried taking photographs of himself so that he could study close-ups of his face. He even tried to pull his ears back and raise his mouth up at the corners to make it look wider. He felt that his mouth looked less obviously small when he was smiling or laughing, so he tried to do so as frequently as possible.

He described himself as a shy, sensitive, quiet young man who had a tendency to brood. He was perfectionistic in his work and had no girl friends because he felt too shy and nervous to ask someone out. There was no evidence of a formal thought disorder and no family history of nervous or mental illness.

COUVADE SYNDROME

The couvade* syndrome may be described as a state in which various physical symptoms occur in the husbands of pregnant women. The symptoms are of psychogenic origin, usually occurring in about the third month of pregnancy and disappearing when the child is born. The symptoms are commonly related to the gastrointestinal tract, for example, loss of appetite, nausea, and vomiting. In some dramatic instances, such as the one given below, the patients may even mimic pregnancy, and indeed, such symptoms symbolize pregnancy. Trethowan and Conlon (1965) described one of their patients:

A 26-year-old soldier was admitted to a military hospital with a swollen abdomen without tenderness, and occasional dry vomiting. Search for an etiology was fruitless. The symptoms disappeared dramatically when the patient was given intravenous amytal, only to return when the effect of the drug wore off. It was learned from the patient that he had recently married while on leave, and shortly before the onset of these symptoms he had received news that his wife was pregnant. She had writ-

*Couver, French for "to brood or to hatch." Ritual couvade is practiced by many primitive races throughout the world.

ten to him complaining of severe morning sickness and wanted
him to come home to be with her, but this was not possible.
The patient's symptoms were benign but persisted for almost a
year-and-a-half, until he returned home for the first time after
becoming a father. The marriage subsequently foundered for
various reasons; the patient's mother-in-law lived with them
and interfered greatly, and the couple's sexual relationship was
highly unsatisfying to both of them. When they separated
several years later, the symptoms recurred but followed a less
prolonged course.

Factors that contribute to the etiology of this syndrome may include ambivalence in the marital relationship, parturition envy, and, more importantly, identification with the pregnant partner. There is an interesting
similarity between this syndrome and that of pseudocyesis in women.

IMPOSTOR SYNDROME

The following is from an article entitled "Lost Identity," in *Time* magazine.

In a department store, the store detective nabbed a man she
thought was about to steal some clothing. He said his name
was P. S. and produced identification as evidence. The police
booked him and discovered later that he was actually P. L., a
local FBI agent. As part of an FBI operation, Mr. L. used the
alias P. S. for 3 years while masquerading as a pornography
distributor and hobnobbing with gangsters. The operation ended
in fifty-four arrests but for Mr. L. the charade had become
muddled with reality. He kept bank accounts in his pseudonym
and regularly introduced himself as P. S. He had realized during the undercover operation that he had submerged himself
into the fantasy, and went to a psychiatrist. His friendships dissolved; he separated from his wife.

Another case entitled "Space Impostor: An Unusual Clinical Case"
related the following story (Wittenberg and Grinols 1964):

The pregnant wife of a 27-year-old Air Force sergeant left him
at the base to be with her parents until the child was born. Six
months later she reunited with her husband. On the day of her
return, the sergeant told her that he would not be able to spend

the evening with her because he had become involved in some "secret work" during her absence, of which his attendance was required. This was actually a fabrication: while his wife was away, the patient had been going to the movies two or three times per week, and the night she returned a good picture was playing that he did not want to miss. Once started, it was difficult for him to admit his lie, and over the next six years he continued to elaborate similar stories. After several years it seemed as if his stories had become an intricate part of their life, and he began to worry about how he could extricate himself from them; hence he saw a psychiatrist. On evaluation, the patient revealed superior intelligence and a tendency to intellectualize excessively. He also had a somewhat theatrical air about him. Although he maintained that he had never believed his own stories, occasional slips of tongue betrayed significant involvement. He claimed, however, that he was amazed at his wife's gullibility. Clinical and psychometric assessment demonstrated no formal psychotic symptoms, even though there was a quasi-delusional quality to his fantasy.

The major issue appears to be the inability to separate fantasy from reality. The second patient showed some stress. He had a distant relationship with very busy parents and, as a child, had spent many hours in solitary activity. He had been a voracious reader and harbored a recurrent fantasy about knights. Though he attended college for five years, he did not graduate. Before separating from his wife, he had failed a course in the air force and lost his chance of promotion. The humiliation of this failure may have been relieved by the fantasized reestablishment of integrity. It was determined that his failing the examination had occupied the couple for a whole year and may have been a cause of some marital dissent. The premorbid personality structure, the precipitating events, and the role of his wife in sustaining the fantasy provide some clues into the evolution of this interesting condition.

GASLIGHTING SYNDROME

Gaslighting is behavior in which one individual attempts to influence the judgment of a second by causing the latter to doubt the validity of his or her own judgment (Calef and Weinshel 1981). The motivation may be conscious (Barton and Whitehead 1969, Smith and Sinanan 1972), such as when an individual attempts to make others feel that a second individual is crazy so that the latter will be taken to a mental hospital. In these cases, the "gaslightee" may even become symptomatic. This concept of gaslighting was originally suggested in Patrick Hamilton's 1939 play *Angel Street*, which was later a popular movie, *Gaslight*. The following case report (Smith and Sinanan 1972) is an example of gaslighting:

Mrs. K., age 72, was hospitalized for investigation of blackouts. Her husband complained of considerable inconvenience with his wife's illness. There were discrepancies, however, between the patient's and husband's accounts of some details of the family history, investigation of which yielded some unexpected insight.

Some months before the onset of patient's illness, the husband befriended a woman and offered her temporary shelter. This woman was divorced and had worked in nursing homes. She feigned alarm at some trivial symptoms the patient had, which led the patient to become increasingly hypochondriacal. She accepted hospitalization, and the "friend" looked after the house and husband. Her husband wrote to the children that their mother had a severe illness. When one of the children contacted the hospital directly, a family confrontation ensued in which divisive scheming was attributed to the friend, who disappeared when the couple was reunited.

A broader concept of the term *gaslighting* includes the victimizer's unconscious motivations. Potentially painful mental conflicts may be "dumped" on a second person, the victim, who has a tendency to incorporate and assimilate what others externalize and project onto them (Calef and Weinshel 1981). The concept of projective identification (Meissner 1980) may be a similar clinical phenomenon. Calef and Weinshel (1981) presented an apt clinical illustration, a summary of which follows:

A married woman consulted a psychiatrist for florid fears and strange behavior. Both she and her husband believed that she was an illogical woman whose actions appeared to be on the verge of psychosis. The patient considered her husband to be a handsome, prominent, solid, successful young man who was quietly domineering. She felt that she was scatterbrained even though she had considerable intelligence. The family consensus was that the patient was sick and responsible for increased chaos at home.

As a typical example of the family's behavior, the husband once calmly and nonchalantly drove through the city's streets at 50 miles per hour, repeatedly warning his wife and children to keep an eye out for the police. He was entirely unconcerned for his family's safety. The patient and children were panic-stricken and pleaded with him to slow down. He demeaned them for being anxious and was convinced that he was behaving normally and that the patient was irrationally concerned.

As the patient progressed in therapy and became more assertive, her husband disparaged her. He gradually began to withdraw and developed a series of psychosomatic complaints which led to a brief psychosis. The marrige subsequently broke up, and he married a younger woman who was content to accept a subservient role much as the patient had done. The patient remarried and functioned efficiently thereafter.

Awareness of the varied facets of this syndrome may help not only in recognizing disguised attempts to get rid of an unwanted relative by labeling him or her mentally ill but also in understanding the ubiquitous ways in which individuals attempt to control and manage one another.

STACCATO SYNDROME

The constellation of symptoms seen in the staccato syndrome (Tec 1971) are as follows:

1. Symptoms resemble schizophrenia, yet these patients are fully able to maintain relationships with peers.

2. Hallucinations are sporadic. Temper tantrums are occasional but unpredictable.

3. Verbal communication fluctuates between silence and eloquence.

4. Precipitants for episodes of illness are generally unclear.

5. The course of illness is abrupt, disconnected, and discontinuous.

6. Early development is full of restlessness, poor attention span, low frustration tolerance, and underachievement in school. Visual or auditory perceptual difficulties may be present.

7. Adolescence is complicated by multiple forms of drug abuse.

8. Small doses of phenothiazines may be helpful in treatment.

The development and course of this syndrome is typified in the following case report from Tec (1971):

T. was born with a hemotoma that persisted to age 10 months. His mother was heavily anesthetized during the delivery. T. was the oldest of three children and had a verbal IQ of 128 and a performance IQ of only 113 at age 10 years. He was referred to a psychiatrist because he threatened to kill his father at the time of his parents' separation. The patient's father was intolerant and abusive of him. T. was passively resistant to treatment and was restless. At age 15, after a relatively uneventful period in treatment, he became heavily involved with various drugs (marijuana, LSD, amphetamines) and had periodic episodes of hallucinations and paranoid thinking and made occasional suicide gestures. However, these symptoms were ego alien, his affect was appropriate, and there was nothing bizarre in the clinical picture. Between episodes he was well, despite continued drug abuse and relatively poor performance in school.

COMPULSIVE BORDER CROSSING

There exists a group of disturbed people who cross borders repeatedly and in a driven fashion. They appear to share some characteristics, including a sense of personal insecurity and a lack of stable identity. They attempt to resolve these conflicts by seeking acceptance in a new nation. At various times in their lives, there is a polarization between the idealization of the new country and the repudiation of the old. Compulsive border crossers then flee from real or imagined difficulties with the police or others in the hope of finding a peaceful haven. But they flee also from intimacy, as is borne out by their flights to places sufficiently foreign. They then may initiate some heterosexual involvement that was not permitted at home. Babineau (1972) offered a case report, summarized below:

A 36-year-old man related the following life story. He was born in a British colony and was abandoned in an orphanage. He was arbitrarily assigned a name until, later in life, he determinedly found out his true name. As a young man he worked on the docks and would repeatedly board freighters as a stowaway. He was always turned back promptly at various ports of destination. After nine years he managed to obtain a permit to enter England, where he lived and worked for three years. Toward the end of his stay, he developed the delusion that people thought he was a homosexual and the police were pursuing him to arrest and deport him for this reason. He was hospitalized briefly, and on recovery returned to his home colony. After a brief time he managed to enter the United States illegally, where he worked at unskilled jobs and moved from city to city until he was arrested on suspicion of automobile theft. The judge at the hearing gave him a choice between serving a jail sentence or being drafted into the military. He gladly joined the Army, trained as a clerk-typist, and was subsequently stationed in a unit in West Germany, where he began to feel that he was under suspicion by the military authorities. To escape from this increasingly intolerable situation, he decided to defect to East Germany. He worked in a factory there for six months until he became restive again and sought permission to move to another location. This request was denied, much to his chagrin. Despite repeated protests, the patient continued to work steadily and even entered into a stable relationship with a woman for the first time. He had two children from this relationship. In his fifth year in East Germany, he became very anxious and developed the belief that he was the victim of racial prejudice, which elaborated into frank paranoid and grandiose delusions. The authorities realized that he was mentally unstable and released him to West Berlin.

Crossing an international border is a complicated psychological experience. On a spectrum of this behavior's normative aspects, the ordinary tourist is probably in the middle and at the extreme is a group of restless paranoiacs who travel compulsively to widely disparate environments. The differential diagnosis of this condition must include fuguelike conditions, in which dissociation appears to be predominant, as well as chronic schizophrenia, in which patients are nomadic, drifting aimlessly across long distances.

JOB PHOBIA

There is a striking resemblance between the symptoms of school phobia and those of job phobia. Certain descriptive features, such as familial pattern, age of onset, and psychodynamic elements, however, distinguish the job phobia. Its symptoms are mainly somatic, usually occurring in the morning and being relieved when the individual decides not to go to work. They are usually worse on Monday and taper off by Friday. Symptoms may exacerbate in the presence of authority figures. When somatic symptoms abate with treatment, then anxiety, anger, depression, and feelings of humiliation may become more pronounced. Radin (1972) related a typical case history, summarized here:

W. was a 23-year-old married man with three children. One of his children died of congenital heart disease. Following this event, the patient found it increasingly difficult to go to work. Every morning he felt anxious and fearful of losing control and passing out. If he decided not to go to work, his symptoms would subside. He became very dependent on his wife and was eventually unable to leave home without her. If he did go to work, he spent the entire day in the plant clinic. Although he had been conscientious and perfectionistic in his work, he now began to worry that he would lose his job due to his deteriorating health.

W. was a small, youthful man who had a kyphotic deformity of the spine as a result of childhood polio. He had been an active child until age 12, when he contracted polio and had to be hospitalized for about six months. After this long confinement, he withdrew from his friends because he felt self-conscious. His mother was very protective of him, and in contrast his father was very strict. He always attended school regularly, possibly because his father would not have tolerated his not doing so. He grew up to be a shy young man who felt indebted to his wife for marrying him. Until the death of his child, he had been a responsible and committed father and husband.

The background of such patients reveals that as children, they learned to be submissive in order to please unyielding, perfectionistic parents. Reaction formations abound, and with adulthood comes the competitiveness and stress of acquiring and supporting a family. Significant traumas that strike at the core of job phobics' rigid ego structure cause regression and symptom formation.

CINDERELLA SYNDROME

The following are typical features of the Cinderella syndrome (Goodwin et al. 1980):

1. The patients are young girls who seek help, complaining of abuse from their adoptive mothers.

2. These complaints are often simulated or exaggerated and are reminiscent of the woeful saga of the fairy tale heroine.

3. These children are generally unable to deal with their grievances in fantasy or play.

4. There is a history of the death of a mothering figure when these children were about age 6.

5. The adoptive mothers themselves often were abused as children and therefore are appalled at being regarded as "bad" mothers. Adoptive fathers are usually aloof. Sibling rivalry is intense.

6. Frequent changes occur in the fostering environment to the detriment of the emotional development of these patients if this condition is not recognized and appropriately treated.*

Here is a case history from Goodwin et al. (1980) of a patient suffering from the Cinderella syndrome:

A 9-year-old semiclad girl was found wandering the streets by a policeman who took her to a child protection agency. The child alleged that her adoptive mother had locked her out of the house because she had been unable to finish the chores assigned to her. She spoke bitterly of the treatment she received at home. Her mother, she said, left her alone at home while she took her other children on outings.

Investigation of the patient's story revealed that her biological mother had died when the patient was 1 year old. An alcoholic, abusive aunt raised the child for the next five years, until the aunt died. At age 6 the patient was adopted by her current parents.

Her adoptive mother was an anxious, compulsive woman who had been abused as a child. She resented the patient's difficult behavior and denied any abuse of her. Other children in the family were also angry with the patient for upsetting their mother. The patient admitted later in therapy that in the inci-

*There is some controversy about who described this syndrome first (Lewin 1976, 1981). Contributing to this confusion is the recent appearance of a best-selling book, *The Cinderella Complex* (Dowling 1982), about women's hidden fear of independence and Cinderellalike expectations that something external will happen to transform their lives.

dent above she had taken her clothes off, hidden them, and left her home in a huff after an argument.

It may be postulated that the loss of mother in the oedipal phase led to the child's unconscious fear that she had caused her mother's death. The resulting feelings of guilt were defended by total idealization of the lost mother and displacement of all negative feelings onto the adoptive mother or stepmother. Grief for the lost mother became the central issue, and sibling rivalry naturally was intense because the patient felt that the other children were preferred to her, someone guilty of murder.

Although child protection workers are understandably reluctant to decide that a child is lying about parental abuse, cases of simulated abuse do occur. Timely recognition of it may prevent the futile search for an elusive "good" foster family for these children.

CONCLUSION

To understand the evolution of a psychiatric syndrome, one must study the complex interrelationship of the intrapsychic factors with the extra-psychic ones. This interrelationship is apparent in many of the cases described above. The motorcycle syndrome appears to be a social phenomenon generally found in blue-collar communities. It is unlikely, however, that such young men with the requisite ego deficits exist only in such communities. Certainly, sociocultural variables, aspirations, and expectations must interact in a special way with developmental deficits. The Phaedra complex has a ring of universal truth but is significant because the United States' increasing divorce rate has had a tremen-dous impact on family relationships. The incest taboo must surely have a different meaning in a stepfamily. Assassination of powerful political figures, on the other hand, is a timeless phenomenon. Whether demo-cratic forms of government provide greater exposure of these leaders and render them vulnerable to the displaced archaic rage of a disenchanted, unhappy individual is worth consideration. The couvade ritual is ancient, and it remains to be seen if the changing family stereotype and the eman-cipation of women and the effect it has had on the mothering role will influence the nature and intensity of this ritual's symptoms. It is inter-esting, too, to contemplate how the diversity and extremism across bor-ders sustains the maladaptive conflicts inherent in a compulsive border crosser and, to a lesser extent, in a more ordinary traveler.

The gaslight phenomenon is noteworthy because illness has such great impact on those around the sick individual. Often, psychiatric care is criticized for, and occasionally becomes, custodial care. This may, in part, be the reason for increasing civil rights activism in the area of involuntary commitments. The Cinderella syndrome has a similar connotation, with a twist. The lines between actual neglect, perception of neglect, and the fantasy of it must be particularly difficult for a child psychiatrist to determine.

There is a special category, however, of syndromes in which socioenvironmental variables appear to have minimal influence. Dysmorphophobia is one such example. Is it a symptom of an impaired sense of self, or is it a disease entity in itself? In job phobias, developmental and personality factors appear to have a clearer role. In the description of the staccato syndrome, there is a hint of organicity, which is significant in view of increasing interest in the sequelae of minimal brain damage in adulthood.

REFERENCES

American Heritage Dictionary. (1980). Boston: Houghton Mifflin.

Andreasen, N. C., and Bardach, J. (1977). Dysmorphophobia: symptom or disease? *American Journal of Psychiatry* 134:673–675.

Arieti, S., and Bemporad, J. R. (1974). Rare, unclassifiable and collective psychiatric syndromes. In *American Handbook of Psychiatry*, vol. 3, ed. S. Arieti and E. B. Brody, 2nd ed., pp. 710–722. New York: Basic Books.

Barton, R., and Whitehead, J. A. (1969). The gas-light phenomenon. *Lancet* 1:1258–1260.

Babineau, G. R. (1972). The compulsive border crosser. *Psychiatry* 35:281–290.

Calef, V., and Weinshel, E. M. (1981). Some clinical consequences of introjection: gaslighting. *Psychoanalytic Quarterly* 50:44–66.

Dowling, C. (1982). *The Cinderella Complex: Women's Hidden Fear of Independence.* New York: Summit Books.

Fenichel, O. (1945). *The Psychoanalytic Theory of Neurosis.* New York: Norton.

Goodwin, J., Cauthorne, C. G., and Rada, R. T. (1980). Cinderella syndrome: children who stimulate neglect. *American Journal of Psychiatry* 137:1223–1225.

Hamilton, P. (1939). *Angel Street.* New York: Samuel French.

Hay, G. G. (1970). Dysmorphophobia. *British Journal of Psychiatry* 116:399–406.

Lewin, P. K. (1976). Cinderella syndrome. *Canadian Medical Association Journal* 115:109.

———. (1981). Cinderella syndrome—coining the term. *American Journal of Psychiatry* 138:1000.

Meissner, W. W. (1980). A note on projective identification. *Journal of American Psychoanalytic Association* 28:43-67.

Messer, A. A. (1969). The "Phaedra complex." *Archives of General Psychiatry* 21:213-218.

Meth, J. M. (1974). Exotic psychiatric syndromes. In *American Handbook of Psychiatry*, vol. 3, ed. S. Arieti and E. B. Brody, 2nd ed., pp. 723-742. New York: Basic Books.

Morselli, E. (1886). Sulla dismorfofobia e sulla tafefobia. *Bulletin of Academy of Medicine* (Geneva) 6:110-119.

Nicholi, A. M. (1970). The motorcycle syndrome. *American Journal of Psychiatry* 126:1588-1595.

Radin, S. (1972). Job phobia: school phobia revisited. *Comprehensive Psychiatry* 13:251-257.

Riding, J., and Munro, A. (1975). Pimozide in the treatment of monosymptomatic hypochondriacal psychosis. *Acta Psychiatrica Scandinavica* 52:23-30.

Rothstein, D. A. (1964). Presidential assassination syndrome. *Archives of General Psychiatry* 11:245-254.

———. (1966). Presidential assassination syndromes II. *Archives of General Psychiatry* 15:260-266.

Smith, C. G., and Sinanan, K. (1972). The "gaslight phenomenon" reappears—a modification of the Granser syndrome. *British Journal of Psychiatry* 120:685-686.

Tec, L. (1971). The staccato syndrome: a new clinical entity in search of recognition. *American Journal of Psychiatry* 128:647-648.

Time. (1982). Lost identity. 119:24

Trethowan, W. H., and Conlon, M. H. (1965). The couvade syndrome. *British Journal of Psychiatry* 111:57-66.

Wittenberg, B. H., and Grinols, D. R. (1964). Space imposter: an unusual clinical case. *American Journal of Psychiatry* 120:160-165.

Index